The Masonic Magician

The Life And Death Of Count Cagliostro And His Egyptian Rite

Philippa Faulks
Robert L D Cooper

16pt

Copyright Page from the Original Book

First published in the UK in 2008.
This edition published in 2017 by
Watkins, an imprint of Watkins Media Limited
19 Cecil Court, London WC2N 4EZ

enquiries@watkinspublishing.com

Text Copyright © Philippa Faulks and Robert L D Cooper 2008, 2017

Philippa Faulks and Robert L D Cooper have asserted their right
under the Copyright, Designs and Patents Act 1988 to be identified
as the authors of this work

All rights reserved.
No part of this book may be reproduced or utilized in
any form or by any means, electronic or mechanical,
without prior permission in writing from the Publishers.

1 3 5 7 9 10 8 6 4 2

Designed and typeset by Paul Saunders

Printed and bound in Finland

British Library Cataloguing-in-Publication data available

ISBN: 978-1-78678-013-3

www.watkinspublishing.com

TABLE OF CONTENTS

ACKNOWLEDGEMENTS	iv
INTRODUCTION	xii
PART ONE: THE LIFE AND TIMES OF CAGLIOSTRO	1
CHAPTER ONE: THE EARLY YEARS	1
CHAPTER TWO: THE MASONIC MAGICIAN	32
CHAPTER THREE: THE FINAL YEARS	94
CHAPTER FOUR: THE MAN, THE MYTHS, THE LEGEND	159
PART TWO: THE ORIGINS AND HISTORY OF FREEMASONRY	187
CHAPTER FIVE: THE PHILOSOPHER'S STONEMASONS	187
CHAPTER SIX: THE MAKING OF MASONIC HISTORY	238
CHAPTER SEVEN: A LEGACY OF PERSECUTION	274
PART THREE: CAGLIOSTRO'S EGYPTIAN FREEMASONRY	318
CHAPTER EIGHT: EGYPTIAN FREEMASONRY	318
CHAPTER NINE: THE RITUAL OF EGYPTIAN FREEMASONRY	357
CHAPTER TEN: A COMMENTARY ON CAGLIOSTRO'S EGYPTIAN RITUAL	434
CONCLUSION	509
ENDNOTES	519
APPENDIX 1	543
APPENDIX 2	549
GLOSSARY	551
BIBLIOGRAPHY	557
Index	575

PHILIPPA FAULKS is a researcher, historian and author of seven books. Her passion for seeking out the stories of others compels her love of travel. She currently splits her time between the UK and the rest of the world.

ROBERT L D COOPER FRSA BA FSA (Scot) is a Scottish Freemason and Curator of the Grand Lodge of Scotland Museum and Library in Edinburgh. He is the keeper of the oldest Lodge records in the world, dating from 1599. He writes and broadcasts on all aspects of Freemasonry, and has lectured on the topic throughout the world. Of his many books to date, the most recent include *The Rosslyn Hoax?* and *Cracking the Freemason's Code*. www.robertldcooper.com

Other books by Robert Cooper

Cracking the Freemason's Code
Freemasons, Gardeners and Templars
Introduction to the Origins and History of the Order of Free Gardeners
The Rosslyn Hoax?

Dedicated to my daughter Rowan

PF

*Dedicated to all Freemasons wherever they may be
— on the land, the sea or in the air*

RC

ACKNOWLEDGEMENTS

The scope of this work ensured that a number of people were involved; some only occasionally, others throughout the entire process. Michael Mann and Penny Stopa of Watkins Publishing fall into the latter category and we take the opportunity to thank them for having the vision to see the merits of this book before a single word had been written. Our very special thanks go to our editor John Baldock, whose expertise and insight were invaluable in bringing the finished book together. Thanks to our agent Fiona Spencer Thomas, who has devoted her time and expertise in bringing this publication to the attention of the reading public. Gratitude also to the team at TRANSCEN, Middlesex University Translation Institute, who did a superb and precise job in translating Cagliostro's 18th-century French Ritual, without which this book could not realistically have been published.

As co-authors we each have different sets of people to thank.

Philippa Faulks would like to give very special thanks to all those who have encouraged and supported her throughout the writing of the book – her parents and siblings for their unstinting love and encouragement; Julian Rees, Yasha Beresiner and Brent Morris for their kindness and Masonic expertise; Julian Chater for his continual support and help with the Latin. Thanks also to Geraldine and Bali Beskin at Atlantis Bookshop for finding rare texts.

Robert Cooper wishes to record his thanks to all the staff at the Grand Lodge of Scotland for their assistance and encouragement, in particular that of the Grand Secretary, David M Begg, CA. The staff at the Edinburgh Central Library together with their colleagues at the National Library of Scotland have at all times been helpful and courteous.

Special thanks are expressed to Bernardino Fioravanti, of the Library of the Grand Orient of Italy, for his expert assistance on the life of Cagliostro and most of all for permission to reproduce a copy of the original Notice of Condemnation which sealed Cagliostro's fate.

LIST OF ILLUSTRATIONS

Figure 1. Ouroboros

Figure 2. An example of Cagliostro's Serpent Seal – the original was destroyed by the Inquisition

Figure 3. Mason's mark on the tomb of William Schaw in Dunfermline Abbey

Figure 4. An 18th-century engraving of St John the Evangelist, the patron saint of Scottish Freemasonry. Robert L D Cooper

Figure 5. *Vitruvian Man* by Leonardo da Vinci

Figure 6. Egyptian 'mason' = modern Freemason?

Figure 7. Engravings showing the torture of John Coustos by the Inquisition from *Sufferings John Coustos for Freemasonry*, 1746. Robert L D Cooper

Figure 8. Cagliostro's magical seals

Figure 9. The alphabet of the Magi

Figure 10. Personal crest of Charles Morison, who rescued the Ritual manuscript from Revolutionary France. Taken from *Cagliostro's Ritual of Egyptian Masonry*. Yvonne Cooper

Figure 11. Magical Consecration of a Sword from *The Key of Solomon*

LIST OF PLATES

1. Count Alessandro di Cagliostro Public domain – http://en.wikipedia.org/wiki/Image:Alessandro_Cagliostro.jpg
2. Cagliostro's Bronze Seal http://altreligion.about.com/library/glossary/symbols/bldefscagliostroseal.htm Permission to use from Jennifer Emick, about.com
3. Seraphina Felichiani, Countess Cagliostro From *Cagliostro*, by W R H Trowbridge, Brentano Publishers, New York, 1910 (originally from a rare French print)
4. The Symbol of the Rose Cross from *The History and Practice of Magic*, Paul Christian, France, 1870
5. The Chariot of Hermes. From *Transcendental Magic – Its Doctrine and Ritual*, by Eliphas Lévi. (Trans. A E Waite) London, 1923. Robert L D Cooper
6. *A Masonic Anecdote* by James Gillray, published by Hannah Humphrey, hand-coloured etching, published 21 November 1786. Robert L D Cooper
7. Declaration of Sentence issued by the Holy Inquisition 1791. The official document issued by the Vatican condemning Cagliostro to death for being a Freemason.

Reproduced with kind thanks to Bernardino Fioravanti. Private Collection

8. Castel Sant' Angelo, Rome. Photograph by Robert L D Cooper Feb2007
9. Fortress of San Leo, Urbino. Reproduced by kind permission of Rachael Vorberg-Rugh (www.flikr.com)
10. The prison cell of Cagliostro, fortress of La Rocca, in San Leo, Italy http://commons.wikimedia.org/wiki/Image:San_Leo-la_cella_di_Cagliostro.JPG#file photo by YUMA (public domain wikimedia)
11. Cagliostro's cell – trapdoor seen from above, Fortress of San Leo. Reproduced by kind permission of Rachael Vorberg-Rugh (www.flikr.com)
12. Looking up from inside Cagliostro's cell, Fortress of San Leo. Reproduced by kind permission of Rachael Vorberg-Rugh (www.flikr.com)
13. Airlie MS 1705 (one of the oldest Masonic Rituals in the world). Robert L D Cooper
14. Masonic Symbol Chart c.1900. Robert L D Cooper
15. Stonemasons at work. Note the Masonic symbolism. Robert L D Cooper
16. Frontispiece from the *Constitutions of the Free-Masons*, 1723. Robert L D Cooper

17. Masonic Initiation, 18th-century engraving. Robert L D Cooper
18. The Freemason as a Symbol. Robert L D Cooper
19. Masonic apron, c.1790. Note the plethora of Masonic symbolism. Robert L D Cooper
20. The only known official image linking modern Freemasonry with Egypt. Robert L D Cooper
21. Scottish Masonic Knight Templar Seal Box c.1850. Robert L D Cooper
22. Frontispiece from *The Pocket Companion and History of Free-Masons* by J Scott, 1754. Robert L D Cooper
23. Robert Burns in Lodge Canongate Kilwinning, 1787. Reproduced by kind permission of the Grand Lodge of Scotland.
24. Imaginative 17th-century depiction of King Solomon's Temple. From *Orbis Miraculum, or the Temple of Solomon*. London, 1656. Robert L D Cooper
25. Divine Geometer. One attempt to depict the Supreme Being known to Freemasons as the Great Architect of the Universe (TGAOTU). Reproduced with kind thanks to John Baldock

26. Papal Bull 1739. The Papal Bull issued against Freemasonry in 1738 and printed and distributed in 1739. Reproduced with kind thanks to Bernardino Fioravanti. Private Collection
27. Title page of *Memoirs, Illustrating the History of Jacobinism*, by Abbe Barruel, 1797. This was one of the first books that introduced Masonophobia into the world. Robert L D Cooper
28. Statue of Giordano Bruno (1548–1600) in the Campo de' Fiori, Rome, on the spot where he was burnt at the stake for heresy. Robert L D Cooper
29. A Serbian anti-Semitic/Masonophobic stamp issued during the Nazi occupation. Robert L D Cooper
30. Another version of a Serbian anti-Semitic/Masonophobic stamp issued during the Nazi occupation. Robert L D Cooper
31. Nazi propaganda poster depicting a Jew dressed as a Freemason as a puppeteer making the world (east and west) dance to his tune. Robert L D Cooper
32. Alchemical Serpent, drawing by Theodoros Pelecanos, from an alchemical tract titled *Synosius*, 1478.

33. Masonic Ouroboros (cover design) Kirchweger, Anton Joseph. *Annulus Platonis (Aurea catena Homeri oder physikalisch-chymische Erklärung der Natur)* 1781
34. The Great Symbol of Solomon. From *Transcendental Magic – Its Doctrine and Ritual* by Eliphas Lévi. (Trans. A E Waite) London, 1923. Robert L D Cooper
35. Title Page of *Egyptian Masonry*. Yvonne Cooper

INTRODUCTION

The life and death of Count Alessandro di Cagliostro is still somewhat of a mystery. He appears as an enigma, a challenge, an unfathomable puzzle. Freemasons love mysteries; they are always debating where, when and who they originated from. Historians love a mystery, always hoping there will be untold hidden depths to their research. This is why the legend of Count Cagliostro still tantalizes us and continues to evoke such strong opinions. Born in the progressive Enlightenment era of the 1700s, he was just one of a multitude of 'characters' that brightened the gloom left over from the Restoration period of the century before. He was an unquenchable flame of a man, existing ahead of his time, worshipped and condemned in equal measure. However, Cagliostro's light continued to flicker where others faded away, his role as world traveller and philosopher gave way to the more important work as gifted healer and 'rejuvenator of mankind'. His involvement in the moral work of Freemasonry triggered a vision of a kind of utopia whereby every man and woman could become divinely perfect. After much study of Hermetic philosophy, Cabala and alchemy, Count Cagliostro produced a Masonic ritual like no other; a ritual that would ultimately lead to his downfall and condemnation at the hands of the Inquisition. In 1789, he was arrested, tortured and condemned to death by the hand of the Roman Catholic Church. The crime was that of heresy ... and of being a Freemason. His death sentence was mysteriously commuted to life imprisonment by Pope Pius himself, and he was incarcerated in the Inquisition fortress of San Leo in a rural area of Urbino, Tuscany, until his death in 1795. His memory lives on in that small village, his cell still visited and flowers laid in homage to a misunderstood and underestimated visionary.

Cagliostro saw himself as a reformer of mankind; he truly believed that it was his divine mission to spread the wisdom of Freemasonry throughout the world. However, it was a particular brand of Freemasonry that he discovered was to be his life's work. His immense knowledge of ancient teachings led him to found his Rite of Egyptian Masonry, whereby he claimed that his followers could reach a state of spiritual perfection. Cagliostro was deemed to be a spiritual Master and his work as a healer and mystic was legendary throughout Europe. Letters of official commendation followed him on his travels and several very well-heeled dignitaries were indebted to him, becoming his sponsors. His mystical séances were popular amongst genteel society and his clairvoyant prophecies were uncannily accurate, often to the dismay of the recipient.

Deified by some and condemned by others, it did not take long for the tide to turn against him and some very unwelcome attention came in the form of a public accusation that he was in fact a notorious conman named Giuseppe (Joseph) Balsamo, a forger and thief born in humble surroundings in Palermo, Italy. Cagliostro's own 'memoirs' recall a more noble beginning to his life, with his belief that he was brought up as an orphan by various dignitaries and his mentor, the alchemist Althotas. He answered the accusation in this way:

> All over Europe I called myself Cagliostro. Concerning this noble title, one should judge according to my education and consider the honours which I received from persons so distinguished as the Mufti Salahaym, the Sherif of Mecca, Grand Master Pinto, Pope Rezzonico Clement XIII and other European greats. Isn't therefore my title rather an underestimation than an exaggeration?

The shadowy figure of Joseph Balsamo has continued to follow him, and in modern times if you ask most people, particularly Italians and Freemasons, 'Who was Count Cagliostro?' they will invariably say, 'the charlatan, Giuseppe Balsamo.' This popular consensus has sprung from various books written over the centuries which have often documented conflicting views and evidence as to the true identity of Count Cagliostro. For all the terrible things that have been reported about Cagliostro over the centuries by various biographers and commentators, there are those accounts that have taken his actions beyond face value and have read clearly between the lines. If we consider the works of W H R Trowbridge, Henry Ridgely Evans, Manly P Hall, Kenneth Mackenzie and possibly Arthur Edward Waite, they contain a much more sympathetic view. Not only were these authors able to see the good within the man but they understood Cagliostro's spiritual values and his belief in an important 'divine' mission. It is very easy to dismiss him as just a mere charlatan or 'an arch quack', if only the negative qualities are discussed. After all, it is neither particularly exciting nor fashionable to be a good, spiritually inclined philanthropist — much more fun to peddle the image of a cheating, manipulative revolutionary with the intent to ruin nations and a 2,000-year-old religion.

We do not wish to attempt to prove this theory one way or another; one book could never contain *everything* about Cagliostro, and so our aim is to concentrate on the Count's Masonic and spiritual work that in turn will reveal the teachings of *Egyptian Freemasonry*.

Forgotten for decades, the hand-written French manuscript of Egyptian Masonry has lain in the Library and Museum of the Grand Lodge of Scotland. It was donated by the widow of Scottish surgeon and Freemason, Charles Morison, who had recovered the text along with many others from the ruins of the Parisian Lodges destroyed during the French Revolution. It is thanks to the swift recovery of the manuscript by Morison, that we are now able to offer the first full English translation of one of the most important mystical rites of the past 300 years.

Within the Ritual of *Maçonnerie Egyptienne* we found a wealth of knowledge and wisdom; a path of initiation, of alchemical transmutation, a journey to enlightenment. Cagliostro had imbued his work with a hybrid of ancient wisdom; the teachings of the Old Testament, the arcana of Egypt and Persia, the eternal secret of alchemy. His vision was of perfection for mankind; could he be the man to show a way to eternal life? It was a very dangerous vision to have in 18th-century Europe and to the Catholic Church it implied heresy!

The term 'heresy' can be quite subjective and obviously for Cagliostro and his wife, being Catholic by birth and upbringing, they would be in severe trouble for breaching the doctrine. Not only did they risk excommunication but, if they continued with their heretical path, they would be prone to imprisonment, or worse – sentenced to death.

Soon a volatile mixture of unorthodox political and religious ideas crept into Cagliostro's life and, combined with his often bombastic and over confident proclamations, it ensured that his life would be, to say the least, eventful. This man was destined to do great things but his character would also cause him to make powerful enemies.

On 28 April 1738, Pope Clement XII (1716–40) had issued a papal bull to make Masonic allegiance a sin and one for which a Roman Catholic would be immediately excommunicated. It has been said that certain secret societies existed in Europe during the 1700s, of which the most infamous were those of the *Rosicrucians,* the *Hermeticists* and the *Illuminati.* The Catholic Church and many of the aristocrats of the time were convinced that the Illuminati, along with the Freemasons, not only were in league to bring down the monarchy but were attempting to destroy the Catholic faith. The Catholic Church vehemently believed that Freemasonry was a serious threat, not only to the faith but also to the political system. Pope Clement specifically declared in the bull that he:

> ...condemned Freemasonry on the grounds of its naturalism, demand for oaths, religious indifferentism, and the possible threat to Church and State.

Eventually Cagliostro's involvement in Freemasonry and mysticism were to be his downfall. Revolution was imminent and the Holy Church was becoming unnerved by the movement of radicals throughout Europe. Cagliostro's move to Rome in 1789 was a powerful mistake and he was watched by the eagle eye of the Roman Inquisition. On 27 December 1789, Cagliostro, his wife and his secretary were all arrested and taken to the Castel Sant' Angelo in Rome, to await trial and sentence.

The most serious charge laid at the feet of the Count was of being a Freemason and allegedly an 'Illuminate'. He was also accused of being 'an Enchanter occupied with unlawful studies', of deriding the holy faith, of doing harm to society, and spuriously of having large amounts of money from unknown sources.

We have not been able to see the Vatican's official minutes of the interrogations of Count Cagliostro or his wife; the only testimony we have is from the edited version of the interviews and trial which was compiled by a Vatican notary, Father Marcello, and published as an official booklet under the title *La Vie de Joseph Balsamo* (*The Life of Joseph Balsamo*) and distributed throughout Europe in 1791. However, the couple would have been interrogated at the hands of the Inquisition, which leaves no doubt that the evidence gained may well have been 'encouraged'.

The Inquisition was probably one of the most dangerous and creative inventors of torture to have ever been assembled in the name of religious justice. First established in 1184, it was effectively a tribunal or institution that would stand as judge in the case of heresy against the Catholic Church. The main weapon would be to employ torture which was deemed a legitimate means of extracting confessions, names or other information from those arrested on suspicion of heresy. The 'extraction' of information was enforced by jailers, officially only carried out for 15 minutes at a time and supposedly under the supervision of a doctor. The methods used were barbaric and intensely painful, often leading to premature death before the victim had even achieved a trial. In 1542 the Roman Inquisition was established by Pope Paul III with the title of 'Congregation of the Holy Office', and flourished until the mid 1800s. In 1908 the 'Holy Office of the Inquisition' became 'The Sacred Congregation of the Holy Church', and then changed once again in 1965 to the 'Congregation for the Doctrine of Faith', which it is called to this day.

The most famous cases to have been tried by the Inquisition included the philosopher, priest and occultist Giordano Bruno (1548–1600), who was found guilty of heresy and burnt alive at the stake on 16 February 1600; and Galileo Galilei (1564–1642), physicist and philosopher, who maintained that the Earth revolved around the Sun. Unfortunately for Galileo, this was contrary to Holy Scripture which stated that the Earth was immovable, and he was condemned as a heretic in 1633 and placed under house arrest for the remainder of his life, which ended on 8 January 1642. The Church has gone some way to make amends for Galileo's treatment: in 1737 he was reburied on sacred ground, Pope Benedict XIV rehabilitated him in 1741 allowing publication of Galileo's complete published works, and finally on 31 October 1992, Pope John Paul II, as a result of an official investigation, expressed regret for the way the affair was handled. Other victims of the Inquisition, including Giordano Bruno, were also 'honoured' with an expression of 'profound sorrow' over their treatment, but there was no hope of rehabilitation for their views were still considered profoundly against those of the Church. It is unlikely therefore that Alessandro Cagliostro will ever receive the same sympathy.

The trial of Cagliostro was prolonged and drawn out further by the Inquisition's inability to provide any real proof of his 'crimes'. Nonetheless, after 15 months languishing in the Castle of St Angelo, he was condemned to death on 7 April 1791. After the verdict was read out, all his documents, Masonic Regalia, diplomas from foreign Courts, family relics, books, instruments and, most distressingly, his manuscript of Egyptian Freemasonry were burnt before a large crowd in the Piazza della Minerva. Why did the Church hate Freemasonry so much? Was his 'heresy' in fact nothing more than an excuse to persecute one in a long line of groups stretching as far back as the Knights Templar? Over the centuries Freemasons have repeatedly been attacked by others, not just the Catholic Church. How many people are aware that during World War II, about 80,000 Freemasons perished under the persecution of Adolf Hitler (1889–1945) and Benito Mussolini (1883–1945), either shot or consigned to concentration camps along with the Jews, gypsies and other unfortunates? How many of us know that Freemasonry has been banned in many countries over the centuries? Catherine II of Russia (1729–96) had a hatred of

Freemasonry. She eventually ordered the closure of the Lodges in the 1780s. However, her son and successor Emperor Paul I (1754–1801) re-instated it during the early 1800s. It was forbidden in Spain from 1740–80, Austria followed suit in 1764 until 1780; Switzerland banned it from 1744–98 and in recent times General Franco (Francisco Franco Bahamonde 1892–1975) suppressed Freemasonry.

Today Masons are still faced with opposition, not only from the Church but also from individuals and the media. Anti-Masonry lives on; its legacy provides the means to make Freemasons the only group to have to declare their membership when applying for governmental jobs. Anti-Masonry is a fairly innocuous term. It does not, however, convey the hatred, spite and prejudice held by those who, for a variety of reasons, attack Freemasonry. Henceforth throughout this book we will use the words: Masonophobe; Masonophobic and Masonophobia where previously anti-Mason, anti-Masonic, etc. would have been used.[1]

Our main concern when writing this book was to show the positive sides to a man who has long been denigrated and denounced as an imposter or charlatan. We wished to give credence to the altruist and mystic, the visionary and 'friend of humanity' – to offer an insight into the spiritual work of an Enlightenment hero who never recanted his Freemasonry or his magic. Hopefully we have achieved that.

PART ONE

THE LIFE AND TIMES OF CAGLIOSTRO

CHAPTER ONE

THE EARLY YEARS

ENOUGH ILL HAS BEEN said of Cagliostro. I intend to speak well of him, because I think this is always preferable, providing one can.[1]

BARON DE GLEICHEN

Count Cagliostro left an account of his early years in a booklet published in Paris in 1785. It was issued in his defence during the trial of the Affair of the Diamond Necklace when he was falsely imprisoned in the Bastille before being acquitted of all charges.

According to his own memoirs, Cagliostro admitted that he knew neither the name of his parents, nor the place of his birth. He states quite emphatically:

I do not know the place where I was born nor the parents who gave me birth.

Different circumstances in my life have aroused in me doubts and suspicions which the reader may share. But I repeat that all my researches in this respect have resulted only in giving me, it is true, great but vague and uncertain ideas as to my birth ... My tutor always told me that I was left an orphan at the age of three months, and that my parents were noble and Christians, but he kept the most absolute secrecy as to their name and the place of my birth. Some words spoken at random have made me suspect that I was born at Malta, but this is a matter which it has always been impossible to verify.

This would seem to be not merely vagueness nor an attempt to deceive but a frank admission of his lineage. If we look at his writings there are hints that he was not, in fact, an orphan as there are several prominent people who feature in his life that would appear to be candidates for his father, none of which have ever been proved.

In addition to the account given by Cagliostro, we have a vitally important piece of information – evidence from the *Memorial or Brief for the Count Cagliostro*[2] that a newspaper of the time, the highly regarded *Courier de l'Europe*,[3] stated authoritatively that Cagliostro's parentage was that of the Prince (and presumably the Princess) of Trebizond. Parkyns Macmahon, a former subeditor of the *Courier de l'Europe*, recorded this statement in the Introductory Preface of *Memorial or Brief...*

Comte de Cagliostro leaves the public in perfect darkness about his birth and parents; hence so many conjectures made by idle spectators. One of them, determined at all events to give a father, at least, to the Comte, has fixed upon the late Grand Master of Malta, Pinto. He gravely tells the world, that a Maltese galley captured about 37 years ago, a Turkish pleasure boat with several young ladies of the first distinction on board, one of them exchanged hearts with the Grand Master, who by his holy vow of celibacy could make of his fair capture any thing but a lawful wife. Some little time after, the Grand Signor, by the interposition of the French Court obtained that the ladies should be returned to their disconsolate parents. They all set off together, not even the Grand Mistress excepted. The latter could not easily conceal her shame; she was now brought to the bed [gave birth] of a boy. Her father enraged at this, though a very common accident would have destroyed the fruit of his daughter's unlawful amour; but she found means to have the child put in a place of safety and soon after died by poison or a broken heart. Thus runs the tale of the day. But I am happy to have it in my power to refute the above fiction, by an account of

Cagliostro's real birth. My author is the *Courier de l'Europe* of the 10th instant, a paper which in point of French information, I look upon as the only criterion of authenticity. The imperial family of the Comnenes had long reigned independently over the Christian Empire of Trebizond;[4] but, by process of time they became tributary to the Turks. From that source Comte de Cagliostro derives his origin. This is now proved beyond any dispute. He was born in the capital of that empire, and is acknowledged to be the only surviving son of the Prince who, about 35 years ago, swayed the precarious sceptre of Trebizond. At that period, when Comte Cagliostro was in, or near the third year of his age, a revolution took place, the reigning Prince, his father, was massacred by the seditious, and himself, by some trusty friend to the weaker party, carried to Medina, where the Sherif had the unprejudiced generosity to have him brought up in the religion of his Christian parents.

Whether Comte de Cagliostro has thought proper, from political reasons, to remain, as it were, in a cloud, or actuated by the spirit of a becoming pride, has disdained to gratify the curiosity of a nation, where he has been treated with so much indignity; certain it is, that his high descent is no longer contested; but even circumstantially proved in his memorial, wherein he recites that the black slave in his service told him of all things to beware of the city of Trebizond and predicted the misfortunes that were to befall him after his departure from Mecca.

For the early part of his life Cagliostro relates that he was brought up in the home of the Mufti[5] Salahaym in the ancient city of Medina. Cagliostro's given name was Acharat and he was attended by:

> ...four persons, a tutor aged from 55 to 60 years, named Althotas, and three servants, one white, who served me as valet, and two blacks, of whom one or other was with me day and night. Althotas, whose name it is impossible for me to pronounce without emotion, had for me the care and affection of a father. It was a pleasure for him to cultivate the tendencies for the sciences which I showed. I can say that he possessed them all, from the most abstract to that of ornaments of dress. Botany, physics and medicine were those in which I made the most progress.

Althotas was obviously a very prominent mentor in Acharat's life. Allegedly an adept in Eastern philosophies and alchemy, Althotas instructed his young charge in the various sciences, taught him to speak several languages fluently and, as mentioned, he introduced Acharat to the mysteries:

It was he who taught me to adore God, to love and serve my neighbour, and to respect religion and the law in all places. I wore the Mahometan [Islamic] dress as he did, but the True Religion was impressed on our hearts, although we professed Mahometanism in appearance.

The 'True Religion' he speaks of could be that of his Christian parentage. Or were Althotas' teachings derived from a much older, more esoteric tradition that lay beyond the conventions of institutionalized religion? If so, this would explain Cagliostro's interest in the ancient teachings of *Hermes Trismegestus*, also known as the Egyptian god *Thoth*. For the Hermetic teachings were to play a very important role in the lives of Cagliostro and his 18th-century contemporaries.

Mecca

In 1760 when Cagliostro reached the age of 12, he and Althotas embarked on their travels. Their first port of call was Mecca where they lived for three years within the palace of the Sherif.[6] From Cagliostro's reminiscences we can deduce the inference that the Mufti, the Sherif, or some other wealthy individual from Trebizond was his father. It must have caused much pain to have never made the acquaintance of, nor even discovered the true identity of his parents, something that perhaps is reflected in the demeanour of Cagliostro in later years through his constant attention seeking. Cagliostro recalls the emotion he felt when he was in the presence of the great man:

> We arrived at Mecca and alighted at the palace of the Sherif. They made me dress in clothing more magnificent than any which I had worn up to that time. On the third day after my arrival, my tutor presented me to this sovereign, who gave me the most tender caresses. At the sight of this Prince, an inexpressible emotion took possession of me and my eyes were filled with the sweetest tears I have ever shed in all my life. I was witness to the effort he made to retain his own composure. The moment was one of the events of my existence which it is impossible for me to recall without the most vivid emotions.
>
> I remained three years at Mecca. Not a day passed that I was not admitted to the Sherif and each day saw his attachment increase and my gratitude also. Often I surprised him with his eyes fixed on me, then raising them toward Heaven with all the marks of pity and emotion. I turned from him, pensive and devoured with a fruitless curiosity. I did not dare to question my tutor, who reprimanded me with severity as if I could not without offence seek to know the authors of my being and the place of my birth. At night I sometimes

talked with the negro who slept in my apartment, but in vain I tried to pierce his secrecy. If I spoke of my parents he would become deaf to all the questions I might ask him. One night when I pressed him harder than usual, he told me that if I ever left Mecca I would be menaced with the greatest of misfortunes, and above all I should beware of the city of Trebizond.

My desire for travel prevailed over his gloomy forebodings. I was weary of the regular life I led at the Court of the Sherif. One day I saw him enter the apartment I occupied. My astonishment was extreme at receiving such a favour. He clasped me in his arms with more tenderness than he had ever shown, recommended to me that I should never cease to adore the Eternal One and assured me that in serving Him faithfully I would finish by being happy and would know my fate. Then he said, bathing my face with his tears: 'Adieu, unfortunate child of Nature.' These words and the tone in which he pronounced them will remain eternally engraved in my memory. It was the last time I was able to enjoy his presence. A caravan expressly prepared for me was waiting for us; I departed and left Mecca, to return no more.[7]

Adieu, 'unfortunate child of Nature' indeed.

Egypt, Asia and Africa

In 1763 Acharat and his mentor headed to Egypt whereby they could immerse themselves in the most ancient and sacred teachings in the world. Cagliostro recalls:

> ...we visited the famous pyramids, which are to the eyes of superficial observers only enormous masses of marble and granite. I made the acquaintance of the heads of the different Temples, who were kind enough to introduce me into places where ordinary travellers never penetrated.

It is implied that he was initiated into the Hermetic mysteries during his stay in Egypt and participated in a ritual within the great pyramid (Giza). This would explain his lifelong passion in these mysteries and would sow the seed for his Egyptian Freemasonry in later years.[8] From Egypt they travelled to Asia and Africa eventually alighting on the island of Malta. There they made the acquaintance of Pinto, Grand Master of the Knights of Malta, and were admitted to his palace where they stayed for some time; Acharat practising the art of the sciences and Althotas receiving the insignia of the Order. Again there is a hint that the Grand Master knew something of Acharat's heritage; some have even speculated that Pinto himself was his father and his mother a noblewoman from Trebizond. Unfortunately Althotas died whilst in Malta and the young man, bereft of his master, found his life on the island lacking and decided to once again embark on further travels, this time accompanied by the Chevalier Luigi d'Aquino (1739–83).

 ...Grand Master Pinto gave me, as well as my tutor, lodgings in his palace, and I recall that the apartment I occupied was near his laboratory.

 The first thing that the Grand Master did was to invite the Chevalier d'Aquino, of the illustrious house of the Princess of Caramaniea, to be kind enough to accompany me everywhere and to do the honours of the island for me. I assumed then for the first time, with the European dress, the name of Count de Cagliostro, and was not a little surprised to see Althotas invested with the habit of an ecclesiastic and decorated with the Cross of Malta. The Chevalier d'Aquino had me make the acquaintance of all the Grand Crosses of the Order of the Knights of Malta. I even remember to have dined with M. the Bailiff de Rohan, today the Grand Master. I was then far from foreseeing that twenty years later I would be arrested and taken to the Bastille for having been honoured with the friendship of a Prince of the same name. I have every reason to believe that the Grand Master was informed as to my origin. He spoke to me several times of the Sherif of Mecca and Trebizond, but never wished to talk plainly on this subject. Nevertheless he always treated me with the greatest respect and offered me the most rapid advancement in the Order of Knights of Malta in case I should decide to take the vows. But my desire to travel and the influence which inclined me to practise medicine made me refuse offers so generous and honourable.

It was in Malta that I had the misfortune to lose my best friend, my master, the wisest and most enlightened of mortals, the venerable Althotas. Some moments before his death he grasped me by the hand and said, in a voice nearly extinct: 'My son, always have before your eyes the fear of God and love of your neighbour; you will very soon learn the truth of all I have taught you.'

The island where I had lost the friend who had long held the place of father to me now became an insufferable place of abode. I asked permission of the Grand Master to leave it and travel through Europe. He consented to this with reluctance, and made me promise that I would return to Malta some day. The Chevalier d'Aquino was kind enough to take charge of accompanying me in my travels and supplying all my wants. In fact I departed with him. We visited at first Sicily, where the Knight procured me the acquaintanceship of the nobility of the country. From that place we visited different islands of the Italian archipelago and after looking over the Mediterranean again, we landed at Naples, the native country of the Chevalier d'Aquino. His affairs requiring some individual journeys, I departed alone for Rome with letters of credit on Sir Bellonne, a banker of that city.

Rome

It was in Rome that Cagliostro met Cardinal Orsini and Pope Clement XVI. Whilst there, at the age of 22, he also met a beautiful young girl by the name of Seraphina Feliciani (1755–94?), the 15-year-old daughter of a prominent Roman merchant. Falling desperately in love, the young Count persuaded Seraphina's father of his good intentions and they were married soon after. Cagliostro speaks of his love for Seraphina in his memoirs:

> I was then in my twenty-second year. Chance procured me the acquaintance of a young unmarried lady of quality, named Serafina Felichiani. She was scarcely emerged from childhood; her budding charms kindled in my heart a passion that sixteen years of married life have only tended to strengthen.

London – Cagliostro the Freemason

Some authorities suggest that Cagliostro's initiation into Freemasonry took place while he was in Malta. Others maintain the setting was Germany or The Hague. We do, however, have some evidence that suggests one initiation took place in a room at the King's Head tavern in Gerard Street, in Soho, London on 12 April 1776. Esperance Lodge number 289 was of the Rite of Strict Observance, which was not a part of regular Freemasonry. Three other members were also received into the Lodge at that time, namely Pierre Boileau, a valet; Count Ricciarelli, a musician, and the Countess Cagliostro. Cagliostro wrote in his Lettre au peuple anglais (Letter to the English People):

> For a long time I had known the zeal of the English for Masonry. When I came to this island, my first care was to visit their Lodges. I made inquiries as to the names of those among them where French was spoken. The Loge d'Esperance was indicated to me as one of the most regular. This information was sufficient for a real Mason, and it never entered my head to inquire about the social position of each member of that Lodge. In order to study better the English method, I wanted to present myself as a postulant. I confess that I was

completely satisfied, that I found in the Loge d'Esperance excellent Masons, and that whatever is the social position of the good men of whom it is composed, I shall always pride myself on bearing the title of their brother.[9]

This statement implicates that he *was* already a Mason: '...information sufficient for a real Mason...'; '...wanted to present myself as a postulant'; and that he had no social airs and graces and was happy to be amongst brothers who were mostly domestic servants or small artisans, not nobles or aristocracy.

The following account of this initiation was written in 1786 by Theveneau de Morande, the highly disreputable editor of the biweekly Anglo-French newspaper the *Courier de l'Europe*, in his famous denunciation of the Count, and it would not be surprising if it is spurious. According to de Morande's version of events, the Countess was received first, took the required oath and 'was given a garter on which the device of the lodge, *Union, Silence, Virtue*, was embroidered and ordered to wear it on going to bed that night'. Cagliostro was subjected to a slightly more bizarre initiation consisting of being hoisted into the air on a rope and unceremoniously dropped to the floor. He was then hoodwinked and a loaded pistol given to him after which he was instructed by 'Brother' Hardivilliers to blow out his brains. Unsurprisingly the Count was loathe to pull the trigger and was taunted by cries of 'coward' from the assembled brethren. Apparently to give him the courage necessary to proceed, he was made to take the oath, as follows:

> I (Joseph) Cagliostro, in the presence of the Great Architect of the Universe and my superiors in this respectable assembly, promise to do all that I am ordered, and bind myself under penalties known only to my superiors to obey them blindly without questioning their motives or seeking to discover the secret of the mysteries in which I shall be initiated either by word, sign or writing.[10]

De Morande relates that the pistol was then returned to his grip, albeit this time an unloaded one, and he was again instructed to discharge it. Somewhat reassured he placed the gun to his brow and pulled the trigger. A sound of a report was heard and he received a blow to his head, but, unharmed, he removed the blindfold to reveal himself a newly made Freemason. He was duly given his certificate for which he paid the price of five guineas. All in all, the Count achieved the degrees of Apprentice, Fellow Craft, Master and Scotch Master.

Esperance Lodge, into which Cagliostro had been initiated, was affiliated to the Order of Strict Observance, a society founded earlier in the 1700s by the German Baron von Hundt. Its objective was to revive the *Order of the Knights Templar* whom, of course, had been subject to papal and monarchical tyranny having been disbanded in the 14th century by Pope Clement V. Their Grand Master Jacques de Molay was burnt alive by King Philip of France. The Order of Strict Observance carried with them the taint of rebellion and antimonarchism and was therefore not exactly popular with the Church. The establishment believed that Freemasonry was a tool whereby the ruination of the Church and the Monarchy was encouraged and that the Brotherhood conspired to 'trample the lilies underfoot' – a reference to the use of the initials L D P on Cagliostro's seal showing a serpent, pierced by an arrow, with an apple in its mouth. The initials are believed to have stood for *Liberté de Passer*, Liberty of Passage.

Cagliostro's path on the road of Freemasonry started innocently enough but would ultimately lead to the tragic consequences in store for him in years to come. However, in England, the Rite of Strict Observance lodges were purely social and philanthropic and more importantly for Cagliostro, steeped in the teachings of occultism. The overall importance of these lodges was such that the Count was able to make use of their sister lodges all over Europe during his travels. During this time the Count happened to purchase a booklet on Egyptian Freemasonry, reputedly by one George Coston (or Cofton) of which nothing else is known. He found it overwhelmingly inspirational and with renewed passion for Egypt and his new love of Freemasonry, his mission was now to purify, restore and elevate Masonry to its true level. His early travels in Egypt and the possibility that he was indeed initiated into the inner mysteries by Temple Priests, gave him some kudos when it came to the resurrection of his particular rendition of Egyptian rites within Freemasonry. The teachings that had come out of Egypt over the past centuries were those of Hermetics, of which the aim is the moral and spiritual regeneration of mankind. As one erudite Masonic authority put it:

> [Cagliostro's] system of Masonry was not founded on shadows. Many of the doctrines he enunciated may be found in the Book of the Dead and other important documents of ancient Egypt. And though he may have committed the fatal error of matching himself with the policy of Rome and getting the worst of it, I have not yet been able to find one iota of evidence that he was guilty of anything more reprehensible than an error of judgment during his various journeys.[11]

During this period, the Cagliostros took on a suite of apartments in Whitcombe Street, Leicester Fields, and they proceeded to live in a comfortable way, the Count submerging himself in his love of alchemy and Seraphina whiling away her time with her attendant Madame Blevary, a woman of reduced circumstances who also resided in the same house. As the Countess could speak no English, Madame Blevary managed to worm her way into their lives by offering herself as an interpreter and companion, seeing a good opportunity when it presented itself. Having then introduced to the Cagliostros a certain 'Lord' Scot and his accomplice Miss Fry, the three fraudsters proceeded to find a way to relieve the Count of his perceived wealth.

Within a short space of time, the Cagliostros were inundated with new 'friends', all eager to know more about the new arrivals and intrigued by the assertion from the professor (Scot) that the Count could transmute metals in his laboratory. On finding the Cagliostros so susceptible to dupe, the conversation turned one evening to the idea of the lottery. Cagliostro then was reminded of a cabalistic formula he had once read that could predict winning numbers. Naturally his friends begged him to reveal such a remarkable talent and after much pressure, he relented, and to test the system Scot 'risked a trifle' and won over a hundred pounds. Cagliostro was ambiguous to the results; much more concerned with his alchemy he shunned the response of his acquaintances, viewing their scrabbling for money as of a low nature. He was then subjected to several months of petty recourses by the likes of Scot and Fry until, in their desperation, they had him brought before the bench on trumped-up charges, the outcome of which was a month's stay in the King's Bench Prison.

From London to Brussels

Following Cagliostro's short stay in prison, it was decided that he and his wife would leave England for less stressful shores. In late 1777 Alessandro and Seraphina left for Europe with less than £50 to their name, having allegedly been fleeced of over 3,000 guineas by his so-called friends during his time in London. The Count states:

> My fifty Guineas, which was all that I possessed on leaving London, took me as far as Brussels, where I found Providence waiting to replenish my purse.

Unfortunately he did not embellish further what it was that Providence provided or indeed where it came from, so we can only go by the unreliable and prejudiced views of his Inquisition biographer in implying that it was from disreputable sources. It is more likely that he made good contacts and coinage through his healing work and through the brethren of the Lodges in Brussels.

The Hague, Netherlands and Germany

After Brussels, the Cagliostros made themselves at home in The Hague in the Netherlands and once more the Count embarked upon his Masonic career, being admitted to

Perfect Equality Lodge of the Order of Strict Observance. Soon after, Cagliostro made his first speech and it was here that his vision of Egyptian Freemasonry would be fulfilled; he made several impassioned speeches which led to his Lodge adopting the Egyptian Rite for both men and women. His lifetime obsession and great work had begun. Countess Cagliostro presided as Grand Mistress over the female lodges, while the Count made forth to convince as many Freemasons as he could that his 'new' ritual was the true way to the moral and spiritual rejuvenation of humankind. Baron de Gleichen, a trustworthy and knowledgeable man of the time, declared that:

> Cagliostro's Egyptian Freemasonry was worth the lot of them, for he tried to render it not only more wonderful but more honourable than any other Masonic Order in Europe.[12]

Cagliostro believed that by unifying the Lodges in the manner of the true path of the Egyptian mysteries, all would become equal – the commoner and the nobleman, the worker and the prince could come together in mutual alliance to bring about an enlightened age of tolerance and the highest ideals for mankind. This, perhaps, was his most noble but effectively naïve aspiration – there were those who saw this as the beginning of revolution.

From The Hague, the couple travelled to Nuremberg and whilst in a hotel there, the

Count exchanged Masonic signs with a fellow traveller. When the man inquired as to the Count's identity, Cagliostro sketched the design of a serpent biting its tail as his reply.

Figure 1 Ouroboros

The sign is the *Ouroboros* (tail-devourer), which is an ancient alchemical symbol depicting a snake or dragon swallowing its own tail, thereby constantly creating itself and forming a circle. The symbol has survived from antiquity and can be traced back to ancient Egypt, where it was called *The Circle of Necessity*. On recognizing the symbol, the Mason knew that Cagliostro was a man of profound esoteric knowledge, and pressed into his hand a large diamond ring.

Moving on, the Cagliostros arrived in Leipzig, a large city in the state of Saxony, southeastern Germany. They were welcomed there by a local Masonic Order who lavished on them a sumptuous banquet fit for a visiting dignitary.

After the dinner, Cagliostro made a speech outlining his system and its significance for Masonry, and he called upon the brethren there present to adopt his Rite, but the Master of the Lodge, Herr Scieffort hesitated. The Count warned them that the time had come for a choice to be made and prophesied that the Master's life was in the balance, stating that if they did not embrace Egyptian Masonry then Herr Scieffort would not survive longer than a month. Scieffort refused to make any modifications and, strangely enough, committed suicide several days later. Some contemporary commentators say that, in fact, Scieffort had died several months before Cagliostro arrived on the scene and it was a suitable tale to tell.

Mittau

Cagliostro continued through Germany, into Poland and Prussia and was warmly received by other Lodges of the Order of Strict Observance. In both Danzig (Gdansk) and Konigsberg (formerly the capital of East Prussia but now known as Kaliningrad in Russia) he was welcomed as a dignitary. From here the Cagliostros pressed on, arriving in Mittau, the capital of the Duchy of Courland (an historical Baltic province now part of Latvia) in February/March 1779.

There were many Masons keen to make their acquaintance, amongst them two brothers, the Counts von Medem. One of Cagliostro's most serious future disciples was the writer (Elisa) Charlotte Elisabeth Konstantia von der Recke (1754–1833), the respective daughter and niece of the two aforementioned Counts. Elisa was later to write her memoirs documenting her relationship with Cagliostro but they were not published until 1787, eight years after her meeting with him. By this time Cagliostro's name had been blackened by his alleged role in the Affair of the Diamond Necklace (see section entitled "The Affair of the Diamond Necklace") and Elisa seems to have become somewhat disillusioned after her initial enthusiasm, for her writings are more of an exposé.

Meanwhile, the Cagliostros were invited to stay with the von Medems and the family endeavoured to introduce him to many influential persons. Due to a long-standing interest in alchemy and the occult, the von Medems begged Cagliostro to demonstrate his rumoured psychic and healing powers. Reluctant at first, the Count eventually succumbed, giving some astonishingly accurate predictions and providing proof of his acclaimed medicinal cures. On one occasion he offered to hold one of his famous séances and asked if there was a young boy who could act as the medium. One of the von Medems agreed that his six-year-old son could assist.

Elisa von der Recke provides us with an account of the experiment:[13]

Cagliostro poured into the child's left hand and on his head some liquid which he called the Oil of Wisdom, and, after reciting some prayers and psalms, declared that by this ceremony the boy was made a clairvoyant. Then Cagliostro wrote some mysterious characters on the boy's hand and head, and instructed him to look steadily at his anointed palm. Just before the beginning of the séance, Cagliostro had asked Count von Medem – the boy's father – so that the boy could not hear him, what kind of apparition the Count wished his son to see, to which the father replied that, in order not to frighten the boy, he would prefer him to see the apparition of his own mother and sister. In about ten minutes, after the conjuration, the child suddenly exclaimed that he saw his mother and sister. Cagliostro asked him what his sister was doing, and the child replied: 'She pressed her hand to her heart as though it were aching.' A while afterwards the child exclaimed: 'Now my sister is kissing my brother, who has just come home.' The experiment took place in a house many streets away from the house in which the boy's sister lived, and his brother was supposed to be many miles away from the town, and was not expected home that day at all. Great was, therefore, the surprise of the gentlemen present at the séance when, having returned to Count von Medem's house immediately after its end, they learned that at the very moment the boy saw his sister pressing her hand to her heart she actually had a bad heart-attack and felt quite ill, and that very soon afterwards the boy's brother had come home unexpectedly and was kissed by his sister.

He often performed séances for the crowds that gathered from his social circle and on more than one occasion made some astonishing claims that proved to be extraordinarily accurate. In later years Elisa von der Recke was to pour cold water on these predictions by asserting that Cagliostro must have made secret enquiries of persons concerned, either consciously or unconsciously, relieving them of the information by way of hypnosis, or even going as far as to accuse him of administering poison to a member of her family so as to execute an accurate prediction of illness.

In addition to the founding of Lodges of Adoption (Lodges for female Masons), Cagliostro also offered instruction in the occult sciences via a private audience of small groups. In his naivety and enthusiasm he became quite animated in his talks and managed to offend several of the ladies present with his views on the alchemical *conjunctio* or 'sacred marriage'[14] and instigated subjects that many of his followers believed to be bordering on black magic. When his perturbed audience protested at the subject matter of his lectures he realized he had overstepped the boundaries and declared that he was testing them. Unfortunately this shook the confidence of several of his admirers, including Elisa, and the tide began to change. The Mittau Masons however, although eager to support Cagliostro's Egyptian system soon became greedy for more and more phenomena. Eager to prove that spiritual forces were at work, the Count exercised his powers on frequent occasions, but soon began to feel like a performing bear and refused to honour any further requests. The attitude towards him changed from wonder to cynicism and he was for the first time called 'imposter' and 'quack' for his refusal to perform on demand. Explaining to the Masons that magical powers were to be used for the good of mankind and not for idle amusement or gratification, he was suddenly no longer in favour and he decided to move once more.

St Petersburg and Warsaw

On arriving in St Petersburg, he was soon admitted into a Lodge but the members did not warm to his system of Egyptian Masonry. Disinclined to perform occult phenomena he refused all requests, and although the Masons witnessed several of his medical cures they were more inclined to think of him as a healer than a magician. However, Cagliostro did manage to bring himself to the notice of the Russian Empress Catherine II, better known as Catherine the Great. Due to her deep mistrust of all things mystical (and indeed democratic) which to her included Freemasonry, she was extremely wary of this exponent of the Craft and took an almost instantaneous dislike to the Count. This she took even further, when it seemed that he was having a positive effect on several highly influential persons of the court, including her son Paul, by writing and publishing three satirical plays based on his metaphysical and Masonic traits entitled *The Deceiver, The Deceived* and *The Siberian Shaman*. In later years she would resolve to wipe Freemasonry from the face of Russia. Cagliostro, aware that the Empress's favour was against him, sensibly decided to leave.

Moving onwards into Warsaw, the response was more favourable and he met with Count Moszynski (1738–1817) and Prince Adam Poninski (1758–1816), with whom he stayed. The Prince accepted the idea of Egyptian Freemasonry and as a result a large number of Polish Masons followed suit. A Lodge of the Egyptian Rite was founded within a month and on this basis he was received on several occasions by King Stanislas Augustus Poniatowski (1732–98), a former lover of Catherine the Great. At court he successfully described past and future happenings for a lady who doubted his powers. She herself confirmed the past events as being true and history itself proved the latter to be correct.

Strasburg

After leaving Warsaw (due to the unwanted solicitations of Prince Poninski toward Seraphina) the Cagliostros set forth for Strasburg and it was here that Cagliostro primarily became known for his healing and charitable work; setting up a clinic for those impoverished by circumstance and unable to afford medical care, endeavouring to serve the poor in whatever way he could. With his knowledge of medicines and imbued with the healing powers of divine providence, he was reputed to have cured over 15,000 men, women and children during his stay. It has to be noted that he never received payment from these people, relying solely on gifts and subsidies from his wealthier patrons.

During his stay he had the opportunity to make the acquaintance of many dignitaries and influential persons of which one was Louis René Édouard, the Cardinal de Rohan (1734–1803). Cagliostro's relationship with the Cardinal started uneasily with de Rohan pestering Cagliostro to see him so that he may witness his professed powers. After several refusals the Cardinal was seized by a severe attack of asthma and Cagliostro agreed to help cure him. Soon they became friends and Cagliostro cemented the bond further by predicting the death of Empress Maria Theresa of Austria, thus proving his extraordinary clairvoyance beyond doubt. The Cardinal then invited Cagliostro to lodge at his palace where there was an impressive alchemist's laboratory. When questioned as to the wisdom of having such a man within his vicinity, the Cardinal was quoted as saying that he had on many occasions seen Cagliostro produce gold in a crucible and that he had never 'asked nor received anything from me'.[15] The common bias that many held against Cagliostro was that they regarded him as a flagrant conman, extracting money from his patients and friends. This was denied not only by Cardinal de Rohan, as stated previously, but also by another prominent nobleman, Baron de Gleichen who related that:

> To one that knew him [Cagliostro], his ordinary conversation was agreeable and instructive, his actions noble and charitable, and his curative treatment never a failure and generally admirable. He never took a sou from his patients.[16]

The Count's reputation for healing was further confirmed when he came not only to the aid of the Marquis de Lasalle, Commandant of Strasburg, who was suffering from a severe case of gangrene, but also to Cardinal de Rohan's cousin who was seriously ill in Paris. Begging Cagliostro for help when all other physicians had failed, the Cardinal escorted Cagliostro to Paris incognito whereby he restored the cousin to health within the week. It was only after the cure that Cagliostro's identity was revealed, much to the amazement, and no doubt envy, of the Parisian physicians.

Unfortunately, this jealousy was to infect many aspects of his life and once back in Strasburg he befell yet more misfortune. Taken in by a poor young man named Sacchi, Cagliostro employed him in the clinic as a pharmacist but, within a week or so, it emerged that he was in fact a spy for some rival doctors and had been blackmailing patients to discredit the Count. When Sacchi was removed from the clinic he threatened Cagliostro's life and was then expelled immediately by Commandant de Lesalle. In revenge, he published a libellous account in which he exhorted that Cagliostro was the criminal offspring of a Neapolitan coachman – another ridiculous accusation but one that would haunt the Cagliostros for the rest of their lives.

Several weeks later a letter arrived to inform Cagliostro that his former companion in Malta, Chevalier d'Aquino, was gravely ill. Rushing to be at his side, the Count arrived in Naples only to discover that his great friend was already dead. Cagliostro and Seraphina stayed in Naples for several months but then Cagliostro accepted an invitation to Bordeaux where he was received with an almost royal reverence by Duc de Crillon and the Maréchal de Mouchy. He stayed almost a year, healing the poor and spending time with his titled friends. Sometime during the year, he had a deeply spiritual vision and reflected that it was time to concentrate on his Egyptian

Freemasonry in earnest. He chose Lyons, the city of Illuminism, as the place for his vision to become reality. Here he would find followers of Martinez de Pasqually, Emanuel Swedenborg and Louis Claude de Saint-Martin and hopefully meet up with his contemporary, Dom Pernety, the founder of another system of esoteric wisdom.

On arrival in Lyons he was warmly welcomed by local dignitaries and townsfolk alike, people poured through his doors to be cured and he was admitted to the Lodge in Lyons with great ceremony and invited to found a lodge of Egyptian Freemasonry. With help from the local Masons, construction started immediately and the *Lodge of Triumphant Wisdom,* Mother Lodge of Egyptian Freemasonry, was born.

However, Cagliostro was not to witness the full completion of his design for he was summoned to Paris to take part in a Masonic convention at which Wolfgang Amadeus Mozart, the healer Franz Anton Mesmer and Saint-Martin were reputed to be present. It was while he was in Paris that Cagliostro's fortunes began to change course, for within eight months of his arrival he found himself a prisoner in the infamous Bastille. We shall be returning to the events that took place in Paris in Chapter 3, but first we shall take a closer look at the various influences that had led Cagliostro to create Egyptian Freemasonry.

CHAPTER TWO

THE MASONIC MAGICIAN

Magician [Magus] – a person skilled in the mysterious and hidden art of magic, the ability to attain objectives, acquire knowledge, or perform works of wonder using supernatural or nonrational means.

Magic, sometimes known as sorcery, is a conceptual system that asserts human ability to control the natural world (including events, objects, people, and physical phenomena) through mystical, paranormal or supernatural means. The term can also refer to the practices employed by a person asserting this influence, and to beliefs that explain various events and phenomena in such terms. In many cultures, magic is under pressure from, and in competition with, scientific and religious conceptual systems.[1]

Scientists have for centuries given us an insight into the underlying laws of the physical universe and revealed the hidden workings of the world in which we live. Cagliostro and his mystical contemporaries had a similar goal, but for them it was the unseen world that would reveal its mysteries. Inspired by ancient esoteric texts, such as *The Corpus Hermeticum* (also known as *The Hermetica*), they were convinced they could discover the secret workings of the universe directly from its Creator, by becoming at one with the Mind of God. Cagliostro also had a personal vision to fulfill, one that he believed would not only revive Freemasonry, as he then saw it, but would lead to the regeneration of the whole of mankind through moral and physical rejuvenation.

To set the scene for Cagliostro's vision, we need to look further into the era he was born. The 1700s were aptly named the 'Age of Enlightenment'. Long gone were the Dark Ages of the thousand years prior to the Renaissance, and the oppression of the pre-Restoration era was receding with every decade. The time for radical thinking and the nurturing of the wonders of science was blossoming. Philosophers and free thinkers were in abundance and they felt more liberated in their ability to voice their new and exciting doctrines. The Renaissance had been the literal rebirth of pagan philosophy and theology, but it had been overshadowed by the genuine fear of reprisal from members of the orthodox religion who were ardent subscribers to persecuting anyone who was deemed heretical. The term 'pagan' is not to be confused with the modern-day interpretation – it literally means 'country dweller' and those folk would have had their own religious concepts. It is a euphemism for those who held beliefs natural to their environment and culture; it is not an encompassing terminology for Wiccans, witches or neo-goddess worshippers as in contemporary use.

During the Renaissance all manner of radical philosophies blossomed, many rediscovered from the early years of civilization. Neo-Platonism emerged, underpinning all the nonrational aspects and can be considered as the umbrella under which the other elements operated. According to the philosophy of Neo-Platonism, the cosmos is an organic whole in which each part is connected to all the others. The borders between matter and spirit are indistinct and everything on the Earth is alive and imbued with the spirit of the Divine. Man is linked to the universe by a complex system of spiritual influences, forces and connections and an example of this is to be found in the practice of astrology and alchemy, both of which were prevalent at the time. The new thinkers believed that the ancients held the key to the pinnacles of spirituality and Renaissance man strove to recreate those teachings and apply them to the new age – it was quite literally a rebirth of wisdom.

The most obvious candidates for revival of their spiritual and moral philosophy were the ancient Egyptians. At the time they were the oldest known civilization and one that had been revered by many over the centuries. The primary interest lay in the practice of Hermetics;

Cagliostro and his contemporaries themselves followed the teachings of Hermes Trismegistus, the Greek name for Thoth, the ancient Egyptian man-become-god. Thoth was revered as a god of ancient Egypt around 3000BC and is depicted in tomb and temple as the Ibis-headed scribe, messenger of the gods and recorder of the deeds of mankind. In the afterlife court, the Great Hall of Judgment, Thoth would be in attendance to judge whether the deceased had achieved spiritual wisdom and purity and could then accordingly ascribe a place in heaven. He was master of geometry, astronomy, architecture, medicine and religion and was said to have taught these to the Egyptians. It is thought that Thoth wrote a series of texts that would stand the test of time to be discovered by enlightened ones, who would then understand his teachings and be able to transcend themselves from mere mortals to the state of blissful immortality.

It is thanks to the Greeks, in part, that we still have these invaluable teachings, for along with others thirsting for knowledge in the 2nd and 3rd centuries BC, they transcribed the texts of many ancient sages and philosophers. During the third century BC the Greek ruler Ptolemy II instigated the establishing of the great libraries and museums of Alexandria. This magnificent city was founded by Alexander the Great, who was thought of by the Egyptians to be the Son of Ra (the ancient Egyptian Sun god), basically a leader and Pharaoh by divine right. It was to this city of learning that earnest travellers from all over the world flocked to quench their thirst for Egyptian knowledge. Men and women of all religions met to discuss philosophy, mythology and theology and the well-known library at Alexandria was stocked with nigh on half a million scrolls, documenting some of the most important information mankind would ever see. Treatises on Plato, Pythagoras, Buddhism, ancient Egyptian religion, Judaism, Zoroastrianism, astrology, geometry, the Greek myths and very early Christianity were studied and discussed; never before had there been such a hub of knowledge.

The Greeks identified Thoth with their own god Hermes, also a messenger of the gods and the guide of souls in the underworld. In order to distinguish the Egyptian Hermes from their own, they called him Hermes Trismegistus meaning 'Thrice-Great'. It was his collective written knowledge that became Corpus Hermeticum or The Hermetica. This awesome text is perhaps one of the most important spiritual documents ever to have been found, for it indicates how men may transcend themselves and become as gods. A beautiful and poetic text, it describes how Thoth, through his becoming at one with the mind of god (Nous), witnesses the creation of the world and understands the natural law of the universe.

Unfortunately Alexandria's centre of learning was soon to be no more; with the advent of the Roman Empire came intolerance to other religions or forms of worship. Heretics, or those going against the doctrine of the Church, were killed. Libraries and museums were sacked, and the scrolls, papyri and tablets destroyed. Pagan temples were defaced and shut down and book burning became the order of the day. No longer would there be tolerance and free thinking. Ancient Egypt was dead; the Roman Empire was divided into the Western and Eastern Empires. Reunited by Constantine, they divided once more upon his death, the Western Empire gradually collapsed under Germanic invasion and the last emperor was overthrown in ad 476. The Dark Ages descended in the Western world but meanwhile the Eastern Empire continued to thrive under Christian rulers until the 8th-century Islamic conquests weakened their hold. Not until the 16th century would the ancient spiritual doctrines once more re-emerge in Europe with the Renaissance or 'rebirth' of radical thought.

Luckily transcriptions of The Hermetica had travelled out of Egypt when the scholars fled to avoid the Christian onslaught and over the centuries made an impact on various religions both orthodox and nonorthodox. Five hundred years after the fall of the libraries at Alexandria, followers of the Muslim faith created an empire of learning. Philosophy, religion and science were brought together and in Baghdad, at the beginning of the 9th century, the first ever university was created. It was aptly named the House of

Wisdom and it was here that many of the early pagan texts were translated and secretly studied. Once again the texts of ancient Egypt were held in great veneration and The Hermetica was exalted into the highest position, becoming the secret inspiration for various offshoots of the Muslim religion. Some mystic Muslims, known as the Sufi, believed that their ancestry could be traced back to Hermes Trismegistus. The text itself was taken on as the holy book by the unorthodox sect, the Harranian Sabians.

However, once again religious orthodoxy was about to rear its ugly head. Just like the Christians, the Muslims were beginning to call for strict observance to their doctrine and intolerance to other religions was mounting. Heretics were to be punished and they found a perfect example in the Sufi philosopher Yahya Suhrawardi (1155–91) who had dedicated his life linking the 'original religion' to that of Islam. According to authors Timothy Freke and Peter Gandy,[2] Suhrawardi believed that in ancient times there had been a single doctrine that had been revealed to Thoth and that this had been passed down through the generations of sages directly to the Sufi mystic Al Hallaj (c.858–922).[3] This did not impress the orthodox clerics and, like Al Hallaj before him, Suhrawardi was executed as a heretic.

Still largely unheard of today unless you happen to be an Egyptologist or a student of the esoteric, The Hermetica has been handed down through the ages to those who had the spirit to understand its immense teachings. During the 1400s an agent of Cosimo de Medici had been commissioned to seek out and obtain ancient sacred texts and in 1460 he brought back a copy of The Hermetica. The Hermetic revival in the Renaissance can be traced to a Latin translation of 1471 entitled *De Postate et Sapientia Dei* by Marsilio Ficino (1433–99), who was a member of the de Medici court. It was during this period that interest in the life of the Pharaohs and their temple priests was coming to the fore. Obsessed by symbols, the hieroglyphs used by the ancients fascinated the Renaissance thinkers and they believed that the Egyptians had used them as a secret means of communing with the occult world. This was entirely in line with Neo-Platonic thought and it became a challenge to attempt to break the 'code' of the ancients. This in itself fuelled the movement known as *Hermeticism*.

Hermeticism is wide in its scope and contains various trains of thought, including the concepts of cause and effect, reincarnation, duality and the central maxim 'as above, so below'. It is a complex philosophy and one that remains open to interpretation by the individual. It had, or has, no dogma; there is no 'head office', no official detailed or accepted beliefs – however, it is primarily panentheist (all-in-God), that there is *one* god, *one* great cause – the initiator of the universe, to whom the whole world and mankind was attributed, all living things created by and therefore perceived as having a divine spark. It is a beautiful concept and one which many have readily accepted as a companion to Freemasonry over the centuries; its lack of dogma and a belief in a creator being sits comfortably with the views held by Masons. Could there be more to the origins of Freemasonry than most people think? So what was this vision that not only spurred Cagliostro on, but was first received by Hermes, the man, during his direct meditations with the Creator of the universe? During his teachings with the Mind of God, Hermes was initiated into the mysteries of creation and it was then he received his divine mission to become a spiritual guide for mankind. Only through the wisdom of the 'Nous' (the Greek term for the 'mind of god') could those who walk in darkness be brought into the light. This, we believe, was what Cagliostro felt was his mission also; he often talked of bringing the light into seekers' lives and called himself the 'Friend of Mankind'.

The beginning of the vision of Hermes is described as follows, taken from an early translation of The Hermetica, 'The Second Book' called 'Poimandres'.[4]

Hermes begins to meditate:

> My Thoughts being once seriously busied about the things that are, and my Understanding lifted up, all my bodily Senses being exceedingly holden back, as it is with them that are very heavy of sleep, by

reason either of fullness of meat, or of bodily labour.

He then sees a figure and hears a voice ask him what he wants:

> Me thought I saw one of an exceeding great stature, and an infinite greatness call me by my name, and say unto me, 'What wouldest thou Hear and See? or what wouldest thou Understand, to Learn, and Know!' Then said I, 'Who art Thou?'
>
> 'I am,' quoth he, 'Poimandres, the mind of the Great Lord, the most Mighty and absolute Emperor: I know what thou wouldest have, and I am always present with thee.' Then said I, 'I would Learn the Things that art, and Understand the Nature of them and know God.'
>
> 'How?' said he.
>
> I answered, 'That I would gladly hear.'
>
> Then he, 'Have me again in thy mind, and whatsoever thou wouldst learn, I will teach thee.'

He then goes on to describe a mystical vision showing the creation of the universe, which would become the foundation for all his teachings. At first he sees a 'gentle and joyous', all-encompassing divine light, which as he continues to watch, generates a dark swelling water.

> When he had thus said, he was changed in his Idea or Form and straightway in the twinkling of an eye, all things were opened

unto me: and I saw an infinite Sight, all things were become light, both sweet and exceedingly pleasant; and I was wonderfully delighted in the beholding it.

He is later informed that the light is the 'Mind of God' and the darkness of the water is the unlimited creative potential from which the universe will manifest. This is similar to the theory of the Big Bang, the modern scientific creation theory whereby an explosion of light and energy slowly shapes itself to become the void that is space, from where planets, suns and moons and life forms are eventually born. Hermes hears from this turbulent dark water a terrifying cry, reminiscent of the pain of birth.

But after a little while, there was a darkness made in part, coming down obliquely, fearful and hideous, which seemed unto me to be changed into a Certain Moist Nature, unspeakably troubled, which yielded a smoke as from fire; and from whence proceeded a voice unutterable, and very mournful, but inarticulate, insomuch that it seemed to have come from the Light. From the Light is then issued a Word which calms the maelstrom.

The word is 'order', and is the underlying structure for God's creation.

Then from that Light, a certain Holy Word joined itself unto Nature, and out flew the pure and unmixed Fire from the moist Nature upward on high; it is exceeding Light, and Sharp, and Operative withal. And the Air which was also light, followed the Spirit and mounted up to Fire (from the Earth and the Water) insomuch that it seemed to hang and depend upon it. And the Earth and the Water stayed by themselves so mingled together, that the Earth could not be seen for the Water, but they were moved, because of the Spiritual Word that was carried upon them.

The Divine (Poimandres) then asks of Hermes whether he understands what he has just seen.

Then said Poimandres unto me, 'Dost thou understand this Vision, and what it meaneth?'

'I shall know,' said I.

Then said he, 'I am that Light, the Mind, thy God, who am before that Moist Nature that appeareth out of Darkness, and that Bright and Lightful Word from the Mind is the Son of God.'

This piece is probably the most quoted from The Hermetica. It is a very important and basic system of connecting with the Divine and one which almost all religions incorporate in the form of meditation and prayer.

The Hermetica would have been studied by millions of other seekers before Count Cagliostro first discovered its wisdom. In fact the list of the most noted students before and after him reads like a metaphysical, scientific, artistic and philosophical *Who's Who* (see Appendix One). From its beginning in Egypt, this remarkable text has been passed down from society to society becoming absorbed into orthodox and fringe religions along the way. From Egypt the text passed through Chaldea (where it is believed the founders of astrology originated); from here some of the wisdom was absorbed into the Orphic Hymns of Orpheus, which then inspired Zoroaster, Pythagoras and Plato.

Over the centuries Hermeticism blended itself into many of the dogmas and religions in true syncretic form; its framework of magic, alchemy and astrology was bolstered by the Jewish Cabala and Christian mysticism. So when it was 'rediscovered' during the Renaissance it rekindled a revolution in alchemy and once more metamorphosed into a different form with the incorporation of the magical influences of magicians such as Heinrich Cornelius Agrippa (1486–1535), Paracelsus (1493–1541) and John Dee (1527–1608/9). Although the text lives on, it has been changed many times either through poor translation or misunderstanding, but within it we can salvage what remains of true Egyptian teaching, something we should never underestimate. The beauty and wisdom of ancient Egypt has slipped into every spiritual teaching known to man. One example is that of the Christian Psalm 104, which holds many characteristics of one of the Hymns to the Aten dedicated to the monotheistic deity worshipped in Egypt during the reign of Akhenaton (c.1351–4BC). It is believed that Jewish emigrants sang the hymns to keep up their spirits, the spirit of the Aten walking with them out of Egypt.

THE EMERALD TABLET

The teachings of Hermes Trismegistus have always played a huge part in the lives of the alchemists, along with the simple 13-line script engraved on a piece of emerald. Known as *The Emerald Tablet, Smaragdine Table, Tabula Smaragdina*, or the *Secret of Hermes*, it is an ancient Hermetic text, also believed to have been scribed by Hermes. It reveals a similar message to that of Poimandres, the creation of the world and the four elements by the Divine and the mysteries of the micro/macrocosm. However, it also purports to reveal the secret of the primordial substance and its transmutations – the first matter or the philosopher's stone, the holy grail of all alchemists, and the means of turning base metal into gold and for producing the elixir of life.

The translation reads:

> It is true, without any error, and it is the sum of truth; that which is above is also that which is below, for the performance of the wonders of a certain one thing, and as all things arise from one Stone, so also they were generated from one common Substance, which includes the

four elements created by God. And among other miracles the said Stone is born of the First Matter. The sun is its Father, the moon its Mother, the wind bears it in its womb, and it is nursed by the earth. Itself is the Father of the whole earth, and the whole potency thereof. If it be transmuted into earth, then the earth separates from the fire that which is most subtle from that which is hard, operating gently and with great artifice. Then the Stone ascends from earth to heaven, and again descends from heaven to earth, and receives the choicest influences of both heaven and earth. If you can perform this you have the glory of the world, and are able to put to flight all diseases, and to transmute all metals. It overcomes Mercury, which is subtle, and penetrates all hard and solid bodies. Hence it is compared with the world. Hence I am called Hermes, having the three parts of the whole world of philosophy.

Newton's translation

Sir Isaac Newton studied the Tablet's wisdom and a translation made by him was found in his papers relating to alchemy:
1. Tis true without lying, certain

2. That which is below is like that which is above is like that which is below to do the miracles of only one thing.
3. And as all things have been one: so all things have their birth from this one thing by adaptation.
4. The Sun is its father, the moon its mother.
5. The wind hath carried it in its belly, the earth its nurse.
6. The father of all perfection in the whole world is here.
7. Its force or power is entire if it be converted into earth.
7a. Separate thou the earth from the fire, the subtle from the gross sweetly with great industry.
8. It ascends from the earth to the heaven earth and receives the force of things superior & inferior.
9. By this means you shall have the glory of the whole world all obscurity shall fly from you.
10. Its force is above all force, for it vanquishes every subtle thing & penetrates every solid thing.
11a. So was the world created.
12. From this are & do come admirable adaptations where of the means (or process) is here in this.

13. Hence I am called Hermes Trismegist, having the three parts of the philosophy of the whole world.
14. That which I have said of the operation of the Sun is accomplished & ended.

Commentary on the Emerald Tablet of Hermes – The Glory of the World

Many commentaries and/or translations were published by, among others, Johannes Trithemius, Roger Bacon, Michael Maier, Albertus Magnus, and as seen above, Isaac Newton. This mysterious text has survived in our collective unconscious to the present day; its influence has been seen in the work of Carl Jung and most recently in the book and film, *The Secret*.

The following text is a commentary on the Emerald Tablet which was included in the text *Musaeum Hermeticum* of 1625, first published in German as *Gloria Mundi sonsten Paradeiss Taffel*, Frankfurt, 1620.

Hermes is right in saying that our Art is true, and has been rightly handed down by the Sages; all doubts concerning it have arisen through false interpretation of the mystic language of the philosophers. But, since they are loth to confess their own ignorance, their readers prefer to say that the words of the Sages are imposture and falsehood. The fault really lies with the ignorant reader, who does not understand the style of the Philosophers. If, in the interpretation of our books, they would suffer themselves to be guided by the teaching of Nature, rather than by their own foolish notions, they would not miss the mark so hopelessly. By the words which follow: 'That which is above is also that which is below', he describes the Matter of our Art, which, though one, is divided into two things, the volatile water which rises upward, and the earth which lies at the bottom, and becomes fixed. But when the reunion takes place, the body becomes spirit, and the spirit becomes body, the earth is changed into water and becomes volatile; the water is transmuted into body, and becomes fixed. When bodies become spirits, and spirits bodies, your work is finished, for then that which rises upward and that which descends downward become one body. Therefore the Sage says that that which is above is that which is below, meaning that, after having been separated into two substances (from being one substance), they are again joined together into one substance, i.e., an union which can never be dissolved, and possesses such virtue and efficacy that it can do in one moment what the Sun cannot accomplish in a thousand years. And this miracle is wrought by a thing which is despised and rejected by the multitude. Again, the Sage tells us that all things were created, and are still generated, from one first substance and consist of the same elementary material; and in this first substance God has appointed the four elements, which represent a common material into which it might perhaps be possible to resolve all things. Its development is brought about by the distillation of the Sun and Moon. For it is operated upon by the natural heat of the Sun and Moon, which stirs up its internal action, and multiplies each thing after its kind, imparting to the substance a specific form. The soul, or nutritive principle, is the earth which receives the rays of the Sun and Moon, and therewith feeds her children as with mother's milk. Thus the Sun is the father, the Moon is the mother, the Earth the nurse – and in this substance is that which we require. He who can take it and prepare it is truly to be envied. It is separated by the Sun and Moon in the form of a vapour, and collected in the place where it is found. When Hermes adds that 'the air bears it in its womb, the Earth is its nurse, the whole world its Father', he means that when the substance of our Stone is dissolved, then the wind bears it in its womb, i.e., the air bears up the substance in the form of water, in which is hid fire, the soul of the Stone, and fire is the Father of the whole world. Thus, the volatile substance rises upward, while that which remains at the bottom, is the 'whole world' (seeing that our Art is compared to a 'small world'). Hence Hermes calls fire the father of the whole world, because it is the Sun of our Art, and air, Moon, and water ascend from it; the Earth is the nurse of the Stone, i.e., when the Earth receives the rays of the Sun and Moon, a new body is born, like a new foetus in the mother's womb. The Earth receives and digests the light of Sun and Moon, and imparts food to its foetus day by day, till it becomes great and strong, and puts off its blackness and defilement, and is changed to a different colour. This, 'child', which is called 'our daughter', represents our Stone, which is born anew of the Sun and Moon, as you may easily see, when the spirit, or the water that ascended, is gradually transmuted into the body, and the body is born anew, and grows and increases in size like the foetus in the mother' womb. Thus the Stone is generated from the first substance, which contains the four elements; it is brought forth by two things, the body and the spirit; the wind bears it in its womb, for it carries the Stone upward from Earth to heaven, and down again from heaven to Earth. Thus the Stone receives increase from above and from below, and is born a second time, just as every other foetus is generated in the maternal womb; as all created things bring forth their young, even so does the air, or wind, bring forth our Stone. When Hermes adds, 'Its power, or virtue, is entire, when it is transmuted into earth', he means that when the spirit is transmuted into the body, it receives its full strength and virtue. For as yet the spirit is volatile, and not fixed, or permanent. If it is to be fixed, we must proceed as the baker does in baking bread. We must impart only a little of the spirit to the body at a time, just as the baker only puts a little leaven to his meal, and with it leavens the whole lump. The spirit, which is our leaven, in like fashion transmutes the whole body into its own substance. Therefore the body must be leavened again and again, until the whole lump is thoroughly pervaded with the power of the leaven. In our Art the body leavens the spirit, and transmutes it into one body, and the spirit leavens the body, and transmutes it into one spirit. And the two, when they have become one, receive power to leaven all things, into which they are injected, with their own virtue. The Sage continues: 'If you gently separate the earth from the water, the subtle from the hard, the Stone ascends from earth to heaven, and again descends from heaven to earth, and receives its virtue from above and from below. By this process you obtain the glory and brightness of the whole world. With it you can put to flight poverty, disease, and weariness; for it overcomes the subtle mercury, and penetrates all hard and firm bodies.' He means that all who would accomplish this task must separate the moist from the dry, the water from the earth. The water, or fire, being subtle, ascends, while the body is hard, and remains where it is. The separation must be accomplished by gentle heat, i.e., in the temperate bath of the Sages, which acts slowly, and is neither too hot nor too cold. Then the Stone ascends to heaven, and again descends from heaven to earth. The spirit and body are first separated, then again joined together by gentle coction, of a temperature resembling that with which a hen hatches her eggs. Such is the preparation of the substance, which is worth the whole world, whence it is also called a 'little world'. The possession of the Stone will yield you the greatest delight, and unspeakably precious comfort. It will also set forth to you in a typical form the creation of the world. It will enable you to cast out all disease from the human body, to drive away poverty, and to have a good understanding of the secrets of Nature. The Stone has virtue to transmute mercury into gold and silver, and to penetrate all hard and firm bodies, such as precious stones and metals. You cannot ask a better gift of God than this gift, which is greater than all other gifts. Hence Hermes may justly call himself by the proud title of 'Hermes Trismegistus', who holds the three parts of the whole world of wisdom.

You can imagine how the highly creative minds of the 17th century and beyond would have been desperate to unravel the mysteries of the ancients, to know the wisdom of the whole universe, which according to ancient teaching comprised of three parts – *Alchemy, Astrology* and *Theurgy.*

Alchemy

Alchemy – *Al-Kemet* – was believed to have originated in ancient Egypt as coming from *Kemet* which was the original name of Egypt. It is the investigation of nature, along with a philosophical and spiritual practice which combines elements of chemistry, physics, astrology, metallurgy and medicine. Inspired by 17th-and 18th-century engravings, the word 'alchemist' conjures up mental images of robed sages in antiquarian laboratories attempting to transmute lead or other base metals into gold, and indeed this was a large part of it. This process could only be achieved by securing the fabled philosopher's stone (*philosophi lapis*), a mythical substance that was supposedly able to make the transformation. The philosopher's stone could also be used as, or to help create, the 'elixir of life' — a liquid reputed to make someone appear younger or even to achieve a state of immortality.

During the Renaissance period, the search for the philosopher's stone was a major preoccupation for many, particularly those with the disposable income to be able to either set up their own laboratory or pay an alchemist to do it for them. Many dignitaries and members of royalty were the official sponsors of anyone who proclaimed an ability to change lead into gold or produce the much desired youth elixir; something that Cagliostro was reputed to be rather good at. This may appear at first glance to imply that the already rich were greedy for yet more riches and a rather selfish desire for immortality over the less fortunate. But alchemy was much more than a materialistic ideal; it was a deeply mystical and philosophical practice to improve the spiritual state of mankind.

The figurative representation of the alchemist tucked away in his laboratory playing with metals and various other elements, is not much more than a simple visual allegory. Behind the quaintly romantic feel is a quest for spiritual perfection — the transmutation of the metals is symbolic of the state of change required in the human to transcend our base nature and transform into a purer, higher state of being, the moral equivalent of gold. Once again an esoteric practice mirrors that of Freemasonry or vice versa. In the ritual, a rough and a smooth ashlar (block of stone) are used to demonstrate the transformation required for the candidate. The rough ashlar shows the candidate as a non-Mason, who then through the teachings of Freemasonry is able to chip away at the rough edges of his nature to become representative of the smooth ashlar – a perfect square, a perfected human being.

Alchemists from time immemorial have attempted to tap into the hidden spiritual forces that connect everything, to move from the microcosm to the macrocosm. When this was understood, the alchemist could then potentially be able to manipulate these forces for the goodness of mankind. Spiritual perfection was a highly desirable aim because in achieving it, not only would the successful alchemist become as one with the divine essence that imbued everything, he would through his own improvement improve the spiritual wellbeing of humankind.

However, this process was something that needed to be achieved with great secrecy. It was believed that the search for the philosopher's stone could only be undertaken by individuals or groups of adepts skilled in the mystic arts, and secrecy was necessary as the majority of people were simply incapable of understanding the principles of alchemy. The wisdom of the ancients was intended for the pure of heart who would not seek it solely for their own self-interest. Secrecy was also necessary, for misunderstanding of the alchemists' work could also lead to persecution. This preservation of the art led to a large number of secret societies throughout 18th-century Europe wherein the knowledge was contained so that it would not become diluted by the common practice of the populace.

The alchemists and other magicians believed that symbols were keys to the unseen, being able to both reveal and conceal the divine essence. As their meanings could not be successfully put into words, the pictorial references were handed down from generation to generation – so not only did the alchemists meet in secret but they taught and learnt in secret, with signs and sigils that ordinary folk could not decipher. Not just a secret society, but a society with secrets.

Alchemy became so popular that decrees were issued by various authorities to ban its use. The earliest ban had been in 144BC in China. Diocletian banned the production of silver and gold in the 3rd-century ad supposedly out of fear 'lest the opulence of the Egyptians should inspire them [the people] with confidence to rebel against the empire'. Almost a thousand years later, Pope John XXI (c.1215–77) issued a bull condemning the alchemists Thomas Aquinas (c.1225–74) and Roger Bacon (c.1214–94), amongst many others, for their heretical work. Aquinas was already dead but Bacon was imprisoned for 14 years. In the 14th century, Pope John XXII forbade the transmutation of base metals into gold. In 1403 King Henry IV banned alchemy in England, only allowing it to be performed under royal licence. The ban appeared to be a paradox stemming from the fear of production of real gold and the indignation invoked by the fake.

Astrology

Within the writings of Hermes Trismegistus, it is stated that the ancient Persian prophet Zoroaster was the first to comprehend the movements of the celestial bodies, and then passed on this knowledge to the rest of mankind. The Hermetics believed that the movements of the planets had meanings beyond that of their observable orbits – that although the heavenly bodies had an impact on the affairs of mankind, they merely influenced rather than dictated. This influence worked via a variety of occult forces, and knowledge of these forces and their associations allowed them to be manipulated, thereby offering insight and wisdom. This knowledge was not something to be exploited and rather than an individual obtaining an astrologer to draw up a personal horoscope, it was thought that by tapping into these spiritual forces, primarily through the practice of magic and alchemy, spiritual benefits could ideally be obtained for the whole of mankind as well as for the individual.

Theurgy

'The Art of Divine Works' – considered to be the practical aspect of alchemy, involving the use of magical ritual. During the Renaissance, magic was considered to be of two distinct types – black and white. Black magic or *goetia* was the attempt to communicate with and control demons and other evil spirits. If control was not possible, alliance would be the next best thing. Theurgy was the complete opposite, often described as 'divine magic'. This was an attempt by the alchemist or magician to create an alliance with the divine spirits, such as angels, archangels and ultimately God. In modern times we would not categorize this as white magic for it involves the manipulation or coercion of spiritual forces and therefore borders on 'grey' magic. White magic could now be categorized as a purely connective relationship with God.

The use of ritual magic, theurgy, was the key by which alchemical endeavours were brought to fruition, the aim being to achieve 'theosis' or unity with the Godhead. This would bring about spiritual perfection for the magician and therefore achieve the Hermetic principle of spreading this beneficence to all of mankind.

These three parts of the wisdom of the whole universe – alchemy, astrology and theurgy – are often described by the Hermetists as the 'operations' of the Sun, the Moon and the stars.

This is again reflected within Freemasonry, which also makes use of the symbols representing the three heavenly bodies.

THE INSPIRATION FOR CAGLIOSTRO'S MISSION

These teachings were to be the catalyst for Cagliostro, for along with his study of the Hermetic path he saw that there was something that reflected many of these ideals and values – Freemasonry. His love of Egypt (Hermetics), his desire for purity and the transformation of mankind, combined with Freemasonry was a potent force. If he could just amalgamate the three things that he felt were the key to the regeneration of humankind then he would be able to pass on these wonderful teachings for time immemorial. His vision was of a perfected world whereby all religions would be tolerated, wherein all men would be charitable to one another and that communion with the divine essence itself could be realized. The constitutions of Freemasonry mixed with a potent blend of esoterica and the result would be a spiritual utopia.

What an amazing task! What a dangerous notion. These things, as with alchemy and the occult sciences, should ideally have been kept secret. Ordinary people would not understand and so they were not really an issue, but the

Church on the other hand understood far too much, and it was the one to be afraid of. Even in the 100 years after the Renaissance, it was not wise to digress too far from the path of orthodox religion and, although the Age of Enlightenment certainly brought about a new wave of thinkers, it was still prudent to be reasonably covert about your practices. However, there were several rather flamboyant characters that were already setting the stage for Cagliostro; a plethora of mystics, healers, alchemists and philosophers. One was the Count de St Germain, an enigmatic figure who also claimed that he was of an immortal nature.

Acording to one account, the Cagliostros paid a visit to the Count de St Germain. In his usual eccentric manner, St Germain arranged their meeting for the hour of two o'clock in the morning, at which time Cagliostro and Seraphina were to present themselves at the Count's temple of mystery. The Count de St Germain was to be found sitting upon the altar, with two acolytes swinging golden censers at his feet. In the book *Lives of the Alchemystical Philosophers*,[5] published anonymously in 1815, the following is recorded as having occurred between the magicians:

> The divinity bore upon his breast a diamond pentagram of almost intolerable radiance. A majestic statue, white and diaphanous, upheld on the steps of the altar a vase inscribed, 'Elixir of Immortality', while

a vast mirror was on the wall, and before it a living being, majestic as the statue, walked to and fro. Above the mirror were these singular words – 'Store House of Wandering Souls'. The most solemn silence prevailed in this sacred retreat, but at length a voice, which seemed hardly a voice, pronounced these words – 'Who are you? Whence come you? What would you?' Then the Count and Countess Cagliostro prostrated themselves, and the former answered after a long pause, 'I come to invoke the God of the faithful, the Son of Nature, the Sire of Truth. I come to demand of him one of the fourteen thousand seven hundred secrets which are treasured in his breast, I come to proclaim myself his slave, his apostle, his martyr.' The divinity did not respond, but after a long silence, the same voice asked – 'What does the partner of thy long wanderings intend?' 'To obey and to serve,' Seraphina answered. Simultaneously with her words, profound darkness succeeded the glare of light, uproar followed on tranquillity, terror on trust, and a sharp and menacing voice cried loudly – 'Woe to those who cannot stand the tests.' Husband and wife were immediately separated to undergo their respective trials, which they endured with exemplary fortitude and which are detailed in the text of their memoirs. When the romantic mummery was over, the two postulants were led back into the temple with the promise of admission to the divine mysteries. There a man mysteriously draped in a long mantle cried out to them – 'Know ye that the Arcanum of our great art is the government of mankind, and that the one means to rule them is never to tell them the truth. Do not foolishly regulate your actions according to the rules of common sense; rather outrage reason and courageously maintain every unbelievable absurdity. Remember that reproduction is the palmary active power in nature, politics and society alike; that it is a mania with mortals to be immortal, to know the future without understanding the present, and to be spiritual while all that surrounds them is material.'

After this harangue the orator genuflected devoutly before the divinity of the temple and retired. At the same moment a man of gigantic stature led the countess to the feet of the immortal Count de St Germain who thus spoke: 'Elected from my tendrest youth to the things of greatness, I employed myself in ascertaining the nature of veritable glory. Politics appeared to me nothing but the science of deception, tactics the art of assassination, philosophy the ambitious imbecility of complete irrationality; physics fine fancies about Nature and the continual mistakes of persons suddenly transplanted, into a country which is utterly unknown to them; theology the science of the misery which results from human pride; history the melancholy spectacle of perpetual perfidy and blundering. Thence I concluded that the statesman was a skilful liar, the hero an illustrious idiot, the philosopher an eccentric creature, the physician a pitiable and blind man, the theologian a fanatical pedagogue, and the historian a wordmonger. Then did I hear of the divinity of this temple. I cast my cares upon him, with my incertitudes and aspirations. When he took possession of my soul he caused me to perceive all objects in a new light; I began to read futurity. This universe so limited, so narrow, so desert, was now enlarged. I abode not only with those who are, but with those who were. He united me to the loveliest women of antiquity. I found it eminently delectable to know all without studying anything, to dispose of the treasures of the earth without the solicitations of monarchs, to rule the elements rather than men. Heaven made me liberal; I have sufficient to satisfy my taste; all that surrounds me is rich, loving, predestined.'

The illustrious Count de St Germain was often confused with being one and the same as Count Cagliostro; they were both reputed to have discovered and used the elixir of life and some say they were both known as the 'Wandering Jew', a figure from a medieval Christian myth (see section entitled "MYTH OF THE WANDERING JEW AND IMMORTALITY").

Cagliostro's contemporaries were perhaps less colourful in appearance and manner but equally as immersed in the mysteries of the universe.

Martinez de Pasqually was reputed to have been born in 1727. His full name was *Jacques de Livron Joachim de la Tour de la Casa Martinez de Pasqually*. His Rite was cabalistic and Hermetic in its teachings, and was known as the Rite of Elected Cohens or Priests. It comprised the following grades:

1. Apprentice
2. Companion
3. Particular Master (corresponding to the three Craft degrees)
4. Grand Elect Master
5. Apprentice Cohen
6. Companion Cohen
7. Master Cohen
8. Grand Master Architect
9. Knight Commander

Pasqually's work was theurgic and sought union with the Deity. Like Cagliostro, he used the ancient symbols and words and communed with the angelic beings.

According to Arthur Edward Waite:

Pasqually was born somewhere in the parish of Notre Dame, belonging to the diocese of Grenoble, but the date is unknown. He is first heard of in the year 1760 at Toulouse. He carried his strange Rite of Theurgic Priesthood from Toulouse to Bordeaux, from Bordeaux to Lyons, from Lyons to Paris, seeking its recognition everywhere at the centres of Grand Lodges and Chapters.[6]

In 1768 Pasqually settled in Paris, where he established the Sovereign Tribunal of the Rite. Learning that property had been bequeathed to him in the island of San Domingo, he decided to take up residence and he was not seen in Europe again. He established a Lodge in Port-au-Prince, and another in Lêogane. He continued to correspond with the lodges in France and they received in the following years more formulas for magical evocations and procedures that would be used in the higher degrees of the system. In 1773 Pasqually sent a *'Répertoire général des noms et nombres en jonction avec les caractères et hièroglyphes'* to France. This was a general system to be employed in the invocation and evocation of spirits. In 1774 he constructed initiation rituals for women who wished to be admitted to the Order. He died in 1779 at Port-au-Prince.

One of Pasqually's disciples in Paris was Louis Claude de St Martin, subsequently known as the 'Unknown Philosopher'.

Louis-Claude Saint-Martin (1743–1803) was a French philosopher and occultist. It was when based at an army garrison in Bordeaux that he became a student of Pasqually. He left the army in 1771 to become a mystical preacher and he was welcomed around Europe for his sublime oration. He became involved with Jacob Boehme, the German Christian mystic and later translated many of his works into French. Saint-Martin was heavily influenced by Franz Mesmer and Emanuel Swedenborg. It is undecided as to whether Saint-Martin himself founded the *Order of Martinists*. This was an esoteric mystical tradition with an emphasis on meditation. They believed in Christ as 'The Repairer' who would enable individuals to realize a state of innocence such as existed before the Fall of Man. It is more likely that Saint-Martin's disciples continued his teachings throughout Europe and when a young Parisian doctor called Gerard Encausse (later known as Papus) became acquainted with them that the Order became realized.

In 1884, along with some of his associates, Encausse established the Ordre Martiniste. The Order survived until the First World War when Papus died, as did many other leaders of the Order, on the battlefield fulfilling his duty as a doctor. A fragment of the Order remained and splintered into competing groups. The Second World War was almost as disastrous for them due to Hitler's hatred of secret societies and orders, and many of the followers died in the concentration camps. Martinism still exists to this day and is a fast growing organization. Other societies that align themselves with Martinism are the Elus-Cohens (Pasqually's society) and the Scottish Rectified Rite (Chevaliers Bénéficients de la Cité-Sainte – CBCS), originally a Masonic Rite of Strict Observance founded in the late 18th century by Jean-Baptiste Willermoz (1730–1824), a student of Pasqually and contemporary of Saint-Martin. The CBCS is still in existence today as a Masonic rite and as a rite open to women.

Friedrich Joseph Wilhelm Schroeder was a precursor of Cagliostro and a doctor and professor of pharmacology, who was born at Bielfeld, Prussia, on 19 March 1733. He devoted himself to chemistry, alchemy and occultism. In 1766, he founded a Chapter of True and Ancient Rose-Croix Masons at Marburburg. *Mackey's Encyclopedia of Freemasonry* describes him:

> In 1779, he [Schroeder] organized in a lodge of Sarreburg a school or Rite, founded on magic, theosophy, and alchemy, which consisted of seven high degrees; four high degrees founded on the occult sciences being superadded to the original three Symbolic degrees. This Rite, called the 'Rectified Rose-Croix', was only practised by two lodges under the constitution of the Grand Lodge of Hamburg. Clavel, in his *Histoire Pittoresque* (p.183) calls him the Cagliostro of Germany, and Oliver terms

him an adventurer. But it is perhaps more just that we should attribute to him a diseased imagination and misdirected studies than a bad heart or impure practices.

Franz Anton Mesmer was born 23 May 1734. At the age of 9 he entered a monastery school and at 15 won a scholarship. When he was 18, he obtained a place at the University of Ingolstadt, where he studied the writings of Paracelsus and obtained the degree of doctor of philosophy. He studied law for a while in Vienna, but his interest in Paracelsus fired him with a determination to become a doctor and he took up the study of medicine under Dr van Swieten, one of the foremost physicians of the day.

According to a Theosophist Society lecture, Dr Mesmer was 'deeply fond of music, playing with skill the piano and cello'. His home was soon the meeting place of the music lovers of Vienna, Haydn and Mozart becoming daily visitors. When the Director of the Imperial Opera refused to present an opera by Mozart on the grounds that he (then 12 years old) was too young to compose an opera, Dr Mesmer took pity on the young artist and presented Mozart's first work to the public in his own garden theatre. Mozart acknowledged this service by inserting a complimentary reference to Dr Mesmer in his *Cosi fan Tutte*. In 1776 an important event occurred in Dr Mesmer's life. One day a stranger appeared at his door, introducing himself as the Count de St Germain.

'You must be the gentleman whose anonymous letter I received yesterday,' Dr Mesmer remarked as he took his caller into his study. 'Yes,' St Germain replied, 'I am he.' 'You wish to speak with me on the subject of magnetism?' Dr Mesmer inquired. 'I do,' St Germain replied. 'That is why I came to Vienna.' Dr Mesmer then told his guest of his magnetic experiments, confessing that he was still confused about the higher aspects of magnetism. 'Who can enlighten me?' he asked. 'I can,' said the Count, with the assurance, 'it is my duty to do so.' The conversation which took place on that memorable afternoon lasted for several hours.[7]

The scientific work of Mesmer is discussed by all his biographers but his occult involvement is not so well known. Mesmer was not only a Mason, but was also an initiated member of two occult fraternities, the *Fratres Lucis* and the *Brotherhood of Luxor*. But his healing work will be his most remembered mission; he almost gave up everything in the desire to treat the sick and injured, turning his house into a hospital of sorts. However, his methods were curious and opened him to much derision and humiliation.

He first began to use magnets on his patients, but after his talk with Saint Germain, he moved on to the use of 'animal magnetism'. 'Animal magnetism' according to Theosophical teachings is:

> ...a fluid, a correlation of atoms on metaphysical planes, which exudes from every human being in a greater or less degree. Some people have the power to emit this fluid consciously, through their eyes and fingertips, and most of the healing 'miracles' of history are based upon this psychophysical power in man.

Mesmer's unorthodox ways caused him much grief and he left Austria for France where he received the patronage of the aristocracy, not least that of Marie Antoinette. But this did not avert further suspicion and in 1784 he was denounced as an impostor and left France to work as an unknown healer, undisturbed in Frauenfeld:

> a little village about twenty miles from Zurich. There he continued his research work and gave free treatments to his humble peasant neighbours who had never even heard of the famous Dr Mesmer.

Emanuel Swedenborg (1688–1772) was a Swedish scientist, philosopher, theologian and Christian mystic. He was well known as an inventor and scientist. Aged 56 he entered into a spiritual phase, and began to have intense dreams and visions. This brought about a spiritual revelation in him, whereby he claimed he had been appointed by God to write a heavenly doctrine to reform Christianity. He claimed that, with divine aid, he could freely visit heaven and hell and talk with angels, demons and other spirits. In the last 28 years of his life, he wrote and published 18 theological works and several that remained unpublished.

He was a talented psychic and one aspect of Swedenborg's writing that is often discussed is his ideas of marriage. Although a bachelor all his life, that did not prevent him from writing in depth about the subject. 'A righteous marriage,' he argues, 'is intended to be a continuous spiritual refinement of both parties, and such a union would be maintained in the afterlife.'[8] He saw marriage as being fundamentally about union – of wisdom, physically represented in the man, and of love, physically represented in the female.

> Faith is a union of the two qualities of reason (represented by the man) and intention (represented by the female). And, similarly, the wisdom of God has its corresponding part in the love from the Church.

Swedenborg was sharply opposed to the Christian doctrine of the Trinity as three separate persons; he claimed that the three were merely different aspects of the one God. He felt that Divinity was a union within one person that could not be divided. He also believed that salvation was only possible through the conjunction of faith and charity in a person. For Swedenborg the physical world was a result of spiritual cause, the laws of nature reflecting the spiritual laws and the material world reflecting its spiritual counterpart. This is reflective of the Hermetic principle 'as above, so below'. His ideas had an enormous effect on many, including William Blake, W B Yeats, etc. It was also the influence of his teachings and qualities that went towards the founding of the Masonic First Rite of Swedenborg, by Dom Antoine Joseph Pernety (1716–96).

Dom Antoine Joseph Pernety It is possibly Pernety who was the inspiration for Cagliostro's early forays into Egyptian tradition and ritual. Pernety was a French Hermetic alchemist and also, interestingly enough, a Benedictine monk from the Abbey of St Germain des Prés in Paris. He was known for founding a Masonic rite entitled the *Hermetic Ritual of Perfection* which had originally been used by an esoteric Masonic sect called the *Illuminati of Avignon*.

Unfortunately, Pernety was persecuted by the Jesuits and had to leave Avignon for Berlin, where he was placed under the protection of King Frederick II. Frederick was a well-known supporter of Freemasonry, having been initiated in 1738, and so afforded Pernety safety in the position of curator of the Berlin Library. Whilst in Berlin, Pernety practised a form of Hermetic/Egyptian talismanic and astral magic and performed séances for the German aristocracy, for whom he reputedly invoked the power of spirits and angels. Cagliostro made the acquaintance of Pernety whilst staying with some

Masonic patrons in Leipzig and it is likely that they shared many an evening conversing on the higher mystical arts.

It is also possible that during his travels, Cagliostro became acquainted with Prince Raimondo di Sangro (1710–71). Di Sangro, a Freemason and head of a Neoplolitan Lodge, was excommunicated by the Catholic Church for his Masonic activities (later revoked by Benedict XIV) but he was also a master alchemist. During Cagliostro's interviews with the Inquisition interrogators, it is recorded that he had been taught by 'a Prince in Naples who had a great passion for chemistry'. The Holy Fathers did not believe him, but later rumination has provided the idea that di Sangro was that Prince.

It has to be understood that in the libraries of these scholars and magicians were probably also copies of the ancient magical texts such as the *Lesser and Greater Key of Solomon,* Heinrich Cornelius Agrippa's *Three Books of Occult Philosphy* and the works of Paracelsus and other great alchemists and theurgists.

It is also very pertinent that during the 1770s, Germany was a hotbed of secret societies and Masonic orders, including one known as the *African Architects*. This was reputed to have been founded by Frederick von Koppen, who was also believed to have written a peculiar Masonic text called the *Crata Repoa*. This was a work purporting to contain authentic rituals used by the ancient Egyptian priests during initiations within the great pyramids. These rituals are now thought to have been inspired by Jean Terrasson's Masonic novel *The Life of Sethos* published in 1731, which included large amounts of information gleaned from Greek texts relating to the mysteries of Egypt. It is likely that Cagliostro was familiar not only with the novel but with the rituals then incorporated into various Masonic Lodges throughout France during the mid-1700s.

When putting the life and work of Cagliostro into perspective, we must remember that occultists and mystics were reasonably common in an era where new discoveries, both scientific and philosophical, were happening all the time. After the Renaissance there was a flood of free-thinkers, both of a romantic and scientific ilk. Perhaps nowadays we unfairly view true eccentricity as a mental illness not to be tolerated or encouraged, but we are happy to accept the still prevalent 'New Age' concepts as long as they fit in with our ideal view of the world. We effectively still have the charlatans and the fake mediums, the snake-oil salesmen, the badly trained healers offering divine healing and whispering of immortal life. We also, luckily, still have those that are properly trained and skilful in their divine mission, many of whom can be found in the Masonic Lodges of today.

THE MASTER MAGICIAN – PSYCHIC, ALCHEMIST AND HEALER

Cagliostro was by all accounts an accomplished psychic. According to several testimonies, the Count was considerably accurate in his predictions, sometimes extremely so. His mystical séances involved the use of a *dove*; a young boy or girl to act as the scryer (seer). This was exceptionally common, 'doves' having been employed by magicians for centuries; the young person being in a state of virgin innocence that was believed to afford pure communication with the spirit realm. These children would be trusted with the power to command the seven spirits that surround the divine throne and in turn preside over the seven planets. The boy or girl would then kneel in front of a globe of clear water which was placed on a table covered with a black cloth. Another method would be to use a vase filled with water and oil floated on the surface. Concentration on the liquid would invariably lead to a state of partial or complete hypnosis and their clairvoyant abilities would manifest. Cagliostro would make strange mesmeric passes and summon the angels to enter the receptacle, whereby the dove would observe the visions and describe events taking place at the time or ones that would soon come to pass.

On occasions, Cagliostro would use a crystal sphere instead of the water globe or vase, and more rarely a metallic mirror which he carried with him. This was documented on the authority of Madame du Barry, the mistress of Louis XV. After Louis' death, she spent her banishment from the court at her houses in Paris and Versailles. It was in Paris that she was introduced to Cagliostro by Cardinal de Rohan who, after discussing the subject of Mesmer and magnetism, declared:

> My dear Madame ... the magnetic séances of Mesmer are not to be compared with the magic of my friend the Comte de Cagliostro. He is a genuine Rosicrucian who holds communion with the elemental spirits. He is able to pierce the veil of the future by his necromantic power. Permit me to introduce him to you.

Intrigued by her friend's proclamation, Madame du Barry excitedly invited the Count to visit her the next day. The following day, accompanied by the Cardinal, the Grand Copht (Copht or Copt meaning a native Egyptian Christian or one claiming descent from ancient Egypt) arrived resplendent in diamonds and carrying a jewel-encrusted walking stick. Aside from his spectacular, if not somewhat tasteless attire, Madame du Barry was struck by the power she felt emanating from the magician's eyes and she realized that she was in the presence of no mere charlatan.

After discussing the question of sorcery, Cagliostro presented her with a leather case that he took from the breast pocket of his coat. He explained that it contained a magic mirror and that within she may see events from the past and future. He boldly hastened to add that – 'If the vision be not to your liking, do not blame me. You use the mirror at your own risk.'

Madame du Barry proceeded to open the case and inside found a 'metallic glass in an ebony frame ornamented with a variety of magical characters in gold and silver.' The Count recited some cabalistic words and asked her to gaze into the mirror. As commanded, she obeyed and after a few moments fainted clean away! This was recorded in her memoirs, but she gave no clue as to what she had witnessed in the glass.

So what can we conclude from this? The Grand Copht obviously did his job well in as much that Madame du Barry certainly received a visitation in the mirror, but not one to her liking. Perhaps she saw a visitation of her own demise, her head upon the block of the guillotine and then held aloft by its blonde hair for public execration? The magic mirror has held many a vision over the centuries, whether in its glass form or as ink held in the palm of the hand as practised by the ancient Egyptians; whatever the case it seemed to have had a rather definite effect on the ageing Madame for she further writes that she refused to see Cagliostro under any circumstances after that fateful day.

Another description of Cagliostro's hypnotic powers was recounted by the Baroness Henriette Louise d'Oberkirch (1754–1803), who upon first meeting him, was informed:

> You lost your mother a long time ago. You hardly remember her. You were an only child. You have one daughter, and she will be an only child. You will have no more children.

Her attendant that day was, as before, Cardinal de Rohan. The Baroness was naturally miffed at the impertinence of Cagliostro's remarks, but was persuaded to respond to him by the Cardinal. She reluctantly admitted the truth about herself, verifying his prediction about the number of children.

The Baroness was somewhat enchanted, although slightly perturbed, by the extravagant persona of Cagliostro and described him thus in *Mémoires de la Baronne d'Oberkirch*:

> He was not absolutely handsome, but a more remarkable physiognomy has never been offered to my observation. He had a depth of look that was supernatural; I really cannot describe the expression of his eyes, they were at one time all aflame, and at another glazed like ice; he attracted and yet he repelled; he inspired fear and yet excited an insurmountable curiosity ... It is certain if I had not dominated the desire which drew me towards the marvellous, I should myself, possibly, have become the dupe of

this intriguer. You see the unknown is always so seductive! What I cannot disguise is that there was in Cagliostro an almost devilish power, he fascinated the mind, and he took power of the intellect.[9]

Cagliostro's relationship with Cardinal de Rohan was a cordial one. Invited to stay at the Cardinal's episcopal palace, he presented de Rohan with a diamond worth 20,000 livres, which he claimed to have manufactured. On this premise the Cardinal had a laboratory installed in the palace where Cagliostro could undertake his alchemical experiments. It was there that Cardinal de Rohan states that he saw Cagliostro transmute base metals into gold. Spiritual séances were also held at the palace and Baroness d'Oberkirch recorded in her memoirs that Cagliostro also predicted the death of Empress Marie Theresa of Austria.

> He even foretold the hour at which she would expire. Cardinal de Rohan told it to me in the evening, and it was five days after that the news arrived.

His favour with Cardinal de Rohan continued and when he arrived in Paris in 1785, the Cardinal chose and even furnished a house for him. He was received by the Parisians with fervour; desperate for new sensations they welcomed him with open arms, his séances full of noblemen and aristocracy. The house in the Rue St Claude bustled with admirers and his mystical proceedings were held in the specially furnished *Chambre Egyptienne*. Adorned with concave mirrors, statues of Anubis, Isis and the Apis bull and the walls covered in hieroglyphs, it was to create the perfect ambiance for the materialization of the spirits. Cagliostro would appear robed in black silk with hieroglyphs embroidered in red. On his head he wore a turban of cloth ornamented with jewels, and a chain of emeralds lay on his breast, to which were attached scarabs and cabalistic symbols in all colours and metals. Around his waist he wore a sword with a handle shaped like a cross and draped from a red silken cord.

Around Paris he was hailed as a marvel; the sculptor Jean-Antoine Houdon (1741–1828) carved a bust in marble from which bronze and plaster replicas were made and sold. Francesco Bartolozzi (1727–1815) made engravings on which the inscription read:

> *De l'ami des humains reconnaissez les traits*
> *Tous ses jours sont marqués par de nouveaux bienfaits,*
> *Il prolonge la vie, il secourt l'indigence,*
> *Le plaisir d'être utile est seul sa recompense*

> Recognize the marks of the friend of humanity
> Every day is marked by new beneficence,
> He prolongs life and succors the indigent,

The pleasure of being useful is his only recompense.

These were poignant words and reflective of a very powerful and benevolent personality. However, his 'do-gooding' caused a stir amongst certain jealous nobles who, on witnessing his remarkable healing effects, decided to bring him down a peg or two by setting him up for a very public fall. According to one account,[10] Cagliostro was before an audience of illustrious people and three beggars were presented to him asking for a cure to their respective ailments. One was deaf, another blind and the third suffering from a terrible skin condition. The Count blessed them and urged them on their way assuring them of their cure, at which point the three 'beggars' burst into laughter and threw back their hoods to reveal themselves as the young noblemen who had set out to humiliate him. The crowd began to jeer at Cagliostro, to which he responded solemnly declaring that '...if you are not deserving of what I give you, I can take it back!' At that moment the three young men began to panic and cry out, for one had become deaf, the other blind and the third afflicted by painful skin lesions. A lesson learned and one that Cagliostro apparently felt was just, for he forgave them and restored them to their former health. It was said that after this spectacle, no one doubted the healing powers of Count Cagliostro.

CAGLIOSTRO'S ALCHEMICAL OPERATIONS

Cagliostro is remembered for his alchemical operations. Following is an account of how, on 7 June 1780, he transmuted base metal into silver during a visit to a Masonic Lodge in Warsaw. One of the members recorded a description of the experiment:

> Cagliostro made me weigh out a pound of quicksilver which had been my property and had been already purified. Before that he had bidden me distil some rainwater till all liquid had evaporated leaving a deposit which he called Virgin Earth or *secunda materia*. Of this there remained about 16 grains. On his instructions I had also prepared an extract of lead.
>
> After all these preparations were complete he went into the lodge, and he entrusted me with the task of carrying out the whole experiment with my own hands. I did this under his instructions in the following way: The Virgin Earth was put into a flask, and half the quicksilver was poured over it. Then I added 30 drops of the lead extract. When the flask was then shaken a little, the quicksilver appeared to be dead

or frozen stiff. I then poured lead extract into the remaining quicksilver, but this quicksilver remained unaltered. So I had to pour the two lots of quicksilver together into a larger flask. After I had shaken the quicksilver, however, for some time, all assumed the same consistency. Its colour turned dirty grey.

The whole was now shaken into a bowl which it half filled. Cagliostro next gave me a small piece of paper, which proved to be only the outer wrapping of two others. The innermost contained a shining carminecoloured powder, weighing perhaps one-tenth of a grain. The powder was shaken into the bowl, and Cagliostro then swallowed the three wrapping papers.

While this was going on I filled up the bowl with plaster of Paris, which had already been prepared with warm water. Though the bowl was already full, Cagliostro took it out of my hands, added some more plaster of Paris, and pressed it firmly with his hands. Then he gave it back to me to dry it over a charcoal fire.

The bowl was now placed in a bed of ashes over the wind furnace. The fire was lit and the bowl left over it for half an hour. It was then taken out with a pair of tongs and carried into the lodge. The bowl was there broken, and in the bottom lay a lump of silver weighing fourteen ounces and a half.

There have been other accounts to say that Cagliostro faked his operations but whether this was just a case of a jealous rival or indignant colleague, we will never know. Cardinal de Rohan had faith in Cagliostro and so did many of his other sponsors. Perhaps, as with all alchemists who realized that the true operations were in the spiritual actions of the individual, Cagliostro had to 'perform' to satisfy the curiosity of the masses.

Cagliostro was not only an adept in magic but also a proficient herbalist. He made it a priority to help those who were ill or neglected physically. As mentioned earlier, whilst in Strasburg he is reputed to have healed 15,000 people. This he did with a combination of the laying on of hands, using mesmeric passes (magnetic healing) or by the administration of formulas and tinctures. He was particularly famous for his *pommade pour le visage* – a cream for the face that had reputedly remarkable youth-enhancing effects and was exceedingly popular amongst the ladies of high society.

He was, however, famously in possession of the fabled elixir of life, also known as the 'elixir of immortality' or the 'water of life'.[11] This quintessence (attributed to the five elements) was the alchemist's goal: the legendary potion that would give them eternal youth or the power over life and death; related to the myths of

Enoch, Thoth/Hermes Trismegistus, who were all believed to have drunk the *liquid gold* or the 'white drops' and then gone on to achieve immortality. The elixir has been sought all over the world, recipes mainly consisting of the use of gold, a harmless but allegedly potent medicine. The emperors of China paid alchemists huge amounts to discover the formula, often falling foul of toxic recipes that included arsenic and mercury; in India, similar recipes using precious materials exist although it is not known whether alchemy came to India from China or vice versa. In Europe there were several alchemists who were reputed to have used the elixir to excellent effect, the most notable being Nicolas Flamel, his wife Pernelle and the Count de St Germain.

Eliphas Lévi, the famous French occultist, spoke of Cagliostro's mystical elixir of life:

> There was much talk in the last century about an adept accused of charlatanism, who was termed in his lifetime the divine Cagliostro. It is known that he practised evocations and that in this art he was surpassed only by the illuminated Schroepffer. It is said also that he boasted of his power in binding sympathies, and that he claimed to be in possession of the secret of the Great Work; but that which rendered him still more famous was a certain elixir of life, which immediately restored to the aged the strength and vitality of youth. The basis of this

> composition was malvoisie wine, and it was obtained by distilling the sperm of certain animals with the sap of certain plants. We are in possession of the recipe, but our reasons for withholding it will be understood readily.[12]

So far we have not been able to track down the full recipe which Lévi tantalizingly mentions was in his possession!

Cagliostro was a powerfully effective healer by all accounts, and his reputation was such that rich and poor alike flocked to him wherever he took up residence. Dumas Père writes:

> Cagliostro was heard to say to his patients: 'I desire your illness to disappear' and 'I command you to be cured!' ... That secret power he called his 'master stroke' – that of the great initiated, regenerated by Hiram and blessed with the gift of light, of life.[13]

When asked by the famous pastor Johann Lavater about the secret of his art, Cagliostro answered with a motto of Paracelsus – *'In herbis, verbis et lapidibus'* meaning 'in herbs, words and stones'. This is attributed to Paracelsus' famous formulas that consisted of remedies made from herbs, roots and flowering plants; crushed minerals and various powders and the use of the *Word*. The theurgist commands and the *Word* causes an effect. Cagliostro, as did many before and after, believed that the Rosicrucian philosophy of intuition before knowledge and illumination before science was the secret to divine healing. The composer and historian Jean-Benjamin de Laborde (1734–94) gave an account of Cagliostro's healing clinics:

> I have just come from his audience. Picture to yourself a vast hall filled with unfortunate creatures, almost all of them destitute, raising to heaven their hands so feeble that they can barely lift them to beg for the Count's charity. He listens to them, one after another, remembers every word each one says, leaves the room for a minute and then comes back laden with remedies which he dispenses to each of those unfortunate souls, repeating to each one what had been told him about that individual's ills, and assuring all of them that they would soon be well again if they followed his prescriptions faithfully. But those remedies alone would be insufficient, for the patients need soup to give them strength to support themselves. Few of those poor souls have the means to buy anything. The sensitive Count divides his purse among them. Happier to give than to receive, his joy is shown by his compassion. Those wretched people, filled with gratitude, love and respect, fall at his feet, clasping his knees, calling him their saviour, their father, their God. The good man is touched, his eyes fill with tears. He tries to hide them but he cannot. He weeps and the entire

throng bursts into tears with him. Blessed tears that delight the heart, whose charm cannot be conceived unless one has been fortunate enough to weep the same way.[14]

The Magician's Seal

It was amongst Cagliostro's personal effects that the Inquisition found a peculiar seal (see also Chapter 3) bearing the symbol of a snake pierced by an arrow and holding an apple in its mouth. The letters *L* (followed by 3 dots in a triangular formation) *P* (followed by 3 dots...) *D* (followed by 3 dots...) were engraved upon it. The three dots arranged in the triangular form are considered to represent the triune God dwelling in heaven. The practice was begun in 1774 by the Grand Orient of France; Masons who used the symbol as a 'period' after their initials were often referred to as 'Three Point Brothers'. It is still used by Masons in the US, particularly those of the Scottish Rite, although the meaning is not always recognized.

Figure 2 An example of Cagliostro's Serpent Seal – the original was destroyed by the Inquisition

Eliphas Lévi commented upon the apparent symbolism:

> As explained by the cabalistic letters of the names Acharat and Althotas, it expresses the chief characteristics of the Great Arcanum and the Great Work. It is a serpent pierced by an arrow, thus representing the letter Aleph, an image of the union between active and passive, spirit and life, will and light. The arrow is that of the antique Apollo, while the serpent is the python of fable, the green dragon of Hermetic philosophy. The letter Aleph represents equilibrated unity. This pentacle is reproduced under various forms in the talismans of old magic ... The arrow signifies the active principle, will, magical action, the coagulation of the dissolvent, the fixation of the volatile by projection and the penetration of the earth by fire. The union

of the two (the serpent and arrow) is the universal balance, the Great Arcanum, the Great Work, the equilibrium of Joachin and Boaz. The initials LPD, which accompany this figure, signify Liberty, Power, Duty; also Light, Proportion, Density; and Law, Principle, Right. The Freemasons have changed the order of these initials, and in the form of LDP they render them as *Liberté de Penser,* Liberty of Thought, inscribing these on a symbolical bridge; but for those who are not initiated they substitute *Liberté de Passer,* Liberty of Passage. In the records of the prosecution of Cagliostro it is said that the examination elicited another meaning as follows: *Lilia destrue pedibus:* Trample the lilies under foot; and in support of this version may be cited a Masonic medal of the sixteenth or the seventeenth century, depicting a branch of lilies severed by a sword, having these words on the exergue: *Talem dabit ultio messem* – Revenge shall give this harvest.[15]

Again we have a blend of alchemy, cabala, Hermeticism and Freemasonry in this description, all subjects that Cagliostro was proficient in.

Cagliostro himself described the cipher to the Inquisition interrogators:

> ...the serpent with the apple in its mouth, which I have adopted for my crest, and which denotes the cause of original sin, and of the subsequent fall. The redemption

of our Lord Jesus Christ, is the arrow which has pierced the serpent; and this we ought to keep constantly before our eyes and in our hearts.

The symbol of the serpent also occurs within another Masonic and Egyptian-inspired work, Mozart's *The Magic Flute*, where in the first scene, a serpent is slain by the hero. (See Chapter 8 for further significance of this connection).

THE ROSICRUCIAN CONNECTION

Although it has never been officially asserted that Cagliostro was Rosicrucian, it is obvious that he was well learned in their philosophy and modernday Rosicrucians view him as a Master. The present forms of Rosicrucian initiations include many elements of Cagliostro's Ritual, particularly the layout and presentation of the Lodges. The triangular altar, the *Shekinah* (tabernacle) and the use of the 'dove' (the child medium used in séances and rituals) have been adopted by the Rosicrucian Order; the position of 'dove' is held by children of Rosicrucian parents and represents purity of conscience within the temple.

The Rosicrucians believe that Cagliostro was the son of the Grand Master of Malta and that Althotas, his teacher, was also of Rosicrucian origin. They mention that he was a high initiate of all the orders of the time, and given the highest honours in the Rite of Swedenborg, Pasqually's Order of Elus-Cohen, the Secret Degree of the Rose Croix and the position of Grand Master of the Scottish Rite. He worked with Louis-Claude de Saint Martin, the Count de Saint Germain and allegedly initiated a young lieutenant called Napoleon, who later became the Emperor of France.

The Rosicrucian Order write:

> Cagliostro was an emissary of the Great White Brotherhood, dedicated to a mission of transforming the heart of society from what it was at the time.[16]

Wherever the truth lies, Cagliostro has had an enormous effect on the spiritual beliefs of the day, whether we are aware of it or not. He also had a rather strong influence on Freemasonry, not only in the 1700s but also that of our modern day. Later in the book we look at the possible origins and structure of Cagliostro's system of Egyptian Freemasonry and also its relevance to regular Freemasonry both ancient and modern.

CHAPTER THREE

THE FINAL YEARS

THE 'DIVINE' CAGLIOSTRO, one moment the darling of Paris, the next a lonely prisoner in a dungeon of the Inquisition, passed like a meteorite across the face of France

MANLY P HALL[1]

PARIS – RUE ST CLAUDE

Arriving in Paris in January 1785, the Count and his wife rented rooms on the Rue St Claude, a delightful mansion in which they dedicated a *chambre Égyptienne,* decorated lavishly in the style of the temples of Egypt replete with statuettes of Isis, Anubis and Apis. It was here that Cagliostro held his mystical séances and dedicated himself once again to being 'the friend of mankind', curing those who passed through his doors in their hundreds.

Cagliostro had originally been asked to attend a Masonic Convention by the Lodge of Philalethes (Lovers of Truth), the head of which was Savalette de Langes, an influential royal banker and Master of the *Loge des Amis Réunis*. At first he had agreed to attend but changed his mind, and demanded that the Philalethes adopt his constitutions to the Egyptian Rite, burn all their archives and consequentially be initiated into the Mother Lodge at Lyons. Unfortunately, further negotiations faltered and this brief connection with the Philalethes Lodge was severed. Urged by his followers to attend the Convention, in which many prominent Masons from all over Europe were to converge and discuss matters of Masonic importance such as its origins, its esoteric relevance and essential nature, Cagliostro decided to use this as a forum for his Egyptian Freemasonry. Initially this caused a ripple of revulsion amongst the Masons of Paris and he was opposed at all levels, but not being the kind of man to take the line of least resistance, he continued with his persuasive speeches. According to French writer Louis Figuier (1819–94):

> ...his eloquence was so persuasive that he completely converted to his views the large and distinguished audience he addressed.[2]

It would seem that Cagliostro's star had risen but it was a star about to fall.

The Affair of the Diamond Necklace

On the morning of 22 August 1785, Cagliostro was faced with a *commissaire* and eight policemen, who under orders of a *Lettre de Cachet*[3] bearing the seal of Louis XVI, arrested him on charges of complicity in the 'Affair of the

Diamond Necklace'. He was unceremoniously dragged from his house and, at pistol point, ushered into a carriage which took him to the state prison – the dreaded Bastille.

He subsequently found out that his imprisonment was due to the stupidity of his friend the Cardinal de Rohan who had been magnificently duped by a certain Jeanne de Valois-Saint-Rémy, better known as Comtesse de la Motte (1756–91). The Cardinal had unwittingly fallen prey to the clutches of this embittered woman of minor aristocratic birth who, hoping to get revenge on the monarchy, had mastered a cunning plan to extract a huge amount of money from Rohan to buy a diamond necklace in the name of the Queen, Marie Antoinette. The jewellers in possession of the necklace, which had in fact been intended for the neck of the previous King Louis XV's mistress Madame du Barry, twice offered it to Antoinette who refused, insisting that France had 'more need of warships than jewels'.

Fearing bankruptcy and ruin, the jeweller threatened to commit suicide and the whole matter became a source of intrigue amongst the people at court. Knowing that the Cardinal had lost favour with the Queen, and having knowledge of his desire to become Prime Minister, la Motte worked on him pretending to be a confidante of Antoinette's. She eventually persuaded him that the Queen was enamoured with him, and asked if he would guarantee the money she needed to purchase the sumptuous bauble. He agreed on condition that he met the Queen in person. La Motte's husband recruited a young prostitute who bore a remarkable resemblance to Marie Antoinette, and under the cover of darkness they boldly produced the young girl to him in the very gardens of the royal palace. Completely awestruck and smitten, the Cardinal was putty in their hands.

La Motte's perfect machinations went ahead smoothly and the necklace was received and ultimately broken up by her and her husband and sold abroad. Of course, when the first payment for the necklace was due and did not materialize, the Queen was informed by the unwitting jewellers that the debt was in default. She ultimately flew to seek the aid of her husband, Louis XVI, denying all knowledge of the transaction and one by one the pieces fell into place.

The only reason for the Count's, and by now his wife's, imprisonment was the corrupt statement from Comtesse de la Motte implicating them in the theft. La Motte's defence was that Cagliostro and the Cardinal had summoned her to one of their séances and, after much mystical performance, the Cardinal had presented her with a casket of diamonds and directed her to deliver them to her husband and have them disposed of in London. She also used the documented invention of his disgraced druggist Sacchi in an attempt to imply that Cagliostro was merely a jumped-up valet from the slums of Naples whose real name was 'Thiscio'. She continued in a similar vein, insisting that the Count had invented his exotic past and was nothing more than a charlatan peddling pills to those craving immortality, and that his brand of Freemasonry was a way to dupe the wealthy; its obscene rites and profanities would attempt to bring about the downfall of the Holy Church of Rome.

Poor Cagliostro's only crime was that of ignorance; having warned the Cardinal about la Motte when he had been introduced to her, he had no other involvement and, in his defence, had not been in the country at the time of the ploy, arriving the day after the agreement had been made with the jewellers. During his period of incarceration, Cagliostro issued a publication in his defence. At the time the whole affair was of national, if not international, intrigue; newspapers ran pages of scandal in disavowal of one or other of the inmates and lawyers queued to accrue themselves money and infamy. The brief for the Count Cagliostro that ensued was a superb piece of propaganda in his favour, in which the account of his early years was written. After much interrogation, and the subsequent hearing, there was no real cause to hold him or the Cardinal and they were acquitted in June 1786 with honours alongside the Countess Cagliostro, after nine horrendous months.

Comtesse de la Motte did not fare so well and was sentenced to be exposed naked in front of the Conciergerie with a rope around her neck and publicly whipped and branded on each shoulder with the letter **V** – which stood for *'voleuse'* – thief! She also suffered life imprisonment in a prison for abandoned women; however she escaped to London where she fell from a window to her death in 1791.

On his release from prison, Cagliostro returned to find the Rue St Claude thronging with friends and sympathizers. The Revolutionary fire was smoldering and much had been made of the Queen's apparent guilt alongside that of the la Mottes. Printed pamphlets were distributed voicing anger and suspicion at the King and Queen's involvement, not to mention the arrest and incarceration of innocents under the detested power of the *Lettre de Cachet* and so Cagliostro was seen by some as a martyr of liberty. Unfortunately the devotion shown by the masses was not mirrored by the monarchy and the day following his release, the Cagliostro's were banished from France by order of the King. Despite his innocence, his presence would have been an embarrassing and constant reminder of the affair.

BANISHED FROM FRANCE

The couple left French soil, their carriage driven between two lines of silent sympathizers, via the port of Boulogne, where it is documented that he gave his blessing to 5,000 persons who knelt on the beach. He went straight to London and never set foot again in his beloved France, his house in Rue St Claude locked up and abandoned for over 24 years. It survived unscathed throughout the Revolution until, in 1810, the doors were once more opened and the great Comte di Cagliostro's articles of magic and mystery were auctioned off by order of the government. Crucibles and retorts, rare curios and furniture were sold to the highest bidder, then the doors locked once again and the *chambre Égyptienne* was no more. The house is still there, occupied over the centuries by grocers, feather curlers, a furrier, a manufacturer of cardboard boxes and amusingly a brasserie – the Bar de Cagliostro. I wonder if the various occupants of the house, or customers of the bar, knew that Cagliostro – the Grand Copht of Egyptian Freemasonry, who saw his life's mission as the rejuvenation of humankind – had once lived within those same walls.

Paving the way for the return of the Count and his wife to British shores were some favourable reports in the English papers. *The Times* described Cagliostro as 'an excellent scholar' and one 'not with a view to gain, but merely upon a principle of humanity and goodwill to his fellow creatures'. Another exciting source of information was from Parkyns Macmahon's English translation of Cagliostro's 'Memorial...'

produced during his trial and imprisonment in the Bastille, which also included Cagliostro's robust defence against the vicious accusations of Madame de la Motte. The English public loved the little pamphlet and it was read by all manner of people from royalty to the 'lowest mechanic'. As mentioned previously, Macmahon, an editor of the *Universal Register*[4] had past connections with the *Courier de l'Europe* newspaper, which at the time had, for a fairly small publication, an enormous circulation of at least 5,000 copies a week.

Once more in London the Cagliostros found themselves in great favour; nobles, dignitaries and even princes were falling over themselves to make the acquaintance of the Grand Copht of Egyptian Freemasonry. The couple was soon enough taken under the wing of Samuel Swinton, himself the proprietor of the aforementioned *Courier de l'Europe,* who found them a superb villa next to his own house in Knightsbridge. Seeing the Count as a fount of wealth in the form of his rejuvenating 'little red pills' he implored Cagliostro to set up business with him by opening a clinic such as he had in Strasburg. If Cagliostro was contemplating such, it was about to be put paid to by the introduction of a new 'friend' in the form of Charles Theveneau de Morande (1741–1805). Little did they know that de Morande was about to push Cagliostro's star firmly out of orbit and into a horrifying descent.

If the slurs on Cagliostro's identity and character are disparaging enough, then Theveneau de Morande could equally rival them. In his book, *A Literary Low-Life Reassessed: Charles Theveneau de Morande in London, 1769–1791*, Simon Burrows declares:

> As pornographer, scandalmonger, extortionist, and spy, Charles Theveneau de Morande, was one of the most notorious men of the eighteenth century.

So, libeller, blackmailer and eventually a spy for the French Government, Charles Theveneau as he was then known, invented his own supposedly noble heritage and labelled himself after the fictitious lineage of 'de Morande'. He perfected his writer's art amongst the hacks of London, sharpening his pen on the libellous pornographic tracts they produced, aimed at extorting money from their unfortunate targets. He then moved on to work on various other publications, all as vicious and slanderous as the rest. He even went as far as to threaten to publish a pornographic biography of Madame du Barry, Louis XV's mistress; this incited a bodged kidnap attempt by the French King. Determined to silence de Morande, the King eventually followed up with an enormous bribe of 32,000 livres and an annuity of 4,000 livres for life! Not one to be deterred, de Morande continued his trail of slander and eventually became editor of the *Courier de l'Europe* in 1784.

Unwittingly, Cagliostro was setting himself up for the mother of all grillings by de Morande; not only had he misjudged some of the people with whom he had made acquaintance in London but he, at the advice of his French lawyers, started proceedings against the French government over the destruction and confiscation of his remedies and personal articles. A pamphlet soon appeared in the bookshops of Paris, detailing the Count's outrage at his arrest and describing his abominable treatment in prison. This was followed within the week by a personal letter to a friend bemoaning how he felt he had been betrayed by the rulers of France, which was circulated in republican circles. The letter was then printed on both sides of the Channel under the title 'Count Cagliostro's Letter to the French People'.[5]

Cagliostro was slowly inching himself into a political arena that he was not fully equipped to deal with. The mood in Paris was grim, with rumblings of revolt already tangible – the French people wanted to hear tales of the torture and betrayal of innocents at the hands of their rulers, the tide was turning and the poor unfortunate child of nature appeared to be becoming instrumental in the creeping downfall of a monarchy. In the 'Letter' he spoke almost prophetically, stating that he would only return to Paris if the Bastille was torn down and 'turned into a public promenade!' He allegedly talked of revolution, prophesying that it would be brought about when the abuse of power destroys power itself and stating that a prince would come, abolishing all *Lettres de Cachets* by convening the States-general and restoring the true religion. Strong words in a dangerous climate but as usual Cagliostro's bombastic phrasing was perhaps more flowery in prose than the message that was received by the ears of an ever-impatient mob. Attempting to repair some of the diplomatic damage, the chief minister of Paris issued an order to the French ambassador in London to give Cagliostro leave to return to Paris whilst his case regarding his possessions was heard.

In the meantime the Count had made a new acquaintance, again introduced by Swinton; this time it was the nobleman Lord George Gordon (1751–93), son of the Duke of Atholl. Unaware of the reputation of the Lord as one known by the British people as 'Mad Lord George' due to his erratic and subversive behaviour which, amongst other things, sparked off the anti-Catholic riots of 1780, Cagliostro blithely saw only the nobleman's title and Masonic leanings. To the consternation of the French ambassador when he met with Cagliostro to discuss his return to France, Lord Gordon was in accompaniment, resplendent in full Scottish dress and brandishing a claymore. Bellowing to Cagliostro that it was a trap and making menacing movements towards the envoys, the wild-eyed Lord ensured the meeting was thus doomed. The French Government, now needing to do something quickly about this potential danger, set their trap. The Count was soon to receive the biggest blow ever to his reputation and self-esteem. Theveneau de Morande's poison dart hit its target when he published a damning account in the *Courier de l'Europe* entitled 'The Travels of Count Cagliostro before he arrived in France'.

Was Count Cagliostro 'Giuseppe Balsamo'?

In his article de Morande sensationally declared that Count Cagliostro was in fact the alias of a notorious Sicilian rogue and forger, Giuseppe 'Joseph' Balsamo. Balsamo was reputed to have emerged from the slums of Palermo, becoming a talented forger of documents and paintings who, travelling across Europe with his wife, attracted the attention of several authorities with his confidence tricks. This story was also the official line given by the Roman Catholic Church at the time of Cagliostro's arrest in 1789 by the Inquisition, and the accusation was printed, distributed, and firmly lodged in the echelons of history as the infamous pamphlet *The Life of Joseph Balsamo*.[6]

When the parallel lives of Cagliostro and Balsamo are examined, there are so many inconsistencies that we find it hard to believe that a man who attracted so much attention across Europe was never recognized as Count Cagliostro by any of the authorities. On several occasions both the English and French police were in the position to arrest the Count and Countess Seraphina as impostors. Balsamo and his wife Lorenza had come into contact with the authorities more than once for minor misdemeanours, most notably in Paris when Balsamo had his wife imprisoned for impropriety. W H Trowbridge comments on this very theme:

> There is another reason for doubting the identity of the two men. It is the most powerful of all, and has hitherto apparently escaped the attention of those who have taken this singular theory of identification for granted. Nobody that had known Balsamo ever saw Cagliostro.[7]

On no occasion were the Balsamos arraigned for being 'the Cagliostros', nor were the Cagliostros accused of being 'the Balsamos'. Surely, if the couples were as notorious as they were made out to be, somebody, whether officials, dignitaries or those in polite society, would have made a connection between them and identified them as being the same couple? There is one spurious connection but it was made by the lothario Count Giacomo Casanova di Seingalt (1725–98). A thief, manipulator, fornicator and spy for the inquisition – a veritable source of truth? The answer is perhaps best left to conjecture.

Not only did de Morande accuse the Count of being a charlatan and swindler but he also trotted out a list of misdemeanors from Balsamo's supposed visits to London and Europe. He ridiculed Cagliostro's initiation into Esperance Lodge, and in doing so sounded the death knell for Cagliostro's Masonic career in England and beyond. The London Masons decided on the basis of the article that the Count was an imposter and when Cagliostro attended a meeting at the Lodge of Antiquity in Bloomsbury, a character called Brother Marsh performed a vaudeville ritual providing a farcical depiction of the Count as nothing more than a funfair quack. Undeterred, Cagliostro, in his determination to convert his fellow Masons to Egyptian Freemasonry, went ahead and took out an advert in the *Morning Herald* on 2 November. It asked that all true Masons come together to bring about the rejuvenation of English Freemasonry, summoning them to a meeting in Great Queen Street on the following day. It read as follows:

In the Name of 9, 5, 8, 14, 20, 1, 8 [Jehovah]; 9, 5, 18, 20, 18 [Jesus]

The Time is at hand when the Building of the New Temple or New Jerusalem, 3, 8, 20, 17, 8 [Church] must begin; this is to invite all True Masons in London to join in the Name of 9, 5, 18, 20, 18 [Jesus] the only one in whom there is a Divine 19, 17, 9, 13, 9, 19, 23 [Trinity] to meet tomorrow evening, the 3d instant, 1786 (or 5790) at

Nine o'clock at Riley's, Great Queen Street; to lay a plan for the laying of the first stone of the foundation of the true 3, 8, 20, 17, 8 [Church] in this visible world, being the material representative Temple of the Spiritual 9, 5, 17, 20, 18, 11, 5, 13 [Jerusalem].

A Mason, and member of the new 3, 8, 20, 17, 8 [Church]

Unfortunately this announcement coincided with de Morande's humiliating description of the Masonic gathering in Bloomsbury and the meeting came to nothing. Further humiliations followed, including a scathing cartoon attributed to the satirist James Gillray (1757–1815) and an accompanying poem ridiculing all that the Count held dear.

This was the last straw for Cagliostro and after taking legal advice he issued a 'Letter to the English People' attempting to defend himself, whilst also breaching the character of Theveneau de Morande. De Morande, in turn, used every ounce of resourcefulness and decided to have Cagliostro thrown in jail for trumped-up debts. It is interesting to note that in the end Morande had to retract his statement and make an apology, but by then the damage was done, the Count admitted defeat and did what he did best – packed his bags and left the country.

THE FINAL DESTINATION – ROME

The Cagliostros left England for Europe, the Count heartbroken at the betrayal by his fellow Masons and chastened by the public ridicule. The couple settled for some time in Switzerland but times were changing and Cagliostro soon found himself in a land of cold political climate. He was becoming disillusioned by his so-called friends and Seraphina was miserable; now forbidden to practise his particular form of Freemasonry or his medicine in Germany, Austria, Russia and Spain, it was decided that they would return once more to Rome. This was by far the most foolish move that they could make, for Freemasonry itself was a capital offence within the jurisdiction of the Papal States.

Rome, 27 December 1789, the Feast day of St John the Evangelist, author of the Apocalypse and patron of Masons. Count Alessandro di Cagliostro was none the wiser that a pleasant evening spent in deep discussion with friends was about to be torn apart. He was unaware that previously that day the Vatican council had met in the presence of Pope Pius VI, and had already decided to arrest and condemn him to death. Although documentation of the true events are sketchy, it is reported that the secret police of the Holy Office burst into the room and once the Count realized what was afoot he grabbed a pistol and aimed it at the source of his betrayal – his beloved wife. The gun, however, misfired and he was dragged unceremoniously to the prison in the papal fortress of Castel Sant' Angelo. Thinking that she was now in a position of safety, Seraphina was somewhat surprised to be escorted to a nearby convent. The Sisters of Santa Appolonia were to be her protectors and tutors in the devotional practice she so longed for; not quite what the devious Seraphina had planned.

What followed for Cagliostro were 15 torturous months spent in squalid conditions within the sturdy walls of the Castel Sant' Angelo in Rome. After months of interrogation and no doubt coercion to confess, Cagliostro was eventually brought before the Inquisition to hear his final sentence.

Declaration of Sentence of Count Cagliostro – 7 April 1791

Giuseppe Balsamo, attainted and convicted of many crimes, and of having incurred the censures and penalties pronounced against heretics, dogmatics, heresiarchs and propagators of magic and superstition, has been found guilty and condemned to the said censures and penalties as decreed by the Apostolic laws of Clement XII and Benedict XIV, against all persons who in any manner whatever favour or form societies of conventicles of Freemasonry as well as by the edict of the Council of State against all persons convicted of this crime in Rome or any other place in the dominions of the Pope.

Notwithstanding, by special grace and favour, the sentence of death by which this crime is expiated is hereby commuted into perpetual imprisonment in a fortress, where the culprit is to be strictly guarded without any hope of pardon whatever. Furthermore, after he shall have abjured his offences as a heretic in the place of his imprisonment he shall receive absolution, and certain salutary penances will then be prescribed for him to which he is hereby ordered to submit.

Likewise, the manuscript book which has for its title Egyptian Masonry is solemnly condemned as containing rites, propositions, doctrines and a system which being superstitious, impious, heretical and altogether blasphemous; open a road to sedition and the destruction of the Christian religion. This book shall therefore be burnt by the executioner, together with all the other documents relating to this sect.

By a new Apostolic law we shall confirm and renew not only the laws of the preceding pontiffs which prohibit the societies and conventicles of Freemasonry, making particular mention of the Egyptian sect and of another vulgarly known as the Illumines and we shall decree that the most grievous corporal punishments reserved for heretics shall be inflicted on all who shall associate, hold communion with, or protect these societies.

The *Moniteur Universel* published this story:

The sentence has been posted here ordering that the papers and effects of Monsieur Cagliostro should be burned by the hand of the executioner. That order was carried out this morning on the Piazza di Minerva. It lasted three quarters of an hour. The people made a holiday of it. As each article was thrown on the fire — books, posters, licensed documents, Masonic cordons — the multitude clapped their hands and shouted for joy.[8]

These words reverberated throughout Europe where, already bolstered by the Revolution in France, they created a sense of outrage and in turn an outpouring of revulsion in Cagliostro's favour and against the tyranny of the Church. A further statement in an article in *Feuille Villageoise* summed up the general feeling:

The Pope ought to have abandoned Cagliostro to the effects of his bad reputation. Instead he has had him shut up and tried by charlatans far more dangerous to society than himself. His sentence is cruel and ridiculous. If all who make dupes of the crowd were punished in this fashion, precedence on the scaffold should certainly be granted to the Roman Inquisitors.

The trial itself was documented in a small book written by the Vatican notary, Father Marcello, and published under the pseudonym Monsignor Giovanni Barberi. *La Vie de Joseph Balsamo* (translated as *The Life of Joseph Balsamo*) was less a biography of Balsamo/Cagliostro than a direct and vicious attack on Freemasonry. Its depiction of Masonry as a vile and odious society capable of being able to 'open a road to sedition and the destruction of the Christian religion', infuriated the Freemasons of Europe. They responded by issuing a pamphlet in defence of their beliefs.

> This pamphlet ... appeared under the auspices of the Swiss government and produced such a sensation throughout Italy, and particularly in Rome, that the Conclave, terrified at the revolutionary fury it had awakened, instructed its agents to buy up every copy they could find.

In his biography of Cagliostro, W R H Trowbridge declared:

> The Conclave would have been better advised to suppress the work of the Inquisition biographer. The account it contains of Cagliostro's trial completely justifies the popular belief in the bigotry, cruelty, tyranny and total lack of the

Christian spirit that characterized the proceedings of the Holy Inquisition.

Europe was rocked by the condemnation of this well-known Freemason and healer of the sick. The enormity of the situation was terrifying, if only because many feared for their own safety. Cardinal de Rohan, the Archbishop of Bourges, Dom Pernety and Father Joseph – all trembled at the sentence passed upon him.[9]

So why on earth had the Cagliostros sought to return to Rome? In the first instance it was probably Seraphina's desire to visit her aging father and find some form of stability for once. She was sick and tired of inclement weather, having to pawn her jewels when things went wrong and was harbouring a growing disinterest in her husband's vision of Egyptian Freemasonry as a panacea for all ills. Whilst they were on the move once more between Switzerland and Italy, she had been secretly handed some letters from her family in Rome. Her father expressed his concern at her recent trials and tribulations, worried by all the reports that were filtering through Europe, and he implored her to consider her future.

Awash with nostalgia for her childhood home and the warm embrace of her family, Seraphina began to ponder long and hard on her plans for her more mature years. She missed her family and her religion, and while she and the Count were in Roveredo, she met with a priest and made every effort to revert to her Catholic faith.

The priest, Clemontino Vannetti, made note of her piety in his memoirs.[10]

Cagliostro himself did not seem too perturbed by his wife's reversion to Catholicism and when they were next hounded from their lodgings by doctors, jealous of Cagliostro's healing ministrations, Seraphina's newfound faith stood them in good stead. Their landlord from Roveredo provided a letter of introduction which gained the trust of the overlord of the town, a Prince Pietro Virgilio Thun – the Bishop of Trent.

Similar to the connection that had occurred between Cagliostro and Cardinal de Rohan in France, the Bishop had an interest in the occult and it didn't take long for an idea to formulate in Seraphina's mind. Seven years earlier, de Rohan had expressed an idea to the Cagliostros; a casual comment postulating as to whether the Church might ever accept Egyptian Freemasonry as a kind of Catholic side order. Seraphina became quite excited and claimed that surely the Pope was a powerful enough ally to protect them from the heads of state in France who were still baying for Cagliostro's blood. Who would mess with the Vatican, surely not even Marie Antoinette? Amazingly, the Bishop did not dismiss the idea, probably due to the kudos of managing to return one of Europe's most notorious dissidents back to the Catholic flock: not missing a trick the Bishop was envisaging the robes of a cardinal. The Cagliostros themselves were dreaming of the Count becoming a founding father of an order as elite as that of the Order of St John, also known as the Knights of Malta.

However, there was some ground to be covered before any of these ideas could be put in motion, particularly the Count's 'heretical' nature. When questioned on the basics of the Church's catechisms, Cagliostro's knowledge was basic, although his discussions were lengthy and as usual quite bombastic. The task of re-educating the Count was placed in the hands of one Father Ghezzi, who although extremely sceptical at the sincerity of Cagliostro's 'conversion' and the notion that this strange Freemason could hold sway with the Pope, was nonetheless impressed by his application to the catechisms and showing repentance for his sins.

The Bishop was delighted and took the bold step of writing a heartfelt letter of recommendation to the Vatican, asking for the safe return to Rome for the couple. He omitted to mention any ideas concerning the amalgamation of Egyptian Masonry with the Church just for the present. He merely stated that Seraphina was a good Catholic woman who wished to see her ailing father and was concerned that her husband's notoriety would be an obstacle to their entering Rome. He also mentioned that Cagliostro himself had made strong concessions to re-establishing his faith and had taken full confession.

On 4 April, Bishop Thun received a reply from the Vatican. It was certainly a time for celebration – it stated that Count Cagliostro was under no legal restriction to enter the Papal State. Seraphina also received a letter from her father confirming that they would get no trouble from the Catholic authorities. In their joy at such news, no one noticed that the wording of the papal notice was somewhat ambiguous.

Seraphina, bolstered by the news, continued her onslaught of pressure on the Count to return to Rome and this was compounded sometime in May when the Bishop received some unpleasant news. Emperor Joseph II of Austria, the brother of Marie Antoinette, had sent him a scalding letter, incredulous that a man in such a position as the Bishop was harbouring a notorious swindler and member of the Illuminati. It was definitely time to move on, and armoured with the Bishop's recommendation the couple made their way to Rome.

Once in the noble city, the Cagliostros were greeted with great enthusiasm; nobles from France who missed the *joie de vivre* of the Parisian social circus, and Italians anxious to mingle with fabled celebrities. The Count was overjoyed to be remembered by various members of the Knights of Malta, in particular Father François-Joseph de Saint Maurice. He had been an advocate of Cagliostro's for some time and had allegedly predicted that he would meet the Count in Rome, which amazingly now was true. As he was also experiencing a slump in his career, he was very happy to be aided by

Cagliostro who, in return, appointed Saint Maurice as his secretary.

However, according to some sources, Seraphina was not enjoying her return to her homeland as much as her husband. It is implied that the Countess, becoming more and more disillusioned with her situation, decided to betray her husband. She began to make detailed notes of any impropriety that he may have commited and was rumoured to have had their servants and other acquaintances employed as spies against the Count. Not only was she furious that the plan to introduce Egyptian Freemasonry into the Catholic Church had gone awry, and Cagliostro had not been granted an audience with the Pope, but she wanted to rid herself of her husband so that she could remarry.

The most obvious thing for her to do would be to have him convicted of blasphemy and if this is indeed what Seraphina planned and executed, then it was the ultimate in betrayals to a man who, although flawed, had always been a good husband to her. The story goes that Seraphina noted every impropriety and blasphemous action that Cagliostro committed, allegedly cajoling him into the utmost of lewdities and satirical jibes at the Catholic faith, and then faithfully reported them to her scandalized family, who in turn passed on the information to their priest, who ultimately made it known to the most dangerous ears of all – the Inquisition.

The trap it seemed had been laid and now the bait was prepared. Seraphina continued to bemoan their impoverished state and finally Cagliostro decided to fall back on Freemasonry. He made some friends amongst the artists of Rome and found that one of the painters had formed a small Lodge. Now having to operate on a mercenary level, Cagliostro carefully announced the revival of Egyptian Freemasonry to his trusted friends. He hoped to invite the Marquise Vivaldi to become Grand Mistress, in doing so ensuring that she would then enroll her wealthy companions. At a secret meeting in September 1789, he explained his vision of rejuvenation to his carefully selected guests and although they were intrigued by his words, only two were willing to pay for the privilege of their initiation diploma. The two men were Carlo Antonini, a friend of the Felicianis, and Matteo Berardi, a governmental lawyer. Unbeknownst to Cagliostro, Carlo Antonini was reputedly not only Seraphina's lover and prospective husband, he was also a spy. Rumours that the Countess was attempting to betray him reached Cagliostro's ears and he asked his friend, Saint Maurice, to keep an eye out for him. He did not really doubt his wife's love and believed that she was merely upset with him, as often she was, for allowing their finances to dwindle. Little did he know that Seraphina had allegedly already asked to make a deposition to the Holy Office for the repose of her conscience. If this were the case, she would be seen as the pious sheep returning to the flock and Cagliostro would be doomed.

Meanwhile, in Europe, the political wheels were turning, with the rumblings of Revolution becoming louder. News of rising political reformers reached Rome, and Cagliostro once more felt that it could be possible to initiate the true moral rejuvenation of mankind through Egyptian Freemasonry. With the monarchy in France losing its footing, his enemies from the Diamond Necklace trial meeting a rather unpleasant end at the hands of the mob and, much more importantly, his previous ally the Cardinal de Rohan elevated to a position of power within the Revolutionary Assembly, it was appearing likely that Cagliostro could return to France and catapult his star back into orbit. He and François-Joseph de Saint Maurice decided to write a petitioning letter requesting permission for their return to France. For Cagliostro, the proposition of returning to the country he loved, now free from superstition and religious fanatics, was a dream come true. He would reunite with Cardinal de Rohan and reinstate himself as Grand Copht, bringing enlightenment and moral salvation to the newly liberated land.

Seraphina, on the other hand, was aghast; all her plans would be ruined if they were to leave Rome and her family had arranged for her to give her deposition. She needed to act fast and so she employed her greatest skill – seduction. Poor Saint Maurice was like a sitting duck;

Seraphina 'unburdened' her secret love for him and in doing so ensured that his 'surveillance' of her took on a whole new perspective. One day in November, with the knowledge that the Count would be absent from the house, Seraphina's cohorts brought a priest, who would take her deposition from her, to the courtyard outside her bedroom. After having questions shouted up to her, Seraphina would hastily respond whilst a Church official scribed the whole conversation.

This deposition, in addition to inflammatory testimonies from her father and the two recent Egyptian Rite initiates (see section entitled "Declaration of Sentence of Count Cagliostro – 7 April 1791"), was deemed enough for the Inquisition to act. On 27 December 1789, various members of the Holy Office met at the Cardinal de Zeleda's house. They were awaiting the presence of Pope Pius VI, who had just finished attending the mass of the Feast of St John. Normally such a procedure would have been left in the hands of the officials of the Church, so it was a notable matter of great urgency and importance that the Pope himself had deigned to appear. After an address from the Pontiff, the council unanimously concurred with his decision to have Cagliostro and his secretary arrested forthwith and their dwelling searched for damning evidence. In a letter from Lorenzo Prospero Bottini, dated 2 January 1790, he records:

> Last Sunday secret and extraordinary debates in council took place at the Vatican.

No one knows exactly what transpired but it was obvious from the arrest of the Count and Countess, what the context was likely to be. Cagliostro had been betrayed, not only by his wife but also by François-Joseph, his secretary and friend.

BETRAYAL AND SERAPHINA'S CONFESSION

Cagliostro languished in a squalid, cramped cell for 15 months during his interrogation and trial. Devastated by his wife's betrayal, he repeatedly lurched between misery at having been abandoned by her and consolation that she must have been tricked into betraying him. He was obsessed by her and it tormented him almost as much as the interrogators themselves. Even his hardened jailers were moved by his devotion to her and testified to such. He was allowed no contact with the outside world and specifically denied any communication with his wife, even though he pleaded with his torturers to allow him to see her or for her to be allowed to share his cell. The conditions for the Count in the Castel Sant' Angelo were pitiful and a far cry from his previous incarceration in the Bastille; not only was he denied any shaving or grooming tools, for fear that he would harm himself or others, but he was also deprived of writing implements. It was filthy, cramped and festering with waste and food matter, but this was minor in comparison to his misery and pain from torment and torture at hearing his wife's confession.

Seraphina's testimony was reported as tantalizingly sensational; she described how she had been groomed from child-woman to apparent harlot, with Cagliostro as an immoral 'pimp'. The gloating minutes record her admission that:

> ...the first lessons which the young bride received from her husband, were intended (according to her own confessions) to instruct her in the means of attracting and gratifying the pleasures of the other sex.

Father Marcello, the Inquisition biographer describes how Cagliostro, on one occasion, instructed Seraphina to go to the chambers of another man and subsequently became incensed when he learned that she had not performed as required, allegedly stating '...adultery is no crime in a woman who commits it on account of her interest, and not simply through affection to another man'.

The testimony of Seraphina continues in a similar negative vein but she does not anywhere describe why she tolerated her husband's alleged brutalities for 16 years, nor indeed why she did not leave him on any occasion even though, if we are to believe the story that she was continually playing the coquette with men of means, she had every opportunity to abscond with someone richer and more handsome. The

Church ridiculed Cagliostro's appearance, rendering him so ugly and repugnant that no woman, '...unless she was either old, or so ugly that she could never have expected a lover, had not such a man as Balsamo been in existence...' would have glanced twice at him. How strange that he managed to endear himself to Seraphina, a woman described as a genteel beauty, for 16 years of marriage.

The interrogators continued with this account:

> Let us ... hear the depositions of his wife. She declared upon oath that many of the pupils [seers] had been prepared beforehand by her husband and had their lesson given them in regard to every question about which they were to be interrogated but that some however had been chosen unawares to him; and that, in regard to them, she imagined that he could only operate by the intervention of magic.[11]

With this statement, is the Church implying guilt for being a charlatan and duping his audience or for his use of magic on the other occasions, or both? Why did Seraphina go to such lengths to betray her husband? Maybe she *was* thoroughly disenchanted with him but after 16 years of marriage, would she have wanted to see him destroyed so readily? Perhaps her initial accusations that led to his arrest were given in the naïve belief that he would have been jailed for a short period, enabling her to have secured a divorce and escape to a richer and more desirable beau. Was she really the calculating *femme fatale* the Holy Office led us to believe or was she encouraged to render a drowning man to the depths? Was she really as naïve as to think that *she* could get away with having been firmly embroiled in Freemasonry herself?

If you can, imagine the scenario of a middle-aged 18th-century woman, caught between her desire for freedom and most likely her life, and the interrogations of one of the most terrifying inquisitors known to man. She would have *at least* been shown 'the rack', the infamous implement of torture. There is no record of the 'encouragement' offered her to reveal evidence against her husband but, if resistant to confession, she may well have been subjected to violent means, such as the obscene practice of the 'Ordeal of Water'. This odious torture was often used on women as it left no physical trace to be witnessed afterwards. It consisted of laying the woman over a bench, face up, with a funnel inserted into the mouth and the nostrils blocked with rags. Copious amounts of water were then poured into the funnel until the stomach was about to burst; the inquisitors would then beat the victim's grossly swollen stomach until they confessed. If you were really unlucky the water would have been mixed with urine, pepper or diarrhoea.

Aside from any torture inflicted she would have been held in despicable conditions, kept without food or water for periods of time, possibly in the dark with just the rats and insects for company amongst her own waste; frightened, sleep deprived and undoubtedly verbally abused. A perfect recipe for confession!

THE EVIDENCE AGAINST CAGLIOSTRO AS STATED BY THE INQUISITION

Cagliostro was subjected to 43 interrogations during the months he was held in Rome. The Vatican spared no expense, employing so-called expert theologians to study his Egyptian Freemasonry, legal investigators to trawl through every bit of evidence and medical experts to dissect his herbal preparations. According to some, it took this long to be able to scrape together enough detritus to condemn the poor man. He was allowed no witnesses to defend his name and the Vatican appointed two lawyers in his defence who, ironically, pleaded that Cagliostro was guilty and deserved punishment – no fair trial, no justice. The Inquisition did not need to give proof of its judgments and no interference was tolerated – case closed. Selected details of the trial were published in the official Inquisition publication *The Life of Joseph Balsamo* (*see* section entitled "INTRODUCTION"). The full transcript of the interrogation and trial is in the Vatican secret archives and is not available to the public. *The Life of Joseph Balsamo* makes difficult reading. It was meticulously put together to cast as black a shadow as possible, not only across Cagliostro but also over Freemasonry in general. It is pertinent to note that there were other Masons in Rome during this period, many of whom were well known to the Vatican, some of whom were in fact Catholics. Rumoured to be members of the Order of St John (whose Grand Masters included Pinto and Emmanuel de Rohan, great uncle of Cardinal de Rohan), several men fled from the city as soon as they realized the seriousness of the situation. Those who remained in Rome were neither called as witnesses at the trial nor were they prosecuted for their involvement in Freemasonry.

The Inquisition biographer says of Freemasonry:

> What is the object of the Free Masons [sic], and those phrenetic [sic] societies called the Illuminati, with their plots, their secrets, their invocations and their ridiculous rites?[12]

The Church were obsessed with the idea that Cagliostro was a major player in the Bavarian Illuminati, due to his admission that he had been invited to join. However, a few months after Cagliostro's imprisonment, a German Illuminist J Johann Christoph Bode (1730–93), refuted the theory in an anonymous treatise, stating that there was no documented proof of any deep involvement in the Illuminati by Cagliostro.[13]

The Illuminati have long been the subject of conspiracy theory and conjecture but there is no real evidence that they were any more responsible for revolution and the overthrow of orthodox religion than any of the other political movers and shakers of the time. The Holy Father further stated that Cagliostro, after being acquitted of wrong-doing in the Affair of the Diamond Necklace, had harboured a terrible vengeance against the Bourbon regime and that revolution trailed in his wake, spurred on by the followers of his diabolical Freemasonry. His return to Rome was intended as an incendiary to ignite revolution within the Papal States and to bring about the fall of the Catholic faith, for according to rumour, his fellow brethren would rise up and strike against the Church, using money from Cagliostro's sponsors to fund a fleet of 5,000 ships so as to lay siege against Rome! Did it not occur to the Church that instead of Freemasons and free thinkers as the propagators of revolution, maybe it was just subordinated people with a mind of their own that turned against the bourgeoisie?

Elsewhere in the text we find evidence of the Holy Church's ignorance towards Freemasonry and its historical roots. In one case, the biographer relates a short history of Freemasonry, including the mention of Bishop

Cranmer as the founder of Freemasonry and later remarking on Oliver Cromwell's patriotism. This statement induced an amused footnote from the English translator, who quipped:

> The Holy Father seems to be little acquainted with either the history or mysteries of Freemasonry ... in this paragraph, we find a new charge against Cranmer and a new virtue attributed to Oliver Cromwell, for we learn that one was a Free Mason [sic] and the other a patriot![14]

The Holy Father continues with the presumptuous assertion:

> Many persons who have carefully examined and scrutinized the lives of the Free Masons [sic], declare that they have found them all, and particularly their leaders, to be men of bad character, ignorant and equally destitute of morality and religion. But laying conjecture aside, we shall have recourse to facts only...[15]

This sentence contradicts itself. If many people have declared the facts why would they need to lay aside conjecture? It was somewhat ambiguous to assert that *all* Freemasons are bad, ignorant and morally destitute. For a growing society aimed at perfecting the art of morality, it would seem slightly incongruous to be able to tar them all with the same brush. The Church also produced spurious evidence against Freemasonry from unnamed witnesses who allegedly came forward after Cagliostro's arrest. They state:

> It results from many spontaneous declarations from the depositions of witnesses, and other papers held in our archives, that while, among those assembled under pretence of occupying themselves about the business of the society, some openly profess the most daring contempt for religion and the most avowed and abominable libertinism, others attempt to overturn the yoke of subordination and destroy the principles of the monarchy.

Whilst doubting that any depositions given to the Inquisition were 'spontaneous', we can also assume that information extracted was the result of the witnesses' fear for either their liberty or their lives. The other 'papers in our own archives' would never reach the light of day and these witnesses never appeared at the trial itself.

Cagliostro had allegedly been warned of his imminent arrest and the trial made full use of the fact that he did not destroy any of his Masonic manuscripts, certificates or regalia. It was with some contempt that they wrote:

> ...not withstanding these warnings, Cagliostro never dreamed of flying; nay, he did not even destroy those numerous papers which have since served as vouchers of his crimes, and have furnished the most ample proofs of his complicated guilt.[16]

A lasting comment, made by the translator of the English edition of the Inquisition text, was entitled 'Advertisement by the English Translator' and placed at the beginning of the book:

> Whatever motive may have influenced the Court of Rome, it will be lasting reproach on the reign of Pious VI to have detained, tried and inflicted the punishment of perpetual imprisonment on a man, against whom he could only prove the crime of being a Free Mason.

THE CHURCH'S CONDEMNATION OF CAGLIOSTRO'S EGYPTIAN FREEMASONRY

The following quotes regarding Egyptian Freemasonry are taken from the Inquisition biography *The Life of Joseph Balsamo*. The full Ritual is published in English for the first time in Part Three, allowing the reader a chance to make up his/her mind as to the truth.

The Holy Church despised Freemasonry but in particular they were contemptuous of Cagliostro's Egyptian Rite, branding it:

> ...as containing rites, propositions, doctrines and a system which being superstitious, impious, heretical and altogether blasphemous, open a road to

sedition and the destruction of the Christian religion.

To the Catholics it was intensely heretical – here was a man, not a pope, cardinal or priest, who was offering men and women the chance to perfect themselves morally and physically to achieve spiritual enlightenment. Not subordinating themselves to a priest who knows best and is the only one who can guide a soul to heaven; no confessional and absolution – just hard work and the dedication to truly improve oneself and achieve the immortality of the soul as first described by the ancient Egyptians.

The Church describes Egyptian Freemasonry:

> It may be necessary to enter into some details concerning Egyptian Masonry. We shall extract our facts from a book compiled by himself, and now in our possession, by which he owns he was always directed in the exercise of his functions, and from which those regulations and instructions were copied, wherewith he enriched many Mother Lodges. In this treatise, which is written in French, he promises to conduct his disciples to perfection by means of physical and moral regeneration, to confer perpetual youth and beauty on them, and restore them to that state of innocence which they were deprived of by means of original sin. He asserts that Egyptian Masonry was first propagated by Enoch and Elias, but that since that time it has lost

much of its purity and splendour. Common masonry, according to him, has degenerated into mere buffoonery, and women have of late been entirely excluded from its mysteries; but the time had now arrived when the Grand Copht was about to restore the glory of masonry, and allow its benefits to be participated by both sexes.

The statutes of the order then follow in rotation, the division of the members into three distinct classes, the various signs by which they might discover each other, the officers who are to preside over and regulate the society, the stated times when the members are to assemble, the erection of a tribunal for deciding all differences that may arise between the several lodges or the particular members of each, and the various ceremonies which ought to take place at the admission of the candidates.

The objections with regards to the Ritual are clear – blasphemy; tolerance and acceptance of other faiths and races; communing with spirits (angels) and heresy.

The Church comment on the blasphemous aspect:

In every part of this book the pious reader is disgusted with the sacrilege, the profanity, the superstition, and the idolatry with which it abounds – the invocations in the name of God, the prostrations, the adorations paid to the Grand Master, the fumigations, the incense, the exorcisms, the emblems of the Divine Triad, of the moon, of the sun, of the compass, of the square, and a thousand other scandalous particulars, with which the world is at present acquainted.

The use of Christian terminology and references to biblical figures in the Ritual did nothing to appease the Church, in fact it only served to fuel their wrath – this was blasphemy, impiety, but in many esoteric groups, the Christian faith was still of great importance to them and an overlap of symbolism and allegory was par for the course.

The trial commentary continues:

The Grand Copht, or chief of the lodge, is compared – to God the Father. He is invoked upon every occasion; he regulates all the actions of the members and all the ceremonies of the lodge, and he is even supposed to have communication with angels and with the Divinity. In the exercise of many of the rites they are desired to repeat the *Veni* and the *Te Deum* – nay, to such an excess of impiety are they enjoined, that in reciting the psalm *Memento Domine David*, the name of the Grand Master is always to be substituted for that of the King of Israel. Common masons have been accustomed to regard St John as their patron, and to celebrate the festival of that saint. Cagliostro also adopted him as his protector, and it is not a little remarkable that he was imprisoned at Rome on the very festival of his patron.

The reason for his veneration of this great prophet was, if we are to believe himself, the great similarity between the Apocalypse and the rites of his institution.

Cagliostro, for the most part, did indeed consider himself a Christian. He may not have conformed to the ideal of the Catholic Church but he was far from the religiously destitute and ignorant creature they portrayed him as. If anything he was deeply religious – just not quite how the Church deemed appropriate.

Here follows a question posed by the Inquisition:

> Q: Has not your conduct tended to debase and disgrace the great work of the redemption and the death of our Lord Jesus Christ?
>
> A: No, never. For in my primitive system and in all my operations, I made the most honourable mention of the serpent with the apple in its mouth, which I have adopted for my crest, and which denotes the cause of original sin, and of the subsequent fall. The redemption of our Lord Jesus Christ is the arrow which has pierced the serpent; and this we ought to keep constantly before our eyes and in our hearts...[17]

The Church also had issue with the fact that Cagliostro's Egyptian Freemasonry, along with regular Freemasonry, accepted and embraced the admission of those from all faiths and races.

The Holy Father comments:

> People of all religions are admitted into the society of Egyptian Masonry – the Jew, the Calvinist, the Lutheran are to be received into it as well as the Catholic – provided they believe in the existence of God and the immortality of the soul, and have been previously allowed to participate in the mysteries of the common Masonry.

The doctrine of Egyptian Freemasonry promotes tolerance. But for the Holy Church, tolerance brings with it the necessary recognition of other faiths, of other ideals that if widely understood and accepted may well 'open a road to sedition'. However, nowhere in the Ritual itself is there reference to encouraging sedition or the destruction of the faith. If we look at the Ritual (see Chapter 9), there is in the eighth point of doctrine the phrase, 'The images of the Divinity are supreme; Egyptian Masons respect them and cherish yours above all else, never speak against the Laws of the country where you live, or against the Religion which prevails in that place.' It is clearly stated, as in regular Freemasonry, that the law of the land and respect for the official religion is expected of its members.

Cagliostro was quoted as saying he 'loved the Jews exceedingly and was used to affirm that they were the best nation in the world'. Certain factions within the Church have never been able to contain their dislike of the Jewish race and this probably did nothing to change their opinion, especially considering the alleged financial connection between the Jews, the Freemasons and the Illuminati – the perfect conspiratorial union to bring down the monarchies of Europe and the Catholic faith. There is much speculation as to the role of Freemasons, the Jews and the Illuminati with regard to the French Revolution and other social disintegration, but there is no conclusive proof, merely prejudice, conjecture and thinly veiled anti-Semitism. Much will continue to be discussed and published regarding the 'New World Order' and other such conspiracies but the purveyors of such theories hold the very same kind of manipulative coercion and dangerous leadership that they are accusing their subjects of.

The Church also makes comments on the Ritual with regard to the communication with the seven archangels:

> We must here observe that when any of his disciples were admitted into the highest class, the following execrable ceremony took place. A young boy or girl, in the state of virgin innocence and purity,

was procured, who was called the pupil, and to whom power was given over the seven spirits that surround the throne of their divinity and preside over the seven planets. Their names according to Cagliostro's book are Anael, Michael, Raphael, Gabriel, Uriel, Zobiachel, and Anachiel. The *pupille* is then made use of as an intermediate agent between the spiritual and physical worlds, and being clothed in a long white robe, adorned with a red ribbon, and blue silk festoons, he is shut up in a little closet. From that place he gives responses to the Grand Master, and tells whether the spirits and Moses have agreed to receive the candidates into the highest class of Egyptian masons.

The Holy Fathers were equally contemptible when it came to the subject of immortality:

> In his instructions to obtain the moral and physical regeneration which he had promised to his disciples, he is exceedingly careful to give a minute description of the operations to which they have to submit. Those who are desirous of experiencing the moral regeneration are to retire from the world for the space of forty days, and to distribute their time into certain proportions. Six hours are to be employed in reflection, three in prayer to the Deity, nine in the holy operations of Egyptian Masonry, while the remaining period is to

be dedicated to repose. At the end of the thirty-three days a visible communication is to take place between the patient and the seven primitive spirits, and on the morning of the fortieth day his soul will be inspired with divine knowledge, and his body be as pure as that of a new-born infant.

Obviously, the Church could never condone the idea that anyone other than the Almighty himself could confer immortality, and it was only through the guidance of a priest that the individual could find salvation. Cagliostro, however, as a conduit of the Divine, believed he was able to guide his followers to a similar goal.

The Official Objections of the Holy Roman Church with regards to Count Alessandro di Cagliostro (as stated in The Life of Joseph Balsamo*)*

This was a general summary of the Church's case against Cagliostro:

> *First – on all occasions he manifested the most obstinate hatred and contempt for the Catholic religion, its ministers and ceremonies.*
>
> *He attacked the majesty and perfection of God, the divinity of Jesus Christ; his death, the grand work of redemption, the virginity of Mary, the efficacy of the sacraments, the dignity of the Church, in short everything that is most venerable and most respected either in heaven or on earth.*

From what we have discovered about Cagliostro, he had many close associates and admirers who were not only Catholic but held positions of high office, for example Cardinal Rohan and Bishop Trent. He included certain tracts from the Catholic Mass in his Ritual, which although heretical, was obviously not contemptuous – he believed himself to be a Christian. He may well have raged against the Church during his interrogations but that is for the Holy Fathers to prove, should we be privy to the minutes of said examinations. Nowhere in the Ritual or in any of the official quotes is there any attack on God or Christ by Cagliostro. He is devoutly respectful of the Divine and other representatives of that Divinity. Technically he was blasphemous towards the Christian Church by implying that through his system of rejuvenation his followers could achieve immortality, and therefore as a man ahead of his time he sits firmly in the category that many of his mystical predecessors did – as a heretic to the Church and a spiritual visionary to others.

> Second – According to the evidence of a great number of witnesses who have conversed with him themselves, or known others who have done so, he is unanimously represented as a man destitute of religion, whose principles are entirely corrupted, who does not believe in anything, and one who is generally considered an atheist, an imposter, a cheat, a heretic, a deist &c ... absolutely devoid of every principle of religion and morality.

From our research none of the 'great number of witnesses' who conversed with Cagliostro have been recorded as such within the evidence seen, and word-of-mouth evidence from 'others' would or should be totally inadmissible. He was not unanimously represented as destitute or devoid of any principle of religion – it is obvious that he was extremely knowledgeable and had many principles with regard to religion. There are numerous testimonies to his good character, written over the years by dignitaries and noblemen from the various countries he visited. He was, by definition, not an atheist considering the wording within his Ritual and his constant referrals to God or the Divine. The assertion that he was an atheist is then totally contradicted by the accusation of him being a Deist! As to being an imposter and a cheat, that can hardly qualify as anything other than adding insult to injury.

Letters which vouch for the good name of Cagliostro are available from three separate French sources, sent to M Gerard, Judge of Strasburg:

> From Comte de Vergennes, Minister of Foreign Affairs:
>
> M. di Cagliostro asks only for peace and security. Hospitality entitles him to both. Knowing your natural inclinations, I am convinced that you will make haste to see that he enjoys all those perquisites and amenities which he personally deserves.[18]

The second letter was penned by the Marquis de Miromesnil, Keeper of the Seal:

> Conte di Cagliostro has been actively engaged in helping the poor and the unfortunate and I know of a notably humane deed performed by this stranger who deserves to be granted special protection.

The third correspondence was from Marshal de Segur, the Minister of War:

> The King charges you not only that he should not be harassed in Strasburg ... but also that he should receive in that city the full consideration which the services he has rendered the sick and poor fully entitle him to.

These could hardly be construed as vain words from unreliable sources, indeed Marshal de Segur expresses that he is sending the charge of the King.

> Third — Although he strenuously denied all these imputations, yet he has been obliged to confess a variety of circumstances which sufficiently indicate his guilt.

Considering that he was faced with one of the most terrifying tormentors known to man, it is hardly surprising that Cagliostro at first denied and then confessed his guilt. He knew that the outcome of his trial had already been decided before his arrest, and that it was improbable, and painfully realistic, that whatever he made admission to or further confessed would have made any difference to his fate.

CONDEMNED TO OBSCURITY

On 7 April 1791, Cagliostro's fate was sealed and a sentence of death was passed upon him. However, this death sentence was almost immediately commuted by Pope Pius himself, by the intervention of a mysterious visitor to the Vatican. According to one account,[19] a man arrived asking to speak with the Pope; not giving his name but merely uttering a word, he was immediately taken to the pontiff's rooms. After a few moments of discussion, the stranger left. Shortly after, Pope Pius instructed his officials to commute Cagliostro's sentence to life imprisonment. This in itself was ultimately a death sentence for Cagliostro, for he would never again see the outside world nor have any public communication with it.

As it was feared Cagliostro would be liberated from Rome, he was escorted by armed guard under the cover of darkness to the Papal State prison of San Leo in Urbino, Tuscany. His faithless wife was still languishing within the walls of the Convent of Santa Appolonia, as her testimonies had left a nasty taste in the Inquisitors' mouths; they deemed that perhaps she was not the kind of woman safe to be left to her own devices and instead should be under the watchful eye of the sisters for the rest of her days.

On arriving in Urbino, it was up to the legate, Cardinal Doria, and the governor of the prison, Sempronio Semproni, to make sure that the Count was securely contained for the rest of his natural life. Doria had brushed up on Cagliostro's life by reading the Inquisition's publication of his life and trial, which had only recently been published and a copy rushed to the Cardinal's side. Doria had been warned that Cagliostro was wily and that extreme caution was to be exercised at all times. He was entrusted to send weekly reports of Cagliostro's behaviour and decorum to Pope Pius, who had been a keen witness and attendee of the interrogations and trial.

Wary of attempts by Cagliostro's followers to ambush the party, strict instructions were given to the guards and eventually they reached the gate to the ancient village of San Leo unscathed. It was here that the Count would have caught the first glimpse of what was soon to be his last residence. Built upon a sheer scarp of rock, the gloomy fortress cast a fearsome silhouette above the village. The only way to approach the awesome pile was via a treacherous stairway cut into the rock. Although the fortress was formidable, boasting walls 7 feet thick and crammed with cells, it was only guarded by a small garrison of 20 men, which was a reasonable amount to guard 8 prisoners but what about the possibility of invaders? Combine that with the need for some serious repairs to be carried out on the old building and it posed something of a security risk. Now that the castle was due to hold a prisoner of Cagliostro's calibre, would security be tight enough to deal with the rumoured plots to release him?

A suitable cell had been arranged for Cagliostro to inhabit by the legate, Doria. It was called the 'Pozzetto', also known as the 'cell of the well' and had previously been the home of several other 'high risk' inmates. It had originally held drinking water and was effectively a 9-feet-square hole that had been hacked out of the mountain, now converted into a part of the castle tower. The view of San Leo's parish church, from a tiny triple-barred window, was hampered by a platform which allowed two sentries to be positioned at all times. The cell had no door and the prisoner had to be lowered in via the same trapdoor that was used to serve food and water. It was a claustrophobic and unpleasant habitat but for the moment it was not to be Cagliostro's.

He was, instead, placed at the opposite end of the prison in the 'treasury cell'. This change of plan infuriated Doria as he had wanted Cagliostro incarcerated within the bowels of the castle, but he was told by the Governor's stand-in that the Pozzetto was in need of repair and that the Count would be safer away from any contact with the outside world in his lofty position high up in the uppermost point of the fortress. The walls of this cell were reputed to be 11 feet thick and would insulate Cagliostro from hearing any chatter from the other prisoners, effectively isolating him completely from human contact aside from his daily confessional.

The treasury cell, however, was not much more pleasant than the current state of the Pozzetto; cold, damp and infested with vermin, it did not bode well for the future health of Cagliostro. It was, strangely, within the Church's interest to keep Cagliostro alive and well, mainly because the outrage of his sentence was still reverberating around Europe and it would cast a distinctly unpleasant shadow over the Holy Office should he die unrepentant in their 'care'. Luckily for Doria, when the governor of the prison returned, repairs were carried out on the Pozzetto and, by direct instruction, a special grille was fixed over the window to discourage Cagliostro from talking to the sentries positioned outside.

Security needed to be tightened within the prison and this too was implemented: no longer would prisoners be allowed to buy their own food or, bizarrely enough, be permitted to eat at the governor's table! Legate Doria made provisions for new guards to be sent and at all times were they warned to keep a vigilant eye upon their celebrated prisoner; he was not to be trusted under any circumstance. Cagliostro's entire regime was scrutinized. He was allowed neither shaving implements nor items for writing; he was forbidden to converse with his jailers and they with him, for it was believed that he could seduce anyone with his words.

All ran smoothly for some months; Cagliostro was even reported showing signs of remorse, although this was largely taken with a grain of salt. However, the climate changed somewhat when it came to the attention of Doria that two noblemen from the locality had allegedly been allowed to see and converse with Cagliostro. He became incensed, didn't the governor know that the Count was a dangerous subversive, with intent to inflame the public with revolutionary ideals and, more importantly, could arrange for an attempt to liberate him from the fortress? This news had unfortunately reached the Vatican and Doria was instructed in no uncertain terms to investigate as soon as possible. Aware that his position as legate was severely at risk, he made inquiries through his network of spies in the village as to the nature of the rumours — were the men merely curious nobles or, more sinisterly, were they admirers of the Count with tenuous links to Revolutionary France, planning an invasion and the liberation of Cagliostro? What had transpired between the Count and these men, could they have passed anything to him, could he have entrusted anything to them?

Just when Doria had doused the flames of panic, a new drama began to unfold. A message reached him from the governor of a neighbouring village that several Frenchmen had passed through. Apparently they had been overheard discussing how they were admirers of the Count di Cagliostro and were disgusted at his unjust imprisonment. They hinted that he would soon be free to enjoy the pleasures of French wine and tobacco. Doria panicked and immediately contacted Governor Semproni, admonishing him to tighten security and surveillance immediately at the castle in anticipation of a suspected attack by revolutionaries. Semproni's response was not quite what he expected; the governor lightly brushed off the seriousness by replying that he'd have the men locked up swiftly should they indeed show their faces. Doria, close to exploding, forwarded the letter he had received warning that a surprise attack by French revolutionaries in the newly invented hot-air balloons was imminent. Poor Semproni was flabbergasted, this kind of thing was the theme of storybooks – Frenchmen in flying balloons ... in Urbino! Completely exasperated by the whole notion, but terrified of retribution from his superiors, Semproni ordered the guards to be on the alert from aerial terrorists at all times. Needless to say, this remarkable story filtered from the castle to the village and farther afield to end up as sensationalist headlines throughout Europe's press. 'Read all about it! Jacobin revolutionaries attempt air balloon rescue of Count Cagliostro!'

With relief that nothing further transpired, Governor Semproni made the sensible decision to move Cagliostro to the newly repaired Pozzetto in the depths of the castle. He now felt suitably certain that any attempt at release would be nigh on impossible. However, during the transference of the prisoner from the treasury cell to cell-in-the-well, it was discovered that Cagliostro had various items hidden within his clothes. Cleverly secreted they found a tiny almanac and a pen he had ingeniously manufactured from mattress straw. Using candle black that had fallen into the cell and his own urine, Cagliostro had created a usable ink with which to embellish his book. This went entirely against the strict instructions from the Vatican that he must never be allowed access to writing materials! It makes one wonder exactly what could have exchanged hands during the meeting between the Count and the infamous nobles – instructions, teachings, and a manuscript perhaps.

Once again, Doria was furious, this was becoming embarrassing and threatening to his credibility and position. He ordered a thorough search of the treasury cell, and was amazed to find further items including a pen hidden in the window frame and a piece of bone, sharpened so that it could be used to extract blood for writing. Doria had to come up with a solution to this dangerous problem, fast. The solution came in the form of Corporal Marini, a jailer, one-time soldier and general thug. He was given the task of bringing Cagliostro into line, mentally and physically. He was ordered to make irregular, unannounced and thorough inspections of the prisoner and his cell.

Within a week or so of Cagliostro's move to the Pozzetto, courtesy of a peephole made in the trapdoor of the cell, Marini discovered that the Count had already made several hiding places by hollowing out niches in the walls. It is rumoured that in one of the hiding places an eggshell was found containing a mysterious golden liquid (most likely urine for making his ink). From further observation he was seen to tear the wood from his bed to obtain a piece of dowel which he was later seen to be attempting to sharpen. This would have made a perfect implement for him to use upon his jailers. As the bed now needed to be replaced with one that could not be dismantled and the hollowed-out hiding holes replastered, Cagliostro was transferred back to the treasury cell. It was also decided that, due to the continual problems with the prisoner, a shackle and chain would be cemented into the wall of the Pozzetto so that any further attempts at insubordination would be futile.

Admittedly, Cagliostro was not an easy prisoner, but then, being unjustly condemned to life imprisonment would encourage most not to give up without a fight. To irritate the governor further he would make unfeasible and almost ridiculous demands of a physical and spiritual nature – he requested a prayer stool to prevent his knees from getting damp, a wooden crucifix instead of a crudely made papier mâché one, he objected to the face of Christ on that one and wanted it replaced so that he might meditate more piously upon it. He undertook regular daily confession and, to the priests in charge of his repentance and salvation, Cagliostro appeared to be penitent and reforming quite nicely, but Doria believed it was just a devious way of manipulating them and that they should all be wary of his every move.

He was becoming somewhat obsessed with his celebrity prisoner and his letters to the various cardinals reflected this, stating that Cagliostro 'knows all too well how to ... surprise and deceive'. This fear was justified soon after Cagliostro's return to the Pozzetto, when a metal spike was discovered within the privy hole, fashioned into a perfect stiletto point, with just the nail head as a handle to give a clue to its origin. The instrument was mentioned in another letter from the Ambassador Bottini, who called it a 'marvel!' The man was a genius inventor but it was almost too much for Doria – he ordered that the room be almost literally torn apart, every inch to be combed for weapons or other tools. It was official; Cagliostro was seriously undermining Doria and the Governor.

Cagliostro's subtle war on his tormentors continued – he took up a holy fast, insisting on just water. His confessors were impressed by his seemingly genuine spirituality and penitence; Doria was not convinced and as the Count's weight dropped off alarmingly he was forced to bring in outside help to attempt to stave off what he thought might be an impending hunger strike. A Dominican priest was brought in and after a lengthy confession Cagliostro decided to return to his normal diet. However, during his confession he had managed to slip a letter written in candle-black ink on a torn scrap of linen to the priest, complaining of the brutal treatment by Marini.

The Count's backlash against his imprisonment continued – he painted alchemical and Masonic murals on his cell walls, improvising with paint made from rust flakes and urine, and applied with a crude brush or wood stripped from his bed. He made startling prophecies, often shouting through his barred window to the villagers below. His prophecies were so disturbing that even his jailers could not resist repeating them and, needless to say, they reached the ears of Legate Doria. Cagliostro's uncanny knowledge of the unfolding drama of the Revolution in France was disquieting; where was he gaining information, or was he indeed amazingly psychic? Doria passed on all the information to Rome, particularly one prophecy concerning the possible assassination of the Pope, all the while implying that Cagliostro was a mocking fool verging on the edge of insanity.

Maybe after years of imprisonment, wallowing in betrayal and torn apart from his wife, Cagliostro was beginning to lose his mind. He had earlier implied that he thought Seraphina was in a cell next to his and he had implored the guards to be gentle with her. He would call to her through the walls, telling her of his love for her, how he had forgiven her betrayal. Many of the jailers believed he had lost his mind, even the prison doctor concluded that his misery was genuine. Doria, however, was as convinced as ever that Cagliostro was a fake, his obsessive hatred of him clouding all reason or compassion. The Count's behaviour became increasingly bizarre and violent; so much so that Doria ordered the governor to have him chained to the cell wall and if this was ineffective, he was to be beaten into submission. Cagliostro's screams, however, were to be heard in the village below and he was then moved back to the aerial position of the treasury cell so as to quell the disquiet that was growing.

As the Revolutionary armies grew ever closer, Doria's fears grew ever greater. Cagliostro's prophecies were unnervingly accurate. Suddenly in the spring of 1794, Doria was relieved of his position. Soon after, the jailers and the governor began to admit defeat with regard to the Count's behaviour, his priest no longer took his confession due to his impious rages and the guards let him continue with his blasphemous paintings and ravings. Mad or bad, no one could tell for certain, but in the early hours of 26 August 1795, Cagliostro did the Holy Church a favour and suffered a stroke. Still alive but seriously ill, he was offered the last rites in an attempt to 'save his soul'. It is recorded that he refused all administrations and he died an 'impenitent man'. After four years, four months and five days of torturous confinement, the divine Cagliostro was dead.

The Vatican released a statement of his demise on 28 August 1795. Even then they could not allow themselves a simple death certificate. They had to drag his name and reputation through the mud one last time – 'a heretic famous for his wicked ways'. He was mocked for his death by apoplexy (stroke) as punishment for 'having a hard and impenitent heart'. He was, they stressed, 'born in distress, lived more distressingly and died very miserably'. The Holy Church received a public supplication for the rehabilitation of his soul and that an ecclesiastical burial be performed but they wrote without pity that they had denied this to him.

He was buried at 11pm in the evening, 'at the top of a mountain ... inclined towards the west, about equal distance between two buildings destined for Sentinels known as Il Palazetto and Il Casino on the soil of the Roman Apostolic Curia'.

There are various stories surrounding Cagliostro's death and burial. A Tuscan diplomat, Luiggi Angiolini wrote:

> At last, that same Cagliostro, who made so many believe that he had been a contemporary of Julius Caesar, who reached

such fame and so many friends, died from apoplexy, August 26 1795. Semironi had him buried in a wood barn below, whence peasants used to pilfer constantly the Crown property. The crafty chaplain reckoned very justly that the man that inspired the world with such superstitious fear whilst living, would inspire people with the same feelings after his death, and thus keep the thieves at bay...[20]

Some accounts say that he did not die in San Leo due to reports that the custodians of the Castel Sant' Angelo in Rome (where he was incarcerated during his trial) used to show inquisitive tourists a little square hole where Cagliostro was said to have been confined and died. This is probably more a case of confusion, or merely that the guards may have earned a few lire for the privilege! Others dispute that the Count died at all and that he had escaped from his aerial prison and the Church was forced to spread news of his death and burial. Some say he was strangled by the guards as they feared him and his 'sorcery' so much. He had allegedly made two predictions before his death; one concerning the fall of San Leo, which consequently was blown up in 1797, another prophesying the fall of the papacy. Rumours also abound of his immortality due to his imbibing the elixir of life. Seen in the salons of Paris, or living as an immortal in India? We will never know for sure.

There is an unpleasant account that when the Revolutionary armies arrived at San Leo in 1797, General Dombrowski demanded to know where the great Cagliostro was held. Informed of his death, he ordered the remains to be dug up and the skull of the Count to be filled with wine so that they may toast his memory!

Bottini asked, as did many others, when Cagliostro was condemned and confined to his prison:

> Why, if he really possessed the powers claimed, has he not indeed vanished from his jailers, and thus escaped the degrading punishment altogether?

Why indeed? Theosophist Helena Blavatsky retorted to the same question:

> We have heard of another prisoner, greater in every respect than Cagliostro ever claimed to be. Of that prisoner too, it was said in mocking tones 'He saved others; himself he cannot save ... let him now come down from the cross, and we will believe' ... How long shall charitable people build the biographies of living and ruin reputations of the dead...!

Poor Cagliostro! He died a broken man, ravaged by torture and misery, estranged from his beloved wife who, unbeknown to him, went insane in her convent prison and died in either 1794 or 1796 – the dates are unknown. Neither the Count's nor the Countess's bodies have ever been publicly found; neither of them has been laid to rest with respect or love. Maybe one day that will be possible, maybe one day the Church will allow that.

Here follows an account given by an official of Napoleon regarding Cagliostro's fate:

> The galleries ... which have been cut out of the solid rock, were divided into cells, and old dried-up cisterns had been converted into dungeons for the worst criminals, and further surrounded by high walls, so that the only possible egress, if escape was attempted, would be by a staircase cut in the rock and guarded night and day by sentinels.
>
> It was in one of these cisterns that the celebrated Cagliostro was interred in 1791. In recommending the Pope to commute the sentence of death, which the Inquisition had passed upon him, into perpetual imprisonment, the Holy Tribunal took care that the commutation should be equivalent to the death penalty. His only communication with mankind was when his jailers raised the trap to let food down to him. Here he languished for three years without air, movement, or intercourse with his fellow creatures. During the last months of his life his condition excited the pity of the governor, who had him removed from this dungeon to a cell on the level with the ground, where the curious, who obtain permission to visit the prison, may read on

the walls various inscriptions and sentences traced there by the unhappy alchemist. The last bears the date of the 6 th of March 1795.

CHAPTER FOUR

THE MAN, THE MYTHS, THE LEGEND

AS ONE COMING FROM the South and the brilliant light of noon, with full knowledge of nature and active communion with God, I now go toward the North into the fog and, abandoning at every step a piece of myself, giving way, diminishing at each stop, leaving a little more light for you, a little more clarity and warmth, a little more vitality, until the end of my journey when the Rose blossoms in its fullness on the Cross.[1] I am Cagliostro.

THE MAN

More than 200 years have passed since Cagliostro's death in the Vatican prison of San Leo and we are still not much nearer to solving the riddle that is the identity of the infamous Alessandro, Conte di Cagliostro (pronounced kalyo-stro). Many have tried to fathom his true origins but at every turn there are contradictions that call into question even the latest evidence. Trowbridge states that there is 'no other equally celebrated figure in modern history whose character is so baffling to a biographer.'[2]

There have been a number of accounts of the life of Cagliostro and many of his biographers have come, during the course of their research, to either love or hate him.[3] The contemporary evidence against the Count is represented in an almost entirely hostile manner and therefore obscures any positive sides of his character. No one, or so we believe, is all bad, but this is what we are confronted with when researching the life of Cagliostro. It is almost impossible to find early references that do not defame or mock, except those which have been written by the Count himself. This does not prove that he was all bad, merely that the campaign to blacken his name worked. Within letters written by dignitaries from the various countries he visited, there is much more positive information about him. The majority of these correspondents praise his altruistic and kind nature, his almost devoted attitude towards caring for the poor and needy.

Exploited and caricatured since his death, this extraordinary figure burst onto the European stage, a peacock of a man, resplendent in theatrical cloth and character. To his detriment he was lacking in discretion and maturity. His flamboyant nature and, at times, bombastic speech were enough to raise the hackles of the more restrained members of the communities which he sought to impress. But perhaps we should remind ourselves that this was the century of great change, of flamboyance and deadly decadence that was to lead a head of state, aristocrats and others to the guillotine, and cause wars to erupt between classes, states and continents.

Thomas Carlyle (1795–1881), a cynical essayist of the time, described the era as:

> ...the very age of impostors, cut-purses, swindlers, double-goers, enthusiasts, ambiguous persons, quacks simple, quacks compound; ... quacks and quackeries of all colours and kinds. How many Mesmerists, Magicians, Cabalists, Swedenborgs, Illuminati, Crucified Nuns, and Devils of Loudon![4]

In the still bright light of the once glittering Renaissance period, alchemists, sorcerers and mesmerists (named after the hypnotist Franz Anton Mesmer who used the power of animal magnetism to induce a trance-like state in his patients, hence the term 'mesmerized') were much in vogue, although they were slightly more cautious of the ever-roaming eye of the papal Church, which finally caught its esoteric quarry embodied in the fateful Comte di Cagliostro.

Cagliostro's travels took him and his young wife Seraphina (1756–96) across Europe; from Rome to London, where he was initiated into a form of Freemasonry known as the Rite of Strict Observance in Ésperance Lodge, in Soho. They then moved on to Holland, Germany, Poland, Russia and Strasbourg before returning to France. In Paris once again he ignited the political fire by being implicated in a plot to defame the Queen, Marie Antoinette in the celebrated Affair of the Diamond Necklace of 1785. Proclaimed innocent of theft and misdemeanour, but banished from French shores by a furious King Louis, we can see that perhaps not only was he quite a sensation in the Masonic and social circles but he was also an inflammatory presence in Europe – a Europe that was like a powder keg set to explode. Within just a few years the French Revolution would begin and the very people who had banned the Count from the country would be led to that terrifying instrument of death – the guillotine.

MYTH OF THE WANDERING JEW AND IMMORTALITY

Cagliostro's life was part of the dramatic events of the century which saw wars, revolutions, agricultural and industrial innovations, all of which preceded the emergence of modern industrialized Europe. It was an era of intrigue, flamboyant decadence and a whole host of 'alternative' ideals and fashions – he was not the only alchemist, philosopher or radical thinker to be considered outspoken or eccentric. There is an almost endless list of characters that flitted across the Western world during the 18th century, one of which, the Comte de Saint

Germain (c.1710–84), was to fare slightly better than Cagliostro in reputation.

St Germain was, like Cagliostro, another highly enigmatic and mysterious fellow who trailed myths and wonder in his wake. Attributed with initiating Cagliostro into a Rosicrucian Order, he too travelled throughout Europe and beyond, changing names as often as his contemporary. In the 18th century it was common to have several aliases, whether to avoid creditors or merely to employ intrigue. It has even been intimated that Cagliostro was one of a number of guises adopted by St Germain. Quite often these men of mystery also manufactured romantic or mystical past lives to further add a frisson to their image. In fact these supposed 'fantasies' were often linked to various spiritual traditions that included initiatory rituals or rites of passage and were allegorical and symbolic in nature. Interestingly enough, the Comte de St Germain, when faced with those unlikely to take his version of immortality seriously without due evidence, commented to the Baron de Gleichen:

> Those stupid Parisians imagine that I am 500 years old ... and I encourage them in that thought because I see it pleases them.

Due to their claims of supernatural ability and claims of immortality, both Cagliostro and St Germain have been compared to 'The Wandering Jew', a figure from a medieval Christian mythos which has persisted into the modern age. Supposedly 'the Jew' is the man who offended Jesus on his way to the Crucifixion, and was subsequently cursed by the Son of God to walk the Earth alone until the Second Coming. The character tends to vary from tale to tale; he appears as a shoemaker or other tradesman, the doorman on Pontius Pilate's estate or occasionally, Jew becomes Roman. He goes by an assortment of names, the three most common are Malchus, Cartaphilus and Ahasuerus (Ahasverus). There are innumerable renditions of the tale and each one is slightly different, but in every case the Jew's 'crime' varies. According to one legend, as a man bearing the name of Cartaphilus, he mocks Jesus on the way to Calvary, striking him with the back of his hand and sneering 'Go quicker, Jesus, go quicker; why do you loiter?' and Jesus, looking back on him with a severe countenance, said, 'I am going, and you shall wait till I return.'[5]

A later European version of around 1547 tells of a sighting of the Wandering Jew. Now named Ahasverus, who was originally a shoemaker, he is described as having:

> ...lived in Jerusalem at the time of the crucifixion of Christ, whom he had regarded as a deceiver of the people and a heretic ... [On the road to Calvary, Christ passed by Ahasverus' house and], bowed under the weight of the heavy cross, He tried to rest a little, and stood still a moment; but the shoemaker, in zeal and rage, and for the sake of obtaining credit among the other

Jews, drove the Lord Christ forward and told him to hasten on His way. Jesus ... looked at him and said, 'I shall stand and rest, but thou shalt go till the last day.'[6]

From a biblical standing, there are two points of reference that could be attributed to the traditional myths. Immortality becomes a curse and eternal punishment when in John 18:22, Malchus, the servant of the High Priest 'strikes Jesus with the palm of his hand' no doubt incurring the same punishment as Ahasverus. However, in Matthew 16:28, eternal life is given as a blessing and a reward, when Jesus promises a disciple: 'Verily I say unto you, there be some standing here, which shall not taste of death, till they see the Son of man coming in his kingdom.'

The tale of the Wandering Jew may be an allegorical representation of the Jewish Diaspora, the expulsion of the Jews from their homeland and the subsequent scattering of the people across the globe. If it indeed represents the displacement of the Jewish people, as a Christian punishment for their part in the Crucifixion, then the myth becomes a perfect vehicle for anti-Semitism. Another theory is that 'the Jew' represents the personification of anyone who has come to see the error of their ways and forever walks in punishment of their sins against humanity until they receive absolution. Whatever the case, there have been numerous reputed sightings and encounters with the Wandering Jew over the centuries, leading to the premise that it is in fact an allegory for a pilgrim in need of redemption.

An excellent account of a conversation concerning his immortality between Cagliostro and the Duc de Richelieu is quoted by Sax Rohmer, writer and member of the Hermetic Order of the Golden Dawn, in an anecdote from his book, published in 1914. Regarding Cagliostro, he relates the following:

> Among the many anecdotes bearing upon this phase of his career, the following is worthy of citation, if only because so many versions exist, and for the reason that an episode almost identical is related of the celebrated Comte de Saint Germain.
>
> One day, then, whilst passing along the picture-gallery in the Louvre – so one account tells us – Cagliostro halted before the picture by Jouvenet, The Descent from the Cross, and began to weep. Several of his companions questioned him as to the cause of his emotion. 'Alas!' he replied, 'I shed tears for the death of this great moralist, for this man so good with whom I have had intimate intercourse. Indeed, we dined together at the house of Pontius Pilate.' 'Of whom do you speak?' inquired the Duc de Richelieu, stupefied. 'Of Jesus Christ. I knew him well!'

That Cagliostro spoke of his immortality came to the attention of the Inquisition:

To some he affirmed that he was born before the deluge, and to others that he had assisted at the Marriage of Cana in Galilee ... He spoke of his travels, his studies, his learning, in a manner at once emphatic and sublime. His conversation was normally replete with his travels to Arabia, Egypt and he also frequently mentioned his discoveries in regard to the pyramids and the various secrets of nature which he had obtained knowledge. When his name or condition was demanded he would answer 'I am what I am' and would show his cipher – a serpent pierced by an arrow holding an apple in its mouth.[7]

The Inquisition makes specific reference to the fact that when asked his name, Cagliostro replied 'I am what I am', and they would instantly have realized that this was almost identical to that part of Exodus when Moses asked God for his name as the reply is: 'I am that I am' (Ex. 3:13–14). It is unlikely that Cagliostro, in using these words, was actually claiming to be the Creator. What then was he doing? It seems more than likely that he was trying to find out if the person asking the question was an adept of some kind ('I AM' pertaining to be a symbolic term of having reached a state of perfection). In other words he was expecting a specific response.

These claims to apparent immortality offended some, including Duc de Richelieu, but no doubt this intrigued others. At the very least this kind of statement got the attention that Cagliostro craved. Note, however, that he does not claim to be immortal. Instead he refers to dining in the house of Pontius Pilate with Jesus Christ. The implication reached by many would be that he was claiming to have been alive some 1, 800 years earlier. However, when it is remembered that by this time Cagliostro had been admitted to a lodge belonging to the Rite of Strict Observance and would be well acquainted with the Masonic use of allegory (saying one thing to explain something else) things begin to become a little clearer. He allegedly said: 'Of Jesus Christ. I knew him well.' This might be interpreted as meaning that Cagliostro was well acquainted with Christ's teachings and his mission among humankind.

As well as making shocking statements to gain attention he may well have been taking note of the reaction of people to such apparently outrageous statements. Those who reacted badly would be quietly avoided whereas those whom he thought receptive would be cultivated and encouraged.

Cagliostro was rumoured, at this time (a similar rumour was attributed St Germain), to have had in his service a valet who, by his mysterious silence, considerably added to the impression created by his master. M. d'Hannibal, a German noble, one day seized this fellow by the ear, and in a tone half jesting and half angry cried:

'Rascal! You will tell me now the true age of your master!' But the valet was not to be bullied; and after a few moments of earnest reflection he replied: 'Listen, monsieur – I cannot tell you the age of M. le Comte, as it is unknown to me. He has always been to me as he appears to you; young, gay, buvant sec. All I can tell you is that I have been in his service since the decline of the Roman Republic; for we agreed upon my salary on the very day that Caesar perished at the hand of the assassin in the Senate!'[8]

Many people wonder why supposedly adept magicians seem unable to defend themselves when caught in the ultimate situation whereby ruination, imprisonment and death are inevitable. Why does their Divine Providence not intercede and save them? Why do they not make themselves vanish using their magical powers or conquer their enemies with a single word? Why did the clairvoyant not know she was going to be hit by a truck? Simply, their 'magic' is not what most people believe it to be.

Magic, to the mystics, occultists or Hermetists was not in the image of 'black magic' or 'witchcraft'; it was to perfect the art of manipulating the natural elements and/or attaining a state whereby they could achieve resonance or oneness with the Mind of God. The higher purpose was not to personally escape or be saved from death or misfortune, it was something quite different — it was to help save humanity, achieve divine perfection and be spiritually immortal. If this were not so wouldn't Jesus have escaped crucifixion? Osiris would not have been slain and all the other martyrs and adepts would have escaped their terrible fates. Joan of Arc (1412–31) and Giordano Bruno (1548–1600) would have extinguished the flames; Czech healer and magician Franz Bardon (1909–58) would have liberated himself from prison.

We have no way of knowing what these people's divine mission entailed in their entirety. We can understand the Christian concept of 'free will', and therefore we can surmise that Divine Providence or God assists in the plan but cannot interfere with mankind's own machinations. This is not to say that those who did not escape the gallows, the stake or the Inquisition were impostors and fakes, we must merely conclude that there were greater forces at work. There are however, rumours that Cagliostro and his wife did indeed escape from their prisons and were seen to be dining in Paris some 70 years later. According to Endreinek Agardi of Koloswar:

> Count d'Ourches, who as a child had known the Cagliostros, swore that Monsieur and Madame de Lasa, the toast of Paris in 1861, were none other than the Count and Countess Cagliostro.[9]

There has also been talk that the Count was liberated from his cell by fellow Masons and that he fled to India where he continued his spiritual path and, indeed, is rumoured to be still living as the immortal he always claimed to be. It was whispered that due to Cagliostro's miraculous disappearance, the authorities were forced to issue a declaration of his demise. On 6 October 1795, a small paragraph appeared in the Paris *Moniteur* announcing the news 'it is reported in Rome that the famous Cagliostro is dead'. However, reports of his death were not believed and it took an official investigation ordered by Napoleon to eventually quell further rumours.

THE CONSPIRACY THEORIES

Much has been made of the various conspiracy theories relating to Cagliostro and his Egyptian Freemasonry. There are three main theories that can be explored further to attempt to understand why he was and remains reviled by some.

Revolutionary and Agent of the Illuminati

One theory is that Cagliostro was an agent of the Illuminati and a major cause célèbre in the downfall of the monarchy of France and the instigation of the French Revolution.[10] This is a very convoluted theory and involves many of the major players in Cagliostro's life, but does that confer responsibility on him by association?

If we unravel the various threads we can begin to see some obvious but tenuous links.

Cagliostro knew several of the leading names said to have been involved in some way in the Revolutionary proceedings – Paul Savalette de Langes (1746–98); Duke of Montmorency-Luxembourg (1737–1803) (chief administrator of the Grand Orient of France and official protector of Cagliostro's Rite); Philippe II, Duke of Orléans (1674–1723) (King Louis' cousin and the Grand Master of Grand Orient Freemasonry); Benjamin Franklin (1705–90); Antoine Court de Gébelin (1725–84); Mirabeau (1749–91).

The Loge des Neufs Soeurs (The Lodge of Nine Sisters (or Muses) was founded in 1776 in Paris by Joseph Jérôme Lefrançais de Lalande (1732–1807) and l'Abbé Cordier de Saint-Fermin and was one of the most influential Lodges in France. The French mathematician, poet and philosopher Claude Adrien Helvétius (1715–71), although not recorded as being a Freemason, was a prominent member of the same social circle. After his death in 1771, his wife, Anne-Catherine, supported Lalande in establishing the Nine Sisters Lodge as well as organizing Le Salon de Madame Helvétius. Anne-Catherine was well known in Parisian society for her 'salons' held to discuss philosophy and these were much respected by the intellectuals who became members.

The Nine Sisters Lodge attracted a similar membership including the writer Voltaire (1694–1778), Court de Gébelin, the sculptor Jean-Antoine Houdon (1741–1828) and Benjamin Franklin, who joined during his time as ambassador in Paris. He later went on to become Master of the Lodge in 1779. Franklin also used these gatherings to find like-minded men who would be of use to him and the emerging New World of America. The Marquis de Lafayette (1757–1834), a young man of 19, was a frequent visitor to Mme Helvétius' salons and was soon recruited by Franklin and sent to America to serve under George Washington. He was a Freemason by the time he arrived in America in 1777. It appears that there was enough activity between the French Masons and those involved in the American Revolution to give the impression that there was a definite link to the following years of upheaval in France. However, it does not give solid evidence to link Freemasonry with the catastrophic events that were to erupt. There were obviously a multitude of factors involved – social, economic and political. It would be unsurprising if groups of free thinkers debating on how best society should be run, or envisaging a Utopian dream of equality and tolerance, would be prime suspects when radical change occurred. It was clear to see that the 'ordinary' folk of France were already thoroughly disillusioned by the oppressive weight of monarchy, ruling bourgeoisie and unproductive clergy. It would not take too much to explode the already ticking time bomb of revolution. King Louis (1754–93) and his extravagant wife, Marie Antoinette (1755–93), had done little to hide their grossly decadent lifestyle and if Cagliostro's 'heroism' of escaping life imprisonment in the Bastille during the Affair of the Diamond Necklace was anything to go by, the general populace were already looking for a hero who would become the bomb's fuse. Was it merely a case of being in the wrong place at the right time or was Cagliostro rather more to be reckoned with?

In Cagliostro's 'Letter to the French People', written after his release from the Bastille where he had been falsely imprisoned during the trial of the Affair of the Diamond Necklace, he has often been quoted as saying that the people of France should make a 'peaceful revolution', asking that the Bastille be destroyed and that it should be replaced with a temple to Isis. Other writers, particularly the Inquisition biographer (see Chapter 3), have gone as far as quoting him as writing 'the Bastille shall be destroyed and become a public walk...' and that 'a prince shall reign in France who will abolish *Lettre de Cachet*, convoke the States-general and re-establish the true religion'. As mentioned in previous chapters, Cagliostro's brilliance for predicting future events was extraordinary, but was this particular outburst a psychic pre-diction or a chilling warning?

Cagliostro's biographer W H R Trowbridge believes that there is a different reality:

> Nearly all who have written on Cagliostro have erred in stating that the letter contained [predictions] all of which occurred three years later, in 1789. The predictions are the invention of the Inquisition biographer, to whose shortcomings, to put it mildly, attention has frequently been called. Cagliostro merely says that if in the future he was permitted to return to France he would do so only provided the Bastille was destroyed and its site turned into a public promenade.

Needless to say the letter caused a profound reaction regardless of its true intentions.

Arthur Edward Waite said with regard to the Revolutionary conspiracies aimed at Cagliostro:

> Egyptian Masonry was an occult Rite, belonging to Hermetic Masonry and more especially designed to sustain the claims of Cagliostro as possessing the Great Secret of the Universal Medicine. I observe the egregious author of the article under notice identifies unconditionally the 'Grand Copht' with Joseph Balsamo, so he has not read the evidence against this view produced by Mr W R Trowbridge, who is not a Mason and has no job in Romanism or Revolution questions.

Jesuit Agent

This was a rumour from one of Cagliostro's former disgruntled students wishing to discredit him in the lead-up to the French Revolution. This theory was patently absurd as Helena Blavatsky stated:

> Cagliostro was naturally born in a family of Roman Catholics, no matter what their name, and was brought up by monks of the 'Good Brotherhood of Castiglione', as his biographers tell us; thus, for the sake of dear life he had to outwardly profess belief in and respect for a Church, whose traditional policy has ever been, 'he who is not with us is against us', and forthwith to crush the enemy in the bud. And yet, just for this, is Cagliostro even today accused of having served the Jesuits as their spy; and this by Masons who ought to be the last to bring such a charge against a learned Brother who was persecuted by the Vatican even more as a Mason than as an Occultist. Had it been so, would these same Jesuits even to this day vilify his name? Had he served them, would he not have proved himself useful to their ends, as a man of such undeniable intellectual gifts could not have blundered or disregarded the orders of those whom he served. But instead of this, what do we see? Cagliostro charged

with being the most cunning and successful impostor and charlatan of his age; accused of belonging to the Jesuit Chapter of Clermont in France; of appearing (as a proof of his affiliation to the Jesuits) in clerical dress at Rome. Yet, this 'cunning impostor' is tried and condemned – by the exertions of those same Jesuits – to an ignominious death, which was changed only subsequently to lifelong imprisonment, owing to a mysterious interference or influence brought to bear on the Pope![11]

Cagliostro and the New World Order

This is a more modern take on Cagliostro's life and beliefs. His Egyptian Rite is rumoured to have been an influence on the fraternal societies such as The Order of Skull and Bones, founded at Yale University in 1832 (previously known as The Brotherhood of Death). This would not be a preposterous idea considering the influx of Masonic teachings into the USA during the late 1700s, early 1800s, which had a major influence on a number of the fraternal societies still functioning today. There are also some rather more bizarre connections insinuated by conspiracy theorists on the web, very spuriously connecting the use of the 'Pentagon' in Cagliostro's magical operations, created for physical and moral perfection, with that of the US government – i.e. the design of the Pentagon building and the supposedly esoteric geometric layout of Washington DC.

It is also inferred that Cagliostro's teachings have been incorporated into the teachings of the Mormon Church (Church of the Latter Day Saints of Jesus Christ) via their founder Joseph Smith Jr (1805–44). Smith was an ardent student of Hermetics and Cabala, had strong interests in Egyptology and, as mentioned previously, Masonic ceremonies had a profound effect on many 19th-century free thinkers.

THE MAKING OF A LEGEND

Cagliostro's enemies and detractors may have sought to blacken his name. There were others who perpetuated his memory in a variety of ways, portraying him as a supernatural or sinister figure, but every so often the higher ideals and his humanity shine through, such as in Mozart's *The Magic Flute* and the persona in the popular comic book and film *Spawn*.

The following are important examples of the influence Cagliostro has had on the creative minds of the past 220 years.

The celebrated French sculptor Jean-Antoine Houdon made an eternally famous bust of *The Divine Cagliostro* in 1786, which graced the mantle of many a Parisian home during the Count's more popular years and numerous artists' engravings were available from street vendors of the 1780s.

Johann Wolfgang von Goethe (1749–1832) wrote a play about him entitled *Der Gross Cophta*. One of three satirical comedies based on Freemasonry, it was not particularly successful when staged in 1791. It was effectively a thinly disguised version of the Affair of the Diamond Necklace, with Cagliostro portrayed as the main culprit of the event.

Wolfgang Amadeus Mozart (1756–91) was said by some to have based the character of Sorastro from *The Magic Flute* (1791), on Cagliostro. An opera dedicated to Freemasonry with some Egyptian themes, it can hardly have been based on anything other than Cagliostro's Egyptian Rite. It has been implied that in the opera, the reason for female infiltration of Sorastro's Lodge was inspired by Cagliostro's determination that women should be allowed to be admitted to the mysteries. If one looks deeply at *The Magic Flute*, the connections to the Egyptian Rite are obvious and will be discussed further in Chapter 8.

Artists, too, longed to capture the mysterious enigma – Cagliostro's friend Philippe Jacques de Loutherbourg created over 100 illustrations representing the spiritual teachings and reminiscences of Cagliostro. In his work *The Ascent of Elijah* (1814–15) he depicts Cagliostro being taken up to heaven in a chariot adorned with Masonic symbols, representing the 'raising' of the Master into the immortal realms of paradise. His most important work included eight watercolours depicting the initiatory steps of the female Egyptian Rite.

The poet and artist William Blake (1757–1827) was deeply inspired by Cagliostro's philosophy and created many pieces that depicted these ideals.

Alexandre Dumas, père, made Cagliostro a main character in his novels *Memoirs of a Physician* (aka *Joseph Balsamo*, and *The Elixir of Life*, 1846) and *The Queen's Necklace* (1849), which was a romantic dramatization of the disastrous events of 1785 when Cagliostro was implicated, amongst others, to be the orchestrator of a plot to deceive the Queen of France, Marie Antoinette. In his novels Dumas made much of the conspiracy theory of the time that Cagliostro was the leader of the Illuminati and portrayed him and seven European Chiefs pledging almost demonic oaths to the effect of bringing about Revolution and the downfall of the monarchy.

During 1875 Johann Strauss wrote an operetta called *Cagliostro in Vienna*. Some years later the Soviet writer Alexei Tolstoy (1883–1945) wrote a supernatural romance called *Count Cagliostro* where a long-dead Russian princess is brought back to life by the Count using only her portrait. Baron Edward Bulwer-Lytton (1803–73) wrote a Masonic Rosicrucian novel called *Zanoni* in 1842, including a character reminiscent of Cagliostro.

The roll call of honours continues with the accounts from various renowned spiritualists and magicians either laying claim to being his new incarnation or to having direct psychic dealings with him, amongst them:

Eliphas Lévi (Alphonse Louis Constant 1810–75) – the famous French occultist studied the work of Cagliostro and was believed to have direct psychic communion with him.

Hélène Smith (Catherine Elise Müller 1816–1929) was a renowned French psychic who believed that she was in direct contact with Cagliostro. Her séances included her channelling the Count, replete with double chin and Italian accent and performing automatic writing. Unfortunately her credibility was questioned when she failed to come up with any consistent dates or information that could be verified as being Cagliostro's and there were several inconsistencies between the writing of the 'visiting' Cagliostro and the real one. Hélène also laid claim to being the reincarnation of Marie Antoinette.

Helena Petrovna Blavatsky (1831–91) – the Founder of the Theosophical Society believed that Cagliostro had been misunderstood and unfairly maligned. In 1890 Blavatsky made it clear that she did not agree with the writings of Theveneau Morande or the Inquisition biographer, boldly declaring that 'whoever Cagliostro's parents may have been, their name was not Balsamo!' She attributed his downfall to his weakness for an unworthy woman [Seraphina] and to his possession of certain secrets of nature which he had refused to reveal to the Church. Although she felt that 'having made a series of mistakes, more or less fatal, he was *recalled*', she also declared that Cagliostro's justification 'must take place in this century!'

Cheiro (aka Count Louis Hamon 1866–1936) – a famous clairvoyant and palmist of the 20th century. Helena Blavatsky believed he was the reincarnation of Cagliostro. He went on to become extraordinarily popular as a psychic, working for many prominent names in entertainment and eventually wrote a book on the Count called *The Romance of Cagliostro*.

Aleister Crowley (1875–1947) – the author and magician claimed an impressive line-up of past lives, Cagliostro being one.

The Count's name has also been adopted in the world of stage magic for various conjury items – including the *Cards of Cagliostro*, the *Casket of Cagliostro* and more recently one called the *Skull of Cagliostro* which involves the 'skull' being 'imprisoned' in red cords symbolizing his incarceration in the prison of San Leo. Using 'magic' you then release the skull from its bonds! The famous conjurer Robert-Houdin used to perform a séance for King Louis Philippe, which made splendid use of Cagliostro's serpent seal. In 1891, two magicians calling themselves the 'Wizard of the South' held a magical show in London bombastically named *Cagliostromantheum*. A stage magician named Caroly performed an ingenious trick called the 'Mask of Balsamo' at his conjuring exhibition at the Capucine Theatre in 1893. Henry Ridgley Evans, a historian and conjury expert, witnessed the performance:

> The prestidigitator brought forward a small, undraped table, which he placed in the centre aisle of the theatre; and then passed around for examination the mask of a man, very much resembling a death-mask, but unlike that ghastly memento mori in the particulars that it was exquisitely modelled in wax and artistically coloured. 'Messieurs et mesdames,' remarked the professor of magic, 'this mask is the perfect likeness of Joseph Balsamo, Comte de Cagliostro, the famous sorcerer of the eighteenth century, modelled from a death-mask in the possession of the Italian Government. Behold! I lay the mask upon this table in your midst. Ask any question you please of the oracle and it will respond.' The Mask rocked to and fro with weird effect at the bidding of the conjurer, rapping out frequent answers to queries put by the spectators. It was an ingenious electrical trick!

There is also a tarot card deck named in his honour. Initially manufactured in Italy in 1912, the deck was later released using the name 'Cagliostro', probably due to its Egyptian theme. There is nothing to assume that it has any real link to the man himself other than the symbolic nature of the cards.

The Count's spectre lived well on into the 20th century. Two films were made in 1910 and 1912 respectively, by Pathé films – the first was *Cagliostro, Aventurier, Chemiste et Magician*, the second, *Le Paravent de Cagliostro* (*Cagliostro's Folding Screen* – English version). In 1916 Mikhail Kuzmin wrote a novella entitled *The Marvellous Life of Giuseppe Balsamo, Count Cagliostro*.

A black-and-white silent horror movie, *Der Graf von Cagliostro*, was made in Germany in 1920 by Micco Film. Following in 1929 was *Cagliostro – Liebe und Leben eine Grossen Abenteurers* (Life and Loves of a Great Adventurer).

He was immortalized by Orson Welles in the 1949 horror movie, *Black Magic* (released in Italy under the name *Cagliostro*). An episode in the US series *Suspense*, starring Jack Palance, appeared in 1953 with the intriguing title of *Cagliostro and the Chess Player*. The Italian artist, filmmaker and biographer Piero Carpi featured Cagliostro in his famous comic books *Cagliostro* (1967) and *Il Maestro Sconosciuto – the Unknown Master* (1971). He also penned the screenplay for a film based on his own novel, simply entitled *Cagliostro*, which was made in 1974 by Twentieth Century Fox. Howard Vernon portrayed him in *Erotic Rites of Frankenstein*, 1972. Cagliostro was portrayed in the fantasy film *Spawn*. His role as mentor to Spawn appears as a mystical fiery glow and a voice from the ether. The characters battle against the unholy creatures from hell; a portrayal

Cagliostro would have been most amused and hopefully complimented by! In 1988, Cagliostro featured in the comic book, *The Phantom*. The story 'The Cagliostro Mystery' was written by Norman Worker and illustrated by Carlos Cruz.

DC Comics also took on the character of Count Cagliostro, featuring him as an immortal descendant of Leonardo da Vinci in *JL Annual 2*, whereas Marvel Comics 'hired' him as Dracula's archenemy in the *Tomb of Dracula* series.

Further fictional titles include – *The Historical Illuminatus Chronicles*, by Robert Anton Wilson. In *Foucault's Pendulum* (1988) by Umberto Eco, he is mentioned on several occasions and he also appears as a character in Alfred Bester and Roger Zelazny's novel *Psychoshop* (1998).

The most recent big-budget film to have portrayed Cagliostro is *The Affair of the Necklace* (Warner Brothers 2001) starring Hilary Swank as the notorious Madame de la Motte and an excellent performance by Christopher Walken in the role of the Count. Cineco Cinema produced *Il Ritorno di Cagliostro* starring Robert Englund in 2003.

Probably the most comprehensive and comparative study of the life of Cagliostro was published in 2003. *The Seven Ordeals of Count Cagliostro* (also under the title *The Last Alchemist*) by Iain McCalman, covers many of the theories and portrayals of the Count throughout his life.

Whoever Cagliostro really was and however fascinating we have found his enigmatic persona, this is only one aspect of his life; what we are really interested in is his vision of the 'Rejuvenation of Mankind' to which end he created Egyptian Freemasonry. We will return to the Egyptian Rite in Part Three, but to understand fully why Cagliostro chose Freemasonry as the vehicle for his 'Rejuvenation', we will now examine the origins and history of Freemasonry.

PART TWO

THE ORIGINS AND HISTORY OF FREEMASONRY

CHAPTER FIVE

THE PHILOSOPHER'S STONEMASONS

What is Egyptian Masonry, why did Cagliostro create it and what secrets does it contain? The origin and development of the ritual used by modern Freemasons is an obscure subject but is one that has been well researched. We have previously briefly touched on the origins and development of Freemasonry but it is Masonic ritual that will provide a useful insight to what Cagliostro was attempting to do with his 'Egyptian Masonry' as ritual is used primarily to initiate new members and convey certain esoteric knowledge. The various debates about Masonic ritual need not be repeated here but an outline of the history of the earliest Masonic rituals should prove useful in understanding what Cagliostro was attempting with his Egyptian Rite.[1]

Our starting point, however, is not the rituals themselves, of which more later, but certain characters and events from an even earlier period of history. We turn our attention to the end of 16th-century Scotland and one person in particular known as the founding father of Freemasonry – William Schaw (1550–1602). Born to a family of minor nobility, William came to the attention of the court of James VI at an early age and was sufficiently skilled to be trusted to serve wine at the King's table. He must have been at least capable, for at the age of 33 he was appointed the King's Maister o' Wark (Master of Works). In this position he was responsible for looking after all the properties owned by the Crown. He, therefore, had to ensure that all the buildings were properly maintained and occasionally he would be required to oversee the erection of new buildings.[2] Schaw was obviously trusted by his king as he was selected to undertake diplomatic missions to France as well as to entertain the Danish ambassador and his delegation when they visited Scotland in 1585 (they came in the hope of returning the Orkney and Shetland Isles to Denmark).

Further proof of his abilities is shown by the fact that he accompanied his king to Norway in

1589 for his marriage to Anne of Denmark (1574–1619), younger daughter of Frederick II (1534–88, King of Norway and Denmark 1559–88), which took place on 23 November 1598. After a month of feasting and celebrations the couple moved to Elsinore where the newlyweds were received by dowager Queen Sophie and King Christian IV who was then 12 years old. If further proof of his worth to his king is required it is in the fact that James sent him on ahead to prepare for the Scottish part of the wedding celebrations. He was later appointed to be the Queen's Chamberlain and seems to have undertaken the duties of that office in conjunction with those of Maister o' Wark.

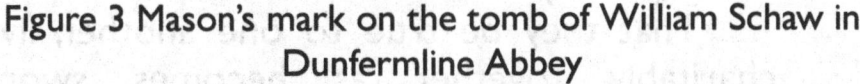

Figure 3 Mason's mark on the tomb of William Schaw in Dunfermline Abbey

In the course of his duties Schaw was in regular contact with stonemasons, and documents still exist bearing his signature showing payments to stonemasons (and other tradesmen) for work done at his command. On 28 December 1598 and again 28 December 1599 Schaw drew up documents now known as the First and Second

Schaw Statutes.[3] The first significant point is that they are addressed to stonemasons' lodges in Scotland and that, in turn, tells us that lodges were already in existence and located in most of the populated areas of the country. In other words, a network of stonemasons' lodges was spread across much of Scotland and Schaw, who was not a stonemason, also had access to that network. His statutes are, at first glance, instructions to lodges on practical matters concerning stonemasonry: the need to keep scaffolding secure to avoid injury to workers; the period an apprentice must serve; fines for breaking certain rules and so on. However, some of these instructions have nothing to do with what we would today call 'health and safety', for example:

> ...that they observe and keep all the good ordinances set down before concerning the privileges of their craft as set down by their predecessors of fond memory.

And especially

> That they be true to one another, live charitably together as becomes sworn brethren and companions of Craft.

The fact that this instruction is the very first and is contained within the first statute indicates its importance.

It is these documents that are the foundations on which modern Freemasonry is based and so they, the author, and the people to whom they were addressed, are of crucial importance for our understanding of later developments within Freemasonry, including Cagliostro's Egyptian Rite.

But why two statutes? Could Schaw not get it correct the first time round? Although something of a digression, the story of how the Second Schaw Statute came to be written is interesting, particularly as it still resonates within modern Freemasonry.

The first statutes were drawn up at a meeting of members of the lodge of Edinburgh on 28 December 1598 and the resultant instructions were despatched to all known lodges in Scotland. Given that the lodges were secret, it is not known how Schaw's instructions were distributed except in one case, there appears to be positive proof that they were received by the lodge of Kilwinning. Kilwinning had not been represented the previous year when the first statutes were issued. On 27 December 1599, one year after the first statutes were created, the lodge sent a representative by the name of Archibald Barclay to Edinburgh, supplying him with a letter of authority on its behalf, ostensibly to seek an audience with the King. He was not in Edinburgh at the time and so was received by William Schaw instead.

The 'patron saint' of Scottish stonemasons is St John the Evangelist whose feast day is 27 December. This was the traditional day for the principal yearly meeting of Scottish stonemasons and was, in effect, their Annual General Meeting

(AGM) at which all important matters were discussed and decisions made. Other meetings may have been held throughout the year, as and when required, but references are few, suggesting that if such meetings were held they were 'rubber stamped' at the AGM. But, the statutes are both dated 28 December, the day after the AGM. Here is what we think happened.

The lodge members would have convened as usual on the 27th, St John the Evangelist's day, and Schaw asked them to discuss his suggested statutes at that meeting. Once agreement had been reached on all the various points, he met with them again the following day when he presented them with the document recording everything that they had agreed to the previous day. Here is the mind of an efficient civil servant at work. It is inconceivable for such an able civil servant to have drawn up such a document in the knowledge that it would be another 364 days before the lodge would hold its next AGM and then give its official approval. Schaw was too able an administrator to allow that to happen so he had the stonemasons agree to the statutes whilst the contents were still fresh in their memory. This would explain the importance of the statutes and their dates immediately following the AGM, also that Schaw was present at the meeting although he was not a stonemason. It is not impossible that he was initiated at that meeting.

Figure 4 An 18th-century engraving of St John the Evangelist, the patron saint of Scottish Freemasonry

What would have happened had a meeting taken place between Barclay and the King rather than Schaw we will never know but we can deduce that the meeting resulted in the second Schaw Statutes and, as we shall see, these contain details of major importance which link the Father of Freemasonry and what was happening in Scotland with Cagliostro some 200 years later.

We now know that Schaw was in regular contact with stonemasons and took a very active interest in their working practices but he was also particularly interested in the affairs of their lodges. He was sufficiently motivated to draw up the two sets of rules (statutes) for the governance of their lodges. The question is why? Why bother? What was in it for him? It may have been that Schaw simply used his abilities to try to improve the lot of stonemasons who were, by any account, pretty well down the social scale. He may also have wanted to produce a more efficient workforce which would have helped him in his position of Maister o' Wark. But, there is the suggestion that there were other motives at play here and that a clue to what they were are contained in part of the second statute, especially that which reads:

> That ye [the] warden of ye lug of Kilwynning, being the second lug in Scotland, tak tryall of ye airt of memorie and science yrof [thereof], of everie fellowe of craft and everie prentice according to ayr of yr vocations; and in cais yat [that] yai [they] haue losy ony point yrof dvied to thame To pay the penalie as followis for yr slwethfulness [slothfulness], viz., Ilk fallow of craft, xx s [20 shillings] Ilk prentess x s [10 shillings] and that to be payit to ye box for ane commoun weill [common good] zeirlie [yearly] & yat conforme to the

commoun vs and pratik [use and practice] of the commoun lugs of this realm.

Translation

The Warden of the Lodge of Kilwinning, being the second lodge in Scotland will test every fellow craft and every apprentice in the art of memory and its science according to their status and if any of them fail on any point thereof they are to pay the following penalty for their laziness: Fellow of Craft[s] 20 shillings and apprentices 10 shillings. This money is to be paid into the lodge box [safe] each year and used as is the common practice of the lodges in this realm [of Scotland].

Here the lodge is being instructed to test every member annually on their ability to remember 'something'. More's the pity the 'something' is not explained but it seems pretty clear to us that it is the ceremonial, or ritual, used by stonemasons. How we come to this conclusion is a matter of deduction. There are to be no exceptions – every member of the lodge is to be tested and this means that it is something unique to stonemasons because if it was common knowledge there would be no point in an annual test about something that was known to everyone.

But why have an annual test? This is probably partly due to the fact that most stonemasons of the time were illiterate. Whatever was to be memorized was clearly not a short or simple piece: *'in cais yat yai haue losy ony point yrof dvied to thame To pay the penalie as followis...'* [in case that they have lost any point thereof given to them [they are] to pay the penalty as follows:]. In other words failure to remember each and every point will incur a penalty. Schaw believes that the stonemasons require some reason to memorize the 'something' and he institutes a system of fines to provide the necessary motivation! A fine of 10 shillings for every point failed by an Entered Prentice and 20 shillings for every failure by a Fellow Craft could have made a significant dent in anyone's pocket. He clearly knew how to motivate his fellow Scots! It seems likely therefore that there must have been something quite lengthy to be memorized and we come to the almost inescapable conclusion that this must be the stonemasons' ritual (including all the words, handshakes, etc.) because that was exactly the function of a lodge. The 'art of memory' is therefore central to Schaw's plans for the stonemasons of Scotland and we shall return to that subject in more detail later in this chapter.

A stonemason earned his living by building churches, houses and castles as well as more humble tasks such as adding stairways or chimneys to existing structures. These tasks were performed during daylight hours. Contracts still exist documenting what these hours were, depending on the time of year. The stonemasons, although economically weak, did attempt to form organizations for mutual defence and support. These are most often referred to as guilds and some consider them to be a form of proto-labour union. Guilds in Scotland are more usually known as Incorporations and most trades with some economic power formed themselves into Incorporations. It was these bodies that regulated each particular trade by setting wages and periods of apprenticeship, setting minimum standards of workmanship and negotiating with employers. Yet, as we have just discussed above, Schaw set down these kinds of rules in what we now call the *Schaw Statutes* but he did not send them to the very people who would have to implement them. He did not send them to the Incorporations instead he sent them to lodges. Here we reach a significant point which suggests why Freemasonry developed in the way it did whereas other trades had nothing equivalent.

The Reformation arrived relatively late in Scotland and was a 'root and branch' reform of the religion of the country.[4] All the pomp and ceremony of the Catholic Church, including the 'mystery plays' enacted by Incorporations, was swept away. The Church no longer provided a spectacle and the Reformed Church focused almost exclusively on the most efficient means of educating the people as to the word of God. This new way of seeing the relationship between God and people was that all church ornamentation, statues, sumptuous costumes, etc. were an impediment to knowledge of the Godhead. The new Protestant form of worship was much plainer and simpler, so much the better to allow the Church to speak directly to the laity without distractions. The Incorporations had played a major role in staging mystery plays based on their favourite parts of the Bible. For example, the Master Mariners enacted parts of the Book of Genesis which related to Noah and the Ark. These were usually held on the feast day of a particular saint and repeated on other major religious festivals (for example, All Saints Day). Other processions, such as those of confraternities of the Church were also abolished and so it ought not to be thought that only specific groups (such as Incorporations) were the targets of the Reformed religion.

There is a theory, and it is only that at this point, that the sudden disappearance of rather splendid festivals, processions and mystery plays (all of which were often accompanied by a great deal of eating and drinking) created a vacuum that the new Reformed Church would not fill. As the Church controlled religious observance throughout Scotland it was simply not possible to stage such events. All the trades and their Incorporations were under the careful scrutiny of both Church and civic leaders. Yet there was one group which did not take part in public 'performances' of a religious nature, was not part of the Church and was not an Incorporation.

We refer of course to the lodge. Only stonemasons had two organizations: one, the public 'face' – the Incorporation, and the other private, secret – the lodge.[5] As we have discussed above, the lodge could only have been for private ceremonials. The Incorporation dealt with practical, economic matters and, like other trade Incorporations, took part in the various religious festivals of the pre-Reformation Church. It is essential in this discussion to realize that only stonemasons had lodges as well as Incorporations.

It is not unreasonable to believe that the ceremonials performed in lodges, only for stonemasons, became a substitute for the Church festivals lost at the Reformation. Now we can return to the clues mentioned in the Schaw Statutes. The very first, that stonemasons should 'live charitably together as becomes sworn brethren and companions of Craft'. This instruction, the first that Schaw sent to all lodges in Scotland, tells us that these stonemasons, that is those who were members of lodges (and not all were), had taken an oath or obligation – 'sworn brethren'. This first, and by implication therefore, the most important instruction to lodge members is that they must treat each other in accordance with their obligation. By implication this also suggests that the oath was taken as part of a ceremony that all other members had previously experienced.

The Reformation had swept away all the pomp and ceremony associated with religious festivals enjoyed by the common people and actively supported by specific groups who took part. William Schaw had taken a great deal of interest in stonemasons' lodges, even going to the extent of writing detailed guidance as to how to conduct their affairs. It seems that because of Schaw's interest in stonemasons, and more particularly what they did within their lodges, he decided to make them reorganize their lodges. Exactly what motivated Schaw to do this we will now never know for sure but we think that the clues in the Schaw Statutes, the life and career of Schaw himself, and the times during which he lived can give us some insight as to his motives. Let us begin with his death. His tomb stands in Dunfermline Abbey and the epitaph reads: WILLIAM SCHAW, Live with the Gods, and live for ever, most excellent man;

This life to thee was labour, death was deep repose.

To his most upright Friend,

ALEXANDER SETON, Erected DEO OPTIMO MAXIMO

(To God the Best and Greatest.)

This humble structure of stones covers a man of excellent skill, notable probity, integrity of life, adorned with the greatest of virtues – William Schaw, Master of the King's Works, President of the Sacred Ceremonies and the Queen's Chamberlain. He died on 18 April 1602.

Among the living he dwelt fifty-two years; he had travelled in France and other kingdoms for the improvement of his mind; he wanted no liberal training; skilful in architecture; was early recommended to great persons for the singularity of his mind; and was not only unwearied and indefatigable in labours and but constantly active and vigorous, and was most dear to every good man who knew him. He was born to do good offices and thereby to gain the hearts of men; now he lives eternally with God.

Queen Anne ordered this monument to be erected to the memory of this most excellent and most upright man, lest his virtues, worthy of eternal commendation, should pass away with the death of his body.

Powerful words by any measure and his epitaph informs us that he had travelled abroad for the 'improvement of his mind' and was 'skilful in architecture'. Again, the question we ask is what was it that attracted him to the stonemasons and their lodges?

The Renaissance

Let us consider the period during which Schaw lived and during which he created modern Masonic Lodges. The Renaissance is generally accepted as being the period which spanned the 14th to the 17th centuries, but these are artificial divisions as there are indications of Renaissance elements before and after this period. It was marked by cultural advancement in a number of areas such as art, literature and architecture and most historians agree that it commenced in what is now northern Italy, dispersing across most of Europe.

Although marked by developments in a variety of fields such as art, architecture and mechanics (as examples) it was people who made those advances possible. The Renaissance can therefore be identified not only by referring to inventions, beautiful art and advances in philosophy but also by examining a number of people (often recognized as geniuses). In the Italian Renaissance context we need only think of the likes of Filippo Brunelleschi (1377–1446); Donato Donatello (c.1386–1466); Sandro Botticelli (1445–1510) and Leonardo Da Vinci (1452–1519).[6]

Whilst many of the Renaissance geniuses have made an indelible stamp on history, others who are of interest to us in this work include the likes of Giordano Bruno and Christian Rosenkreuz (1378–1484), the former propagating a form of Hermeticism and the latter being the legendary founder of the Rosicrucian movement.[7] Yet there are others: Henry C Aggripa (1486–1535); Jakob Boehme (1575–1624); Robert Boyle (1627–1691); John Dee (1527–1608) and his son, Arthur Dee (1579–1651); Paracelsus (c.1494–1541); Sir Walter Raleigh (c.1554–1618); Alexander Sethon (?–1604) and Alexander Dicson (Dickson) (1558–c.1604). Some of these names may be familiar but the majority are not and although forgotten for want of a famous piece of art or magnificent building they, as we shall see, are remembered here for entirely different reasons.

Given the previous discussions regarding stonemasons, their lodges and what secrets they may have possessed, it must be of interest to us to at least mention developments in architecture during the Renaissance. First and foremost the revival of interest in the work of an ancient Roman architect by the name of Marcus Pollio Vitruvius must be considered. He apparently lived during the first century BC and he wrote a book of 10 volumes entitled *De Architectura*.[8] This revival was due to Andrea Palladio (1508–80) and his design of a number of houses and palaces centred on Vicenza (he also designed a number of churches in Venice). His work was based on the writings of Vitruvius and he claimed 'his' style attempted to revive Roman architecture by using classical Roman forms, symmetry and proportion as advocated by Vitruvius. Soon others took up Vitruvius' (Palladio's) style as reflected in, for example, Donato Bramante's (1444–1514) Tempietto in Rome, where tradition informs us St Peter was crucified. The Tempietto was based on Vitruvius' explanation of the Doric order of architecture.[9] It is the effect that this revival of interest in ancient Roman architecture had on other areas which, as we shall show, fed directly back into Freemasonry and Cagliostro's Rite.

Leonardo Da Vinci (1452–1519), famed for all sorts of inventions, works of art and drawings of mechanical devices, also took an interest in Vitruvius and applied his description of the proportions of the human body which came to be one of Leonardo's most famous drawings – the *Vitruvian Man* (see below). Leonardo's application of ancient Roman architectural practice to the human body demonstrates, in no better way, how science and art could be combined to produce something that advanced human understanding (or at least beauty!) beyond the separate parts. In particular he shows his fascination with proportion. Here we see the rational dimension of the Renaissance which is often considered to be the dawn of the scientific, logical and rational age. Later we shall discuss why this is misleading. In this example Leonardo appears to be reaching for something more profound than simply drawing the human form accurately. He described his image as a *'cosmografia del minor mondo'* (a cosmology of the microcosm) and believed that the human body's processes were analogous with the processes of the universe.

Vitruvius described the human form and Leonardo seems to have drawn this based on Vitruvius' text:

> The navel is naturally placed in the centre of the human body, and, if in a man lying with his face upward, and his hands and feet extended, from his *navel as the centre*, a circle be described, it will touch his fingers and toes. It is not alone by a circle, that the human body is thus circumscribed, as may be seen by placing it within a square. For measuring from the feet to the crown of the head, and then across the arms fully extended, we find the latter measure equal to the former; so that lines at right angles to each other, enclosing the figure, will form a square.[10]

It is possible that Leonardo, by depicting the human body in this manner, was symbolizing material existence (the square) and man's spiritual existence (the circle).

This Renaissance view of the relationship between architecture and the human body is important for what follows, particularly in relation to William Schaw and events in Scotland.

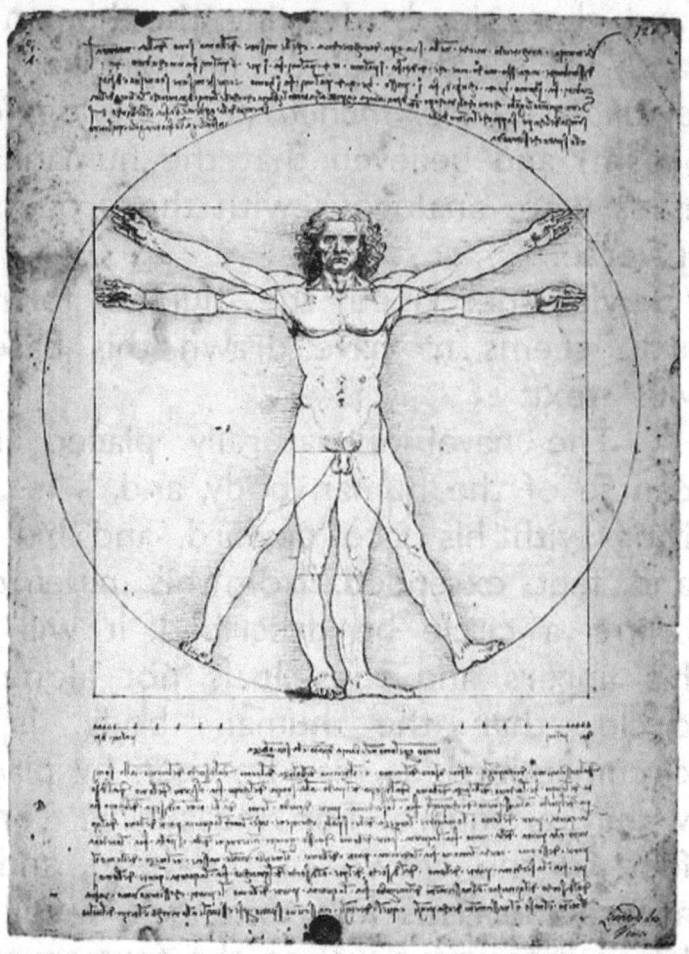

Figure 5 Vitruvian Man by Leonardo da Vinci

The Art of Memory

We have seen how Schaw specifically instructed stonemasons to perform the 'art of memory'.

It is thought that the *Art of Memory* originated in ancient Greece but this is debatable because much of what we know of it is to be found in Roman sources. Put simply the Art of Memory was devised as a technique which greatly aided memorizing long texts and speeches. Before books existed, orators gained a living by 'reading' a book to you from memory. No doubt some could recall, word for word, a book or two, but to make a living the orator needed a substantial repertoire of titles. Clearly any method that allowed him to mentally store a large number of books or other texts would be of great value.

The Art of Memory was a technique which required the individual to create a mental picture of a building with its rooms and passages. Such a building was usually one with which he was familiar. In each room, passageway and perhaps even in a surrounding garden assorted articles were strategically placed. The orator walked through his 'building of the mind' in a particular route. One route was followed for a particular book, another route would be followed for a different text. It is not known exactly but it seems that each room presented the chapter of the book concerned. Particular articles would remind the orator of the contents of a page or perhaps even a paragraph. The technique was likely to be even more specific for prompting an event, person or action. A statue of a sportsman may indicate the Olympic Games, a horse could suggest travel, and wine and food laid out on a table a festival, and so on. Frustratingly, we shall never know with certainty how any particular orator used the technique as they developed their own methods and probably had their own imaginary buildings — although it is possible that actual buildings were adopted for this purpose.

The Art of Memory did impose its own problems. Longer, complex pieces needed a larger building (although conceivably adding new rooms may have been an option) but more difficult was the addition of more and more objects, all of which had to be different with their own special attributes. To deliver a speech the person would mentally enter the building and 'walk' through the rooms on a predetermined route, for example, by walking clockwise round the ground floor rooms in a certain sequence, noting the object(s) in each room. The object would prompt the speaker to recall the next part of his speech. In order to imprint the image of the object more forcefully on the mind of the speaker, the object selected would often be striking in some way — grotesque, crude or rude, brutal or erotic, as best suited the subject matter. This method enabled very complex and lengthy orations to be delivered and the Romans developed the art to such an extent that every word of a book could be recalled by this method.

Today most of us would find this technique bizarre, even absurd, because the amount of time and effort required to remember the huge amount of imagery — building(s), rooms, corridors, gardens, all of which had to contain a multitude of objects — seems ridiculous for the end result, the reading of a book. However, the amount of material which survives from the Roman period shows that the technique worked well and was widely used. One reason might be because the human mind is not always logical in how it processes information – remembering complicated calculations but forgetting what happened yesterday. For the sake of the argument here, we can divide memory into two types: natural and artificial. Natural memory is untrained and could be considered as the unconscious, whereas artificial memory is trained and tends to have had thoughts, ideas and facts forced into it. Learning multiplication tables by rote is one way of forcing material into the artificial memory. Mentally walking round a building noting a variety of diverse, apparently unassociated, objects is another. One further point is the capacity of the human mind to recall images much more easily than a large chunk of text. 'A picture is worth a thousand words.'

Schaw's use of the term the 'Art of Memory' is interesting and can indicate firstly, that he was aware of the technique and secondly, that he wanted the stonemasons to put it to a particular use. Remember they were largely illiterate and this system of memorization is well suited to retaining large amounts of material. One must suspect that he wanted the stonemasons to use the system for a particular reason (otherwise he could simply have said you will all remember the ritual from beginning to end) and that was to remember the ritual in a particular way and, perhaps more importantly, in a particular order.

The Renaissance (the word means 'rebirth') was essentially a process of rediscovering material from ancient Egypt, Greece and Rome that had been lost for centuries. A huge range of subjects was rediscovered including architecture, philosophy, astronomy, mathematics and much else besides. As we shall see, some of these contradicted the contemporary teachings of the Church.

Underpinning the Renaissance was a whole range of nonrational beliefs, in particular: astrology, magic, alchemy and Neo-Platonic philosophy. Many of these beliefs had lingered since antiquity, some as parts of folklore, whereas others were considered much more seriously. It was during the Renaissance that these began to be studied in a more rigorous manner. Nonrational, here, does not mean what it does today — irrelevant, illogical or not sensible. Renaissance thinkers considered everything and anything worthy of study — for the study of 'everything' could, potentially, lead to a greater understanding of the world and the universe. The division of what was studied into rational and nonrational is an artificial one imposed by us on the past.

This whole range of nonrational beliefs existed under a philosophical umbrella known as Neo-Platonism. This new version of Platonic thought considered the whole of creation (or the 'cosmos') to be an 'organic whole' in which each part is connected to all the others.[11] Parts of the 'organic whole' were material whilst others were spirit. The innumerable points at which matter and spirit intersected were indistinct. The world and everything in it, on it, or in any way part of it, were considered to be alive, to be animate, and particularly that the divine imbued all matter. Man, the microcosm, was linked to the macrocosm, the universe, by an enormously complex system of spiritual influences, relationships, forces and connections. An example of how this process operated was that planets and stars had a direct effect on people's activities through a variety of occult forces.

In their attempts to understand the universe (and all that was within and without it) they turned to the ancient Egyptian civilization and its religion. The reason was simple. Egyptian civilization (and therefore its religion) must have been the best in the world because it was the oldest known, certainly the oldest known during the Renaissance. Being the first, and therefore the original and the best, created a huge interest in everything Egyptian. This coincided with the Renaissance preoccupation with symbols and the belief that they had the potential to gain access from the material world into the spiritual world (from the microcosm to the macrocosm). Egyptian symbols (hieroglyphs), must logically therefore be the original and most powerful symbols. In this sense they were considered to be keys, able to unlock the doors between worlds.

These ancient symbols or hieroglyphs could not be understood, but that merely ensured that many who tried to decipher them became convinced that the ancient Egyptians must have had a special, secret means of communing with the occult world of the macrocosm. This way of thinking, although somewhat wishful, fitted neatly with the prevailing belief system. The very fact that the Egyptian hieroglyphs could not be interpreted added to their mysterious nature and many took up the challenge to break the 'code' of the ancients and be the first to gain full access to the occult world. The belief that all matters relating to ancient Egypt was the most effective means of connecting with the macrocosm was given full force by the movement known as Hermeticism, which we discussed earlier (see section entitled "THE MASONIC MAGICIAN").

On rediscovering the Art of Memory, the Hermetists of the Renaissance added an entirely new twist. In their attempts to achieve their ultimate goal of *theosis*, oneness with the divine spirit, they harnessed the Art of Memory as a means of contacting the occult world. Giulio Camillo (1480–1544), a Hermeticist, produced a Memory Theatre made from wood. This large model permitted an individual to walk into it to view, physically, the Hermetic concept of the order of the cosmos and the place of the world within it, much as one could view a Roman amphitheatre from the stage.[12] Camillo's theatre had, in addition, a number of biblical and Hermetic influences. The auditorium had a standard layout, but on each step or level, there were figures or objects. These were placed on the rising 'steps' between (on the first level) the seven 'planets' then known as – Sun, Moon, Mercury, Venus, Mars, Jupiter and Saturn. True to the Art of Memory, these depictions were not only intended to remind the viewer of the planets important in astrology, but also indicated the seven essential measures, or first causes of creation from which all other things derive. The 'highest' level in height and importance is the seventh which is devoted to the arts.

Camillo had therefore taken the imaginary building used by the individual and given it a physical form. Unlike the Greek and Roman objects in the mental building he endowed the objects with Hermetic meaning. They, in effect, became talismans with which man could attempt to gain an understanding of occult influences and use them in a variety of ways – the unscrupulous to improve their own lives whereas the genuine Hermeticist hoped to improve the lot of man.

Scottish Hermeticism

William Schaw lived within the Renaissance period all his life and it is known that he travelled to France and Denmark and 'other kingdoms for the improvement of his mind'.[13] It is known that Schaw was in France in 1584, in the company of Lord Seton, the year after Giordano Bruno had left Paris for England. Schaw died in 1602, two years after Bruno. It is not impossible that Bruno and Schaw met even in passing but sadly that must be speculation until more information comes to light. It is known that Bruno was in England during 1583–85 and that his third work, *Sigillus Sigillorum,* was published there in the year of his arrival.[14] This work aroused a great controversy and what is of importance to us here is that his staunchest defender was a Scot, Alexander Dicson (Dickson) (1558–c.1604). He had been born in Perthshire and studied at St Leonard's College, St Andrews. After graduating in 1577 he moved to England but maintained close contact with Scotland. His first recorded defence of Bruno was a critique of Bruno's first work on memory (*De umbris idearum* published in 1582 in Paris, France).[15] Dickson published a second defence under a pseudonym, perhaps because his first open defence made anonymity desirable. Regardless of whether the two ever met, Bruno was clearly aware of Dickson's support and considered Dickson to be a disciple, describing him as such in subsequent works. Of paramount importance is the fact that Dickson's first work places his description of the 'classical art of memory' in a very obvious Hermetic Egyptian setting. In this he outdid Bruno himself. Dickson understood both forms of the Art of Memory – that of classical antiquity and the 'new' Hermetic Egyptian form developed during the Renaissance. In 1592 he published a work on the Art of Memory which contained no Hermetic content whatsoever, yet it is known that he taught the Hermetic technique to a variety of students for a fee, demonstrating that he was a true master of this art. He was also involved in some shadowy pursuits, possibly spying for money, and one can but wonder if his Art of Memory was of assistance to him in this activity. By 1592 he was back in Scotland and at the royal court. This was something known to have worried English agents monitoring his activities who, in reports to England, described him as being a 'Master of the Art of Memory'. He continued to observe the old faith and he was in close contact with the Catholic earls of northeast Scotland for whom he may have undertaken spying missions overseas. This ensured that he was always a figure regarded with some suspicion – apparently by both Scots and English. He was not discreet regarding his religion and this brought him into conflict several times with the reformed Church of Scotland which, on one occasion, had him imprisoned. Eventually he was rehabilitated and was accepted at court, becoming a servant to James VI.

As we have seen, William Schaw had been appointed the King's Master of Works in 1583. Both he and Dickson were of a similar age and both worked at the royal court. Significantly, both had knowledge of the Art of Memory but, whilst we know Dickson was an expert in the subject, the extent of Schaw's knowledge is not so clear. Yet Schaw and Dickson were not the only individuals at court who had an interest in the Art of Memory. The year after Dickson graduated from St Leonard's College, St Andrews, so too did William Fowler (c.1560–1610). He subsequently wrote a treatise on the Art of Memory and also seems to have actually taught the technique to James VI. At exactly the same time that Schaw is employed at the royal court and is involved with the stonemasons of Scotland (and their lodges) there are four men with a deep interest in the Art of Memory – one of them apparently no less a person than the King.

Anne of Denmark married James VI in 1589 and as Schaw accompanied his king to Norway this is a good indication of the King's trust in him. When it is known that Fowler also accompanied James VI to Norway, and both stayed with the royal retinue at the Danish court on the return journey, it is clear that James had no difficulty with being closely associated with servants steeped in the Art of Memory. Schaw later became the Queen's chamberlain and at about the same time Fowler was appointed her secretary. Two practitioners of the Art of Memory were close to the King for a number of years and then both were made close servants to the Queen. Unfortunately there is nothing extant to inform us of what Hermetic influence they exercised over the Queen. Nor is the exact nature of the personal relationship between Schaw and Fowler known yet, given their responsibilities in the Queen's household they must have known each other well and worked professionally together on a variety of projects as and when required by a member of the royal family.

This was the background in which Schaw lived and worked but the question is, what effect did all this have on his dealings with Scottish stonemasons and their lodges? We have previously seen that Schaw instructed lodges to test annually all the members in the Art of Memory, and instituted a system of fines with specific sums applied to every point of failure. Although it is not impossible that stonemasons had used the Art of Memory before Schaw became involved, he certainly formalized its use by instructing Scottish lodges to do so. But the question remains: which form of the Art of Memory was being used? If Schaw required the Hermetic form, adapted from the classical type devised during the Renaissance and as practised by Bruno, Dickson and others, then the conclusion is inescapable – Schaw chose to introduce Hermetic elements to the lodges. If it was simply the practical technique as an aid to memory, then any inclusion of Hermetic elements would have been accidental. Following Schaw's death, lodges probably used his statutes as guidance especially in the absence of any central 'guiding hand'.

We have previously argued that stonemasons' lodges operated in secret because the special knowledge passed from generation to generation was for them alone. Guarding one's 'intellectual property' today is common, but unlike us they could not use contracts to do so, using instead the best method available – the Art of Memory. This had the added advantage of ensuring that their secrets were more secure by the mere fact of never being written down; no ritual was written for almost 100 years, the first being the Edinburgh Register House [ERH] MS of 1696.[16] The technique also preserved the information in a certain order or sequence.

We believe that there remains one other very poetic reason why Schaw wanted this method adopted and in particular what it was to contain. We confess that this must be speculation but we believe that it is a most interesting and legitimate one.

Schaw needed to devise a system to allow stonemasons to be able to recall their ritual. He was familiar with the Art of Memory and that system was familiar to at least three other senior members of the royal court including the King himself.

In order for the system to work uniformly, a *single* building had to be selected. Unlike the classical and Renaissance practitioners who could choose or invent a building that suited them,

Scottish stonemasons had to choose a single building with which they were all familiar. Given the central position of King Solomon's Temple (KST) in the lore of the stonemasons and revealed within the earliest known rituals it is inconceivable that any other building was chosen. The Art of Memory, using KST as a construct of the mind – room by room, step by step, object by object – in order to recall in detail the ritual ('every point thereof') would have been irresistible. Not only was KST the oldest stone building in the Bible, it was therefore the first.[17] One can almost see in one's mind's eye the proud attitude of stonemasons standing in their kirks when the minister read portions relating to KST from Kings and Chronicles. The folk memory of the stonemasons therefore stretched back as a far as the golden age of King Solomon himself. They had built and beautified the most famed temple in the world.

Their predecessors had not only built KST, but Schaw's Hermetic Art of Memory showed the stonemasons a way that they could stretch back to that golden age and perhaps learn something of Solomon's famed wisdom for themselves. In the process they also sought to improve their mental abilities and their moral and spiritual lives by specific reference to the same working tools that would have been used by their ancestors in the building of KST. Schaw's way linked the Art of Memory to the stonemasons' particular lore and made them special and unique like no other craft or trade. Truly these were secrets worth preserving and this is why we are convinced that stonemasons, and only stonemasons, held lodges, being recognized and worthy brothers who could receive the wisdom of Solomon.

On a practical level, as the ritual was committed to memory using KST and the Art of Memory, the parts of the ceremonial became fixed as did their relative importance one part to another. KST therefore became a fixed, central point within the lodge. The permanence and 'position' of important elements was further reinforced once the ritual came to be printed in the first part of the 18th century. However, you may have noticed that we still have not addressed what these secrets actually were; what was the esoteric knowledge or, perhaps, the wisdom of Solomon? Exactly what was considered so important that only certain stonemasons could receive it and lodges were held in secret?

The Masonic Preservation of Hermeticism

Hermetic ideas were tolerated, especially if not pushed to extremes and not repeatedly discussed in public, as to do otherwise could lead to the same fate as poor Bruno![18] The principal reason for this tolerance by the Church was due to the widely held belief that

Hermeticism was a precursor to the true faith – Christianity. This proto-Christianity had a number of parallels with the Christianity as taught by the Church. In other words, Hermeticism was an interesting relic from before the time of Christ. Interesting to some perhaps, but no threat to the true faith. However, this was all premised on the proven 'fact' that the Hermetic texts were from ancient Egypt, from a time which long predated Christianity.[19]

Isaac Casaubon (1559–1614), born in Geneva of French Huguenot refugee parents, had no formal education until he was 19, but thereafter his intellectual abilities were rewarded by various positions at the universities of Geneva, Montpellier, Lyons and Paris. By 1610 he had gained the reputation of being, after Joseph Justus Scaliger (1540–1609), the most learned man of the age. In 1614 he analysed the language used in various Hermetic texts, particularly the most philosophical entitled Corpus Hermeticum (The Hermetica), which he dated to around ad300 and certainly no earlier than ad200.[20] This destroyed the basis on which Hermetic writing had previously been accepted as not only legitimate, but legitimate for Christians to discuss and study. The parallels with Christianity were now seen to be due to the accidental and coincidental inclusion of some biblical themes and episodes.

Casaubon's anlysis showed that in total the Corpus Hermeticum comprised Jewish, Greek and Egyptian thoughts and ideas which circulated in Alexandria particularly during the Hellenistic period. Hermeticism was therefore discredited as a plausible explanation of how the world 'worked', as the rise of a more rigorous scientific method in the 17th century was being developed. However, if some elements of Hermeticism had been inserted into the lodges of Scottish stonemasons (by accident or design) then there is the intriguing idea that Hermeticism, albeit adapted and modified, remains an element within modern Freemasonry today. This is the view of several eminent historians including Frances Yates and David Stevenson.[21]

Early Scottish Lodges

The lodge is the basic 'unit' of Freemasonry. In the 16th, 17th and well into the 18th centuries this was the only unit used by stonemasons for initiation ceremonies. The earliest known rituals date from the late 17th century and are known as 'catechisms'. The first three of these are:

Edinburgh Register House MS (1696)
Airlie MS (1705)
Chetwode Crawley MS (c.1710)

These manuscripts are Scottish and contain details of two ceremonies used by stonemasons' lodges of that time and earlier. The *Entered Prentice* and *Fellow Craft* ceremonies are now the first and second degrees in modern Freemasonry, although still often referred to by their full titles. There are no compatible texts from England at this time and this suggests that a transition took place from stonemasonry to Freemasonry only in Scotland, and also that once that transition was underway this form of pre-Grand Lodge Freemasonry was transmitted to England to become modern speculative Freemasonry.[22]

The only 'fly in the ointment' with our idea is the rather long gap of almost 100 years between when Schaw was instructing stonemasons in the Art of Memory (the ritual used to initiate new members into their lodges) and the 17th-century catechisms; how could we be sure that these rituals were unchanged for 100 years. The short answer is that we could never be certain, but we quickly realized it was safe to assume that they were the same *because* Schaw had instructed the stonemasons to memorize the ritual and therefore there was no need to ever write it down. Support for this view comes from the ritual itself which contains specific instructions, in long flowery language, that the ritual is never to be written, recorded or in any other way delineated. These early rituals have been reproduced elsewhere and need not be repeated here.[23] What is necessary, however, is to provide those parts of the ritual which are relevant to the links between William Schaw and Comte di Cagliostro.

The oldest rituals (ERH MS, etc.) are multifunctional. They are made up of a catechism (questions and answers) and a description in two parts, the largest being the reception of the candidate as an Entered Prentice. The remaining part refers to the Fellow Craft ceremony which is much shorter (apparently because it repeats much of that contained in the Entered Prentice ceremony) but the words and postures are different. The parts which describe the ceremony are of some interest for they contain the oath or obligation and are reminiscent of that part of the Schaw Statutes which refer to 'sworn brethren and fellows of Craft'. The rituals are incomplete, for example they provide very little detail as to the number of participants or their positions or movements. We believe that they were written as an aid to a lodge member, probably the Master, in order to keep him on track within the ceremony; unlike the illiterate stonemasons addressed by Schaw in his statutes of 100 years earlier these individuals could read and write, so a written 'prompt sheet' was much more useful to them.

The question-and-answer section is where our interest lies. All these rituals consist of 14 or 15 questions and commence with simple enquiries such as 'Are you a Mason?, Answer: Yes.' But soon they become complex and are clearly esoteric in nature for both questions and answers. Those that are of interest to us are reproduced below:

Que 5. What makes a trew and perfect Lodge: An: seven masters and five entered prentices a days joueirny [journey] from a burrghs toun without barke of doge or crow of coke [cock].

Que 6. does no less make a true and perfeit [perfect] Lodge. An: yes five masters thre[e] entered apprentices & C.

Que 7. What is the nam[e] of your Lodge? An: The lodge of Killwinin.

Que 8. How stands your Lodge. An: e[a]st and west of the temple of Jerusalem.

Que 9. Wher[e] was the first Lodge. An: In the porch of Solomon's temple.

Que 10. Are there any light[s] in your Lodge. An: yes, three The north east: S: W: and the Eastern passage. The on[e] denot[e]s the master mason. The other the wariden The third The fellowcraft.

Que 11. Are there any [blank] in your Lodge: yes: the perpend Esseler a square pavement and a brobid ornall.

Que 12. Where [will] I find key of your Lodge: yes: three foot and half from the Lodge dore under a perpend Essler and and [sic] a green divit [divot].

Que 13. What meain you by a perpend Essler and a grein divit: An: I meain not only under a perpend Essler a green divit but under the lap of my Liver wher[e] all the secreits of my heart ly.

Que 14. Which is the key [of your] Lodge. An: A weill hunge tongie.

Que 15. Where lys the key. An: In the bone box.

Much of the above does not make much sense; more precisely, it does not make much sense to the uninitiated. Some are clearly simple instructions to hold lodge meetings in isolated areas where the activities of the lodge members cannot be seen or heard. But even that instruction is couched in rather odd terms – 'a day's journey from a borough town without bark of dog or crow of cock' – as it would hardly be practical for members of a lodge to trek far enough from human habitation to hold a meeting even if this required a day's journey. Rather, it seems that this is more likely to be a coded (what would someone who was not a lodge member make of such an instruction?), if colourful, exhortation to take the utmost care to keep the lodge meeting secret.

It is here then that we think we come to the crux of what Schaw was attempting to do via his 'new style' lodges, and that was the instruction of alchemy. Perhaps we should qualify that statement also. We think he was at least trying to preserve alchemical ideas but we have no way of knowing if he was actually trying to turn Scottish stonemasons' lodges into alchemical laboratories. If that was his intention, and that is a highly speculative suggestion, then he most likely failed for the simple reason that he died three years after writing the second Schaw Statutes. This was simply insufficient time to instruct poorly educated men in this complex process. There are, however, some very small clues to which we turn later that offer no more than a hint that he had some small success.

When we think of alchemy and alchemists we, certainly in the West, conjure up an image of an old man, during the Middle Ages, shuffling among the paraphernalia of a laboratory, but no laboratory in the modern sense. There are glass flasks bubbling away, steam or some other vapour being emitted from kettles and so on. But there are also animals, usually small ones such as toads and rats. There are also potions, some obnoxious (to us) in the extreme, and concoctions which include blood and occasionally human blood. But what would have been very noticeable was a plethora of symbols; drawn on the floor, the walls, on scraps of paper and etched into everyday objects such as knives and other instruments. Symbols were seen as keys to unlock the doors from the microcosm (this world) to the macrocosm (the spiritual world) and could potentially unite the two worlds leading to inestimable improvements for humankind. This solitary figure, although occasionally with an assistant or apprentice, was attempting to change base metal, usually lead, into gold. It is no wonder that the alchemist lived a solitary existence for his secret was literally worth its weight in gold. But like lead, this is a base idea of the alchemist. The true alchemist was not interested in obtaining a valuable metal but pursued his interests for the most altruistic motives – to advance mankind in the widest possible sense. The alchemist sought other things, particularly the philosopher's stone (which would allegedly aid transmutation) and the elixir of life (occasionally equated with the philosopher's stone) which would confer immortality. The true alchemists believed that for every small advance they made, everyone benefited from that advance. Changing lead to gold was therefore an allegory for changing the base animal nature of humans into the pure gold of spiritual union with the Godhead. As well as being quiet about creating gold they remained silent about the possible alternative of union with God – something over which the Church had sole claim.

When alchemists worked they not only did so quietly and in solitude, but their 'language' was not one readily understood by the casual observer. Strange, even frightening, creatures were commonly used as symbols. Even someone not a 'casual' observer would have great difficulty, for much of the 'language' was in the form of symbols or combinations of letters from different languages, and just to confuse matters further, some of the words were pure invention understood only by alchemists themselves. A more detailed discussion of alchemy takes place elsewhere but this is sufficient for comparison with Masonic ritual.

We can perhaps just begin to see some points of comparison between the alchemist and

Schaw's lodges. As a starting point let us compare the rules for both, in so far as they are known. The Alchemical Rules are those stipulated by Albertus Magnus (1193–1280), see the table opposite.

There are without doubt parts of the early rituals which have major esoteric elements.

For example:

> Que 12. Where [will] I find key of your Lodge: yes: three foot and half from the Lodge dore under a perpend Essler and and [sic] a green divit [divot].

Alchemical Rule	'lodge' rule	Airlie MS 1705
He should be discreet and silent, revealing to no one the result of his operations.	The masons will not discuss any matter relating to Freemasonry when non-Masons are present.	Questions and answers 2 and 3. Also included in the obligation.
He should reside in an isolated house in an isolated position.	Lodges only to be held a day's journey from the nearest town.	See above. Where a lodge owned a building it had to be in an isolated position and the servant (tyler) had to live there also.
He (the Master) should choose his days and hours for labour with discretion.	See above. The apprentice is at the service of the Master on every day other than Sunday.	Included in the obligation
He should have patience, diligence and perseverance.	The delay between becoming an apprentice and fellow craft.	Inherent in the ritual divided into two parts.
He should perform according to fixed rules.	Schaw laid out very specific rules.	The Airlie MS (and the other early rituals) are very specific as to the procedures for admission to a lodge.
He should only use vessels of glass or glazed earthenware (The alchemist must use 'working tools').	Freemasons use the working tools of the stonemason antecedents.	The working tools (square and compasses) are referred to in the obligation.
He should be sufficiently rich to bear the expense of his art.	The Schaw Statutes lay down specific costs for failing the annual tests.	There are hardly any administrative details (including costs) in the ritual.
He should avoid having anything to do with princes and noblemen. This is one of the rules that alchemists ignored at their peril occasionally with fatal consequences.	Initially stonemasons' lodges did not admit non-stonemasons. When they did, they were selective and once begun continued to the extent that they were no longer stonemasons' lodges, although there were many exceptions.	The ritual makes no mention of the social status of the candidate, the assumption being that they were all stonemasons. Like alchemists the nature of lodges changed once members of the nobility began to join lodges.

Alchemists were convinced that by using certain symbols at particular times (often determined by the use of astrology) and calling on certain saints, they could unlock the hidden connecting door between the microcosm (our world) and the macrocosm (the spiritual world). The alchemists therefore considered symbols to be keys and, as we know, keys unlock things (doors, safes, chests, etc.) to reveal things which are otherwise hidden. The earliest Masonic rituals mention keys three times, a significant number in a short document. Question 12, above, asks where the key to the lodge is to be found – by what means are the secrets of the lodge to be unlocked. Cryptic directions are provided in the answer which leads to a green divot.

Alchemists believed that gold, and other metals, grew like plants inside 'Mother Earth'. These metals grew at an incredibly slow rate, being one of the reasons why so many wanted the alchemist's secret of transmutation, for it meant that they would no longer have to wait for gold (and silver) to 'grow' naturally.[24] Even this simple question and answer suggests more than it reveals. Suidas, who wrote during the 9th century, explained that the word 'alchemist' is a descriptive term used to identify people who have knowledge of the Egyptian art (of alchemy). He also claims that *chemi* (alchemy) actually means black land or black soil, specifically black soil on the banks of the Nile, which at each annual inundation turned from black to green and so gave life to the people. Does this mean that the secret of the lodge (gold) is buried in black soil under a covering of green grass?

Even this explanation is qualified:

Que 13. What meain you by a perpend Essler and a grein divit: An: I meain not only under a perpend Essler a green divit but under the lap of my Liver

The questioner says, yes I hear your answer but what does it mean? The response is very revealing. Not only is the secret under the green divot but also 'under the lap of my liver where all the secrets of my heart lie'. This phrase 'lap of my liver' has puzzled many students of Freemasonry. The common meaning of 'lap' is 'lobe' and is often used when referring to specific the organs of the human body – *'lap [lobe] of the ear, liver, lungs'*. An obsolete definition of 'lap' is: *'To involve, to imply, include; to implicate; to wrap up in a disguise'*. The definition of the word 'liver' is also suggestive – *'As vital an organ as brain and heart.'* Could it be that the members of the lodge were playing with words not only for amusement but also to further confuse the non-Masons? However, we think that the first overall meaning is intentionally clear: members of the lodge are bound to keep certain things secret.

Here, however, we come to a point that in our view reinforces the idea that lodge ritual as it existed during the time of Schaw (1550–1603) contained not only Hermetic elements but specific references to alchemy. In order to explain this, another historical digression is required.

Claudius Galen (c.AD130–c.216) presented all known ancient medical knowledge and argued that the fundamental principal of life was something called *pneuma*. This was comprised of three types with three actions:

Animal spirit *(pneuma psychicon)* located in the brain – the centre of sensory perception and movement

Vital spirit *(pneuma zoticon)* found in the heart – regulated blood flow and temperature

Natural spirit *(pneuma physicon)* existed in the liver – the centre of nutrition and metabolism

Galen believed that the heart distributed blood through arteries in one direction and that the blood returned through the veins via the liver. He thought that these two organs controlled two separate systems: the heart pumped blood in one direction and the liver in the other.

On this premise the liver and heart were two of the most important organs of the body. The third was the brain, being the centre of the senses. Galen's medical ideas influenced medical practice for centuries. In the Middle Ages the 'knowledge' that the body functioned in this manner led to the widespread belief that the plague (black death) was caused by infected vapours (gases) entering the body.[25] Vapours were carried by the blood to either the brain, the heart or the liver, where they lodged causing various illnesses and often death. It was known that each of these organs had a corresponding excretory duct. In the case of the brain this was either the throat or ears. The heart's was the armpit (oxter) and the liver's the groin. Buboes (infection of the lymph nodes) which formed in those areas revealed which organ had been attacked by the vapours. The most common treatment was normally blood-letting or cauterization. Blood-letting was considered necessary in order to balance the 'humours' of the body. The notion of body humours and their need to be in balance dated from the time of Pythagoras (c.580–c.490BC) and they were said to comprise *phlegm, blood, choler* (melancholy) and *bile*.[26] All four had to be in balance in order to enjoy good health.

The Hermetic idea that the human body could be affected by celestial bodies meant that astrologers and alchemists were essential for the accurate diagnosis and treatment of an illness.

We have seen that question and answer 12 (above) is all about secrecy – indicating not only where the secrets of a lodge lie but also that every Freemason must take those secrets to the grave rather than divulge them. We had one further thought. The liver's excretory gland was in the groin, and as that is one of the most secret parts of the human body then that may well have suited the esoteric 'word-players' of the lodge. However, the reference to the liver as being the place where a Freemason keeps the secrets cannot of itself suggest that Freemasonry, then and now, contained alchemical elements.

William Harvey (1578–1657) discovered the heart was a 'muscular pump' which caused the blood to circulate, and in fact circulated in one direction only.[27] His work dispensed with the idea once and for all that the liver moved blood around the body. From that point on, the liver ceased to be considered as one of the three principal organs of the body. Yet here it is referred to in the earliest of Masonic rituals. We have seen that alchemists and astrologers ascribed certain attributes to certain organs. The fact that the organs were now shown to have a different function did not mean that their occult attributes had changed.

As has already been discussed, the three principal organs had particular attributes, but there were others. The brain is the seat of the intellect and senses, the heart the location of the soul. The soul in alchemy is the passive presence in all of us that survives through all eternity and is therefore part of the original substance (first matter) of the universe. The soul was considered to be beyond the four material elements and was conceptualized as a fifth element (or quintessence). The liver is the place where the secrets (of the heart) are kept. These earliest rituals show that decades after the liver was no longer considered one of the three important organs of the body – the stonemasons continued to do so. They also continued to refer to the heart in the very same question that the liver is prominently mentioned.

There is one final fact that leads us to strongly believe that alchemical elements were incorporated into early Masonic ritual. In 1755 an article was published in *The Scots* magazine entitled 'The Mason's Confession' and the anonymous author explains that it is a lodge ritual given to him by a member of a lodge.[28] Freemasons will be familiar with this 'revelation' of Masonic ritual which has been taking place for almost as long as Masonic records began.[29] 'The Mason's Confession' is interesting for many reasons, but it remains essentially a reproduction of the earliest Masonic rituals we have discussed elsewhere in this book.[30] It is not possible to reproduce 'The Mason's Confession' here but the one small piece that is of paramount importance is:

Q. Where keep you the key of your lodge?

> A. Between my tongue and my teeth, and under a lap of my liver, where all the secrets of my heart lies; for if I tell anything in the lodge, my tongue is to be taken out from beneath my chowks [cheeks] and my heart out from beneath my left oxter [armpit].

Here, for the first time, we believe is a direct reference to Renaissance alchemical medicine within a Masonic ritual — and a very early one at that. You will recall that the heart's corresponding excretory duct was the armpit. The ritual is saying, in other words that if the Freemason reveals the lodge secrets (and the question and answer also refer to the lap of my liver) he must have a diseased heart for that is where 'all the secrets' lie. The method of removal is through the left oxter [armpit] which fits exactly with the treatment of heart problems as diagnosed and practised by Hermetic and alchemical medical practitioners.[31]

CHAPTER SIX

THE MAKING OF MASONIC HISTORY

We have just seen that the roots of modern Freemasonry may well lie within the Renaissance form of Hermeticism, perpetuated by a number of individuals using, for example, the Art of Memory. More recently this possible origin of Freemasonry has been largely ignored in favour of a number of entirely different ideas. These relatively new ideas have taken up thousands of pages in innumerable books, journals, magazines and more recently the internet. Some of these 'theories of origin' are considered to be without merit whatsoever but several others are presently the subject of intense research. During the course of the last 25 years or so, one has dominated that debate – that modern Freemasonry (and in particular that practised in Scotland) has a direct lineal descent from renegade French Knights Templar who fled from France to Scotland in 1307. It is thought that Robert I (1286–1329), following the battle of Bannockburn (1314), invented Freemasonry into which all Knights Templar in Scotland were integrated. There is little need for us to go into more detail here as there is already an enormous amount of material available in the public domain.[1] It is arguably more important for us here to make the point that this romantic and speculative view of the history of Freemasonry is now by no means universally accepted.[2]

At the same time that this view of the origins of Freemasonry was being developed in the popular media, another theory was undergoing a revival, but one which was outside the scrutiny of the popular press. This is known as the *Transition Theory*. Again there is no need for us here to go into great detail as much has already been written and published but, for the purposes of this book some details must be provided in order for one of the central claims to be made clear.

The earliest written records of lodges, that is stonemasons' lodges, exist in Scotland. The oldest are those belonging to Lodge Aitcheson's Haven and which commenced on 9 January 1599. That Lodge ceased to exist in the mid-19th century and therefore the oldest records of a lodge which remains in existence are those of The Lodge of Edinburgh (Mary's Chapel), No.1. The first entry in the minute book is dated 31 July 1599 and those records are continuous to the present.

The first speculative Freemason (that is someone who is not a stonemason but who joins a lodge and 'speculates' as to what stonemasons are doing) is nearly always claimed to be Elias Ashmole (1617–92) who joined a lodge in

Warrington, Cheshire, in 1646 (*see also* section entitled "THE 1700s – THE NEW SYSTEM OF FREEMASONRY"). Unfortunately, the actual records of the lodge, and therefore his initiation, are lost, if they ever existed, and we are left with only a short entry in his personal diary as proof of the event. Yet this repetitive claim takes no account of what was taking place in Scotland at about the same time. It is worth mentioning at this point that Scotland was a separate country with its own parliament and other national institutions. It was united with England only in the person of the Scottish king, James VI (1567–1625, b.1566) who became James I of England in 1603.

The fact that two separate countries, with different laws, customs, religion, currency and so on, and which existed on the same island, had developed two distinctly different forms for Freemasonry ultimately had an effect on what *kind* of Freemasonry was exported to Europe. In the event, it was the English type that predominated and it was that form of 'Freemasonry' (albeit containing considerable French embellishments) which was taken to another level by Comte di Cagliostro. A subsidiary, but yet important, argument is that which claims that only men who were not stonemasons but who joined a lodge made up entirely of working or operative stonemasons could be considered Freemasons in the modern sense. This point is important. A stonemason is engaged during his day on building a church or a castle, etc., but after work attends a lodge where he does none of that physical work by which he makes a living and supports his family. According to this argument, because he does not perform such physical tasks in the lodge, he cannot be what we now call a 'speculative Freemason'.[3] In Scotland, records maintained, and often still owned by the lodges concerned, show that non-stonemasons joined stonemasons' lodges and, unlike Elias Ashmole, they continued to attend the lodge after they had been admitted.

In 1634 William, Lord Alexander, and his younger brother Anthony Alexander and Sir Alexander Strachan were made Entered Apprentices and then Fellow Crafts at the same meeting. In the following decade several more non-stonemasons joined Scottish stonemasons' lodges including Sir Robert Moray (1608–73), first president of the Royal Society (founded 1660), who was admitted to the Lodge of Edinburgh in 1641, together with Alexander Hamilton, general of artillery.[4] The scale of activity, and we have only touched the surface in this brief introduction, has, as we shall see, a major bearing on Cagliostro's Egyptian Masonry and what he intended it to achieve.

THE 1700s – THE NEW SYSTEM OF FREEMASONRY

The 18th century was a time of radical change for Freemasonry and indeed the entire political system of Britain (the Scottish and English parliaments were united in 1707) and Europe. Although there is documented evidence of Freemasonry existing before the 1700s, it was in 1717 that organized or 'regular' Freemasonry began with the establishment of the first Grand Lodge. The story goes that four London Lodges gathered together at the Goose and Gridiron alehouse, in the shadow of St Paul's Cathedral, and decided that they would form into a Grand Lodge. At first it was designed merely to provide an annual feast for London lodges and they elected a gentleman by the name of Anthony Sayer as their Grand Master. Gradually things changed and in 1721, with the Duke of Montagu (1690–1749) in the chair of Grand Master, the Grand Lodge had evolved itself as a regulatory body for lodges all over England. It began to acknowledge the quarterly meetings, usually determined by the spring and autumn equinox and the summer and winter solstice. St John's Day – 24 June – therefore became important, important enough for St John to be adopted as the patron saint of Freemasonry.

This, it was assumed, dated back to the Freemasonry of previous years – believed to be descended from the guilds of stonemasons. In fact this was a significant departure from the Scottish stonemasons' use of St John the Evangelist as the patron saint of stonemasons and whose feast day was 27 December (as mentioned earlier) – something confirmed by the records of Scottish lodge minute books from the late 16th century and throughout the 17th century to the present day. These lodges consisted of highly trained stonemasons who, in order to distinguish themselves from untrained workers, used a system of passwords and hand grips to identify themselves as either apprentice, fellow craft or master masons. This was similar to our use today of Personal Identification Numbers (PIN) or biometric identification methods. Gradually these trade lodges began to admit non-practising members who eventually took over. One of the earliest recorded initiations of an English Freemason was in 1646, when Elias Ashmole (1617–1692), an antiquarian, was initiated into a lodge at his father-in-law's house wherein there was not one stonemason present. This seemed to become the norm with more and more 'accepted' brethren, i.e. non-stonemasons, frequenting the Lodges.

The revival of the quarterly feasts would have appealed to elite men, for the early 1700s were becoming known for an increase in convivial social meetings, whether in the clubs or the coffee shops of the time, therefore it would seem logical that a social and moral club would be of great interest to those men of standing. Such were the members of the four lodges who came together to 'reform' Freemasonry on that day in the Goose and Gridiron. The unification of the lodges caused a definitive split between 'operative' or working masons and 'speculative' or non-trade Masons (the term 'speculative' pertaining to their speculation as to what the rituals, working tools, and symbolism of the stonemasons may have meant). Now it was no longer necessary for lodges to be made up of both stonemasons and non-Masons as described in documents as early as the 1660s[5] whereby it was stipulated that a lodge must be properly consisted of at least five accepted brothers and a minimum of one who was an active master of the trade. In the constitutions laid down in 1723, the charges do not stipulate this; they do, however, state that a lodge can only be deemed to be 'regular' if under the jurisdiction of a Grand Lodge, or specifically the directorate of the Grand Master or his deputies. A certificate would then be issued and the lodge documented in Grand Lodge's records.

Regular Freemasonry was a resounding success and by 1730 there were 70 lodges affiliated to the new Grand Lodge. There were 'irregular' Lodges in operation, but not being under the jurisdiction of the Grand Lodge meant that 'regular' Masons were discouraged from joining them. Provincial Grand Lodges headed by

Provincial Grand Masters were established and central Grand Charity was created.

Freemasons in the 18th century did not see the centralization of lodges under a Grand Lodge as returning to the origin of Freemasonry – in fact they saw it as something much older. As we have seen, there is documented evidence of Freemasonry in the years before the establishment of Grand Lodges, and the establishment of the first Grand Lodge was an exceedingly important event in Masonic history. The official explanation from the current United Grand Lodge of England is that Freemasonry originated from the amalgamation of the stonemasons' guilds and that there is nothing that suggests it has any earlier origins, particularly nothing of a mystical or esoteric nature. If, however, lodges of stonemasons were the foundation for modern Freemasonry (especially those in Scotland) then there would most likely have been some form of esoteric learning ceremony. Considering that the physical laws of architecture include arcane methods, some dating back to the building of the pyramids, then we might imagine that some of the religious or mystical connotations were also passed down, generation to generation.

In every 'origin' of Freemasonry there is to be found some esoteric knowledge. Ceremonies in stonemasons' lodges involved the use of biblical 'plays' as a way of learning not only about the Bible but specifically the parts relevant to their trade. So, for the stonemasons, the creation of the first biblical stone building was immensely important and it was here that the relevance of King Solomon's Temple was found. Imagine the pride of knowing that their predecessors had created such a masterpiece and furthermore that the Master Mason who designed it was reputed to have been taught (and initiated?) by the undisputed masters of architecture, the ancient Egyptians. The imagery of King Solomon's Temple is still an important part of modern Masonic ritual and learning but there are other mysterious elements in ceremonies and symbolism that may have equally important lessons.

There is no written evidence of any Grand Masters before the official Grand Lodge, although historians are eagerly awaiting absolute proof that Sir Christopher Wren[6] (1632–1723), the architect of St Paul's Cathedral and an Accepted Mason, was not only a Freemason but also a Grand Master. Wren was a founding member of the Royal Society and a gifted mathematician, scientist and architect. He personally oversaw the work on St Paul's Cathedral from 1675 to its completion in 1710 and in total he left a legacy of 50 churches and many buildings in Oxford and Cambridge attributed to his talent. According to the Royal Society archives, he was initiated into the Fraternity of Accepted Masons on 18 May 1691 and records of the Lodge Original No.1 (now Lodge of Antiquity No.2) mention him as being in the position of Master of the Lodge. Officially, the first Grand Lodge of England was conceived established on St John the Baptist's day, 24 June 1717. The four lodges involved were as follows:

The Goose & Gridiron, St Paul's Churchyard, established 1691

Crown Ale House Lodge, Lincoln's Inn Fields, established 1712

The Rummer & Grapes, Channel Row, Westminster, later known as Horn Lodge

The Apple Tree Tavern, Covent Garden, now known as the Lodge of Fortitude and Old Cumberland No.12

There is also some argument as to whether this indeed happened as described. The first written account was by the Reverend James Anderson (c.1680–1739) in his *Constitutions of the Free-Masons* (1723). He was born in Aberdeen and his father was, at various times, Master and Secretary of the Lodge of Aberdeen.[7] Anderson was a major player in the 'revival' of Freemasonry along with John Theophilus Desaguliers (1683–1744) and his influential friends. Anderson was a Scottish preacher, who arrived in London sometime in 1709 where he then took over the lease on a Presbyterian chapel in Swallow Street. He was a member of Horn Lodge but is most famous for accepting the task of the new Grand Lodge to 'digest the old Gothic Constitutions in a new and better method'. This is where we begin to tread on dangerous ground by discussing the two subjects that are inherently banned from idle discourse in a lodge – politics and religion. Yet we, as historians, can hardly be expected to ignore the impact of politics and religion on Freemasonry, even if one of their principal rules is that neither politics nor religion can be debated within a Masonic lodge. One can hardly gloss over the obvious connection between the new and improved Freemasonry and the predominance of Whig supporters within its ranks; Whigs being the liberal supporters of King George I. George was not particularly well liked but he was Protestant and, as such, a useful barrier to papacy. He was dependent on his Whig supporters and left his detractors very obviously out in the cold. The other main political party of the time was the Tories, of which a large percentage was in favour of putting a king from the Stuart lineage back on the throne. If it is true that Sir Christopher Wren had indeed been Grand Master of English Masonry, then that would support the notion that Desaguliers and Anderson believed that Wren, being an old Tory, had neglected the growth of Freemasonry and therefore they were just the men to be the new salvation from the dark era of before the Reformation.

In 1715 there was an attempted rebellion by the Jacobites, who were supporters of the House of Stuart, to return James II (the exiled Stuart king) to the British throne. By 1716, a year before the establishment of Grand Lodge, the country was only just starting to recover from the Jacobite revolt but there were still threats of insurrection in Ireland and the ever-dominating spectre of interference from France. Desaguliers was accompanied by men of aristocracy, predominantly Whigs, such as the Duke of Montagu and the Duke of Richmond, both of whom were close to the King. Between Anderson, Desaguliers and the second Grand Master, George Payne, they set about transforming the balance of power in Rummer & Grapes Lodge.

These early years of the new organization seem to have reflected the political climate of the time. John (1690–1749), 2nd Duke of Montagu, a Whig, was installed as Grand Master in June 1721 and was the first member of the aristocracy to lead the Grand Lodge. Under his leadership, the fledgling organization began to blossom. However, much to the dismay of Anderson and Desaguliers, in June 1722 he was succeeded by Phillip James (1698–1731), 1st Duke of Wharton, a Tory (with strong Jacobite leanings). At the end of February 1723 the *Constitutions of the Free Masons* was published by James Anderson with a dedication by John T Desaguliers, Deputy to the previous Grand Master, the Whig Duke of Montague. Although the *Constitutions* were apparently authorized by the Duke of Wharton it was clear that those holding Whig attitudes were making a clear statement regarding the political basis on which the new Grand Lodge rested. This was further reinforced when Wharton was succeeded by the Whig, Francis Scott (1694–1751), 2nd Duke of Buccleuch in 1723 and then by Charles Lennox (1701–1750), 2nd Duke of Richmond and another leading Whig.

By then, unfortunately for Wharton, more Jacobite plans had been revealed and Jacobite advocator, the Bishop of Rochester, was arrested and taken to the Tower charged with high treason. Wharton defended him openly in Parliament and was then subsequently implicated in a further conspiracy; he later left England for France in 1724. The severance from the old branch of Freemasonry had begun; slowly the new form would emerge, gradually absorbing the old, thus furthering the redirection of power from the old trade guild association to the new and improved Free and Accepted Masonry. In doing so it did not imply that there had not been any Accepted Freemasons before the 18th century but the clever manipulation of ignoring the original charge of having at least one stonemason in the lodge and then reintroducing it in later years, gave the impression that there had not been any innovation. Gone were the independent stonemasons' lodges, now replaced by a centralized Grand Lodge system with the merest nod to its origins and heritage.

All the while though, a thorough revolutionary overhaul had been in progress. Anderson even went as far as to 'backdate' the existence of Grand Masters. The bright and shining phoenix of new Freemasonry had emerged from the ashes of the dark ages, resplendent and relieved of its 'archaic' past. To negate any reflections that this was some kind of coup, Anderson blamed the need for revival on the blatant neglect showered on Freemasonry by his predecessors. He asserted that it was the original four lodges (founding the first Grand Lodge) which had decided on the need for unification to allow Freemasonry to flourish and grow for the benefit of *all* brethren. His take on it was that the Grand Lodge was merely restoring the glory of ancient Freemasonry and that, of course, these higher ideals had always existed above and beyond the actions of men, i.e. there had always been a higher point to Masonry than just that of a tradesman's guild that imparted levels of knowledge of a fundamental nature. So the Mason's Company grew up from a method of identifying and sharing secrets amongst tradesmen, to becoming a lofty and philosophical society that just so happened to erect its foundations on the principles of building. A perfect piece of restoration work!

The ideals of new Freemasonry were not dogmatic in either politics or religion; it was utilitarian and pacifist and encouraged social integration. The constitutions state that discussion of state politics and religion were forbidden; brethren must have no involvement in civil plots and allegiance was to the Crown and government. These 'new' noble ideals created an exciting time for all involved; proposed members being initiated into an entirely new organization – one that was free of the main causes of dispute and often violence – politics and religion.

The constitutions were enlightened but nonspecific in various 'gritty' issues such as those of spirituality and politics. For example, the First Charge asks the Mason 'to obey the moral Law and if he rightly understands the Art, he will never be a stupid atheist, nor an irreligious Libertine'. It further states that although in ancient times Masons were required to follow the religion of their country, now it was necessary only to 'oblige them to that Religion in which all Men agree, leaving their particular Opinions to themselves'. This was interesting in that it implied that as long as they were 'good Men and True', regardless of their denomination or persuasion, they were now at liberty to converse and socialize with others, whom they may previously have been distanced from, within the *Centre of Union* (see below) of Freemasonry. Without stating what the 'religion on which all Men agree' actually was, they were able to avoid providing a definition and neatly sidestepped any religious divides. In effect, as long as members remained good and honest men, religious and political persuasions were irrelevant. As Freemasons' doctrines actively encouraged the members to be as good and honourable as possible, this was a perfect solution to the maelstrom created by assorted debating societies, political parties and various religious sects. For a Freemason, therefore, common social divisions were to be left outside the lodge.

The concept of the Centre of Union was a powerful one; imagine all men, of all religious and social persuasions, coming together to learn how to further their moral and spiritual standpoint. A truly revolutionary way to transcend the base nature of mankind by employing the principles of religious, political and social tolerance that could theoretically pave the way for a more humane and tolerant world, without the need for tenacious dogma and cruel retribution for those deemed worthy of heresy. Retrospectively, we can now see why so many religions and a host of assorted other groups have viewed Freemasonry with some suspicion over the years. It was, after all, attempting to create a world without divides, a world where men could strive for near perfection without need for the intervention of religious or political intermediaries. Many a man of the cloth and politician would have been out of a job. This was a very chilling concept for those opposed to the liberation of human souls by their own spiritual efforts, and it allowed for a slipping in control of perhaps the largest dominant religious force of the time – the Church.

In 1738 the new constitutions, also published by Anderson under the authority of the Grand Lodge, made the forceful observation:

> ...avoid Politics and Religion ... our politics is merely to be honest and our Religion the Law of Nature and to love God above all things, and our Neighbour as ourself; this is the true, primitive, catholic and Universal Religion, agreed to be so in all times and Ages.

Quite a statement, but one which on examination was cleverly able to encompass not only the main tenets of Freemasonry but also allowed Anderson to appear as the Masonic expert on such matters. It could be seen to be attempting to persuade some that Masonry was a religion in its own right, but in reality it was setting down the ethos of Freemasonry and allowed Masons to aspire to be of a high moral standing themselves. Its almost biblical approach of loving 'God above all things, and our Neighbour as ourself', was intended not only to appeal to Christians, but to the large Jewish population of London.[8] It made its point in not excluding anyone from its doors as long as they complied with the basis of Regular Freemasonry:

> Be a free man of mature age (18–25 years old depending on the jurisdiction)
> Be of good morals and sound reputation
> Have a belief in a Supreme Being

The transition from stonemasonry to the new Grand Lodge system, the origins of the 'Craft' (as it was coming to be known), still drew heavily on the lessons that would have been taught in earlier years. Initially, to those unfamiliar with the principles of Freemasonry, the allegory of the stonemasons' working tools and associated practices may seem bizarre, but the process of Freemasonry utilizes beautiful symbolism and reveals important moral lessons – something that only previously existed within a small group (stonemasons) – and has now been preserved by the Freemasons of today. Perhaps without this new 'speculative' Freemasonry, this wisdom, knowledge and morality would have gradually faded away as the craft of stonemasonry gave way to new building methods.

Regular Freemasonry today has three degrees of teaching that the initiate must complete; each comes with a ritual consisting of a moral play, and catechisms (questions and answers) that must be observed.[9] The purpose is that, through participating in the ritual, the candidate, in a state of heightened emotion, will be able to absorb the symbolism and allegory, thus learning the valuable lessons, which is, after all, the whole point in becoming a Freemason. This process, which has a recorded existence of at least 400 years, is designed to inspire every candidate to learn more of the hidden mysteries of Freemasonry and what each degree represents. It is appropriate to mention that originally there were only two degrees. The degrees are as follows:

First Degree – Entered Apprentice

Second Degree – Fellow Craft

Third Degree – Master Mason

The degrees represent stages of personal development. No Freemason is told that there is only one meaning to the allegories; as a Freemason works through the degrees and studies their lessons, he interprets them for himself, his personal interpretation being bound only by the constitution within which he works. A common symbolic structure and universal archetypes provide a means for each Freemason to come to his own answers to life's important philosophical questions.

Freemasons meet as a lodge – not an actual place but as a group that meets in a location where the candidate receives his three degrees; it can be any building designated for this use. Within the lodge is a temple – in all temples can be found the altar, on which is placed the Volume of the Sacred Law. This holy book can be whatever candidates desire depending on their faith – the Bible, the Torah (Jewish), The Qur'aan (Muslim), The Hermetica (Hermetisist), The Bhagavad Gita (Hindu), the Guru Granth Sahib (Sikh) or the Triptaka (Buddhist). Some other texts have been used by those not of a religious denomination, such as poems by Rudyard Kipling.[10]

THE AGE OF ENLIGHTENMENT

John Desaguliers, like Wren before him, was a member of the Royal Society of London,[11] being awarded its highest honour, the Copley Medal, for his discovery of the properties of electricity. A natural philosopher and scientist, he was a contemporary of Sir Isaac Newton (1642–1727) and one of his most staunch advocates. Newton rediscovered the mathematical *Divine Code*; he and his followers believed that the original religion was divine science and if a return to this was possible then all religious divides would be relinquished – after all, without dogma these geometrical teachings would be suitable for everyone. So came the Masonic letter 'G', the symbol that hangs above the brethren in all Masonic temples, standing for either *God*, or *Geometry – the Great Architect of the Universe*. The Age of Enlightenment was dawning, and Anderson, Desaguliers and the antiquarian and Freemason Reverend Dr William Stukely (1687–1765) were poised to revolutionize the Craft.

Stukely was another Fellow of the Royal Society and suspected that Freemasonry was a remnant of ancient mysteries, and he subscribed to the *pristine religion theory* (Hermetics). He believed that the Druids had possessed knowledge of the original patriarchal religion to which he hoped Freemasonry had links. All three men held almost evangelical ideas as to the revolutionary aspect that divine science could attribute to the mysteries of Freemasonry. This would mirror the very convictions of Cagliostro and his desire to revive the rituals.

Why then was there a deep need for the *true* spiritual and mystical aspects of Freemasonry to be renewed? Anderson and Desaguliers apparently did not wish to infer that there were any particular clues to mystical or spiritual teachings included in Freemasonry. They pretty much described it as a convivial club and form of 'relaxation' away from the trials of life, but it was obvious to those with any *nous* that there were definite teachings to be learned.[12]

To those with a deep interest in Freemasonry it is clear that there is more to it than just a moral and social society; the very rituals used as morality plays to inspire the faithful are full of symbolism far beyond mere analogy. Is it just 'a peculiar system of morality veiled in allegory and illustrated by symbols'? Why, based on the principles of building a strong foundation, the references to Solomon's Temple? If no longer an 'operative' society, why the all-important, all-pervasive interest in construction? Perhaps stonemasons had esoteric knowledge much more potent than any possessed by any other group.

A trip to Egypt can perplex the observant adventurer; on the walls of one of the tombs of Rameses II, he is seen wearing what may appear to be the apron of a Master Mason, and the positions of various pharaohs and deities are perhaps similar to those a Mason might adopt.

Figure 6 Egyptian 'mason' = modern Freemason?

The Egyptian Book of the Dead (often buried with the deceased as a hopeful guarantee for guiding them through the afterlife) has references similar to those mentioned in Masonic ritual. The symbolism and various trials also strike a rather familiar chord. Various signs and symbols can be seen on temple and tomb walls that resemble those connected with Freemasonry, and artifacts found in the tombs of stonemasons who constructed the pyramids and temples show that there was indeed a working society of stonemasons. Many other areas of Masonic symbolism have been equated with the antiquities of ancient Egypt – for example, there are temples that are built with half in rough ashlars (the unhewn block i.e. before it has been carved and smoothed) and half in smooth ashlars (the hewn block i.e. smoothed and shaped), two objects that are of great importance in Freemasonry and which symbolize the Mason who seeks to smooth the rough edges of his personality.

Masonic symbolism often begins with King Solomon's Temple; it is central to the oldest known Masonic ritual known as the Edinburgh Register House MS (dated 1696) and progressively develops (especially during the 18th century) from that building, and parts of it, such as the two pillars which stood outside the Temple.[13] The now famous (and often ridiculed) rolling up of the trouser leg in Masonic ritual is figuratively interpreted by some Freemasons as representing one of those pillars. However, as is discussed elsewhere, because Freemasonry has no dogma there are other interpretations held by other Freemasons which are equally valid. The same 'pillar symbolism' is found in ancient Egyptian writings; in fact the fully balanced enlightened man was called 'the Master of Two Legs', representing the concept that, when both pillars of the self were mastered, one could walk a good life. There are other parallels. For example, the Masonic Square, which is presented to every candidate of the second degree and to which specific moral lessons are associated, was placed over the heart of mummified Egyptians. As always, caution has to be exercised in making comparisons between the meaning of a symbol in one culture and the same symbol used by another.

None of this proves a direct lineal connection between ancient Egypt and modern Freemasonry. What it does suggest is that there may be some traits common to both and it is that possible link that we shall investigate when discussing Cagliostro, his mission, his purpose and, of course, his ritual.

There is an undeniable obsession with ancient Egypt throughout the history of Freemasonry and parallels that cannot be ignored. That is not to say that it unequivocally originated from Egypt but that the supreme wisdom of the Egyptian philosophy and culture has endured throughout the millennia to find itself entwined in this wonderful society. Whether purely in symbolism or on a more deeply esoteric level, the teachings of the Egyptians have penetrated each and every religion, leaving a trace of its beauty and arcane knowledge in all doctrines. This is most likely due to the fundamentally crucial text known as The Hermetica.

Famous 18th-Century Freemasons

Freemasonry is unique in that it allows men of all walks of life to become brethren; no particular dogma; no bar on colour, race or creed and the wonderful ability to encourage diversity of thought in all areas of life. During the 18th century the possibilities for discovery were endless; of course many ideas and inventions had already come into operation but there was a huge scope for investigation on all levels. Within this scope fell the two opposing views of spirituality and science; Freemasonry housed the extraordinary ability of allowing these two ideals to coexist. Not only in the teachings but also in the role call of Masons who were in the separate camps. On the one hand there were the rationalists, the scientists, doctors, lawyers and businessmen; on the other were the romantics, for want of a better word, the writers, artists, musicians and poets.

A brief list includes:

The Rationalists Dr Desaguliers, Rev. James Anderson, Edward Jenner (1749–1823), James Watt (1736–1819), Erasmus Darwin (1731–1802), Thomas Dunkerly (1724–95), Jaques-Etienne Montgolfier (1745–99) and Joseph-Michel Montgolfier (1740–1810)

The Romantics Alexander Pope (1688–1744), Robert Burns (1759–96), Voltaire (1694–1778), Sir Walter Scott (1771–1832), Johann Wolfgang Goethe (1749–1832), Wolfgang Amadeus Mozart (1756–91), William Blake (1757–1827) and George Gordon Byron (1788–1824)

FREEMASONRY GOES GLOBAL

So while the beginnings of regular Freemasonry were unfolding and becoming firmly established in many countries around the globe, Count Cagliostro was only a twinkle in his fabled father's eye! But by the time of his birth in 1748, things were already in a state of flux and offshoots from regular Freemasonry were becoming the norm, especially in cosmopolitan Europe. Various new orders were being developed, with the traditions of Scottish Masonry and its links to the Knights Templar assuming some importance. Rosicrucianism was also flourishing and adding a whole new dimension to some of the Masonic lodges. All lodges that were established abroad had to be affiliated with The United Grand Lodge of England, otherwise they were deemed to be 'irregular'. Regular or Grand Lodge affiliated Masons were not at liberty to join these irregular lodges and doing so would terminate their right to be a member of regular Freemasonry. Accordingly, all overseas Grand Lodges and their sister lodges were obliged to follow the Grand Lodge constitutions, any aberration from regular Freemasonry would mean that Grand Lodge would withdraw its recognition.

From 1723, modern Freemasonry spread from provincial England abroad, via deputations to its previous colonies in Spain and India and obviously across the Channel to Europe.

Scottish Freemasonry

Although Masonry itself (i.e. the lodges of the stonemasons and their rituals, symbolism, etc.) is undoubtedly traceable to Scotland, modern Freemasonry (that is Grand Lodge Freemasonry) emerged soon after in England within the first decade of the 18th century. Scottish Freemasons insisted on their own Grand Lodge, which was duly established in Edinburgh in November 1736, being the last to be formed in Britain despite the oldest lodges existing there.

Irish Freemasonry

Ireland established its own Grand Lodge in 1725 and the jurisdiction was for the entire country, both north and south; as far as it was concerned Ireland was, and still is, one undivided country. Its constitutions were modelled heavily on Anderson's.

France

Modern Freemasonry crossed the Channel in around 1725, where it was greeted with much enthusiasm by the French aristocracy and many learned thinkers. The first French Grand Lodge was set up in Paris in the years 1725–30. The first Grand Master of France was inaugurated in 1728 and was the Duke of Wharton, the former Grand Master of the Grand Lodge of England, who had left British shores after his brush with the wrath of Hanoverian power and consequent incarceration in the Tower of London. Wharton had found his feet in Paris and was notably surrounded by Jacobite sympathizers. He died in 1731 after founding the first lodge in Spain. Unfortunately Wharton's tomb was desecrated by order of General Franco shortly before Franco's death in 1975.

With their typically stylish invention, the French managed to creatively adapt the rituals into various different forms. Primarily there was that which corresponded broadly with regular Freemasonry and is still represented today by the National Grand Lodge of France. This dominated the scene for some time until more exotic forms began to spring up throughout the country. One thing that seemed to bring about this further renaissance of Freemasonry in France was that the constitutions of Anderson's 'modern' Freemasonry had almost de-Christianized the Craft. This appeared to leave a void for many French Masons who, wanting to return to a more Christian philosophy, were happy to develop it into something that resembled a system more akin to the chivalric orders of the Knights Templar; they classified themselves with terms such as 'Chevalier'. This concept inspired side orders influenced heavily by the chivalry of the Scottish Rite or Ancient & Accepted Rite which, unlike regular Freemasonry, consisted of 33 degrees. France, also being a major player in the colonization of the globe, quickly ensured the spread of all branches of Freemasonry throughout the continents, which is why there is still such a heavy influence of French-originated orders in far-flung centres of the world.

The Masonic Convention in Paris

In 1785, the Order of Philalethes organized the General Convention of Universal Masonry. They invited and encouraged prominent Masons from all over Europe to attend including:

> Tassin, the banker, and Tassin, an officer in the royal service ... Princes (Russian, Austrian, and others), fathers of the Church, councillors, knights, financiers, barristers, barons, Theosophists, canons, colonels, professors of magic, engineers, literary men, doctors, merchants, postmasters, dukes, ambassadors, surgeons, teachers of languages, receivers general, and notably two London names – Boosie, a merchant, and Brooks of London – compose this Convention, to whom may be added M. le Comte de Cagliostro, and Mesmer, 'the inventor', as Thory describes him (*Acta Latomorum*, Vol. II. p.95) 'of the doctrine of magnetism!' Surely such an able set of men to set the world to rights, as France never saw before or since![14]

A summons had been sent to Cagliostro to attend the convention, and he had assured the messenger that he would take part. However, he suddenly changed his mind and demanded that the Philalethes adopt the constitutions of the

Egyptian Rite, burn their archives, and be initiated into the Mother Lodge at Lyons. In doing so he intimated that they were not availing themselves of true Freemasonry.

He wrote:

> ...The unknown Grand Master of true Masonry has cast his eyes upon the Philaletheans ... Touched by their piety, moved by the sincere avowal of their desire, he deigns to extend his hand over them, and consents to give a ray of light into the darkness of their temple. It is the wish of the unknown Grand Master to prove to them the existence of one God – the basis of their faith; the original dignity of man; his powers and destiny ... It is by deeds and facts, by the testimony of the senses, that they will know GOD, MAN and the intermediary spiritual beings *created* between them; of which true Masonry gives the symbols and indicates the real road. Let then, the Philalethes embrace the doctrines of this real Masonry, submit to the rules of its supreme chief, and adopt its constitutions. But above all let the sanctuary be purified, let the Philalethes know that light can only descend into the Temple of Faith, and not into that of skepticism. Let them devote to the flames that vain accumulation of their archives; for it is only on the ruins of the Tower of Confusion that the Temple of Truth can be erected.

As you can imagine, this diatribe was not greeted heartily, a lengthy correspondence took place and eventually the Philalethes sent Baron de Gleichen to see the Count to inquire further what was required of them and also to ask members of the Lodge of the Egyptian Rite to attend the convention. Much correspondence took place but Cagliostro would not recede from his stance and finally three delegates travelled to Lyons and were initiated into Egyptian Freemasonry. They reported back in the positive that 'his [Cagliostro's] doctrine ought to be regarded as sublime and pure: and though without having a perfect acquaintance with our language, he employs it as did the prophets of old'.

The negotiations, however, fell through, and Cagliostro severed his ties with the Philalethes for good, the correspondence ending on this note:

> We have offered you the truth; you have disdained it. We have offered it for the sake of itself, and you have refused it in consequence of a love of forms ... Can you elevate yourselves to (your) God and the knowledge of yourselves by the assistance of a Secretary and a Convocation?...[15]

Cagliostro, however, did appear at the Convention and delivered a speech that astounded the assembly (see section entitled "THE STRUCTURE OF CAGLIOSTRO'S

EGYPTIAN FREEMASONRY") and his presence was indeed prominently felt.

Italy

Modern Freemasonry reached Italian shores in 1729. A lodge was founded in Florence by a group of Englishmen headed by Charles, Duke of Middlesex and also Tommaso Crudeli, a local physician, who was the first Italian Martyr of Freemasonry. In 1736 the lodge was investigated by the Roman Catholic Church and consequently condemned on 25 June 1737. Tommaso Crudeli was arrested on 9 May 1739 and subjected to torture in an attempt to force him to reveal Masonic 'secrets'. He was imprisoned until April 1741 when he was released, a physically broken man. He died several years later in 1745.

In 1738, the first papal bull against Freemasonry was issued by Pope Clement XII. It prohibited Masonic activity, and if you were a Catholic entertaining the idea of becoming involved in Freemasonry, then you would be committing a mortal sin and would face excommunication from the Church. However, many Catholics ignored the ban, which even went totally unheeded in Venice.

Germany

Germany saw the introduction of Craft Freemasonry in 1730, with one of the most important initiates being Frederick II. He was an avid supporter of the Craft and when other countries were issuing bans against it, he was a wellknown protector of fellow Masons within his realm. It was during this time that several influential spin-offs of regular Freemasonry emerged in Germany.

Karl Gotthelf Hund, Baron von Hund und Alten-Grotkau (1722–76) originated the Rite of Strict Observance, a branch of Freemasonry that originally worked a system of six degrees; the first three were comparable to the regular three degrees but the latter were based on those of the Knights Templar. It is noted that Cagliostro was initiated into a Lodge of Strict Observance whilst in London in 1777. The Rite was governed by an 'Unknown Superior' or the 'Knight of the Red Feather' and herein lay the roots of its demise.[16] The 'unknown superior' was unknown even to Von Hund, and this lack of leadership and accountability eventually led to claims for fraud. Von Hund seems to have been a dupe more than a villian but the order was overcome by dissention and was reformed under the direction of the Duke of Bismark at the Convention of Wilhelmsbad in 1782. Placed on a proper Masonic footing it became known as the Reformed Rite of the Beneficent Knights of the Holy City.

A member of Hund's Rite of Strict Observance was Frederick von Koppen, who started his own rite, that of the African

Architects. This also coincided with the anonymous publication of a mysterious text entitled the *Crata Repoa*. This purported to detail the initiation into the ancient Egyptian priesthood and was a system of seven grades, which showed some influence of Masonic practice.

However, the most infamous of the German pseudo-Masonic orders was that of the *Bavarian Illuminati*, founded by Jesuit-taught lawyer Adam Weishaupt. An off-shoot of the *Enlightenment* movement, it was filled with freethinkers, which may have contributed to its reputation as a conspiracy to overthrow European governments. Also known as just the Illuminati, the movement itself was termed Illuminism or the 'enlightened ones'.[17] Today the term *Illuminati* is often used to refer to groups or so-called 'secret societies' that conspiracy theorists believe have control over governments or corporations, however, there is no concrete proof that any Illuminati are responsible for any actions relating to the fabled 'New World Order'.

United States of America

Regular Freemasonry may have arrived in the US before 1730 as there are a number of references to Masonic documents and meetings prior to that date. In particular there were said to be papers relating to the Kings Chapel in Boston dated 1720 which showed that a lodge met there at that time. However, these and other documents, presuming they ever existed, are now lost. Freemasonry therefore officially began in the US about 1730 when the Grand Lodge of England appointed Daniel Coxe the Provincial Grand Master for New York, New Jersey and Pennsylvania. The Americans took on Anderson's constitutions almost verbatim and indeed these were the inspiration for the Founding Fathers' American Constitutions.

Benjamin Franklin, one of the most important of the Founding Fathers was a prominent Freemason, initiated in 1731; he became a Grand Master in 1734 and in the same year edited and published James Anderson's *The Constitutions of the Free-Masons*. Between 1776 and 1785, he spent his time in Paris as an ambassador, forging an alliance with the French that was crucial to the success of American Independence. During his stay he became Grand Master of the Loge Neuf Soeurs alongside such luminary members as Voltaire, Jean-Antoine Houdon and Jean-Nicolas Démeunier.

It can be seen, therefore, that from late 1720s onwards, Freemasonry continued to spread across the globe – to the East Indies and Bengal in 1729 and then in the 1730s to Belgium, Denmark, Gibraltar, Holland, Malta, Turkey, Minorca, Switzerland, Russia, Gambia, Cape Coast and Coast of Africa. Then followed Bombay (1764), Madras (1767), China (1767) and Sumatra (1796) and in many instances it was British Regimental lodges that took the Craft wherever they were posted. It is noteworthy that it became popular amongst men of different creeds, classes and faiths and, although the process was not universally smooth and occurred at the same time in different places, in due time the Craft existed in most parts of the world and accepted a huge diversity of men.

The Age of Enlightenment had indeed dawned and this exciting and vibrant era was the perfect stage to receive a character equally as stellar – the Comte di Cagliostro: Mason, Magician and Martyr.

CHAPTER SEVEN

A LEGACY OF PERSECUTION

To provide definitive accounts for each country would merit a book in its own right. What is reported here is therefore merely indicative of the sufferings of Freemasons across Europe and even then takes no account of the situation in countries not considered to be part of Europe.

Why should such a group, Freemasonry, raise the ire of religions, political parties, trades unions, the media, even consumer groups together with a host of assorted others? This is something which has puzzled Freemasons themselves ever since attacks on Freemasonry began, yet during the course of those hundreds of years Masons themselves have been unable to offer a comprehensive answer. Freemasons, as a group, are at a complete loss to understand why anyone, even someone as odd and unusual as Comte di Cagliostro, would be condemned to death simply for being a Freemason.[1] We shall offer our opinion but fear that, like others before us, no complete answer is, or ever will be, available.

The earliest stonemasons' lodges (as reorganized by William Schaw) dated from the very end of the 16th century, a period when interest in Hermeticism, alchemy and astrology were at their height. As Professor David Stevenson put it:

> The pursuit of this quest through alchemy reached its peak in the decades before and after 1600; alchemy has been described as the greatest passion of the age in central Europe. The search for the philosopher's stone was not, in the hands of the true alchemist, merely a materialistic search for ways of turning base metals into gold, but an attempt to achieve 'the moral and spiritual rebirth of mankind'.[2]

These meetings of 'Schaw's' lodge were secret meetings for stonemasons only. Perhaps the use of that word 'secret' continues to cause problems to this day – but originally no one else was interested. Their meetings were therefore private rather than secret, yet today, at every turn, every report in the media refers to Freemasonry as 'secret' or as a 'Secret Society' and yet everyone knows about the Freemasons, their lodges, etc.

The first non-stonemasons to join stonemasons' lodges did so in 1634 and quite a number followed in subsequent decades. The lodges were obviously not, therefore, secret (how could a non-stonemason join otherwise?). It is likely that the existence of these lodges 'leaked' out once non-stonemasons were acquainted with members of such lodges. In fact, in 17th-century Scotland there were a number of references by non-stonemasons to the existence of the Masons' Word. This shows that some people had become aware that members of lodges, and *only* members of lodges, possessed a 'secret'. The situation had therefore changed from that of lodges being secret, to the members of lodges possessing a secret (the Masons' Word). Secrecy had returned in a completely different guise.

It is perhaps here that the root cause of all the suspicions about Freemasonry is to be found. Approximately 350 years ago it became known that members of lodges (stonemasons or not) possessed a secret, a secret that could only be gained by becoming members of a lodge. Yet membership was restricted and controlled. This meant that people were aware that there was a secret (actually probably several) known only to lodge members. The existence of such an organization caused curiosity but, certainly initially, no animosity.

When Freemasonry came into being, it developed and expanded in a Protestant country – Britain (England's Protestant Reformation took place in 1540 and Scotland followed in 1559) – where it suffered only relatively minor problems, such as ridicule, and copy-cat organizations.[3] During the period when Schaw reorganized the stonemasons' lodges of Scotland it was an entirely separate country with a separate monarchy and political system, but the two countries soon began to forge much closer links. The countries became united under one king in 1603 and several attempts at further integration continued throughout the 17th century until the Union of Parliaments took place in 1707, thereby creating Great Britain. It was perhaps no coincidence that the modern, Grand Lodge, system of Freemasonry came into being just ten years later with the establishment of the Grand Lodge of England in London. However, when Freemasonry spread to the continent things changed.

The Holy Office (Inquisition) held a conference in Florence, Italy during 1737 which was under the auspices of Pope Clement XII (Lorenzo Corsini) (1730–40; b.1652). Clement XII was, himself, a native of Florence.[4] The secret conference had only one subject to discuss – Freemasonry. Florence may have been chosen due to the possibility of a lodge having been established there by English merchants. As far as can be ascertained no Freemasons were invited to give evidence and so were condemned in secret, with no defence offered on their behalf.

Andrew M Ramsay (c.1686–1743) a Scot from Ayrshire, managed to become the Orator to the Grand Lodge of France, and in that capacity was expected to deliver erudite lectures on Freemasonry at meetings of the Grand Lodge.[5] Ramsay was raised a Presbyterian in his native Scotland but, in 1706, left to serve in the army of the Duke of Marlborough

(1650–1722) in France during the War of the Spanish Succession (1701–14). During 1710 he came to know François Fénelon (1651–1715), Archbishop of Cambrai. Because of Fénelon's *Quietist* philosophy, Ramsay converted to Roman Catholicism. His first oration was due to be delivered at the Grand Lodge of France in Paris on 20 March 1737 but he first submitted the text to André-Hercule, Cardinal de Fleury, Bishop of Fréjus (1653–1743) and Prime Minister of France, who instructed Ramsay that it was not suitable, despite Ramsay revising the text to counter what he anticipated Fleury's objections to be. The text was again returned to Ramsay with a pencil comment by Fleury: 'The King does not wish it.' It seems that Ramsay thought that Freemasonry could be used to advance the Catholic cause but the Church, in the guise of Fleury in particular, did not agree. We shall discuss this point more fully in the conclusion. Of course Ramsay could not have been aware that Freemasonry had already been condemned by a secret conference of his own Church.

It is thought doubtful that the lecture, now known as Ramsay's Oration, was delivered at the Grand Lodge of France although there is some debate about this.[6] The rejection of Ramsay's Oration put an end to his career as a Freemason and he never again was involved. This is perhaps the first official indication that the Church did not view Freemasonry with favour, certainly in France.

Those who were members of the Grand Lodge of France were generally of the aristocracy and not greatly moved by the opinions of the Church. In fact, despite the Church's obvious suspicion of Freemasonry, the Order began to expand at a dramatic rate. The speed of expansion seems to have been one reason for the Church's concern, probably through fear of being unable to 'keep up' and exercise any control over a new organization which they had not yet had the chance to analyse. The papal bull of 1738 gives no theological basis for a ban on Freemasonry and its main expression of concern was that meetings were secret – in other words secret from the Church – and again is suggestive of concerns over the ability to exercise any control over Freemasons who were Catholics.

On 28 April 1738, Pope Clement XII issued a papal prohibition against Freemasonry which is reproduced in full below:

CLEMENT, BISHOP, Servant of the Servants of God to all the faithful, Salutation, and Apostolic Benediction.
Since the divine clemency has placed Us, Whose merits are not equal to the task, in the high watch-tower of the Apostolate with the duty of pastoral care confided to Us, We have turned Our attention, as far as it has been granted Us from on high, with unceasing care to those things through which the integrity of Orthodox Religion is

kept from errors and vices by preventing their entry, and by which the dangers of disturbance in the most troubled times are repelled from the whole Catholic World.

Now it has come to Our ears, and common gossip has made clear, that certain Societies, Companies, Assemblies, Meetings, Congregations or Conventicles called in the popular tongue Liberi Muratori or Francs Massons or by other names according to the various languages, are spreading far and wide and daily growing in strength; and men of any Religion or sect, satisfied with the appearance of natural probity, are joined together, according to their laws and the statutes laid down for them, by a strict and unbreakable bond which obliges them, both by an oath upon the Holy Bible and by a host of grievous punishment, to an inviolable silence about all that they do in secret together. But it is in the nature of crime to betray itself and to show itself by its attendant clamour. Thus these aforesaid Societies or Conventicles have caused in the minds of the faithful the greatest suspicion, and all prudent and upright men have passed the same judgment on them as being depraved and perverted. For if they were not doing evil they would not have so great a hatred of the light. Indeed, this rumour has grown to such proportions that in several countries these societies have been forbidden by the civil authorities as being against the public security, and for some time past have appeared to be prudently eliminated.

Therefore, bearing in mind the great harm which is often caused by such Societies or Conventicles not only to the peace of the temporal state but also to the well-being of souls, and realizing that they do not hold by either civil or canonical sanctions; and since We are taught by the divine word that it is the part of faithful servant and of the master of the Lord's household to watch day and night lest such men as these break into the household like thieves, and like foxes seek to destroy the vineyard; in fact, to prevent the hearts of the simple being perverted, and the innocent secretly wounded by their arrows, and to block that broad road which could be opened to the uncorrected commission of sin and for the other just and reasonable motives known to Us; We therefore, having taken counsel of some of Our Venerable Brothers among the Cardinals of the Holy Roman Church, and also of Our own accord and with certain knowledge and mature deliberations, with the plenitude of the Apostolic power do hereby determine and have decreed that these same Societies, Companies, Assemblies, Meetings, Congregations, or Conventicles of Liberi

Muratori or Francs Massons, or whatever other name they may go by, are to be condemned and prohibited, and by Our present Constitution, valid for ever, We do condemn and prohibit them.

Wherefore We command most strictly and in virtue of holy obedience, all the faithful of whatever state, grade, condition, order, dignity or preeminence, whether clerical or lay, secular or regular, even those who are entitled to specific and individual mention, that none, under any pretext or for any reason, shall dare or presume to enter, propagate or support these aforesaid societies of Liberi Muratori or Francs Massons, or however else they are called, or to receive them in their houses or dwellings or to hide them, be enrolled among them, joined to them, be present with them, give power or permission for them to meet elsewhere, to help them in any way, to give them in any way advice, encouragement or support either openly or in secret, directly or indirectly, on their own or through others; nor are they to urge others or tell them, incite or persuade them to be enrolled in such societies or to be counted among their number, or to be present or to assist them in any way; but they must stay completely clear of such Societies, Companies, Assemblies, Meetings, Congregations or Conventicles, under pain of excommunication for all the above mentioned people, which is incurred by the very deed without any declaration being required, and from which no one can obtain the benefit of absolution, other than at the hour of death, except through Ourselves or the Roman Pontiff of the time.

Moreover, We desire and command that both Bishops and prelates, and other local ordinaries, as well as inquisitors for heresy, shall investigate and proceed against transgressors of whatever state, grade, condition, order dignity or pre-eminence they may be; and they are to pursue and punish them with condign penalties as being most suspect of heresy. To each and all of these we give and grant the free faculty of calling upon the aid of the secular arm, should the need arise, for investigating and proceeding against those same transgressors and for pursuing and punishing them with condign penalties.

Given at Rome, at Santa Maria Maggiore, in the year 1738 of Our Lord.

The fact that Freemasonry had initially begun and developed in a predominantly Protestant country may have played a part in the Church's dislike of the Order but once it spread to countries where the Church held real power, attitudes changed and hardened. The absence in the bull of any suggestion that the Order was Protestant, and the complete lack of a theological basis for its rejection, suggest that this was a 'knee jerk' reaction to the appearance of a new organization on its territory. Here it is very important to note that theological arguments against Freemasonry were not included in the bull. It is almost as if the Church only later realized that it offered no religious objections regarding Freemasonry.[7]

Ramsay's Oration is considered to be the catalyst for the explosion of new branches of Freemasonry, particularly the Knights Templar and other Masonic bodies with a chivalric emphasis.[8] Not only, therefore, did 'basic' Freemasonry spread but so too did other so-called Masonic ceremonies. Some of these were Masonic but many were not.[9] A Scottish Masonic lodge had been established in Rome prior to 1735 and a number of Catholic Jacobite supporters were members, e.g. George Seton, 5th Earl of Winton (c.1678–1749). Allan Ramsay (1713–84) the famous Scottish portrait painter was initiated in this lodge. However, immediately the papal bull against Freemasonry was issued in 1738, the Lodge closed. This tends to confirm the view that the Church was against Freemasonry and had no concept that there might be different 'types' – Catholic or otherwise. This further suggests a 'knee jerk' rather than a considered reaction.

This, then, was the first major attack by an organized religion (on an organization which denied that it was a religion) and Freemasons, then and now, viewed the attitude of the Church with a combination of dismay and disbelief. However, Freemasons and others should be aware that they were not the only group of people who were then under the scrutiny of the Church – although it is ironic that they were condemned during the course of a secret meeting, secrecy being the main cause of the Church's objection!

That century saw a variety of heretics and schismatics listed by the Church. Unitarians were declared heretics and Wesley and Whitfield were proclaimed heretics because they instigated Methodism. Swedenborgians and the Moravian Church also found themselves on the Roman Church's list of heretics, as was the Quietism promoted by François Fénelon. Individuals too were not immune. François-Marie Arouet (better known by his pen name – Voltaire (1694–1778); Jean-Jacques Rousseau (1712–78); Pasquier Quesnel (1634–1719) and Scopio de Ricci (Bishop of Pistoria) (1714–1810).

However, as the century wore on, more and more individuals and groups jumped on the Masonophobic bandwagon. Many were relatively harmless, merely poking fun, but some made vicious attacks, many without evidence of any irregularity and appeared merely content to follow the lead given by the Roman Church in 1738.

Where the Roman Catholic Church retained some influence the Eminenti Apostolatus Specula (papal bull) was put into effect. For example, in 1740 Spain banned Freemasonry and although the ban was rescinded in 1780 history would repeat itself (albeit in a different manner) 200 years later under General Franco. Philip V (1700–46; b.1683) promulgated the papal bull against Freemasonry. A priest, Joseph Tarrubia, managed to be initiated into a Lodge and commenced gathering information about members, not only of that Lodge, but of other Lodges in Madrid to which he was invited.[10] The information he supplied allowed the Inquisition to apprehend most of the known Freemasons in Madrid who were sent to serve as slaves aboard Spanish galleys. It is unknown how many, if any, survived.

In 1750 the same priest reported to the Inquisition that he estimated that there were at least 97 Lodges active in Spain, and this information induced Philip V's successor, Ferdinand V (1746–59; b.1713), to declare in 1751 that any gathering of Freemasons would be considered as treason. This was the year that a second papal bull against Freemasonry was issued by Prospero Lorenzo Lambertini, Benedict XIV (1740–58; b.1675)

Freemasonry arrived in Switzerland in 1736 and a Scotsman, George Hamilton, was the first Grand Master; in the following year he was appointed Provincial Grand Master by the Grand Lodge of England. However, for reasons that are not entirely clear, the Swiss authorities instructed

Hamilton that he was under no circumstances to initiate native Swiss into Freemasonry.

Francis Stephen, Duke of Lorraine (1708–65) attained the title in 1729 and in 1745 became Holy Roman Emperor. In 1731 he had been initiated into Freemasonry at The Hague by Dr John T Desaguliers (1683–1744), a French Protestant Huguenot who had fled to England with his parents following the revocation of the Edict of Nantes in 1685. This had originally been issued in 1598 and had given French Protestants some protection in a predominantly Catholic country. Desaguliers served as the third Grand Master of the Grand Lodge of England in 1719. The Duke married Maria Theresa (1740–80; b.1717) in 1736. She was the only daughter of Emperor Charles VI (1711–1740; b.1685) who was the last male Hapsburg heir and whose death in 1740 triggered the War of the Austrian Succession (1740–48). Although she had been named as the legitimate heir, confirmed by her father's decree known as the 'Pragmatic Sanction' published in 1724 and accepted by most European rulers, many of them, nevertheless, attempted to annex lands Maria Theresa was due to inherit. The partnership of Francis and Maria Theresa was ultimately successful, winning the war and stabilizing the huge and powerful Holy Roman Empire.

It is not known if Maria Theresa was aware that her husband was a Freemason when the marriage took place, but even if she was not, the tensions for Francis must have been considerable as his wife was a devout Roman Catholic. Despite this he remained an active Freemason.

Initially Freemasons drew no attention to themselves as it was not until 1742 that the first Lodge (the colourfully named Lodge of the Three Skulls in Breslau) was formed. That Lodge then created the first Lodge in Vienna – the Lodge of the Three Firing Glasses – also during 1742. The Duke no doubt became very uneasy after he barely escaped through a rear door of the Lodge just as the police entered the front door. Thereafter there seem to have been few minor incidents involving Freemasonry, which may have been due to the Duke's influence with his wife, even after Benedict XIV's more strident bull was issued in 1751. The Duke died in 1765 and, in the months leading up to his death, the queen took the opportunity to ban Freemasonry. The Duke was succeeded by his eldest son, Joseph II (1741–90) who was a benevolent despot but much influenced by the Enlightenment. Under his rule of the Holy Roman Empire the states' attitude towards Freemasonry became much more relaxed.

There have been many attempts to suggest that Freemasons were responsible for, or at least were very involved with, the French Revolution (1789). Some of these claims are made without any supporting evidence whatsoever, and those that do provide some 'evidence' merely offer the 'everyone knows' variety. What they are implying here is that because Messieurs X, Y and Z (such people were rarely named) were *known* to be Freemasons, therefore Freemasons were responsible for the French Revolution. The assumption being made is that because someone is a Freemason they act in a particular manner. This is an almost unique claim in relation to Freemasonry and is one that is responsible for the beliefs and claims that Freemasons are guilty of particular actions *because* they are Freemasons. As has previously been explained, French Freemasonry was primarily an aristocratic pursuit. It is thought that there were approximately 70 Lodges in Paris at the outbreak of the Revolution with several hundreds scattered throughout the country. The whole character of such Lodges was almost certainly anti-revolutionary (that is they were law abiding) in attitude.[11] Nearly every Lodge in Paris was closed during the Revolution and the Masters executed. One fact has been used to turn this anti-revolutionary attitude on its head. The Grand Master of the Grand Orient of France at the time of the Revolution was Louis Philippe II, Duke of Orleans (1747–93). Seeing the way the wind was blowing, he quickly renounced Freemasonry and adopted a new personal name – Citizen Egalité – and supported the Revolution. None of this saved him from Madame Guillotine.

Freemasons were almost certainly involved in the French Revolution but in a personal capacity, and there is certainly no evidence that Freemasonry as an institution was in any way 'organized' either for or against. How then has it come to be generally accepted that Freemasonry was one of the prime motivators of the Revolution? Firstly, we must not forget Cagliostro who been banished (see section entitled "BANISHED FROM FRANCE") from France a mere four years prior to the Revolution and by no less than Louis XVI who was a victim of the Revolution and who was guillotined in 1793. Our charismatic and outspoken Freemason no doubt made clear to all and sundry what he thought of his treatment by the upper echelons of French society, even when they themselves had accepted that he was entirely innocent of all charges brought against him. It is more than possible that many people noticed that the revolutionary process began within a very short time following his expulsion from France.[12] However intruiging this may seem, the specific notion that Freemasonry was the engine which drove the Revolution did not come into existence until some time later (see below).

Inevitably people sought reasons why such a social upheaval had taken place, not least because it caused 'moral panic' in other European countries.[13] The idea that the whole of Europe was on the verge of revolution was stoked by a variety of writers, two of whom are of particular interest to us here. John Robison (1739–1805), a physicist, was a notable academic and rose to become Professor of Natural Philosophy at the University of Edinburgh (1773) and also General Secretary of the Royal Society of Edinburgh (1783). Towards the latter part of the 18th century he produced articles for the *Encyclopaedia Britannica* which, in the main, provided accurate information on the then presently known status of mathematical, scientific and technological subjects. He was acquainted with many notable men of his time, including, for example James Watt (1736–1819), and could therefore be described as an intelligent and articulate man of his time.[14] Our interest, however, lies in a completely different direction.

As his modestly distinguished academic career was nearing its end, Robison suddenly became a very enthusiastic conspiracy theorist, going so far as to publish a book on the subject.[15] The book's main thrust was that the whole of European society (government, religion and civic institututions) as it then existed, was poised to be overthrown by an alliance of Freemasons, Illuminati and reading and debating societies. Robison was a Freemason! He had been inititated in a Lodge in Liège by the name of La Parfaite Intelligence during 1770. He seems, initially, to have enjoyed his membership and was invited to attend many different Lodges and other branches of Freemasonry, some of which he seemed to consider to be mere frippery. He takes great pains in his book to differentiate Freemasonry in his own country from that which existed in

Europe. Even if he despised the kind of Freemasonry he found in Europe, and it is clear that he found some parts of it quite acceptable, it is something of a puzzle that it was 27 years later that he 'suddenly' discovered a conspiracy of continental proportions which he deemed necessary to reveal to the public.

After the publication of the book there was uproar in the Scottish (also British) Masonic community that they were conspiring in this way. Robison was forced to admit that the claims made in his book applied solely to the European Freemasons, and that the conspiracy included many other groups but that they too were not British. This reasoning, and the considerable damage it did to Robison as an academic, had the effect of being dismissed as a 'curiosity' with no validity. We shall enlarge on this important point later. The puzzle is not only that he waited 27 years to publish such a book but why he did so in the first place.

At almost exactly the same time, Abbé Augustin Barruel (1741–1820) was working on exactly the same kind of book. Barruel, a Jesuit, arrived in England in 1792 to escape the French Revolution. He found employment in the service of Prince de Conti (? 1734–1814). His work consisted of four volumes, the first two of which appeared in 1797 (in French) shortly before Robison's edition was published.[16] Once Robison's book appeared Barruel hurriedly completed his remaining two volumes which were published in 1798.

As might be imagined, two substantial books dealing with the same subject created enormous interest. Barruel's book was pilloried in Britain, France and Germany, but Barruel was a pugilistic writer of great skill and his responses merely intensified the debate. Robison too had not been idle. His book discussed and compared with Barruel's, went to five editions, and was published in New York, Philadelphia and Dublin as well as London and Edinburgh. Although both works looked to the Freemasons, etc. as the cause of the French Revolution, each approached the subject from slightly different directions. One of the central themes adopted by both was that the Illuminati had infiltrated Freemasonry for revolutionary purposes. Both also base their allegations against Freemasonry on the claim that there was a link between the Illuminati in Germany and Freemasonry in France, and cite alleged meetings between senior members of both groups as proof.

However, Barruel came to the view that the French Revolution was a direct consequence of anti-Christian (specifically anti-Catholic) and antisocial attitudes and principles inherent within so-called 'secret societies' such as Freemasonry and the Illuminati. Robison, on the other hand, appears to be vague, unsure and error prone about Freemasonry in Europe (suggesting a limited stay and involvement there) and the motives of 'the' Freemasons, etc., and their reasons for overthrowing the whole of European society as it then existed. The works of Barruel and Robison are voluminous, riddled with errors, many of them elementary, and although of interest this is not the place to offer a detailed analysis of their work. The emphatic point to be stated here is that both works have been well and truly discredited.

We now return to the reason why the work of these writers is important. Robison is in some ways the least important of the two in that his reasons for attacking Freemasonry (of the continental variety) comes across as a general, inaccurate and vague diatribe against conspiracies in general and those that 'he' knows to be involved. The most worrying dimension must be that this well-educated and respected member of Scottish academia and society could churn out such material. How could that be in the country, Scotland, with the oldest Lodges, the repository of the oldest Masonic records, and where he must personally have known a number of Freemasons? What motivated Robison to write such a book is unknown; he does not appear to have gone mad as he continued to teach and produce academic papers. We could perhaps even guess that Edinburgh Masonic society offended him in some way. Then again we should never, ever, forget the power of mammon. The book ran to five editions and was also published in French.

Barruel's motives are different, somewhat clearer, and arguably more relevant to the main character of this book – the Comte di Cagliostro. Of paramount significance is the claim by Barruel that he was made a Freemason but never took an obligation (a binding oath).[17] As significant, he also reveals knowledge of Cagliostro's Egyptian Masonry but confuses this with the *Ordre Martiniste et Synarchique* (which we cautiously translate as: Christian Transcendentalist Martinists).[18] Not only does this disclose that Barruel was, at best, a collector of Masonic and pseudo-Masonic information, but also he was not very good at linking the various elements into a coherent, accurate account. Barruel makes another reference to Cagliostro when he states that he was invited to attend a meeting of Loge des Amis Réunis (Lodge of United Friends) in Paris in 1771. The meeting to which Barruel refers had been called to discuss the general confusion, disarray and proliferation of Masonic ceremonies which existed at that time (see section entitled "The Masonic Convention in Paris").

This, of course, is nonsense because we know that Cagliostro had not become a Freemason until 1776 (in London). It does, however, show that Barruel had knowledge of Cagliostro very soon after he had been condemned to death and had been so *because* Cagliostro was a Freemason and Barruel's book was published within a few months of Cagliostro's miserable death in San Leo. Whether Barruel was genuinely confused as to what different Freemasons were doing in different parts of Europe or if he deliberately used Cagliostro's activities to further condemn Freemasonry (even if Cagliostro's 'Rite' was not and never was accepted as being part of Freemasonry) we can never be sure.

The conspiracy theory of the Masonic origins of the French Revolution had been laid by Barruel and to a lesser extent by Robison. Admittedly neither did so very well, nor very coherently and certainly unsupported by solid evidence. That said, today many people do retain a vague idea that the storming of the Bastille and the guillotining of Louis XVI and Marie Antoinette (1755–93) was instigated by French Freemasons and that they caused people to think in a different manner. It was said that Freemasons (especially in France) promoted anti-clericalism, free thinking, nondenominational schools and, perhaps most shockingly of all, that groups (Lodges) could be bound to-gether for the common good but should not, indeed could not, discuss religion and/or politics.

Those that hold such erroneous beliefs about Freemasonry miss the essential point that its prime purpose is a revolution of thought, not of political or religious systems. The membership of any particular Lodge, and therefore of Freemasonry itself, is drawn from all walks of life, creeds, colours, faiths and nationalities, and expecting them to act for a specific purpose (such as a revolution) simply could not happen. For the same reason, the mix of so many different types of people means that Freemasonry cannot be 'pigeon-holed' in the same way as any other group. This inability of non-Masons to label Freemasonry has caused suspicion, persecution and even a death sentence as in the case of Cagliostro.

Unfortunately the idea that Freemasonry was, in some unspecified way, responsible for the French Revolution, quickly gained a wide circulation. However, the suggestion that Freemasons and Jews were acting conjointly to create a New World Order did not appear until some time later. Barruel, for example, mentioned the Jews only in passing and that it was Freemasonry which was entirely responsible for the Revoloution. However, there was a later link between Barruel's conspiracy and the Jews. While Barruel was still alive he received a congratulatory letter in 1806 from a J B Simonini who claimed to be an army officer and who had pretended to be of Jewish birth. A group of Jews, convinced of his claim, offered him a substantial sum of money and to make him a general. This was part of a grand scheme of 'disguised' Jews who were planning a political and economic revolution to take over Europe. There was one condition – Simonini had to agree to be initiated as a Freemason, for that was the agency which the Jews would use to stage the revolution.

Simonini has never been idetified and Barruel apparently realized that this was make-believe. He commented that, if Simonini's letter was made public then yet another massacre of Jews might ensue.[19] This is the first known reference to what later became commonly known as The Protocols of the Elders of Zion, and although by now thoroughly discredited, point by point, it still has wide circulation and remains in print in many parts of the world. For that reason it continues to be used by modern writers on conspiracy theories such as Nesta Webster and William Guy Carr, among others, who believe that the New World Order (or some kind of variant of it) will be achieved by the subversion of 'ordinary' groups (that is, Freemasonry) by radical groups, especially Jews. The Simonini letter is incredibly important, although not recognized as such at the time, because this is first time that it was claimed that a Judaic-Masonic conspiracy existed. Once made, that suggestion became accepted as fact. Those who have argued against that 'fact', and produced evidence clearly showing it to be false, have been ridiculed and harrassed.[20]

Freemasonry in general does not become involved in politics or religion and this is one of its most cherished and enduring principles, yet there are occasions when even the most strenuous effort to avoid such subjects are to no avail. An example is that of the Dreyfus Affair. Captain Alfred Dreyfus (1859–1935) was a Jew serving in the French army and seemed destined for senior rank. However, in 1894 he was accused, by anti-Semitic army officers, of passing military secrets to Germany. He was tried and convicted to spend 12 years on Devil's Island (Cayenne). The case divided French society and the army. The right wing of the army, knowing that Dreyfus was innocent, decided that the honour of the army must come first and so Dreyfus must serve his sentence. Those sympathetic to Dreyfus, also in possession of the same proof of his innocence, saw the situation as one of the right-wing French Government, its supporters, the Church, the army and parts of the media being determined to 'uphold the honour of the French nation and its institutions' even if it meant a Jew suffering, for 12 years, the most appalling conditions.

Most of those who supported the Establishment were not Freemasons and a large number who supported Dreyfus were, although it must be stressed that those leading the pro-Dreyfus 'party' had no Masonic connections, for example, Emile Zola, Georges Clemenceau, Victor Hugo, Ernest Renan and Anatole France. Nevertheless the 'battle lines' seemed clear. The majority of those in support of the army and its treatment of a Jewish officer were not Freemasons in contrast to the majority of those demanding the release of Dreyfus. So convinced were the anti-Dreyfusards, as they came to be called, that the Freemasons were a left-wing group, powerful enough to cause the fall of the government and effect the release of Dreyfus, that a petition of 80,000 signatures was gathered demanding that Freemasonry be suppressed. Circumstances conspired to make the organization appear to be a left-wing socialist group, the effects of which are still felt today. Leaving the argument at that, however, plays directly into the hands of Masonophobes who claim that Freemasons are this, that or the other. In the Dreyfus Affair, Freemasons did not act as a body in support of Dreyfus and so Freemasonry could not be accused of 'acting against the state'.[21]

The apparent politicization of French Freemasonry as a direct result of the Dreyfus Affair had far-reaching effects, too many to relate here, but we think it important to show the range and consquences of the need to find 'someone' to blame for a catastrophe. In Hungary in March 1919, under the dictatorship of the Communist Bela Kun (1886–1938) the army stole all that they could from Masonic libraries and museums (including some significant works of art) and destroyed a great deal of Masonic property. Anticipating the Masonophobic activities of Hitler and Mussolini by several years, Lodges' buildings and their contents were seized and used for Masonophobic exhibitions. Masonry was officially outlawed by decree in 1920.

The Fascist regime of Germany remains acknowledged as the main country or society, in modern times, which included genocide as a matter of political policy. It is not possible in a work of this size to provide a detailed account of all the Nazi activities against Freemasons, but we feel that we must provide the reader with some facts at least to show that Nazism was anti-Freemasonry. Quotes from *Mein Kampf*, published by Hitler in 1925, indicate the direction of his thinking at that time and, as can always be the case, opinions, attitudes and actions do not necessarily change with time.[22]

The Frenchman Bernard Faÿ (1893–1978) was a writer on Franco-American affairs. He studied at Harvard, USA, and wrote biographies on George Washington and Benjamin Franklin. His access to American intellectuals allowed him to mix in French intellectual circles when he returned to France in the early 1930s. In 1935 he published a book in which he set out to prove that Freemasons were responsible for the French Revolution. Faÿ's work contains little in the way of supporting fact and essentially he based his contention on the fact that George Washington and Benjamin Franklin (and others around them) were Freemasons and had supported the French Revolution. American Freemasons often accepted Faÿ's claims uncritically and indeed they were often used and quoted in Masonic meetings with a source of pride that Freemasonry had replaced a system of absolute monarchy by 'exporting' its form of democratic government.

The ties between the two countries were indeed strong and so the lack of criticism is somewhat understandable. However, it was not until after the war that it was discovered that Faÿ was a Nazi informant, paid to betray Freemasons to the Gestapo. A newspaper which regularly reported on collaborators revealed that Faÿ had been convicted on an unspecified charge and sentenced to 20 years of imprisonment. Faÿ and his boyfriend, Geuydan de Roussel, had kept a detailed journal of their activities for the Gestapo covering the period 1940–44. The journal was lodged as evidence with the court. Marshal Philippe Pétain (1856–1951) signed an armistice with Hitler and became Head of State of the German portion of unoccupied France known as Vichy France.[23] Almost immediately, Pétain, who had assumed near absolute power, issued a host of laws, one of which banned secret socities. In a speech a year later, an 'Address to the French People', the following paragraph was included:

> ...The troops of the old regime are legion. I rank among them without exception all who place their personal interests ahead of the permanent interests of the State – Freemasonry, political parties deprived of clientele but thirsting for a comeback, officials attached to an order of which they were beneficiaries and masters – or those who have subordinated the interests of the Fatherland to foreign interests.

Pétain had clearly taken his cue from Hitler and Nazi ideology (could he do otherwise?) but as previously discussed, anti-Semetism/Masonophobia (or the so-called Judeo-Masonic world conspiracy) had existed within France for a very long time, the Dreyfus Affair being a prime example. Pétain was merely making use of an established prejudice, on this occasion within France but also by addressing Frenchmen in Europe and elsewhere. This was done, no doubt, in order to curry favour with the Nazi regime.

Following Pétain's speeches, which more or less explained who was 'for or against' the regime, many sought to provide information about others, hoping that the 'Establishment' would consider them in a good light and allow their lives to be as good as could be expected. Faÿ and Roussel, we know not how and why, decided to provide information about Freemasons. Perhaps, because they were homosexuals, they were fearful of discovery and so sought to divert the attention of the Establishment. Faÿ was a regular associate of two lesbians, Gertrude Stein and Alice B Toklas, both of whom were Jews living throughout the war in France and latterly in Vichy France.[24] Faÿ was a supporter and protector of Stein and Toklas.[25]

The names of more than 170,000 men, suspected of being Freemasons, were recorded on a filing system used by the Gestapo to record known Jews. It is unlikely that Faÿ and Roussel could have supplied that number of names within a four/five-year period unless they relied on other informants, although that method would have meant a great deal of duplication. However, the official records show that of the 170,000 named men 60,000 were actually investigated as being potential Freemasons. This disparity in figures does suggest that there was considerable duplication of names and thereby a fairly large number of informants. Of the 60,000 'investigated' (and that term is not explained in a full sense) more than 6,000 were imprisoned. Unfortunately, some of the records do not contain full details as to numbers, places of imprisonment or the exact nature of the offence for which these 6,000 Freemasons were incarcerated.[26] Of those 6,000 Freemasons, and these official figures are precise, 999 were deported but, frustratingly, the records do not contain much in the way of detail. That 'foreign' Freemasons captured in France were repatriated is a suggestion we find laughable. If they had been military personnel they would have been described as such, not as 'Freemasons' who had no military status.

The list of 170,000 named Freemasons (unlikely to be anywhere near a correct figure) was whittled down again to 60,000 who were actually interviewed. Although 6,000 were taken for interrogation we have no knowledge of what form that interrogation took. All 6,000 were incarcerated. We have no information as to the charges and convictions, nor do we have any details of the conditions of confinement, length of sentence or access to legal counsel.

What is now known is that exactly 540 Freemsons were executed in France simply because they had been identified as being Freemasons.

As researchers interested in Freemasonry, and in this particular chapter what Freemason's experiences were during the various battles and wars they fought in, we have marvelled at their unsung, unacknowledged courage on behalf of our modern democractic society. The recorded fact that (at least) 540 Freemasons were executed just because they joined a Masonic Lodge, just as their fathers or grandfathers had done, came as a complete shock.

During our research we have asked, 'who were victims of the Holocaust?' The sufferings of various groups: Jews, Roma and Sinti (Gypsies), East European civilians, Russian prisoners of war (POWs), trade unionists, Communists, political opponents, disabled people, Jehovah's Witnesses, gay men and lesbians and black Germans have all been mentioned. This list of victims was taken from the UK government's website: www.holocaustmemorialday.gov.uk (now redirected to that below). This list is therefore the government's official list of victims. It was subsequently decided a few years ago that Holocaust Memorial Day should no longer be part of a government department (it was part of the Home Office) and it was turned into a charity – the Holocaust Memorial Day Trust (www.hmd.org.uk).

We are now aware that lots of minorities (for example: blacks and Jehovah's Witnesses), suffered during the Holocaust. We in no way trivialize or minimize their degradation, for the simple fact is that Freemasons shared the same horrors.[27] We are now aware that Freemasons suffered in every country occupied by the Nazi regime. They were executed in Norway, Denmark, Holland, Poland, and Czechosolvakia – in fact Freemasons in all Nazi-occcupied countries were presecuted to a greater or lesser extent.[28]

Italy under the Fascist regime of Benito Mussolini (1883–1945) had not made the same link between anti-Semitism and Freemasonry as had existed in Germany. However, the Fascist regime believed Freemasonry and Fascism to be incompatible. In 1924 the Fascist Council demanded that all Fascists who were Freemasons must resign their membership and henceforth no Fascist was permitted to become a Freemason. A campaign against Freemasonry commenced soon after, with lists of names of known Freemasons being circulated and targeted in a variety of ways. In 1926 all Masonic property was appropriated by the state and numerous Freemasons were incarcerated.[29] The Grand Master, Torrigiani, complained directly to Mussolini about violence being directed against Freemasons. A prominent Fascist, General

Cappello (Deputy Grand Master of the *Grande Oriente*, Italy's Grand Lodge) resigned from the Fascist Party in order (perhaps naively) to continue to serve Freemasonry. He was arrested on false charges and sentenced to 30 years imprisonment and died before being released.

It is to be noticed that these attacks on Freemasonry in Italy took place in the years immediately before Hitler seized power in 1933 in Germany. One must suspect that Hitler took considerable interest in the methods of another dictator immediately to the south.

The two places where Freemasons did not suffer the maximum and most horrible of fates were Germany and the Channel Isles. Curious, most curious, until one recalls that during the invasion of the Channel Isles (1940) Hitler was still hoping for some kind of political accommodation with Britain.[30]

The situation in Germany was different in that the regime allowed Freemasons to make a declaration recinding their membership and guaranteeing that no further action would be taken against them.[31] When Hitler seized power in 1933 the information and mechanisms which were later used to identify 'undesirables' (Communists, Trades Unionists, Jews, etc.) had not been developed. The belief in a Judeo/Masonic plot was not an idea created and nurtured by Hitler alone as expressed in *Mein Kampf.* It became embedded in Nazi thinking. Herman Goering stated in 1933 that there 'is no place for Freemasonry' within National Socialist Germany.

Adolf Eichmann (1906–62) had performed a variety of tasks on behalf of the Nazi Party and the SS. On his return to Berlin in 1939 he was assigned to the Reich Main Security Office. This was organized into seven groups. Group IV (the Gestapo) was subdivided into six groups. It is IV B which is of interest here. Section IV B was divided into four subsections. B3 was given the task of 'dealing' with Freemasonry. Eichmann (who possessed extraordinary administrative abilities) was soon transferred to section B4, the remit of which was to 'deal' with the Jews.[32] It was perhaps easier to allow one small group among many to be treated lightly (initially at least) and that is perhaps why German Freemasons were not the main focus of fanatics like Eichmann. We were amazed to discover that a number of Freemasons refused the apparently generous offer by the Nazi Party to allow them to simply resign from Freemasonry without any action being taken against them if they did so.[33]

The brutality of those not in favour was reduced to a symbol. In order to identify people and groups who were not considered to be part of German Nazi society, they were forced, when in public, to wear an identifying symbol. The Jew had to wear a yellow star. Homosexuals were made to wear a pink triangle (point down), lesbians a black triangle (point down) and Freemasons were forced to wear a red triangle (point down). The details maintained by the RSHA supplied information in support of the ethnic, racial and ideological objectives of the SS and they reveal a direct persecution of Freemasons.

Yet even today Freemasons are not generally considered to be victims of holocaust. If one was a Trade Unionist and a Freemason, or a Black German and a Freemason, or a Homosexual and a Freemason, it is not known for which 'crime' the individual ended up in the gas chamber. Was it because you had been denounced as a homosexual or because your name was found in a list of Lodge members? German efficiency regarding the holocaust was not that precise – one classification was sufficient. The fact that Freemasons were compelled to wear a badge of identification indicates that there were sufficient numbers to warrant giving them a separate means of identification. However, as we have said elsewhere, accurate figures are impossible to find and estimates must instead be used. Certainly 80,000 Freemasons were exterminated simply because they were Freemasons during the period 1933–45. This number is achieved by extrapolating figures provided from other occupied countries. The figure is based solely on those men who were put to death because they were Freemasons and for no other reason. We consider the figure of 80,000 to be conservative because we are taking into account the whole of occupied Europe. In some countries

Freemasons were pursued with the same vigour as Jews. Hitler had, after all, stated in *Mein Kampf* that Freemasons and Jews were part of the same 'network':

> ...the governing circles and the higher strata of the political and economic bourgeoisie are brought into his nets [the Jews] by the strings of Freemasonry, and never need to suspect what is happening.[34]

That view expressed in *Mein Kampf* was spreading like a virus across Europe. France had already been infected.

Those who refused to comply with the regime's demands regarding Freemasonry were incarcerated until the commencement of *Operation Barbarossa* (22 June 1941) and those who had survived their imprisonment were marched, prior to an attack, at gunpoint through Russian minefields.

As with other groups, Nazi ideology was not simply concerned with eliminating those who did not fit the plan for the 1,000-year Reich. Their property was of importance. Most, if not all, Masonic property was appropriated by the State. Although, it was claimed, the material was needed primarily for the study of Freemasonry (property belonging to the Jews was often 'required' for the same reason) it was also used to stage Masonophobic exhibitions which the public were 'encouraged' to attend in large numbers. For example, in 1937 Joseph Goebbels (1897–1945) staged a 'Masonophobic Exposition' to display the treasures and objects seized from Masonic Lodges.

The Judeo/Masonic 'virus' was not limited to Europe. In 1938 Japan announced that a 'Judeo-Masonic conspiracy' was the motive behind a potential attack by China. Japan therefore had no choice but to defend itself. The forthcoming war was not to be fought against China but against Freemasonry. The Kempeitai, like the Gestapo, were responsible for rooting out Freemasons. They were numerically few in the Far East and normally within the expatriate population, and the Kempeitai recorded little success in finding those responsible for the war. Freemasons were more common in the armed forces and there is some evidence that when identified they were executed.

The point is that Freemasonry was and can be used for any variety of reasons – for example, to divert attention, create a political or religious bandwagon, or simply because some people must have a 'bogeyman' to blame for all that goes wrong in their lives. The Spanish Civil War was fought 1936–39 and General Francisco Franco (1892–1975) became dictator. Although he had relied on military resources from his fellow dictators Hitler and Mussolini he decided not to beome activily involved in WWII. Franco outlawed Freemasonry in Spain with all known Freemasons automatically receiving a jail sentence of up to six years. With a curious sense of logic the Spanish authorities assumed that Freemasons who had advanced to higher degrees within Freemasonry were even guiltier than those 'lower down the scale', and so received longer prison sentences. It is rumoured that Freemasons in every town in Spain were tortured and murdered, but information is scant.[35] Certain examples are well known if not used or reported by the 'ordinary' media. Teodoro Lopez Serrano was the Grand Secretary of the Grand Orient of Spain and this was the only 'crime' he was accused of in court. Found guilty he was sentenced to 18 years imprisonment.[36] The ban on Freemasonry in Spain continued until Franco's death.

We have seen from the above that Masonophobia ranges from simple ridicule to genocide. The veneer of civilization is thin indeed. We have been shocked and horrified by what we have read regarding the treatment of Freemasons. This barely scratches the surface of the subject, but what we have noticed is that Freemasonry is convenient for all manner of purposes, occasions and people. The majority of Masonophobic attacks are made by those involved in religion and politics (and occasionally by people engaged in both). We wonder, as we have no supportive evidence, is that exactly why Freemasons are abused in this way – everyone knows that one of their fundamental principles is to not become involved in politics or religion? What better 'enemy' to attack than one that informs you, in advance, that they will not defend themselves! This is a strange attitude by anyone's standards, yet one curiosity stands out – Freemasons have survived for at least 400 years despite all the abuse they have suffered.

One final point also became obvious to us as the research progressed. Some people in positions of power came to believe that Freemasonry was a threat. What kind or threat, real or imagined, or manufactured for a particular purpose, is not the essential point. All that matters is that Freemasonry might be a threat, and some countries and their leaders will simply not tolerate the slightest suggestion of such a threat.

Freemasonry exists where tolerance exists. Freemasonry survives where people attempt to understand other people and their cultures. Freemasonry does not exist in places where only one view of the world and how it functions is permitted.

If we were asked for a definition of a 'good' country (we appreciate that this is subjective), a good place to live, we would here answer unequivocally that it would be a place where Freemasonry existed, where there were no impediments to becoming members and people did not churn out Masonophobic hatred in speech and in writing.

TIMELINE OF MASONOPHOBIC PERSECUTION

1736	Florentine Inquisition investigates Masonic Lodge in Florence, Italy – established by English Masons. Lodge condemned in June 1737.
1738	Pope Clement XII issues first Papal Bull prohibiting Freemasonry.
1740–80	Spain forbids Freemasonry.
1743	Lisbon – English Mason John Coustos[37] condemned to four years imprisonment by the Inquisition, three other Lodge members are hanged.[38] Coustos is released by demand of King George II and returns to England in 1744. See illustration below.
1744–98	Freemasonry outlawed in Switzerland.
1764–80	Austria follows suit with Marie Theresa outlawing Freemasonry – the ban was ignored.
1787	Catherine II of Russia decrees a ban on all secret societies.
1802	Hippolyto Joseph da Costa (1774–1823), a Brazilian author and journalist, imprisoned for being a Freemason by the Portuguese Inquisition. He escaped in 1805 and fled to England.
1919	Hungary is under the dictatorship of Bela Kun. Raids by the army destroy or thieve from Masonic libraries, archives and works of art. Several Lodges seized and used for Masonophobic exhibitions. Masonry outlawed by decree in 1920.
1924	Benito Mussolini forces every Masonic member of his Fascist Party to resign from either Freemasonry or the Party.

1925	Mussolini bans Freemasonry in Italy under the declaration that it was a political organization. One of the prominent Fascists, General Cappello (Deputy Grand Master of the Grande Orient, Italy's Grand Lodge) rejected his membership of the Fascist Party in favour of Freemasonry. Consequently he was persecuted and arrested on false charges leading to a 30-year jail sentence.
1928	Miguel Primo de Rivera of Spain, orders the abolition of Freemasonry.
1933	Herman Goering states that there 'is no place for Freemasonry' within National Socialist Germany. An Enabling Act was passed by German Parliament. Adolf Hitler expresses that high-ranking Freemasons are willing members of the 'Jewish conspiracy' and that Freemasonry had played a large part in Germany's defeat in World War I. In Mein Kampf, Hitler writes that Freemasonry had 'succumbed' to the Jews and was an excellent instrument for their cause.
1934	German Ministry of the Interior bans Freemasonry and orders the confiscation of all Lodge property. Any Masons holding office before Hitler came to power in 1933 were banned from any part in the Nazi Party, the paramilitary or public service.
1937	Joseph Goebbels creates a 'Masonophobic Exposition' to display the treasures and objects seized from the Lodges.
1937–45	Freemasons are held in concentration camps as 'political prisoners' and are made to wear an inverted red triangle. Freemasonry banned in all countries allied with the Nazis or under Nazi control. Records kept by the RSHA,[39] who studied the racial objectives of the SS, show direct persecution of Freemasons. It is estimated that 80,000–200,000 Freemasons were exterminated during the war years.

1938 — Japan states that 'Judeo-Masonry' was responsible for China's potential spearheading of an attack against them, justifying its defence in a war against Freemasonry and not a war explicitly with China.

1940–70s — General Francisco Franco outlaws Freemasonry in Spain. Masons automatically receive a jail sentence of up to six years, with longer sentences for those holding higher degrees than the 18th. It is rumored that Masons in every town in Spain were tortured and murdered but figures and details are scant. The ban on Freemasonry in Spain continued until the late 1970s.

1980 — Saddam Hussein orders the death penalty for those who 'promote or acclaim Zionist principles, including Freemasonry'.

Figure 7 Engravings showing the torture of John Coustos by the Inquisition

The following popes issued proclamations or papal bulls outlining their intolerance of Freemasonry:

Pope Clement XII	*In Eminenti*
Pope Benedict XVI	*Providas Rominarum*
Pope Pius VII	*Ecclesiam a Jesu Christo*
Pope Leo XII	*Quo Graviora*
Pope Pius VII	*Traditi Humilitati*
Pope Gregory XVI	*Mirari Vos*
Pope Pius IX	*Qui Pluribus*
Pope Leo XIII	*Humanun Genus*

PART THREE

CAGLIOSTRO'S EGYPTIAN FREEMASONRY

CHAPTER EIGHT

EGYPTIAN FREEMASONRY

I AM NOT OF ANY TIME or of any place; beyond time and space my spiritual being lives an external existence. I turn my thoughts back over the ages and I project my spirit towards an existence far beyond which you perceive, I become what I choose to be. Participating consciously in the Absolute Being, I arrange my actions according to what is at hand. My name defines my actions because I am free. My country is wherever my feet stand at the moment. Put yesterday behind you if you dare, like the forgotten ancestors who came

before you, give no thought to the morrow and the illusionary hope of greatness will never be yours, I will be what I am.
ALESSANDRO CAGLIOSTRO

According to the Inquisition, Cagliostro got the idea for his Egyptian Ritual from a booklet supposedly found in a London bookshop. This text was reputed to have been written by a man called George Coston, an obscure spiritist of whom no one has heard mention since. Another theory is that he learned of Egyptian Masonry from a man called Ananiah, a merchant from Jutland, who had previously lived in Egypt. It is surmised that the Count met Ananiah in Malta whereby he became acquainted with the rite and built upon it for himself. One further contemporary worth mentioning is Rabbi Hayyim Samuel Jacob Falk (1708–82). Falk was a 'wonder worker' known as 'The Baal Shem of London' and a learned student of the Cabala. He was condemned by many Orthodox Rabbis for his leanings towards Sabbatianism[1] and was sentenced to be burned as a sorcerer for performing 'miracles' in front of Christian nobles in Germany. He managed to escape and in 1742 came to England where he spent the rest of his life. It is believed by some that Falk taught Cagliostro various disciplines and so this is another possible source of his enlightenment. John Yarker, a prominent and highly respected

Freemason, however, had reason to believe that Cagliostro's Egyptian Rite was from another source, he states in *Arcane Schools* (Belfast 1909):

> The Rite of Cagliostro was clearly that of Pasqually, as evidenced by his complete ritual [it transpires that the ritual printed was only partial], which has recently been printed in the Paris monthly, *L'Initiation*; it so closely follows the theurgy [of Pasqually] that it need leave no doubt as to whence Cagliostro derived his system; and as he stated himself that it was founded on the manuscript of a George Coston, which he had acquired in London, it is pretty certain that Pasqually had disciples in the Metropolis.

Martinez Pasqually (see section entitled "THE INSPIRATION FOR CAGLIOSTRO'S MISSION") had founded a Masonic Rite in 1754, which included as its seventh degree that of Rose Croix. The rituals were of a magical or theurgic nature and involved communication with spirits. This system of magic dates back to the time of the ancient Egyptians, albeit fragmented and modified over the centuries by the Chaldeans, Greeks and Romans. Egypt was revered to have been the seat of esoteric wisdom and had been visited by all manner of philosophers and seekers, amongst them Homer and Plato. These mysteries had been firmly implanted within the early Christian Church before the tyranny and fear-driven dogma of the Holy Fathers took hold.

Cagliostro would weave his form of Christianity into the occult sciences of the ancients, encompassing the birth, death and rebirth myths of both religions. Isis, Osiris, Hiram Abiff and Christ made comfortable stablemates in Cagliostro's world – and the prophets and mystics Moses, Elijah and Enoch nestled in happily amongst them.[2] It was a concept that many a Christian occultist had nurtured and they had also been sorely punished for their heresy.

Ceremonial magic, although not a far cry from the mystical rites of the Holy Church, was deemed to be a step too far. In comparison it also involved the high priest, clad in consecrated robes, whose role was to open the gates to heaven, to consecrate and empower the holy implements, to know and use the holy words of power and invocation, and to bestow the blessing of God. But it was also the idea that men and women could be regenerated, reborn or enlightened to become sons and daughters of God that inspired Cagliostro. His desire to help humanity to reach its pinnacle of purity and goodness spurred him on to embrace the ancient Egyptian concept of the immortality of the soul, the resurgence of the dead. He believed that man could dissolve his negative qualities and become pure, as humans had been before the 'fall of man'. He was offering a Garden of Eden to humankind, or to those that had the discipline and temerity to apply themselves to the rigorous training involved. The 'old' man could become 'new' through moral, physical and spiritual regeneration.

The wisdom of the Egyptian priests would be supplanted in the temple of Cagliostro – three vitally important magical practices would be the basis for his Regeneration of Mankind; firstly, the convocation of spirits, secondly, the practice of moral, physical and spiritual regeneration, and finally, the use of divination by means of the medium or 'dove' to interpret images sent from the Divine. His system of Egyptian Freemasonry would take the Mason from the mundane to the sublime, from purely speculative to positively transcendental.

The written Ritual of Egyptian Freemasonry, found in the possession of the Count on his arrest in Rome, was given a short summary in the Inquisition biography and then ceremoniously and publicly burnt, but the copies of his manuscript from his Lodges in France survived. There have been other partial translations, one in the French Martinism journal *L'Initiation* (see section entitled "EGYPTIAN FREEMASONRY", as referred to by John Yarker) published 1906–09, which was described in the preface as having come from an original manuscript written in the Count's hand and having been discovered in the archives of the Egyptian Lodge *La Sagesse Triomphante* which was founded by Cagliostro in Lyons in 1785. This is obviously the same as the manuscript that resides in the Museum of the

Grand Lodge of Scotland – the ritual you will read in Chapter 9.

Egyptian Freemasonry began as a fledgling order in 1779 while the Cagliostros were touring Courland (see section entitled "Mittau"). Cagliostro took up the title 'Grand Copht', a name originally used by the high priests of Egypt, and cast himself as founder and initiator of the Rite. He offered the candidate the teachings to achieve perfection by moral and physical rejuvenation (this regime is covered in Chapter 10) and to endow them with the Pentagon which he believed would confer on them a state of restoration to primitive innocence, which had been forfeited by Adam during the Fall. Cagliostro maintained that Egyptian Freemasonry originated with Adam, Enoch and Elijah, who had taught the divine mysteries.

Adam

The first man created by God. There is a correlation between the Christian Creation and the Egyptian, often referred to as the *Mosaic Genesis* and the *Egyptian Genesis*. In the Christian version Adam is made by God in his own image but he is not regarded as a divine being. Therefore the Christians believe there is only one divine being or Son of God, Jesus, and no other human can rise to the inner divinity as shown by Christ. Conversely, within the Egyptian Genesis, man is a divine being at one with the

Creator and capable of becoming divinely 'immortal'. One of the first comparisons drawn between the two geneses was by Marsilio Ficino, the Latin translator of the Corpus Hermeticum. He saw not only the comparison but the differences, but was wary about making much of it as he was accused of 'magic' by Pope Innocent VIII in 1489, the same year his book *De Vita Libri Tres (The Three Books of Life)* was produced. Ficino vigorously defended his innocence against a charge of heresy and is remembered as one of the most influential humanist philosophers, astrologers and member of the Neo-Platonist movement of the Renaissance.

Enoch

Enoch was a direct descendant of Adam and great-grandfather of Noah. He was reputed to have lived for 365 years and was a beloved of God. On transcending to heaven, he was there thought to have been appointed guardian of all the celestial treasure, chief of archangels and the immediate attendant at God's side. He taught all secrets, commanded the angels to do his bidding and carried out the wishes of the Creator. He is believed to have written three apocryphal books – the Books of Enoch – which hold the secrets of magic and immortality. He is often referred to as the angel *Metatron*, identified with *Idris* in the Qur'an and the ancient Greeks believed him to be Hermes Trismegestus due to being the messenger of God and the conductor of souls to heaven.

Elijah

A 9th-century prophet in Israel who appears in the Hebrew Bible, Talmud, Christian Bible and the Qur'an. According to the Books of Kings, Elijah was able to raise the dead, bring forth fire from the sky, and he ascended to heaven on a whirlwind when his work was done on Earth. He is frequently compared with Jesus and John the Baptist and is expected to return to Earth before the Second Coming. Elijah is linked to the Angel *Sandalphon*.

We can now see how Cagliostro came to evolve his own system of Freemasonry.

Some fragments of lectures given by Cagliostro regarding Egyptian Freemasonry were written down by Elisa von der Recke, Cagliostro's former pupil, in 1779 and they expound further on his beliefs:

> Moses, Elijah and Christ are the three chief presiding beings over the earthly globe and the most perfect Freemasons that have existed up until now. Although after successfully attaining their glorious goal here, they have been wafted to higher spheres and there exert their powers and wisdom for the happiness of beings of higher kinds, and although they have now already increased the immeasurable ocean of the

Creation by fresh worlds which they bring forth to the Glory of the Author of all Things, their influence on this globe and their care for us still endure, and each one of them has here his own invisible community, which, however, all meet together at one Chief Point and work against the Principle of Evil through various channels.

Freemasonry is the school in which those who are educated are destined for sacred mysticism, but the lower orders of Freemasons reckon nothing of these matters, and their attention is diverted into various channels in order that their secret superiors can watch them better and can make the worthiest amongst them for higher purposes. A stricter selection of these members is made by the three presiding beings of our globe. These subordinates of Moses, Elijah and Christ are the secret superiors of the Freemasons.

Cagliostro is one of Elijah's subordinates. He has already attained the third grade. Elijah's disciples never die, unless they become perverts to Black Magic, and will, after completing well on their earthly career, be translated to Heaven, as was their lofty teacher. But before they reach the number twelve, they are sometimes purged by an apparent death, but, so to speak, always rise again from their own ashes. In this way, the Phoenix represents the allegory of these beneficent Magicians!

The first class of the adherents of Elijah is chosen from the nursery of the Freemasons. These disciples number seventy-two and they have a specific which rejuvenates and preserves the balance of all the forces of Nature, so that they often attain the age of Methuselah. But they must not impart this specific to anyone without the knowledge of their superiors.

The second degree is gradually selected from these and consists of forty-nine members. The latter possess the secret of the red powder, or, to state the matter more clearly, they possess the means of bringing all metals to the maturity of gold. They also have the power of communicating to their superiors in one moment at a distance of more than one hundred miles anything they may consider necessary.

From these forty-nine the thirty-five are chosen. According to what Cagliostro told us, he had already reached this height, and from these the twenty-four are chosen. These two degrees are the most dangerous, as all evil spirits attack these Members of Magic in order to lure them from the Principle of Good; he who, however attains the fifth and last grade will grow in perfection to all Eternity.

This last earthly degree comprises twelve members only. Now the great moment has arrived, as one of these twelve will, like Elijah, be wafted to higher regions to work in other worlds, and, therefore, the most deserving members of the four grades are to be advanced. Should we hear some time after that he is dead and then again that he is still alive; we can be assured that he has withstood the temptations of the evil spirits and has ascended to the fourth degree.

He amongst us who is the most faithful and righteous and whose soul is devoted to magic only for good aims — be it man or woman — has the prospect of being raised to the seventy-two as soon as the first vacancy occurs.

The Queen of Sheba, whose story in the Old Testament is completely veiled in magical pictures and is only partially represented, would have attained the highest grade of magic which a female soul has ever reached. But at the end she became too weak to withstand the temptations of the evil spirits, and, therefore, her story, which is only intelligible to true magicians, has been related in the story of Calypso ... Solomon, the building of whose temple is an allegorical picture in certain Societies, strayed from the path of virtue in his magical career, but was again saved and snatched from the Principle of Evil. The story of the fall of the angels is only an allegory of the transition from white to black magic.

The divine doctrines of the Greeks, the Zendavesta, the Eddas and the Bible are all books sacred to magic.

The circle and the triangle are sacred magical ciphers. Three and nine, two and seven are holy numbers. He who grasps the power of these numbers and ciphers is near the source of virtue. The word Jehovah contains three in it twice over and possesses immeasurable power.

Just as there are sacred numbers so are there holy letters. The letters I.H.S. should never be contemplated without the deepest awe, as they contain all wisdom and the fount of all bliss. He who grasps the true value of these letters is close to the eternal source of all Good.

There are three chapters missing in the Bible, and these are only in the hands of magicians. He who possesses one of these chapters can command supernatural powers.

He who does not venerate I.H.S., the Sun, the circle and the triangle, two and seven, three and nine and the word Jehovah, and has not attained true knowledge of these letters, numbers and words, will not possess the missing chapters of the Bible.

These contain the highest wisdom by which the world is governed.[3]

Cagliostro's system of Freemasonry, as you will read in the analysis of the Egyptian Rite, was obviously a gateway to the Hermetic teachings involving the magical schooling of the spirit, soul and physical body leading to extraordinary powers and realization of the immortality of the soul (see Chapter 10). His system of magic involved not merely imploring God for his assistance but, as a magician, commanding the angels of the Divine to achieve the results according to the power of God. But this power to command and govern did not come easily; as far as Cagliostro was concerned it was a system of extreme study and contemplation. The initiatory path of Hermetics is not simple and involves overcoming one's base nature, mastery of one's thoughts and the acquirement, through many years of learning, of control over the elements, thus leading to the power over life and death or immortality of the soul.[4]

Whilst in Bordeaux in 1783/4, Cagliostro had a premonition that was a pivotal point in his desire to form his system of higher Freemasonry. Feeling ill one night, he retired to bed and fell into a trance-like state. His vision took him to a place he did not recognize where he was accosted by two men and carried off to an underground passage. He found himself before a door which opened to reveal a beautiful room wherein were assembled a group of men dressed in the robes of Egyptian priests. He recognized amongst the men several Masons whom he knew to be deceased; this he took to mean that he was in the presence of a great Elect. He was clothed in a similar robe and handed a flaming sword, after which he walked forwards into a blazing light. Seated upon a great throne was a Supreme Being and Cagliostro prostrated himself before him, offering up thanks for the honour of being summoned to the company of the Great Elect. A voice then rang out – 'This is what your reward will be in the future, but meanwhile you must work with still more diligence!'

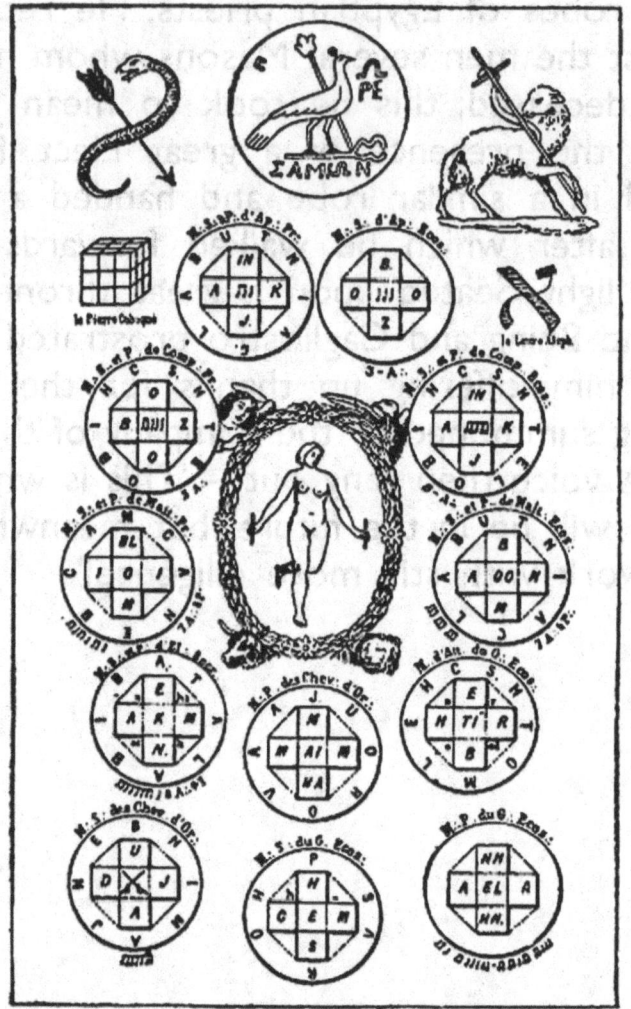

Figure 8 Cagliostro's magical seals

Cagliostro interpreted the vision as confirmation that he was indeed on a divine mission. He then resolved to set his Egyptian Rite in stone, and chose Lyons as the foundation for his Mother Lodge, the home of Egyptian Freemasonry.

When Cagliostro arrived in Lyons in 1784 he was already something of a celebrity. He had a fine reputation as a Master of magic and Masonry and was received with much pomp and circumstance by the Grand Master of the existing Lodge, *La Sagesse,* and its members. They fêted him with an 'arch of steel' with their swords and he was resplendent in his apron, insignia, cordons and sword. He treated them all to a sublime sermon and his divine invocations inflamed their hearts and opened their minds to something beyond mere Masonry. Cagliostro soon demonstrated all his remarkable skills in turn. Not only did he cure a wealthy landowner and convince the Duc de Richelieu of his clairvoyant powers but he managed to astound the members of *Lodge La Bienfaisante* by conjuring the spirit of their recently departed and much beloved Grand Master M. Prost de Royer. The image of the dead man was witnessed by many and de Royer's friends recognized him clearly. Having witnessed these astonishing feats, the people of Lyons clamoured for Cagliostro to found a Lodge of his own rite; to this he acceded and his Egyptian Rite took on a much more permanent home. The Count wished to expand his rite to create unification, a Mother Lodge around which all other rites would revolve. The Rite of Egyptian Freemasonry would eclipse all others.

A subscription was opened and a temple building was erected for the use of the Mother

Lodge – *La Sagesse Triomphante* – Triumphant Wisdom!

THE STRUCTURE OF CAGLIOSTRO'S EGYPTIAN FREEMASONRY

Egyptian Freemasonry was passed under the Craft titles, emulating the use of the three degrees, and it was offered to both men and women, apparently segregated in different temples. Cagliostro required that the male candidates had been passed through all three degrees of Masonry before they could enter, and those of any religion, race or creed were admitted to Egyptian Freemasonry; all that was required, other than the aforementioned regular Masonic degrees, was the belief in God. Three further degrees were bestowed in the Rite, those of Egyptian Apprentice, Egyptian Fellow Craft or Companion, and Egyptian Master.

The male initiates took on the names of the prophets, whilst the women were given those of the ancient Sybils. The men and women held separate Lodges, although the men were allowed to be present at the women's meetings as visitors. Adoptive Freemasonry was the name used to determine the Lodges that allowed women to become Freemasons. The Grand Orient established the first Rite of Adoption in 1774, with the Duchesse de Bourbon becoming

Grande Maitresse in 1775. Napoleon's wife, the Empress Josephine, was also to hold that same office in 1805. As we only have fragments of the female rites it is difficult to ascertain exactly what transpired. It is intimated that both sexes could reach the same level of moral and physical regeneration through Egyptian Masonry, but we need to take into account that in the 18th century women were not as independent or robust as modern women and therefore were not required to undertake the full trials and operations unless they volunteered to do so. It is also evident that the men saw themselves as superior and were probably subject to more vigorous and arduous trials. However, Cagliostro believed that as women had been a part of the ancient Egyptian mystery schools as priestesses, then it was perfectly reasonable for them to be admitted to modern orders such as his Egyptian Rite.

Manly P Hall describes Cagliostro's opinion on Adoptive Freemasonry:

> After creating his Egyptian Rite, Cagliostro declared that since women had been admitted into the ancient Mysteries there was no reason why they should be excluded from the modern orders. The Princesse de Lamballe graciously accepted the dignity of Mistress of Honor in his secret society, and on the evening of her initiation the most important members of the French court were present. The

brilliance of the affair attracted the attention of the Masonic lodges in Paris.[5]

In 1784, Madam di Cagliostro established the Lodge of Isis and during the initiation the women were given this oath:

> I swear before the eternal God of the Grand Mistress, and of all who hear me, never to write, or cause to be written, anything that shall pass under my eyes, condemning myself, in the event of impudence, to be punished according to the laws of the Grand Founders, and all of my superiors. I likewise promise the exact observance of the other six commandments imposed on me; that is to say, love of God, respect for my sovereign, veneration for religion and the laws, love of my fellow-creatures, and an attachment without bonds to our order, and the blindest submission to the rules and code of our ritual, such as they may be communicated to me by the Grand Mistress.

The Grand Mistress would, in turn, breathe upon the initiate from forehead to chin whilst reciting:

> I thus breathe upon you to cause the truths possessed by us to germinate and penetrate within your heart; I breathe upon you to fortify your spiritual part; I breathe upon you to confirm you in the faith of your brothers and sisters, according to the engagements that you have contracted. We

create you a legitimate daughter of the true Egyptian adoption, and of the Lodge...; we will that you be recognized as such by all brothers and sisters of the Egyptian ritual and that you enjoy the same prerogatives with them. Lastly we impart to you the supreme pleasure of being henceforth, and for ever, a Freemason.[6]

According to A E Waite, the women's Adoptive Grades were as follows:

...the ritual of the first two [degrees] was mainly based on legends connected with King Solomon and the Queen of Sheba, and with the serpent of Eden, symbolizing pride. In the second grade the candidate cuts off the serpent's head, and was promised hereafter the power of communicating with celestial spirits. The ceremony of the third grade was similar to that reserved to men alone. The acting Mistress or Chief Officer of the Temple, represented the Queen of Sheba, and she alone remained erect during the invocation of the Supreme Being which first took place. The candidate, lying prostrate on the ground, recited the *Miserere Mei*;[7] she was then raised up, the dove (clairvoyant) was consulted; three sisters sang the *Veni Creator* (*Veni Creator Spiritus* – a famous hymn) and burnt incense about the candidate. The Worshipful Mistress scattered gold leaf with her breath, and said: *Sic transit gloria mundi* ('Thus passes the glory of the world'). A symbolic draught of immortality was drunk by the new Mistress before the tabernacle, and the dove prayed that the angels might consecrate the adornments with which she was about to be decorated; Moses was also invoked to lay his hands in blessing on the crown of roses which was placed about her head.[8]

The temple of the female Masons was designed, in accordance with Cagliostro's wishes, in blue and white with a throne for the Grand Mistress who would wear a blue silk tunic embroidered with the words *'Virtue, Wisdom, Union'*. Her white leather apron bore the words 'Love and Charity' and was trimmed with five blue roses. Surrounded by brethren in uniform and carrying swords, the Grand Mistress would comment on the legend of King Solomon's reception of the Queen of Sheba and of her learning within the Temple, to the 24 Mistresses present. They would learn of Calypso's pride and her punishment, and have the various symbols of the Lodge explained to them. The use of a 'dove' or medium was employed as in the male initiation and the Grand Mistress would instruct the dove to question the angels, but she was forbidden to call upon the spirits of the dead, for this was the exclusive duty of the Grand Copht. Seraphina created an image of sublime loveliness and many ladies of high society in Paris, and indeed the royal Court, were drawn to her majesty and mystery like moths to a flame.

Many modern Masons are merely amused and dismissive of Cagliostro and his Egyptian Rite. Ask most scholarly men within the Craft about Count Alessandro di Cagliostro and they smile and say, 'Ah, Giuseppe Balsamo, the charlatan!' Thanks to the enduring historical inaccuracies and slanders, the resounding response is one of ridicule and dismissive contempt. What was this flamboyant fop trying to do to the Craft? Why on earth did he think he could improve upon something so obviously 'perfect'? There is a pervasive bemusement as to his reasoning and obsessive mission, and unfortunately not much compassion for a man who died attempting to uphold the morals and beliefs of Freemasonry for the benefit of mankind.

So what was Cagliostro trying to do?

The motives for Cagliostro founding his Egyptian Freemasonry have always been in question; many people believed it was an attempt to extract money from unsuspecting spiritual seekers. Many of the world's most popular writers on the subject believe that Cagliostro was trying to *replace* regular Freemasonry. However, none of these explanations seem likely; in fact from reading Cagliostro's own writings, and from the manuscript of his ritual, we can see that his motives are anything but mercenary. He limits the number of members in each Lodge to 72 Apprentices, 24 Companions and only 7

Masters. If income from members was his primary motive it is not a very good strategy. To make matters worse he specifies considerable periods of time to be spent in study and learning between the different initiations for *all* grades within the Order. Cagliostro's critics have made much of the fact that he charged a fee for each of his initiations. It would seem a very illogical move to limit the time it took for each candidate to move onto the next degree, if all he was after was money!

It is also very clear that Cagliostro was not trying to replace regular Freemasonry by the fact that a joining requirement for the male members was that they were Master Masons in a regular Lodge. It seems that Cagliostro was not trying to invent anything new. He viewed Craft Masonry as 'a vestige of the True Mysteries and but a mere shadow of the real illumination' and believed he was *restoring* the original nature of the Craft, rather like one would restore the original form of a broken piece of furniture to its original splendour. When viewing the rites of traditional Freemasonry, he saw the alchemical and Hermetic path. He felt that the teachings had fallen into disrepair and misunderstanding, and was thus attempting to restore them to their original aim and goal. Cagliostro was not of course on his own in this respect; even now many Freemasons see Hermetic and spiritual teachings at the centre of Freemasonry and yearn for the Craft to be more focused on discipline.

In recent times there are a plethora of side orders that Freemasons can join, having completed their journey through the Craft rituals, which offer deeper and, some claim, more lofty teachings. Perhaps many of these Freemasons, if born in Cagliostro's time, would have joined his Egyptian Freemasonry.

Freemasonry for Cagliostro was an ally, not something to destroy; he was trying to offer a higher order to those who wished to continue their spiritual development in a more disciplined environment. When the Ritual of Egyptian Freemasonry is studied, it is obvious that the teachings are predominantly alchemical and full of cabalistic teachings. It is evident to the educated reader that Cagliostro was teaching a path of alchemy and Hermetics, totally congruent with traditional texts on the subject.

If any fault can be ascribed to the Count, it would be the need to be admired and worshipped; that was, perhaps, his main flaw and one that would cost him his liberty and life. The text of the Ritual is littered with adoration and praise towards the founder of the Order – the Grand Copht. We believe that Cagliostro was motivated by a genuine desire to educate and help humanity and it is very obvious that he did possess a deep knowledge of alchemy, Cabala and mysticism.

In his own era, he was also viewed as a bit of a renegade, and various Masonic figureheads were intrigued and not a little concerned by his zeal. Called upon by the Supreme Council of France, it was demanded that Cagliostro prove by what authority he had founded a Masonic Lodge in Paris, independent of the Grand Orient. Due to the Count's superior knowledge, the Supreme Council found it difficult to find a representative qualified enough to discuss philosophic Masonry and the ancient Mysteries that Cagliostro claimed to represent. The time had come to question the self-proclaimed Grand Copht, and Antoine Court de Gébelin – the greatest Egyptologist of his day and an authority on ancient philosophies – was chosen for the task of interviewing him. A time and date were set and the Count invited to attend.

Cagliostro accepted the invitation and presented himself on 10 May 1785, reportedly 'dressed in an Oriental coat and violet colored breeches'. Made to stand before his peers, Cagliostro received the first few questions from Court de Gébelin. A commentary of the meeting was noted:

From the very beginning of the interview Cagliostro's great simplicity and perfect courtesy had attracted the sympathies of the whole assembly. Court de Gébelin was enchanted to recognize in Cagliostro a man with wide knowledge of the traditions of Greece, Egypt, Arabia and Persia. But when it became a question of discussing the points which were to form the basis of the assembly's enquiry, the Sicilian's expansiveness was suddenly damped like a faulty firework; he became cold, reserved, almost inattentive, answering only in vague terms and circumlocutions which avoided the subject under discussion. Pressed by Court de Gébelin, the Duc de Rochefoucauld and Savatte [sic] kindly to explain himself without reserve, after a few moments of silent meditation Cagliostro stood up to speak:

'Gentlemen, in accepting the invitation with which you have honoured me, I did not foresee as dearly as I do now the seriousness of such an interview. If I am not mistaken, you believe that Freemasonry should possess the key to the occult sciences, and, not having been able to discover this key at your lodge meetings, you came here in the hope that I would be able to cast some light on your researches. Well gentlemen, honesty compels me to tell you that you can learn nothing from Freemasonry. The so-called mystery of Hiram is no more than a grotesque absurdity, and the title of Great Architect of the Universe which you give to God is only a name invented by an Englishman lacking entirely in common sense. You yourselves feel that the Supreme Being cannot be defined by such wretched anthropomorphism. The immense variety of the manifestations of Life at the centre of the Universal Order reveals to our consciousness a First Absolute Cause which you are seeking to define in spite of the inadequacy of the human language. Gentlemen, you need seek no longer for the symbolic expression of the divine idea: it was created 60 centuries ago by the Magi of Egypt. Hermes-Thoth fixed the two terms. The first is the Rose, because this flower is spherical in shape, symbol of the most perfect unity, and because its perfume is a revelation of life. This rose was placed at the centre of a Cross, a figure expressing the point at which are united the apices of two right angles whose lines may be produced in our imaginations to infinity, in the triple directions of height, breadth and depth. The material of this symbol was gold, which in occult science signifies light and purity; and in his wisdom Hermes called it the Rose-Cross, that is, Sphere of the Infinite. Between the branches of the cross he wrote the letters I N R I, each of which expresses a mystery.

'I' *[Ioithi* in the sacred language] symbolizes the active creative principle and the manifestation of divine power that fertilizes matter.

'N' *[Nain]* symbolizes passive matter, the mould of all forms.

'R' *[Rasith]* symbolizes the union of these two principles and the perpetual transformation of created things.

'I' *[Ioithi]* symbolizes again the divine creative principle and signifies that the creative strength which emanates from it ceaselessly returns to it and springs from it everlastingly.

'The ancient Magi wore the Rose-Cross hung from the neck on a golden chain; but so as not to reveal to the profane the sacred word INRI they replaced these four letters by the four figures which are brought together in the *Sphinx, Bull, Lion* and *Eagle.*

'Compare with this simple explanation of the Rose Cross of the ancients, the pitiful farce used at your rituals which makes your so-called initiates say in explanation of the word INRI: "I come from Judea, I have passed through Nazareth led by Raphael; I am of the tribe of Juda": Gentlemen, how could such stupid nonsense be accepted by intelligent Frenchmen? If you wish to revive among you the majesty of the doctrines which illuminated the ancient world and rekindle on the heights of human intelligence the beacon of divine radiance, you must first of all destroy the legend of Hiram and your meaningless rituals. You must give up these comic decorations and these titles of Sublime Princes and Sovereign Commanders; four planks under a few feet of earth will show if you are any more worthy than the lowest beggar.'

The assembly was stirred by this pronouncement of Cagliostro's. 'But is it enough,' cried Court de Gébelin, 'to destroy everything in order to prove one's superiority? If Freemasonry is only phantasmagoria, by what signs can you prove to us that the light which is refused to us shines from the mysteries to which you hold the key? If you are the inheritor of the ancient Magic, give us a proof, a single proof, of its power — if you are the genius of the Past, what have you to say for the Future?'

'I reveal it,' replied Cagliostro coldly, 'and if you will give me the Masonic oath, or better, if you will swear yourselves to secrecy on your word of honour, I will prove what I claim.'

'We swear secrecy,' everyone cried, and all hands were raised to confirm the oath.

'Gentlemen,' continued the Sicilian with a magnetic look, 'when a child is born, something has already preceded its entry into life. That something is its Name. The name completes its birth, for, before naming, a king's child and a peasant's are no more than small pieces of organized matter, just as the corpse of the most powerful ruler in the world, shorn of the brilliance of funeral pomps, has nothing to distinguish it from the remains of the lowest slave.

'In modern society are three sorts of names: the family, the Christian and the surnames. The family name is the common impress of race which is handed down, transmitted from one being to another. The Christian name is the sign that characterizes the person and distinguishes the sex. The surname is a secondary qualification, applied to any individual in a family in particular cases. The family name is imposed by civil requirements; the Christian name is chosen by the affectionate intentions of father and mother. The surname is an accidental title, sometimes used only in one lifetime, sometimes hereditary. There is finally the social title, such as prince, count, duke. Now I can read in the ensemble of these personal designations the most outstanding features of any destiny; the more numerous these designations are, the more clearly does the oracle within them speak. Do not smile, gentlemen. My conviction in this respect cannot falter, for it is based on fairly numerous experiments and on proofs too striking to be ignored. Yes, each one of us is named in the heavens at the same time as on earth that is, predestinated, bound, by the occult laws of increate Wisdom, to a series of more or less fatal ordeals before he has even made the first step towards his unknown future. Do not tell me that such certainty, if it existed, would be the certainty of despair ... All your protests will not prevent Predestination from being a fact and the Name a sign to be feared. The highest wisdom of the ancients believed in this mysterious connection of the name and the being who holds it as if it were a divine or infernal talisman that could either illuminate his passage through life or destroy it in flames. The Magi of Egypt confided this secret to Pythagoras, who transmitted it to the Greeks. In the sacred alphabet of *Magism* each letter is linked to a number;[9] each number corresponds with an Arcanum: each Arcanum is the sign of an occult power. The 22 letters of which the keyboard of the language is composed from all the names which, according to the agreement or disagreement of the secret forces symbolized by the letters, destine the man so named to the vicissitudes which we define by the vulgar terms of luck and misfortune.

'But what relationship, you will ask, can possibly exist between mute letters and abstract numbers and the tangible things of life?

'Well, gentlemen, is it necessary for you to know the impenetrable secret of the mystery of generation before you will consent to think, walk, will and act? God illuminates us by means compatible with wisdom, and He always prefers the most simple. Here it is the Word, the work of God, which is the instrument of prophetic revelation.

'One experiment will serve to make me better understood.

> "Est-il possible à l'esprit humain de chercher et de découvrir les secrets de l'avenir, dans l'énoncé littéral de l'Évènement qui vient de s'accomplir, ou dans la définition d'une personne par les noms, titres et actes qui constituent son individualité?"

> "Is it possible for the human mind to seek and discover the secrets of the future in a literal statement of the event which has just taken place, or in the definition of a person by the names, titles and deeds which constitute his individuality?"

'You see only, gentlemen, the obvious or material sense of this question. But, while you ponder, the higher Magic has already read a second meaning which gives the true answer.

Here is the art of unravelling this occult meaning. Remember the invariable RULE.

'The text is made up of 203 letters, to which must be added a progression of numbers ascending from 1 to 203, as follows: E1 S2 T3 I4 L5 P6 and so on.

'All these letters, with their numbers, are placed in a circle, so that the eye may take them all in at a glance. The alphabet of the Magi, which I place before you, fixes the value of the letters. Note that the French language has no double consonants like Th or Ts; we therefore can ignore these for our present purpose. But note also that the letters U and V, the letters I, J and Y, the letters F and P, the letters K and Q, are marked in this alphabet by the same sign; consequently they can be taken one for the other according to the needs of our deciphering. If, for example, there are three U's and one V in the visible text, and if we need two U's and two V's to express the occult text, the third U will do for the necessary second V. If there are three P's and no F's, and if the occult text demands two F's, two of the P's are transformed into F's, and vice versa. All the other letters retain their absolute value.

'With this rule kept in mind, we must let our eyes wander slowly round the circle in a vague contemplation of new groups that the letters may form. Gradually a few words appear: we remove from the circle the letters of which they are composed and note them down, with their corresponding figures. Then we continue the circular contemplation until new words complete the new meaning and exhaust the circle. This operation is accomplished more or less quickly according to the intuitive faculties of the mind – some will be less practised than others. It often happens that the first words we find have no rational meaning or are contradictory. As soon as this is perceived, the letters must be brought back into the circle and the study begun afresh. But as we become more and more familiar with this sort of work the difficulty disappears and, by a mysterious instinct, the mind rejects words created by chance and attracts those born in the light of a second examination.

'Proceeding in this manner, we are able to extricate from the question that occupies our thoughts the following sibylline reply, the metathesis or transposition of the letters in the original text, forming as follows the assembly of elements composing the occult meaning:

"LE 5 13 – VERBE 47 52 57 11 16 – HUMAIN 22 23 24 25 26 27 – EST 29 53 59 – UN 102 107 – REFLET 120 130 131 154 155 3 – DE 177 185 – LA 200 14 – LUMIERE 15 46 116 119 142 145 150 – ETERNELLE 165 168 172 19 67 75 81 88 90 – ECLAIRANT 92 113 118 124 132 153 169 182 187 – ICI 105 114 136 – TOUTE 202 7 122 135 144 – VIE 195 196 203 – LE 12 32 – SAGE 54 64 183 1 – INITIE 4 72 82 83 103 106 – SAIT 111 112 134 161

— LIRE 51 68 69 80 — et 58 84 — RETROUVER 86 96 108 37 158 198 104 98 50 — DANS 139 152 157 160 — LES 63 66 67 — MOTS 97 77 21 126 — ENONCES 167 186 188 190 30 36 60 — LE 64 85 — PROGNOSTIC — 117 164 139 192 45 146 163 176 34 — NON 78 115 125 — LOINTAIN 127 137 162 95 100 128 178 99 — DES 109 110 156 — DESTINS 193 38 166 171 181 133 173 — QUI 174 175 191 — DOIVENT 197 121 194 65 94 138 180 — S'ACCOMPLIR 8 71 79 170 147 159 6 91 201 33 — DANS 40 87 141 179 — CHAQUE 44 31 199 101 140 41 — SPHERE 2 18 35 43 48 55 — DES 61 62 9 — INDIVIDUS 10 148 28 49 93 20 42 184 17."

"*Le Verbe humain est un reflet de la lumière éternelle, éclairant ici toute vie. Le Sage initié sait lire et retrouver, dans les mots énoncés, le pronostic non lointain des destins qui doivent s'accomplir dans chaque sphère des individus.*"

"The human Word is a reflection of eternal light, illuminating all life here below. The wise initiate can read and recover, in the words pronounced, a prognostic not far removed from the destinies which must be fulfilled in each sphere of the individual."

'Thus the Sage, the initiate, not only reads our fate as it is written in the stars; he also finds indications of these very destinies in the simple words announcing a fact or which characterize a human individuality. This is the meaning contained in the Mosaic Genesis[10] a work Egyptian in inspiration, where God makes all living beings pass before the first man, so that he might give each a suitable name; for to *name is to define*.

'Returning to the elements of the occult text, you will see that there remain in the circle 10 letters, namely: T39 C56 D70 D89 N76 D123 D129 P143 N149 and P51. These letters are mute, that is, no word can be made out of them. To extract a meaning from them we must use the procedure of the Sibyls who prophesied in the ancient Roman temples of Fortuna, at Preneste or Antium, and in some way make a prophetic phrase, a human Word, spring from each initial. It will come to us after a few moments of meditation, and, in order to imitate the ancient oracles as closely as possible, I shall think in Latin, and express myself in the following terms:

"*Tacentes Casus Denuntiat Nomen; Decreta Dei Per Numeros Praedicebantur.*"

"The Name announces the events that still remain in the silence of the future, and divine decrees are predicted by Numbers."

'Names and Numbers: these are the foundations of, and the keys to, the sanctuary of the Oracles.'[11]

The speech was an astonishing and utterly profound piece of rhetoric and it quite rightly had a spectacular effect on its audience. According to Manly P Hall, Cagliostro then went on to:

> ...predict to the assembly the future of France in a graphic manner that left no room for doubt that the speaker was a man of insight and supernatural power. With a curious arrangement of the letters of the alphabet, Cagliostro foretold in detail the horrors of the coming revolution and the fall of the monarchy, describing minutely the fate of the various members of the royal family. He also prophesied the advent of Napoleon and the rise of the First Empire. Having finished his address, Cagliostro made a spectacular exit, leaving the French Masonic lodge in consternation and utterly incapable of coping with the profundity of his reasoning.[12]

The alphabet used by the Count was an ancient one inspired by the Magi[13] and resurrected by Paracelsus in the 16th century (see opposite page). It was originally an ancient doctrine of talismans used as protective or healing charms. Derived from the Cabala but probably taken from the arcane sciences of ancient Egypt or Chaldea, the alphabet was inscribed on talismans, along with figures or symbols, and charged with the appropriate planetary or angelic force, on the corresponding metal and at a specific time of day. This is explained in much greater detail in Chapter 10 which gives a commentary on Cagliostro's Egyptian Ritual.

Figure 9 The alphabet of the Magi

The influence of Cagliostro on Mozart

Aside from the Egyptian Ritual, Wolfgang Amadeus Mozart's opera *The Magic Flute* may well be the most lasting and influential effect Cagliostro left behind. The whole opera is based in Egypt and follows the path of a potential initiate into Freemasonry. The Grand Master of the Masonic sect is called Sorastro, who is believed by many to have been based on the Count. The opera libretto (written by Bro. Emmanuel Schikaneder) contains many areas of symbolism that one could trace back to the works of Cagliostro. The opera starts with a scene where a serpent (reminiscent of the seal of the Count) attacks the young initiate Tamino who, overwhelmed with fear, falls unconscious. At this moment he becomes like the sleeping Mercury in the first degree of Egyptian Freemasonry, symbolic of the 'un-awakened' man. When he wakes he doesn't know where he is or who he is.

This isn't the only point of correlation with Cagliostro's rituals; much of the alchemical symbolism can be seen reflected in various aspects of the opera. For example, Papageno the bird man, himself a symbol of basic human nature and weakness, undergoes a trial of having his mouth locked shut; this trial takes place in Cagliostro's Rite and the Rite of Adoption of the female Masons. One of the most striking areas of correlation being when Tamino is to be initiated and he is turned back from various doors before finally being accepted to enter in the Door of Nature. In *The Holy Trinosophia* (an alchemical manuscript attributed to Count de St Germain, but we believe to have been written by Cagliostro) the same trial takes place; the difference being that there are four doors rather than three and that the initiate enters through the Door of the Elements rather than just that of Nature.

The most startling statement in *The Magic Flute*, which seems to be beyond coincidence, is the co-Masonic message of the whole libretto. 'A woman who has no fear of death has a right to join us!' the brethren sing after the couple, Tamino and his lover Pamina, have completed their trials by earth, air, fire and water. There is no doubt that one way or the other *The Magic Flute* was heavily influenced by the works of Cagliostro. The source of the influence is uncertain; although we know Mozart and Schikaneder were Freemasons, there is no evidence to suggest that either was initiated into Cagliostro's Rite. It is likely, however, that they mixed in similar circles; Mozart was rumoured to have been present at the Masonic conference in 1785 when Cagliostro made his famous speech. Egyptology was also an exciting new phase in Europe at the time and various books were in circulation such as Jean Terrasson's *The Life of Sethos* which covered the supposed Egyptian rituals as described by the Greeks. All these were an enormous influence for creative minds as we have seen from the *Crata Repoa* and the *African Architects* rituals.

In the next Chapter we discover the first full English translation of Count Cagliostro's Ritual of Egyptian Freemasonry.

CHAPTER NINE

THE RITUAL OF EGYPTIAN FREEMASONRY

The following ritual is a full translation of a manuscript held in the Museum of the Grand Lodge of Scotland. Discovered in France by Charles Morison, a Scottish Freemason and surgeon (whose name is displayed in the front cover of the book), it was donated to the museum following his death. Morison rescued the Ritual of Egyptian Freemasonry and many other texts from destruction when the Masonic Lodges of Paris were broken up during the French Revolution in 1789.

Cagliostro's Ritual of Egyptian Freemasonry, as mentioned in previous chapters, was intended as an enhancement for Regular Freemasonry not as a replacement. It is structured in a similar way to Freemasonry ritual, both ancient and modern, inasmuch as it involves three degrees and specific catechisms (questions and answers) directed between the Master and candidate.

Figure 10 Personal crest of Charles Morison, who rescued the Ritual manuscript from Revolutionary France. Taken from Cagliostro's Ritual of Egyptian Masonry

EGYPTIAN FREEMASONRY

Dogma

Glory   Wisdom

Union

Charity   Prosperity

You, Grand Copht, Founder and Grand Master of High Egyptian Freemasonry in all corners of the globe

To all those who will see these present Letters we do let it be known

That during the time we have stayed in Lyon, several members of a Lodge of this Orient, following the Ordinary Rite and bearing the distinctive title of La Sagesse [Wisdom], having demonstrated to us the strong desire which they had to submit themselves to our regime and to receive from us the light and the power necessary to know, to prosper and to propagate Freemasonry in its true form and its primitive purity, we are moved to accede to their wish, persuaded that in granting them this mark of our good will and of our confidence, we have the sweet satisfaction of having worked for the glory of the Great God and the good of humankind.

Therefore, having adequately confirmed in the sight of the Worshipful Master and of several members of the said Lodge, the power and the authority which we hold to this effect, we with the aid of these same Brethren found and create in perpetuity in the Orient of Lyon this Egyptian Lodge and establish it as the L.M. [Mother Lodge] for all the orient and all the occident: from henceforth we attribute thereto the distinctive title of La Sagesse Triomphante and naming as its permanent and unmovable officers; to wit:

I.M. St Costner, Worshipful Master, and Gabriel Magneval as his substitute.

B. Magneval, Orator, and Journel as his substitute.

De Croix, Secretary and Auberjonnois as his substitute.

Alquier, Guardian of the Seals, Archives and Funds, and Roi de Cologne as his substitute.

Bessiere, Grand Inspector Master of Ceremonies, and [blank space] as his substitute.

We grant to these officers once and for all time the right and the power to hold an Egyptian Lodge with the Brethren subject to their direction, to carry out all receptions of Apprentices, Companions and Master Masons, Egyptian Masons, to issue certificates, to maintain relations and correspondence with all the Masons of our Rite; and the Lodges upon which they depend in whatever place on earth they may be situated, to affiliate after examination and the formalities prescribed by ourselves the Brethren of the Ordinary Rite who would wish to embrace our regime, in a word to exercise generally all the rights which may appertain and do appertain to the true and perfect Egyptian Lodge having the title and prerogatives and authority of a Mother Lodge.

We nevertheless enjoin the Worshipful Master, the MM, the officers and the members of the Lodge to take unceasing care and give scrupulous attention to the works of the Lodge so that those relating to reception and all others generally of whatever nature may be carried out in conformity with the rules and the statutes decreed separately by ourselves under our sign manual, our grand seal and the seal of our arms. We again enjoin each of the Brethren to walk constantly in the straight and narrow path of virtue and to show by the regularity of his conduct that he cherishes and knows the true principles and the goal of our Order.

In order to validate these we have signed by our own hand and have hereto affixed the Great Seal awarded by ourselves to this Mother Lodge, together with the Masonic profane seal.

Executed in the Orient of Lyon

Statutes and Regulations of the R.L. of La Sagesse Triomphante

Mother Lodge of Egyptian High Freemasonry for the Orient and for the Occident

Constituted as such and founded at the Orient of Lyon by the Grand Copht, Founder and Grand Master of Egyptian High Freemasonry in all parts of the world, oriental and occidental.

***

Our Master sat in our midst and said:

1st You shall reject the heartless man who does not believe in the Supreme Being or in the immortality of the soul; he would sully the Temple and its precincts.

2nd You shall accept him who has nurtured in his heart those two great truths;

whatever else might be his belief and his religion, they are not an obstacle to his initiation.

3rd Whosoever aspires to know the mysteries of high Egyptian Freemasonry shall first of all be received as a Mason in a Lodge of the Ordinary Rite and will justify by certificates from his Masters that he merited the award of the degrees of Apprentice, Companion, Master and Master Elect.

4th If two candidates should present themselves before you at the same time, and one should have higher degrees, of the four degrees above, then you shall receive him first. Let this preference be the reward for the study to which he will have dedicated himself in the hope of improving his mind.

5th A Mason of the Ordinary Rite must be of honest disposition, have a cultivated mind and be of proven integrity, for no man who could not present these essential qualities would ever be part of the Egyptian Rite.

6th In vain would you expect fruit from a young plant; therefore admit as Apprentice only one who shall have reached the age of 25 years; precocious virtues may redeem a few years, but the maturity which comes with age can never compensate for that of the spirit.

7th He who has the happiness to be initiated shall meet his obligation before God and his Masters, to keep our inviolable secret about our mysteries, to maintain silence about everything which shall happen in our Temples or in their environs; to observe strictly the rules of the order. If he should break his promises may he be held in contempt; may he be expelled in shame and may the Great God punish him.

8th The images of the Divinity are supreme; Egyptian Masons respect them and cherish yours above all else, never speak against the Laws of the country where you live, or against the Religion which prevails in that place.

9th Love of one's neighbour is the second duty of man, may every initiate fulfil it in every sense; may he everywhere and at all times be just, beneficent and ready to comfort the poor.

10th Love my children; love them each and all, love with tenderness. Succour and console any of your number who is in distress or suffering affliction: may misfortune befall that brother who shall refuse to help his brother; the Lord shall withdraw his protection from him.

11th　In the primitive purity of Masonry there were only three degrees: you shall recognise and confer only three: Apprentice, Companion and Master.

12th　The Apprentice shall only be received as a Companion after three years of submissiveness study. The Companion shall only attain the degree of Master at the end of five years' work.

13th　Apprentices, you shall be obedient to the Companions; they shall set out your work. And you, Companions, shall take and carry out the orders of the Masters: may jealousy never find a way into your hearts; between you may there only break out a fraternal rivalry.

14th　Masters, to you shall belong the direction and inspection of the work; the government and administration of the Lodge; make yourself worthy of your functions and of your power; order nothing which is not conducive to the glory of my children and to the service of the rest of mankind.

15th　The Apprentices and the Companions shall have two separate workshops, one on the left, and the other on the right of the Temple. The Masters shall gather in the chamber in the centre. May the labourer of lower degree be mindful not to cast imprudent glances at the works of superior degree. May they fear the disastrous consequences of reckless curiosity.

16th The two workshops shall be presided over by a Master who shall be appointed to this effect by the Masters' Chamber; each of them shall elect an Orator, a Secretary and an Inspector Master of Ceremonies who shall exercise these offices for the duration of one year and in accordance with the instructions which shall be given to them.

17th In any election, promotion or operation of any kind whatsoever which shall fall within the competence of one of the workshops, may each labourer make clear his role and his opinion with modesty, but with freedom, and may the freedom of franchise have the force of Law. May the spirit of discord be ever distant from my children. If, however, some differences arise between them may the decisions of the Apprentices be reviewed and amended if necessary by the Companions and may the judgement of the latter be brought before the Central Chamber which shall decide in the last resort (without appeal) with reference to the Masters who shall have presided over the workshops.

18th The Companions shall decide the selection and the initiation of the Apprentices; the Masters shall choose the Companions from amongst the Apprentices.

19th There shall be perfect equality amongst the Masters and the offices with which some of them are invested shall be not so much distinctions as responsibilities; they shall settle everything by a majority. Before making their decision may they take care to invoke the aid of the Great God, and they shall always be unanimous.

20th The most extensive confidence, the most intimate unity shall reside with the Masters in the Central Chamber; may they establish amongst themselves an absolute fraternity. Before planning a venture, in the most interesting circumstances of their lives, may they take the views and the counsel of the Chamber and may the interest of one of its members always and from that moment become the interest of all.

21st Each Master, after three years as a member of the Central Chamber and after having obtained its agreement, shall have the right to create twelve Masters, twenty-four Companions and seventy-two Apprentices.

22nd The Masters shall assemble once every three weeks; the Companions once every five weeks; the Apprentices once every seven weeks.

23rd The number of Apprentices shall never rise beyond 72; that of the Companions shall be fixed at 24 and the Central Chamber shall never comprise more than 12 Masters. If this rule is not observed in truth I tell you, confusion, disorder and laxity shall find their way into your midst.

24th You shall recognise in the Lodge only five grand Officers who shall always be of the class of Master, namely, a Worshipful Master, an Orator, a Secretary, a Guardian of the seals, archives and funds, a Grand Inspector Master of Ceremonies and the *Frère Terrible*.

25th   The Officers shall be appointed for life and shall select, on the advice of the Central Chamber and from amongst those who comprise its membership, a substitute who shall be their replacement in case of absence, and shall be by right their successor in the event of death or retirement.

26th   The substitutes of the grand Officers shall not be able to occupy any other positions and when they act as substitutes they shall have the same rights and prerogatives as the regular office holders.

27th   The Worshipful Master shall preside over the Central Chamber but he shall be here only as the first among equals and his sole prerogative shall be to have two votes instead of one in order to resolve a division of opinions or to expedite discussions and their consequences.

28th   At the head of the grand Officers and the Masters he shall preside over the Lodge when it meets in the Temple on days of celebration or reception. He shall always carry out the initiation ceremonies and he shall ratify under his seal the certificates which are issued to initiates by the Central Chamber.

29th	The Orator shall make a speech at each initiation ceremony and at each general assembly may he impress increasingly upon his Brethren the necessity of drawing close to the Divinity and may he never say anything which is not simple and in harmony with the works in which the Lodge is engaged.

30th	The Guardian of the seals, archives and funds shall be the trustee of the seals which I have granted to you; he shall maintain order in the archives and shall hold the key and administer the Treasury of the Lodge.

31st	The Secretary shall make a record of all the invitations and all the deliberations of the Central Chamber; he shall keep the correspondence: he shall call together the Masters and issue invitations for the general assemblies.

32nd	The Grand Inspector Master of Ceremonies and *Frère Terrible* shall be responsible for the general policy of the Temple and its workshops. He shall oversee the security of the Lodge and shall be responsible for the inspections of the buildings. He shall prepare new members, visit sick strangers and Brethren.

33rd The catechisms, the rules and other instructional manuals shall be deposited in the Central Chamber or they shall be locked with a triple lock. The Masters shall never be able to let them from their keeping, to transport them outside the Lodge nor to transcribe them for their own use. It is also forbidden for Companions and Apprentices to put down in writing what they have remembered after having heard them read out.

34th The Worshipful Master, when he deems it to be prudent and advisable shall be able with the assistance of the two MM to read the Apprentice catechism to Masons of the Ordinary Rite who, being of correct and pure heart, are worthy of knowing the truth; but who, clinging to errors of long standing, need to have sight of it in order to resolve to accept it.

35th All degrees shall be conferred in the form which has been pursued without subtraction or addition. Great care shall be taken not to stray from the path which has been set out in order not to lose the way as our fathers have done.

36th Every year there shall be two general assemblies to celebrate the day of *foundation as an Egyptian Lodge* and the feast of *St John the Evangelist*; the first shall be held on the 3rd day of the 9th month; the second on the 27th day of the 12th month; each of these solemn days shall be marked by an act of charity.

37th May the Lodge of the Ordinary Rite which shall be formed under the title of *La Sagesse* continue on the same footing as that which is before us. May it retain the same officers and the same degrees, its connections and its correspondence but may it avoid in the reception of Apprentices anything which would not have a symbolic or moral value and might cast ridicule on Masonry.

38th May the Worshipful Master and the Officers of this same Lodge be subject to the inspection of the Worshipful Master of the Lodge of the Egyptian Rite; but may concord and love of the common good, inspiring both, establish a perfect harmony in all their proceedings.

39th   Keep ever in your sight the glorious title of Mother Lodge, which I grant to you and render yourselves worthy of the rights which are attached hereto, it is your examples which must attract and change the Masons or the Lodges which you shall be in a position to instruct and to affiliate.

40th   You shall read at each of your general assemblies the Statutes and Rules which I give you.

If you practise what they contain you shall attain knowledge of the truth. My spirit shall not abandon you and the Great Lord shall always be with you.

Reception of an Apprentice of the Egyptian Lodge founded by the Grand Copht

Preparation of the Lodge

The Lodge shall be decorated with sky blue and white without gilding. Above the head of the Worshipful Master there shall be a triangle with the name *Yehovah* and rays.

The Throne of the Worshipful Master shall stand on three steps and the altar shall stand before the Throne.

Upon this altar there shall be a brazier containing a sponge saturated with alcohol, to the right of the Throne shall be the *sun* and to the left, the *moon*.

The tracing board shall be placed at the centre of the Lodge; on this tracing board there shall be painted the door of a temple with 7 steps. On this door shall appear a curtain.

To the right of the door an inscription composed of these words: *Arcanum Magnum* [Great Secret] and to the left these words: *Gemma Secretorum* [Secret Stone]. Before the door a Master Freemason shall be represented, with the red cordon, the green dress coat, vest, breeches and spotted stockings.

The Master shall be standing at the door of the Temple. He shall have the *forefinger of his left hand upon his lips* and in his right hand his sword with which he shall threaten a *sleeping Mercury* who shall be painted on the left of the door.

Above the head of this Mercury shall be engraved the two words *Rough Ashlar*. This board shall be illuminated by 7 candles, three of which shall be on one side, three on the other, and one in the middle.

The Worshipful Master shall be clothed in a robe of white fastened by a girdle of sky blue silk, he shall wear a stole of watered blue silk bordered by a narrow strip of gold lace with the monogram of the founder embroidered in gold spangles at each end; below this there shall be a gold fringe. He shall pass this stole, which shall be fastened, over the arm from left to right, like the Deacons. Over all he shall wear his red cordon. He shall have his sword in his hand.

Reception

The Candidate having been agreed, he shall be placed in the Chamber of Reflection in the middle of which shall be a large tracing board, having in its centre a *large pyramid* at the base of which shall be a cavern; before this cavern shall be represented the figure of Time in the form of an old man with a look of terror on his face and having difficulty in entering this cavern. On the left of this tracing board shall be represented the *horn of plenty,* to the right *some chains and Philosophical instruments.*

When the Candidate is permitted to enter, the Grand Inspector of the Lodge and two apprentices shall enter the Chamber of Reflection, there to prepare the Candidate.

The Grand Inspector, without speaking to him, shall begin to untie the hair of the Candidate, to remove his clothing. He shall order him to take off his shoes and to divest himself of all metals. He shall then deliver to him a speech appropriate to the occasion and in accordance with the tracing board of this chamber. After having made him understand how painful is the path of philosophy and how it is crowded with unpleasant difficulties and torments, he shall ask him if he is full resolved to be initiated in mysteries such as these and to prefer labours, perils and study of nature to the honours, the ease and the wealth of this world. If he persists the Grand Inspector shall take him by the hand and conduct him to the door of the Lodge.

He shall knock 7 times. To the demand which will be made of him he shall reply, "It is a Mason, who, having passed through all the degrees of the ordinary Masonry, presents himself for invitation into the true Egyptian Masonry."

The door shall then be closed and shall not be reopened until the Worshipful Master ordains that the Candidate be brought in.

Opening the Lodge

The Worshipful Master having taken his seat the strictest silence shall be observed. It is forbidden to blow one's nose and even more so to speak.

When the Worshipful Master rises all shall rise at the same time; he shall have his sword in his right hand and it shall not leave his hand whilst he is speaking.

He shall say:

"To order, my Brethren."

"In the name of the Great God let us open this Lodge according to the Rite and constitutions of the Grand Copht, our founder."

He shall descend from his Throne and at 7 paces from the lowest step he shall face the Triangle confirming the Name of God, and he shall say:

"My Brethren, prostrate yourselves as I do, to beseech the Divinity to protect and assist me in the work we are about to undertake."

Having finished the silent prayer, the Worshipful Master shall strike upon the floor with his right hand as a sign to all the Brethren that they may rise.

The Worshipful Master shall resume his Throne and there he shall inform all those present that the Candidate (naming him) who has passed through all the degrees of ordinary Masonry requests and begs the grace of being received and admitted into the true Egyptian Masonry.

If any of the Brethren has anything to allege against the Candidate, he shall, on his honour and conscience, be obliged to declare it. This complaint or reason shall be discussed, and the Worshipful Master shall decide if the Candidate shall be admitted or rejected; but in the event that all give their consent to his reception the Worshipful Master shall send the Grand Inspector and two Brethren as prescribed above, to prepare and conduct the Candidate.

The Speech of the Worshipful Master

The Worshipful Master having given the order to have the candidate brought in, the Grand Inspector shall conduct him before the Throne where he shall cause him to kneel.

The Worshipful Master shall rise and say to him, "Man, you have already been warned that the object of our labours is as far removed from frivolity as that of ordinary Masonry is from true philosophical knowledge. All our operations, all our mysteries, all our proceedings have no other aims than to glorify God and to penetrate into the sanctuary of nature. One achieves this only by much toil. But also, with resignation, with patience and the time fixed by the constitutions of our founder, you shall have the hope of seeing our trials crowned with the happiest success."

"Before being clothed with the sacred habit of our Order and before being recognised as one of our members you shall pronounce with me the solemn oath which I shall cause you to repeat in the presence of God and of all your Brethren."

At the moment when the oath is taken, the alcohol which is upon the altar shall be set alight, and the Candidate, placing his right hand above the flame, shall pronounce the following oath, having knelt down.

Oath

"I promise, I commit myself and I swear never to reveal the secrets which shall be communicated to me in this Temple and blindly to obey my superiors."

***

After the oath the Worshipful Master shall clothe him in an all-white robe, girded by a white cord. Then he shall strike him three times on the right shoulder with this sword and shall say to him:

"By the power which I hold from the Grand Copht, the founder of our Order and by the grace of God I confer upon you the degree of Apprentice of the true Egyptian Masonry and I constitute you guardian of the philosophical knowledge which I shall communicate to you."

The Worshipful Master shall then direct the Grand Inspector to conduct the new brother to the place destined for him. He shall give the sign to all those present to be seated and giving the Orator the Catechism, charge him to deliver the lecture concerning it.

As soon as the lecture is finished the Catechism shall be returned immediately to the Worshipful Master who shall never let it leave his hands or go out of his sight.

That having been completed, the Worshipful Master shall rise from his Throne and together with all the Brethren he shall prostrate himself before the sacred name of the Divinity in order to give him thanks and glorification. He shall then close the Lodge.

Catechism – To recognise the children or subjects of the Grand Founder of the Sublime Egyptian Lodges

Q: Are you an Egyptian Mason?
A: Yes, I am, with strength and singleness of purpose.

Q: From what place do you come?
A: From the depth of the East.

Q: What have you observed there?
A: The immense power of our founder.

Q: What did he teach you?
A: The knowledge of God and myself.

Q: What did he command you to do before your departure?
A: To take two routes: natural Philosophy and supernatural Philosophy.

Q: What is signified by natural Philosophy?

A: The marriage of the Sun and the Moon and the knowledge of the seven Metals.

Q: Did he indicate to you a sure route for arriving at that Philosophy?
A: After having made me acquainted with the power of the seven Metals he added; *Qui agnoscit martem, cognoscit artem* (Whoever recognises Mars, knows art).[1]

Q: May I hope to be fortunate enough to acquire all the light that you possess?
A: Yes, but one must have a right, just and beneficent heart; one must enounce all motives of vanity and of curiosity; finally crush vice and confound incredulity.

Q: Are these virtues sufficient for arriving at this sublime knowledge?
A: No, one must also be loved and particularly protected by God; one must be submissive and respectful towards one's sovereign, and one

---

[1] This has elsewhere been recorded as saying 'Qui agnoscit mortem, cogniscit artem' (he who has knowledge of death knows the art of dominating it) – whether this was an error by the transcriber of the original manuscript or just a different interpretation we are uncertain. Both sayings are equally appropriate for the context.

must seclude oneself for meditation for at least three hours every day.

Q: How should one employ these three hours a day devoted to meditation?
A: In penetrating the grandeur, the wisdom and the omnipotence of the Divinity. In drawing near to him with fervour and in uniting one's physical and moral being so intimately that one may come to possess this natural and supernatural Philosophy.

Q: Before continuing our conversation I require you to give me a proof and a sign whereby I may know if you are really one of the children of the Grand founder of our sublime Lodge.
A: I consent to this, but I shall never give you my sign unless you have first given me yours.

Giving the Sign
This is to bend back the body, to raise the head, to open the eyes and with a strong exhalation pronounce the word *Elohim*.
The response to this sign is to stand on the point of the left foot, with the right foot thrown back and raised, majestically and both arms extended, the left pointing to the ground, the right elevated, throwing the right hand forward with the 5 fingers wide open and separated.

Both being thus mutually recognised they should kiss each other on the forehead, sit down and continue the Catechism.

Q: I beg you my brother, begin giving me instruction concerning natural philosophy.

A: Gladly, but on condition that you cast from your mind every worldly and profane idea, that you shall have no faith in any writer, living or dead, and that you shall be persuaded, as I am, that all men who deny the divinity and immortality of the soul, are in our eyes not only profane but unprincipled.

Q: Having always heard of the Philosopher's stone I earnestly desire to know if its existence is real or imaginary.

A: You did not understand me when I spoke to you concerning the marriage of the Sun and the Moon.

Q: I admit that I did not, and that, my mind not being sufficiently enlightened to enable me to know by my own reflections alone what this marriage may mean, I have need of your aid and light.

A: Listen to me then with attention and strive to comprehend me. By the knowledge given to me by the Grand Founder of our Order I know that primal matter was created by God before he created man, and that he created man only to be immortal, but man having abused the goodness of the Divinity, he determined to accord this gift no longer except to a very small number: *pauci sunt electi* [the chosen are few]. In fact, by the public knowledge that we still have, Elias, Moses, Solomon, the King of Tyre and various other persons cherished by the Divinity came to know about primal matter and about supernatural Philosophy.

Q. But tell me more particularly, I beseech you, what this primal and so precious matter can be?
A. Know that this primal matter always exists in the hands of the Elect of God and that, in order to obtain it, it does not suffice to be great, rich or powerful; but as I have already told you, it is absolutely necessary to be loved and protected by God. I assure you further, by all that is most sacred, that by means of the light communicated to me by our Master, I came to know clearly that one grain of this precious matter becomes a projection to infinity. Open wide your eyes and your ears.

Seven are the transitions for perfecting the matter.

Seven are the colours.

Seven are the effects which shall complete the philosophical operations:

1st   *Ad sanitatem et ad homines morbis* [of purity and of sick mortals]
2nd   *Ad metallorum* [of metals]
3rd   To rejuvenate and repair the lost forces, and to increase the radical heat and humidity.
4th   To soften and liquefy the solid part.
5th   To congeal and harden the liquid part.
6th   To render the possible impossible and the impossible possible.
7th   To procure all the means of doing good, taking at the same time the greatest precautions against working, speaking, acting or doing anything in this connection except in the most reserved and occult manner.

Q: The confidence you inspire in me could not permit me the slightest doubt of the truth of any of your opinions; however, let me make an observation. Our language is so different from that of all those authors who have written concerning the Philosopher's Stone that I find it most difficult to reconcile your discourse with theirs. I have by no means forgotten their commendation which you made to me to have no faith in these authors; but it seems to me that I may make exception in favour of those who enjoy the highest reputation and who have always been considered by the most enlightened, educated and honest men of modern times as true philosophers, such as Hermes Trismegistus, Bazile, Valentin, Treviseau, Arnaud de Villeneuve, Raymond Lully, Cosmopolitus, Philatet, etc.

A: You are neither sufficiently well instructed in the principles of our Master, nor long enough a member of our splendid school that your uncertainties could surprise me; but a few reflections shall suffice to disabuse your mind and fix for ever your feelings about this subject. There has never been, nor will there ever be any man enjoying and possessing this primal matter except those who have been admitted to our society. And the most important, the first, and the most severe of our obligations as you must know, consists in the sacred commitment never to write or divulge any of our mysteries. You should by this be convinced that all the authors that you have cited to me were not true philosophers, or that, if they were, all the books, with manuscripts or printed, that are attributed to them, are entirely false and apocryphal, and that they are no more than the fruit of the cupidity of those who invented them to feed the cupidity of those who believe in them. Moreover, repeat with great exactitude all the operations taught in these books and see if any one of them will ever prosper you. Confine yourself then, as I do, to having pity upon and compassion for these simple and prejudiced ones who believe in and work in accordance with these authors, since they shall all positively end by losing their credit and their fortune, by ruining their health and perhaps, unfortunately, by becoming insane.

Q: In order to come into possession of the secrets of this Philosophy, is it necessary to have recourse to the light of a true philosopher?
A: Yes, but you shall not obtain any help from this man unless the Divinity inspires him in your favour.

Q: What means must be employed to obtain this Grace of God?
A: By adoring Him, by respecting one's sovereign and above all by consecrating oneself to the happiness and comfort of one's neighbour, charity being the first duty of a philosopher and the work most agreeable to the Divinity. To this conduct must be joined fervent prayer in order to obtain this goodness that He might invite one of His chosen Ones to unveil to you the arcana of nature.

Q: What do you mean by the arcana of nature?
A: The knowledge of that beautiful natural and supernatural Philosophy of which I have spoken to you before and of which you shall find the principles concealed in the emblems presented by the Order of Masonry and by the tracing board placed before your eyes in all the Lodges.

Q: Is it possible that ordinary Masonry could provide any idea of these sublime mysteries? I have been a Freemason for 50 years, I have passed through all the degrees and during this long period of time I have never even suspected what you have had the grace to tell me. I have never considered Masonry to be anything but a society of people who gather together to enjoy themselves and who, in order to be more closely united, have adopted signs and a special language. Deign, by your enlightening interpretations, to reveal to me here the true and firm goal of which you have told me.
A: God inspires me, and I am going to raise a corner of the veil which conceals the truth from you. I shall commence by instructing you as to the origin of Masonry; I shall give the philosophical explanation of the Masonic tracing board, and I shall finish by acquainting you with the full extent of the sublime and victorious aim of true Masonry.

Q: Your goodness increases my gratitude and your enlightenment increases my respect; permit me hereafter, rendering you greater justice, to substitute the name of Master for that of Brother. I beseech you, then, my dear Master, to follow your part and to commence by instructing me as to the origin of true Freemasonry.

A: Free Masonry has as its Father *Enoch* and *Elias*; after having been invested with the sublime power which was accorded to them by the Divinity. They implored His goodness and mercy on behalf of their neighbours, so that they could be permitted to communicate His greatness to other men, and the power which he accorded to man above all the beings which surround his Throne. Having obtained this permission they chose 12 dependents whom they called *Elect of God*, one of which, known to you, was called *Solomon*. This philosopher King, after having been inspired, sought to imitate and walk in the path of these two Masters by forming a company of men fitted to preserve and propagate the sublime wisdom they had acquired. Counselling with the other Elect it was agreed that each of them would choose two dependents, making in all 24 *Companions*, the first of whom was Boaz. These 24 Companions had then the liberty to elect 3, whom they called *Apprentices*, which made two supreme chiefs, twelve Masters or Elect of God, – twenty four Companions and seventy two Apprentices. From these last are descended the Templars and from one of the Templars who took refuge in Scotland, the Freemasons who were in principle 13 in number, then 33, etc. Such is the origin and affiliation of Masonry.

Q: This report leaving me nothing to desire, let us pass on, I beg of you, to the explanation of the Masonic ceremonies and the tracing board. On entering the Lodge, why was I blindfolded?
A: In order to make you understand that any man who does not possess the high wisdom which I am teaching you is a blind, restricted man, but having a Worshipful Master as his Master he shall pass out of the dark shadows and know the truth.

Q: Why were my hands bound?
A: To teach you the full extent of the subordination and submission necessary for the orders of your Master.

Q: Why was I divested of part of my clothing and of all metals in my possession?
A: To teach you that every man who desires to become a good man or a true Elect must

renounce all kinds of humours, riches and glory and that to obtain this favour it is not necessary to be great, rich or powerful.

Q: What is the purpose of the gloves given to me?
A: To give you to know that every true Mason shall always have clean hands, that he shall never stain them with blood and above all that he is strictly forbidden to touch primal matter with his bare hands.

Q: What is the meaning of the apron which I was obliged to attach to my belt?
A: It is to teach you that the apron is the first garment used by man to cover his nudity when he had lost his innocence.

Q: Let us now come, I beg of you, to the explanation of the tracing board. What is the meaning of the Trowel?
A: That this is the first implement used by man and it was necessary to enable him successfully to begin his labours on the natural as well as the supernatural.

Q: What is the purpose of the compass?

A: To teach every good Mason that he must never do anything without having the compass in his hand.

Q: What is the meaning of the plumb?
A: That before communicating to a profane the knowledge of the arcana of nature it is necessary to have the exact measure of all his walks and doings.

Q: What is meant by the mosaic section?
A: That in order to avoid all kinds of schism and disunity amongst Masons it is necessary to captivate their hearts by an attachment, a confidence and a boundless fraternal devotion to each other.

Q: What is the purpose of the triangle?
A: To teach you that *Omne trinum est perfectum* [all three are perfect].

Q: What do the two columns mean?
A: These two columns, called Jakin and Boaz are not two columns at all, but in fact two men who sought to learn about natural and supernatural philosophy. Solomon having not found in the first of these the qualities required of a true Mason, he was rejected and placed in an inferior class. On the contrary, Boaz, having

been fortunate enough to recognise the significance of the acacia, by the pleasure of God and with the aid of Solomon, succeeded not only in ridding the rough ashlar of all its impurities but also in rendering it cubical and finally in causing it to become triangular or more than perfect.

Q: I beseech you to explain more clearly to me the significance of the different stones: I know that although on the tracing board there is one rough stone, one cubical and one triangular, but all this being an enigma to me I beg you to give me the key.

A: This is it: the acacia is the primal matter and the rough ashlar is the mercurial part. When this rough ashlar or mercurial part has been thoroughly purified, it becomes cubical; it is then, with this primal matter or this dagger in your hand, that you must assassinate this Master – this rough ashlar which has become cubical; or this Father and this Mother of all the metals. This operation being finished and the body enshrouded it is now a question of purifying it by following the seven philosophical transitions which are symbolised by the seven steps placed before the door of the Temple.

The first 5 which are the primary colours the sixth which is the colour black and finally the seventh which is that of purple, of fire or of fresh blood. It is thus that you may bring about the consummation of the marriage of the Sun and the Moon, and that you shall obtain the Triangular stone and thus the perfect projection. *Quantum sufficit, et quantum appetite* [as much as you need and as much as you have appetite for]

Q: But you have not told me about Adoniram who, according to ordinary Masonry, was assassinated and what is the symbol of the black cordon and the dagger which is awarded in the degree of Elect?

A: Masonry has caused you to err on this point. It was not Adoniram who was assassinated, but rather the liquid part which it is necessary to slay with this dagger. It is also as I have just taught you the volatile, lively and mercurial part which it is absolutely indispensable to solidify. With regard to Adoniram, desiring to convince you of my good faith, my sincerity and my affection for you, I shall tell you the whole story.

Adoniram was the son of *Urabis Raham* and he was called Jokim. Raham, who was working on the superstitions part of Masonry had imparted some information to his son; but he, protected and favoured by God, having come to a knowledge of the superior power possessed by Solomon, both in natural and in supernatural philosophy left the North and came to the South, where the great King resided; and in the hope of attracting attention to himself he stationed himself at the door of the Temple. Solomon having noticed him, asked him what he was looking for, to which he replied: *Adonai*. The king, inspired by God and touched by the respect and veneration shown by this mortal being in thus using with confidence the name *Adonai*, which is the sacred name of the Divinity, not only welcomed him with goodness and beneficence but even caused him to enter with him into the Temple and, knowing that he was well versed in the metallic part, he confided to him the primal matter and changed his name from Jokim to Adoniram which, in the Arabic language, signifies *Son of God*, or *Son of Raham* or *worker in metals*. Adoniram, proud of this flattering description did not have sufficient control over himself to refrain from communicating the fact to Jokim. He informed him and made use of him in all his operations. Jokim, becoming very jealous of the preference which Solomon had accorded to Adoniram, there resulted much discontent and inconvenience.

Solomon, fearing the consequences that this might bring upon his favourite Adoniram, whom he cherished, determined in order to protect him from the doleful effects of jealousy, to initiate him into the spiritual and supernatural wisdom. Consequently he caused him to enter into the sanctuary of the Temple and revealed to him all the mysteries connected with the sacred and perfect Triangle. It was then that he was given the name Boaz under which, as you know to be a fact, he paid the wages of all the Companions and all the Apprentices.

The Temple being finished, Solomon gave him as a reward the Kingdom of Tyre.

Q: I am enchanted by the sublime interpretation which you have just given me concerning the Masonic ceremonies and the tracing board. Nothing seems more obvious or more magnificent to me and I see that it was not possible to misuse more completely the most holy and most respectable establishment than these our present applicants have done to the most sacred object; they have made the most ridiculous mockery of it, and of the most sublime truth they have made a vain and childish illusion.

But permit me to comment that for all the detail which you have just given me you have said nothing concerning the blazing star?

A: This star is the emblem of the Great mysteries revealed in supernatural Philosophy and it is a new proof of the blindness and ignorance of modern Masons, because it ought to be terminated by 7 points or 7 angles, and you shall never see it represented in any Lodge except by 3, 5 or 6 angles. Besides, these poor children of the widow have never discovered any other merit in it than that of containing the letter G, which they have spiritually explained by the word Geometry. Such is the fruit of an hundred years of reflection and the marvellous interpretation of 7 angels who surround the Throne of the Divinity, and the letter G is the presence of the Sacred Name of the Great God called Gehova, Yehova, Adonai, etc.

Q: Grant me, I beseech you, a more profound knowledge of these seven primitive angels.
A: These seven angels are the intermediaries between ourselves and the Divinity; they are the 7 planets, or, more correctly, they direct

or govern each of the seven planets. As they have a particular and fixed influence on each of the realms necessary for the perfection of the primal matter, the existence of these seven superior angels is as real as the fact that man has the power to control these same beings.

Q: My astonishment cannot but increase, like my eagerness to learn more: *the existence of these 7 superior angels is as real as the fact that man has the power to control these same beings.*

But how is it possible for man to command and be obeyed by these angelic creatures?

A: God having created man in his own image and likeness, his is the most perfect of all his works and as long as man preserved his innocence and his purity he was, after the Divinity, the most powerful and superior; and God had not only given him the knowledge of these intermediaries, he had also conferred on him the power to rule and govern them immediately after Himself. Man having degenerated by abusing this great power, God deprived him of that superiority; He made him mortal and denied him knowledge of these intermediary beings.

Q: Were the Elect of God made exceptions to this general judgement?
A: Yes, these were the only ones to whom God has granted the grace to enjoy this wisdom and all the power that he had conferred upon the first man.

Q: Every good and true Mason, such as I glory in being, may he hope to be regenerated and to become one of the Elect of God?
A: Yes, without doubt; but besides the necessity of practising all the moral virtues in the highest degree, such as charity and benevolence, etc, it is further necessary that God, sensible of your adoration, your respect, your submission and your fervent prayers, should move and determine one of His Elect to assist you, to instruct you and to render you worthy of this supreme happiness; for one of the twelve Elect being in repose or being called to the presence of the Divinity, the most virtuous of the 24 Companions succeeds him. Likewise the wisest of the 72 Apprentices takes the place left vacant by the Companion.

Q: Deign, I beg of you, to give me the greatest details concerning this supernatural Philosophy.
A: This Philosophy demands that I divide it for you into three classes:

The 1st is called natural or direct.
The 2nd is called acquired or communicated.
The 3rd is called inferior, low or superstitious.

The *first* is exercised by the man, who in purifying his individual physical and moral parts, succeeds in recovering his primitive innocence and who, after having attained that perfection with the aid of the invocation of the Great name of God and the attributes in the right hand, arrives at the point of exercising man's sublime and original domination, of knowing the entire extent of the power of God and the means of enabling every innocent child to enjoy the power which his estate had given him before the fall of man.

The *second* is possessed by the man, who after having given his obligation to his Master has obtained the grace to know himself, and the sovereign power of God; but the power of this man is always limited; he may act only in the name of his Master and by his power, of the principles of which he knows nothing. This portion of power always demands the necessity of purifying oneself before acting, holding the attributes in the right hand.

It is only with great difficulty and with extreme reservation that I tell you about the *third*. My heart sinks when I am constrained to reveal to you the wickedness of man, who, after having debased his being, seeks to satisfy his pride and his vanity by making use of a sacrilegious, horrible and proscribed power.

Q: Do me the favour of explaining more clearly to me what you mean by the purification of man, and what are the means by which this can be achieved?

A: First it is necessary to being by knowing the spiritual symbols, the invocations to God, the manner of dressing and the method it is necessary to create and prepare the implements of the art, in accordance with the planetary influences; for henceforth instead of speaking to you of these 7 angels I shall use the names of the planets, so that you shall better understand me.

The first implement is this same *Trowel* which you always see in the hands of Freemasons. The *compass*, the *knife*, the *sword* and all the necessary tools, one must know, what is the day of the month and the hours which are the most propitious for the influence of the most suitable planet. It is also necessary to be informed of the day of the month and the most favourable hours for the Benediction of the silken cloth. One must know the Prayers which must be addressed to God, the Invocations to the Angels and the means of taking sufficient control over oneself in order to repel and destroy all the doubts which sully your body and your mind. By conducting yourself precisely in accordance with these procedures you shall succeed in divesting yourself totally of the physical part. You shall be perfectly purified in accordance with the methods of the Elect of God; and with the attributes in your right hand and the assistance of the Master whom God has given to you, you shall without doubt attain the grace to enter into the sanctuary of truth.

Q: Show me, I beseech you, the means of creating these implements?

A: In order to make each instrument it is necessary to await the day and the hour determined by the influence of the regulatory planet. It is further necessary that after the implement comes out of the fire it must be plunged into the blood of the appropriate animal, taking care to ensure that each hour demands a different animal. Remember also that the days and the nights according to our philosophy are entirely distinct from those of the profane, for we divide each day and each night into twelve equal parts, being ordered by the rising and the setting of the Sun in which ever season it may be.

Our first hour commences with the appearance of the Sun and those of the night after its setting. The minutes vary in the same way. You see that according to this calculation the hours of our days are much longer in the summer than in the winter and that they are composed for this reason of more or fewer minutes.

Remember too that the first hour of the day is governed and directed by the Sun. The second by the Moon. The third by Mars. The fourth by Jupiter. The fifth by Venus. The sixth by Mercury. The seventh by Saturn. The eighth by the Sun and so forth for the others.

It is also necessary to know and to conform with the configuration of the aerial circles which must always occur in accordance with the disposition of the four quarters of the earth and by the number 3 or 3 times this mysterious cabalistic and perfect number are likewise indispensable for the quantity of light which is placed before the Sanctuary.

Q: Why do Masons constantly act in accordance with the number 3 times 3 and for what reason do you continually recommend that I should conform to this same number, both for the circles and for the candles of the Sanctuary?
A: My child, it is in memory of the greatest truth; it is one of the most sublime pieces of wisdom which I can obtain for you. It is for you to learn that man was created in three times and that he is composed of three distinct parts: Morality, Physique and Power. It is in the end to make you understand that in order never to err in all the Philosophical operations and to perfect them, whatever you do once you must always start again with 3 or 3 times 3.

Q: But in conforming strictly to all that you have just taught me, will that suffice to enable me to work by myself and succeed?
A: No, because it would still be necessary for an enlightened leader, or a Master in the primitive arts, to instruct you completely and perfectly in all those things which I have only indicated to you.

Q: By what signs shall I recognise a Master in the primitive arts?
A: By the simplicity, by the reality of his actions and by his patience, by his frankness, by his past

and present conduct; by the reality of his actions, by his manner of working in your presence, which must only be that of entreating the Great God, and by commanding the seven primitive angels without ever having recourse to any superstitious or idolatrous way; by his patience, because although a man be entirely devoted to the Divinity he shall never attain all that he wished to know and learn except with patience.

Q: Give me now, I beg of you, some enlightenment concerning the part which is acquired or communicated.
A: Know that any man elected by God has the power to grant you the power which the true cabal obtains, when he has explained to you and confided in you the Pentagon which he formed on the paper of art.

Q: What is the meaning of the paper of art?
A: It is that which the Elect use for all their inventions, operations, etc. There are three kinds of paper which philosophers call virgin paper.

One is the *skin of an unborn lamb* after it has been purified by the complete ceremonies with the silken cloth, on the day and at the hour of the Sun.

The second is *the membrane or afterbirth of a male child born of a Jewish woman* likewise purified with the silken cloth and the complete ceremonies.

The last is ordinary paper but blessed in accordance with the intentions of the Master, always on the day and at the hour of the Sun, holding the Masonic attributes in his right hand.

Having obtained from this Elect of God the marvellous Pentagon it is necessary to carry out everything prescribed by the Drawing Rite and finish with the obligation which you must make to God in the presence of your Worshipful Master.

Q: Shall I be able to make this commitment with a clear conscience?
A: Absolutely, since that oath consists only of the promise to worship God, to respect your Sovereign and to love your neighbour: you shall be obliged to promise also to your Master that you will obey him blindly, that you will never go beyond the limits which he will have prescribed for you; that you will never have the indiscretion to ask questions out of mere curiosity; finally that you will be bound never

to work except for the glory of God and the advantage of your sovereign and your neighbour.

Having completed all these preparations by the invocation on the day and at the hour prescribed, and with the power communicated to you by your Master you shall without doubt achieve all your desires; but do not forget that although you have already obtained the satisfaction that you wish, if you neglect the obligations and the duties which you take upon yourself, not only will you lose irrevocably, in an instant all your power, but instead of raising to a higher and more perfect degree you shall fall into inferiority, imperfection and misfortune.

Q: Shall I therefore be able to hope for a more sublime power?
A: Yes, you shall even be able to become the equal of your Master.

Q: How?
A: With the will, the wisdom, the best conduct and by faithfully fulfilling all your commitments.

Q: My dear Master, to complete my instruction I lack only the knowledge of what constitutes the superstitious part.

A: My child, any man who has only bad principles and who, blinding himself to the choice of means does not put a brake on his greed shall rush headlong into the abyss; he shall sink into vice and end up lowering himself to the point of signing in his own blood a criminal contract which he will make with inferior spirits or intermediaries and which will destroy him for ever.

Q: Would it be indiscreet to ask you what constituted the first operation which you have seen from the Grand Copht our founder?
A: In the proofs which have passed before my eyes.

Q: What are these proofs?
A: This is everything which I can tell you about what has happened in my presence. I have seen the preparation and purification, on various occasions, of mortals, beginning with the invocation and the worship of God, by arranging the Sanctuary in a Masonic way, by dressing the subject in a long garment called a *talaric* tunic [a long tunic – from Latin *talos* meaning ankles]. Then, holding the attributes in his right hand he was successful in completing the work by comparing the persons I have spoken about previously.

I can add nothing further than to wish you as much satisfaction as I have myself experienced, as have my Brethren, witnesses like myself of these miracles.

I vow to you on the Name of the Great God that all I have just communicated to you in this catechism is the most precise truth.

Reception of an Apprentice to the Degree of Companion

Preparation of the Lodge

The Lodge shall be decorated with a tapestry of white and sky blue and gold.

The Throne of the Worshipful Master shall stand on 5 steps, surrounded by his Dais. The altar shall be placed before the Throne.

Above the Throne shall be the flaming star with seven points. In the star shall be inscribed the name of God and in the seven points, if this is possible, shall be seen those of the seven angels.

At the foot of the 5 steps of the Throne shall be traced a circle.

The tracing board shall be placed in the middle of the Lodge, with a heart at its centre. In the heart shall be seen a Temple. To the right of the heart shall be depicted a Trowel and vertically below it, the rough ashlar, the cubical stone and the triangular stone.

To the left, also vertically, a *dagger*, the *Sun* and the *Moon*.

In the lower part of the tracing board shall be painted a Mason struggling against Mercury, plunging a dagger into his heart. This board shall be illuminated by 12 candles arranged 3x3 along the 4 sides.

The Worshipful Master shall be seated on his Throne. The grand officers shall take their seats and the rest of the Masters shall be disposed on the two columns.

The Worshipful Master shall have his right hand armed with the sword, which has a gold handle and a silver blade.

The 7 planets shall be engraved on the two sides of the Moon; it shall also be decorated with a flame coloured ribbon edged in white and a plaque in the form of a Rose bearing all around this inscription:
Primal matter

and the motto

I believe in the Rose

The 12 Masters who comprise the rest of the Lodge shall be decorated with a flame coloured ribbon without a plaque.

On the Worshipful Master's altar there shall be two covered crystal vases: one shall contain red liqueur, pleasant to drink, which may be wine; the other shall be filled with leaves of gold.

Reception

The Candidate having completed his 3 years of apprenticeship shall be presented to the Worshipful Master, bearing the necessary Certificates.

He shall be sent into the Chamber of Reflection. The Orator shall come to help him there and shall assist him to acquire the true knowledge of God, of himself and of the intermediaries between God and man.

The Orator shall then enter into the Temple, deliver his report and ensure that it is acceptable to the Worshipful Master and to the rest of the Masters.

When the member elect has been permitted to enter, the First Inspector shall clothe him in a *white tunic*; he shall have *dishevelled hair* and shall be divested of all metals and girded with sky blue ribbon.

When he is in this state the Inspector shall present himself with the candidate at the door of the middle chamber, knocking 5 times on this door.

The Worshipful Master shall ask who is knocking. The Inspector shall enter and reply:

"It is an Apprentice who has finished his three years and who, bearing his certificates, entreats the Worshipful Master and the Worthy Masters to admit him to the degree of Companion."

During this time the Candidate shall remain alone outside the Temple.

True Opening of the Egyptian Lodge

The Worshipful Master having taken his seat, the greatest silence must be observed; it is forbidden even to blow one's nose and all the more to speak.

When the Worshipful Master rises, the Masters also stand up. He shall have his sword in his right hand and say:

"To order, my Brethren."

"In the name of the Great God let us open the Lodge in accordance with the Rite and the Constitutions of the Grand Copht."

The rest of the Brethren shall bow deeply, along with the 12 Masters, to worship the Divinity. The Worshipful Master, in particular shall beseech Him to grant *Power*, *Strength* and *Wisdom*. Each one in his heart shall say the hymn *Veni, Creator Spiritus* [Come, Holy Spirit Creator].

The Worshipful Master shall rise, then, the Brethren doing likewise, still maintaining a respectful silence and each one shall take his seat.

Then the Master of Ceremonies shall open the door, take the Candidate by the left hand, place in his right hand a lighted candle, and conduct him into the presence of the Worshipful Master, where he shall place him at the centre of the circle described at the foot of the throne.

The Worshipful Master, armed with his sword, which he must hold in his hand every time he speaks, shall address these words to the Candidate.

The Speech of the Worshipful Master

"My child, after 3 years of trials and labours you have beyond doubt learned to cast aside all human curiosity. I think, and I believe with certainty, that it is not this profane motive which brings you to us and that the appearance of zeal does not hide in you the sole desire to know the nature and the sources of the power confided in us."

"Without doubt you have been on your guard, you have raised yourself to the Divinity, you have acquired the knowledge of your own self, of its moral part and its physical portion, and you have sought to know the intermediaries which the Great God has placed between Himself and yourself. Your response?"

The Candidate lowers his head and two Masters positioned beside him, each having a small burner in his hand, giving off an aroma, and purifying him with the smoke, which the

Worshipful Master explains to the Candidate in these words:

"I am now going to purify your body and your mind; this perfume is the symbol of that purification."

After the purification the Worshipful Master shall continue to interrogate the Candidate.

"My child, are you really determined to pursue the course into which you have entered? Is your mind sufficiently strengthened? Is it your true, sincere, and pure wish to come closer and closer to the Divinity, by acquiring a more perfect knowledge of yourself and of the sanctity of the power which is confided in us? Your response?"

The Candidate shall bow.

Then the Worshipful Master shall rise, causing him to kneel down, and the Candidate shall recite his oath as follows:

Obligation

"I promise, I commit myself and I swear never to reveal the secrets which shall be communicated to me in this Temple and blindly to obey my superiors."

After this oath the Worshipful Master shall clothe him in an all white robe girded with a ribbon of white cord, and then shall strike him three times on the right shoulder with his sword and say to him:

"By the power which I hold from the Grand Copht founder of our Order and by the grace of God I confer upon you the degree of Companion and constitute you to be guardian of the knowledge which we shall communicate to you: *D'helios, mene, tetragrammaton* [Sun, Moon, name of God]."

When the Worshipful Master utters these words the 12 Masters present shall fall to their knees and bow their heads deeply. As each of these words is pronounced the Worshipful Master shall strike the right shoulder of the candidate with his sword. This done, those present shall rise and surround the candidate who shall drink the liqueur, raising his spirit in order to understand the following speech which the Worshipful Master shall address to him at the same time.

"My child, you are receiving the primal matter, understand the blindness and the dejection of your first condition. Then you did not know yourself, everything was darkness within you and without. Now that you have taken a few steps in the knowledge of yourself, learn that the Great God created before man this primal matter and that He then created man to possess it and be immortal. Man abused it and lost it, but it still exists in the hands of the Elect of God and from a single grain of this precious matter becomes a projection into infinity.

The acacia which has been given to you at the degree of Master of ordinary Masonry is nothing but that precious matter. And Adoniram's assassination is the loss of the liquid which you have just received and which must be killed with the dagger; it is this knowledge that, assisted by the Great God, shall bring you these riches."

"Sic transit Gloria mundi" ["Thus passes the Glory of the World"].

The candidate rises and the Worshipful Master speaks the following words:

"My child, we use words, signs and grips as symbols of our mutual acceptance with our Brethren belonging to the Grand Copht. Your degree is characterised by the response:

'I am' to anyone who asks who you are.

"The grip consists of taking the right hand of the man who asks you, touching your heart with your left hand, whilst inclining your head."

"The sign is to open your mouth and, looking up at the sky, to exhale strongly."

As he teaches this sign to the candidate the Worshipful Master shall exhale and blow strongly on him 3 times, saying to him:

"And I, with my breath, make you a new man, totally different from what you have been until this day and such as you must be eventually."

Then the Worshipful Master shall finish with a short lecture, if he so wishes and return the new Companion into the hands of the Orator, with the command that the tracing board in the middle be explained to him, with the aid of the catechism handed down by the Grand Copht.

After the speech by the Orator the new Companion shall be placed at the back of the

Lodge facing the Worshipful Master and the Brethren standing to sing the Hymn:

"*Te Deum Laudamus*" ["We praise thee, O Lord" – an early Christian Hymn]

At the end of this Psalm the Worshipful Master shall speak again to confirm the speech of the Orator and shall end by closing the Lodge in the name of the Great God whom they shall worship and from whom he shall request health and prosperity of the Sovereign, of the Lodge, of the new Companion, and requesting it also for the rest of mankind.

Tracing Board of the Master Lodge of Egyptian Masonry Founded by the Grand Copht

At the top of the tracing board there shall be a *Phoenix* in the middle of a *burning pyre*. Below this Phoenix a sword in saltire (crossed) with the *staff of Mercury*.

Below this sword and this staff shall be the figure of *Time* in the form of an old man, big and strong, having two large wings. On the opposite side shall be a Mason wearing the insignia of a Master wearing a green dress coat, vest, breeches and spotted stockings, and hussar boots. The red Cordon and a sword in his right hand, seeming ready to strike or cut the wings of Time. At the feet of this Mason an inverted hour glass and the broken scythe of Time.

***

Reception

For the Order of the Master of Interior of the Egyptian Lodge

The Lodge shall be decorated in sky blue and gold. The Throne shall be raised on three steps and may contain two figures, representing *Solomon* and the King of Tyre. At their feet shall be placed a blue cushion trimmed with gold, with four pompoms or tassels, also in gold. On this cushion shall be the sword, having a gilt silver haft or guard, with the seven planets engraved on each side.

The chamber shall be modest, well decorated and well lit and may contain at least twelve persons, not counting the two Worshipful Masters.

The 12 Masters are called the *Elect of God*, and the two Worshipful Masters are called *God's Cherished Ones*.

The two Chiefs or the two Worshipful Masters shall be dressed in a white tunic with a sky blue stole edged with a golden tassel, having on each side the names of the 7 angels embroidered in gold spangles.

At the end of the point of the stoles shall be embroidered in the same way the sacred Name of God which shall end at the bottom in a golden fringe. The flame coloured cordon, with the plaque from right to left, the hair loose, dishevelled and un-powdered, white slippers or shoes, embroidered and knotted with a blue ribbon, or Rosette, without buckles.

The two Worshipful Masters shall cause the 12 Masters to dress them and these shall sing during the time when they are doing so:

Te Deum Laudamus

The Grand Inspector is the one who shall direct and preside over this ceremony, because it is especially under his inspection.

The 12 Elect shall be dressed decently and if possible in uniform, but they may never enter the chamber with their hat or their cane. They shall present themselves there only with their drawn sword in their hand.

The dressing of the two Worshipful Masters having been completed and the Lodge properly closed and carefully inspected by the Grand Inspector, they shall take their place on the Throne, but without sitting down.

The first Worshipful Master shall then begin with these words:

"To order, my Brethren."

"In the name of the Grand Copht our founder let us seek to act and to work for the Glory of God, from whom we hold wisdom, strength and power; let us try to obtain His protection and his mercy for ourselves, for the sovereign and our neighbours. Join his prayers to mine, to beg on my behalf his help and the light which I need."

Having said this, the two Worshipful Masters shall leave and go to the middle of the chamber, turning to face the name of Jehovah, they shall fall to their knees, along with the others present.

The first Worshipful Master shall make the following invocation:

"O Great God, Supreme Being and Sovereign, we beseech Thee from the depths of our hearts, by virtue of the power which it hath pleased Thee to grant to the Grand Copht our Master, to permit us to make use and to enjoy our share of the grace which the Grand Copht hath given us, by invoking the 7 angels who surround Thy Throne to make them operate and work in unfailing compliance with Thy commands or [without] damaging our innocence."

When this invocation is finished the two Chiefs together with all the others shall prostrate themselves with their face to the ground and shall remain there in meditation until the first Worshipful Master strikes the floor with his right hand, which shall give the sign at which everybody shall stand up. The two Worshipful Masters shall go to sit down on their Throne.

When they are seated the Grand Inspector shall greet them with a bow and then with a movement of his head, but without saying a word. He shall signal to the other Masters to resume their places and sit down.

The first Worshipful Master shall make a speech appropriate to the circumstances telling the Masters that the period of 5 years of

Companionship of Brother _____ has expired and that this Brother requests the grace to be received as a Master. He demands that all shall give him, truthfully and on their conscience, their opinion on the morals, conduct, etc of Candidate _____.

In the event that any one of the Brethren might allege some motives, grievances or complaints against him he shall state them plainly and with frankness in the view of all the assembly and the Worshipful Masters shall decide his fate, either to admit him or to reject him, but if the consensus is unanimous and in his favour, the Worshipful Master shall choose two of the Elect to go into the Chamber of Reflection where the Candidate shall be and they shall prepare him in the following manner.

The Candidate shall be clothed in a modest fashion, his hair unkempt and covering part of his face, before being conducted out of the Chamber of Reflection. The two Elect shall ensure by a carefully designed speech and skilful questioning that they try to discover if the Candidate is sufficiently patient and obedient. They shall tell him that in spite of the time he has spent as a Companion the Masters still need to wait a few more years before admitting him to their midst, but if to all these pretences the Candidate proves by his responses a complete resignation, submission and obedience of his superiors, the two Elect shall give him hope of acceptance. One of them shall go into the Lodge to inform the Worshipful Masters of the favourable condition in which he left the Candidate.

On hearing this report the Worshipful Master shall summon the Grand Inspector and order him to go and find and bring in the Candidate; he shall be found ready and appropriately dressed in a nearby chamber or room.

The Grand Inspector shall conduct him to the feet of the first Worshipful Master who either himself or his substitute, and no other person, shall dress him in the prescribed manner, which is the white tunic, shoes which are also white, edged and knotted with a white ribbon, a girdle of blue silk and the red cordon from right to left. As he dresses him the Worshipful Master shall say to him:

"By the power which the Great God has given to the Grand Copht and by that power which I hold from the Grand Copht I adorn you with this divine clothing."

He shall then make a speech appropriate to the holiness and the grandeur of the mystery which will follow.

Being entirely clothed, the Worshipful Master shall cause him to kneel then, taking his sword in his hand and striking the right shoulder of the Candidate he shall cause him to repeat word for word this speech.

"My God I humbly request Thee to pardon my past faults, I beseech Thee to grant me the grace, by the power which Thou hast given to the Grand Copht and which the Grand Copht has granted to my Master to permit me to act and to work according to his commandment and his intention."

The Worshipful Master shall then blow three times over the head of the Candidate and place him in the hands of the Grand Inspector who shall conduct him to his place, which shall be proper, all white with a stool and a small table before it, upon which shall be placed 3 candles.

The Grand Inspector, after having accompanied the Candidate and having locked him in his tabernacle, shall remove the key, which must be attached to a long white ribbon and he shall present it to the Worshipful Master who shall pass the ribbon round his neck, and he shall place his sword in his hand at the bottom of the steps by which the Candidate shall have ascended.

Immediately this arrangement is finished the first or the second Worshipful Master shall rise and say:

"To order, my Brethren."

All shall stand and one of the Worshipful Masters moving to the centre of the Chamber and turning to face the Name of God shall kneel, as shall all the Brethren to offer his quiet prayer and, having risen, he shall commence the second operation in this way.

He shall use the power which the Grand Copht has given him, to cause the Angel Anael and the others to appear before the Candidate and when he has been informed that they are before him the Worshipful Master shall charge the Candidate, by virtue of the power which God has given to the Grand Copht and which the Grand Copht has granted to him, to request the Angel Anael if the subject proposed for the degree of Master has the merit and the qualities to be received, yes or no?

On receiving the affirmative response from the Angel to the Candidate, the 12 Elect incline their heads to thank the Divinity for the grace which He has accorded them by showing Himself to them by the presence with the Candidate.

The Worshipful Master shall command the Candidate to sit down, together with all the members of the Lodge and he shall then proceed with the reception of the Candidate as follows.

Reception

One of the Worshipful Masters shall leave his seat, sword in hand. He shall position himself in the centre of the chamber and with his sword he shall describe 4 circles in the air at the four cardinal points, commencing in the North, the South, the East and the West.

Then he shall describe another one above the head of each of those present and he shall finish with one in front of the door.

He shall then take the nail which he shall place in the centre of the chamber and to which he shall hold a cord which shall be used with a piece of chalk to trace a large circle of six feet in diameter designated as the place for the Candidate.

In the four sections of the circle it shall be necessary to place burners ready with fire for burning.

In the North – Incense

In the South – Myrrh

In the East – Laurel

In the West – Myrtle

Above these burners shall be placed the four characters known to the Worshipful Masters.

One of them shall remain seated and the other shall remain standing before the Throne with the sword in his hand. To his right shall be the Orator, holding in his hand the four sorts of offering described above.

In this situation the Worshipful Master shall command the Bro. Deputy to return to the Chamber of Reflection to collect the Candidate and to bring him to the door of the Lodge, placing him between himself and his brother. When all three have arrived at this door one of the Elect or the Master shall knock once. The Worshipful Master having heard this shall cause the two doors to be opened, which shall close as soon as the three persons have entered the room. The two Elect who accompany the Candidate shall conduct him into the centre of the circle which was drawn on the floor, where they shall leave him and return to their places.

The Worshipful Master, who shall be standing, shall make the speech already made at the degree of Apprentice, which begins with these words:

"Man, you have already been warned, etc."

After completing his speech the Worshipful Master shall say to the Candidate:

"If you desire sincerely to acquire the knowledge of the Great God, of yourself and of the universe, you must agree to promise and vow to renounce your past life and so to arrange your affairs that you can become a free man."

The Candidate shall kneel and repeat word for word the oath which the Worshipful Master shall dictate to him.

When the oath is finished all the Brethren shall kneel, the Candidate shall prostrate himself at full length with the cord, his face to the ground. The Worshipful Master, accompanied by the Orator, shall cast into each brazier a pinch of each of the perfumes, and returning to the Candidate he shall place his right hand on his head and recite the following Psalm.

"My God have mercy on the man (NN) according to the greatness of Thy mercy.

"And remove his iniquity according to the multitude of Thy tender mercies.

"Cleanse him thoroughly of his sins and purify him of his transgression.

"For he acknowledgeth his iniquity and his crime is ever before him.

"He hath sinned before Thee alone, he hath done evil in Thy sight, so that

"Thou shalt be justified in Thy word, and victorious in Thy judgement.

"Thou seest that he hath been begotten in iniquity and that his mother hath conceived him in sin.

"Thou hast loved the truth, thou hast revealed to him uncertain things and the secrets of Thy wisdom.

"Thou shalt purge him with hyssop and he shall be clean, Thou shalt wash him and he shall be whiter than the snow."

"Thou shalt make him to hear a word of consolation and joy and his bones which Thou hast humiliated shall leap with joy.

"Turn Thy face from his sin and blot out all his iniquities.

"Create in him a pure heart, O God, and renew a right spirit within him.

"Cast him not away from Thy presence and take not Thy holy spirit from him.

"Restore unto him the joy of Thy salvation and uphold him with Thy free spirit.

"He shall teach transgressors Thy ways and sinners shall be converted unto Thee.

"Deliver him from bloodguiltiness O God, Thou God of his salvation and his tongue shall sing aloud of Thy righteousness.

"O Lord, open Thou his lips and his mouth shall show forth Thy praise.

"For Thou desirest not sacrifice; else would he give it; Thou delightest not in burnt offering.

"The sacrifices of God are a broken spirit; a broken and contrite heart, O God, Thou wilt not despise.

"Do good in Thy good pleasure unto Zion; build Thou the walls of Jerusalem.

"Then shalt Thou be pleased with the sacrifices of righteousness, offerings and burnt sacrifices shall they offer on Thine altar.

"We beseech Thee Great God to grant him the grace which Thou hast granted to the Grand Copht, first Minister of the Great Temple."

The Worshipful Master shall then withdraw to his Throne, but remain standing, and shall signal to the Brethren to rise but to remain standing; he shall make another sign to the Orator to go and assist the Candidate to his feet and to conduct him before him.

The Orator shall bring him to the first step of the Throne and shall cause him to put his right knee on this step, with the left knee drawn back. It is at this moment that the Worshipful Master shall create him a Master by blowing 3 times over him, passing the red cordon around his neck, after which he shall have been blessed and touched by the Angels. He shall make him a speech which is similar and in accordance with everything which the Grand Copht, founder, said and did himself to the Worshipful Masters in the same circumstances.

When the ceremony is finished the Worshipful Master shall summon the Orator and direct him to conduct the new Elect to the place which has been destined for him and which shall be on the right of the Sanctuary.

Everybody shall sit down and one of the Worshipful Masters shall make the speech which the Grand Copht will have communicated to him and specified for this occasion. It shall end with this hymn of praise.

> "Lord, remember Thou the Grand Copht, our founder and all the gentleness which he has witnessed as he swore before the Lord and made a vow to the God of Jacob.
>
> "If I enter, said he, into the lodgings of my Palace, if I climb up onto the bed where I must sleep, if I permit my eyes to sleep and my eyelids to slumber, if I rest my head until I have found a dwelling place with the Lord and a tabernacle with the God of Jacob.
>
> "We have heard say that the Ark has been in the land of Ephraim; we have found it in the forest; we shall enter into His

Temple but shall worship Him in the place which he used as a stepping stone.

"Lord, rise from Thy rest, Thou and the Ark of Thy sanctification.

"May Thy Priests be clothed in Thy justice and may Thy Saints be filled with joy.

"For the sake of the Grand Copht, Thy servant, turn not Thy face from Thine anointed.

"The Lord hath sworn to the Grand Copht a true oath and He shall not retract it.

"He hath said, I shall establish on Thy Throne the fruit of Thy virtue: if Thy children keep my word and the precepts which I shall teach them, they and their descendants shall sit eternally on Thy Throne.

"For the Lord hath chosen Zion, He hath chosen it for His dwelling place.

"This is the place of my rest for ever; I shall live here because it is the place which I have chosen.

"I shall shower his widow with my blessings; I shall sate the poor with bread.

"I shall clothe his priests with my beneficent grace and his Saints shall be transported with delight.

"It shall be there that I shall cause the strength and the power of the Grand Copht to shine forth.

"I have prepared a lamp for mine anointed.

"I shall cover their enemies with confusion and with shame and the glory of my holiness shall flourish for ever on their heads."

The Worshipful Master, and all those present, shall rise and the first Worshipful Master going to the centre of the chamber and turning to face the Name of God shall command the Candidate to rise, by virtue of the power which he holds from the Grand Copht.

He shall cause the angels to appear before the Candidate and when informed that they are in his presence, he shall tell the Candidate to ask him if the reception which he has just carried out is perfect and acceptable to the Divinity.

The sign of approval having been made by the Angels to the Candidate, the Worshipful Master and all those present shall in their hearts give thanks to the Great God for all the grace which he has granted them.

The Worshipful Master shall close the Lodge, giving his Blessing in the name of God to the Grand Copht and to all the Masters.

Catechism of a Master of the Egyptian Lodge

Q: From what place do you come?
A: From the interior of the Temple.

Q: What have you observed in the interior of the Temple?
A: A most cherished and favoured dove, a sanctuary bright with light, an allegorical tracing board containing the greatest secrets of Nature and a shining star on the heart of each one of the Worshipful Masters.

Q: What does this star represent?
A: A beautiful rose, around which there are two inscriptions, one consisting of these words:

I believe in the rose
and the other of these words:
Primal Matter

It is the symbol of that precious primal matter which is constantly mentioned in all the writings of our Doctrine and which is in the hands of all the Elect.

Q. What is the use and what are the tasks of the Dove?
A. To serve as the intermediary between the Angel of the Lord and the Elect, to communicate to the latter the Divine will and finally to convince them
of the great power of God.

Q. What does the Sanctuary contain?
A. The Sacred Name of God, placed in the middle of the flaming star.

Q. What does the tracing board represent?
A. A Phoenix being consumed in the middle of a blazing pyre, a sword and the staff of Mercury, Time with wings, a Master Mason Elect of God, an upturned hourglass and the broken scythe of Time.

Q. What is the meaning of the Phoenix?
A. That a true Mason may rise from the ashes, that he can renew himself, be rejuvenated at will like that bird, and that it is with this certificate that one can say—

"*Et renovabitur plumas meas*" ["And you pass bolstered and renewed"].

Q. What is signified by Time and the Master Mason who is clipping his wings?
A. That when a good Mason succeeds in clipping the wings of Time, his life no longer has a fixed term.

Q. What is meant by the broken scythe?
A. That for a man who is immortal the measurement of time becomes pointless.

Q. What were you taught in the interior of the Temple?
A. The most sublime knowledge.

Q. Of what does that consist?
A. After I had received a portion of the power which God desired to grant to the Grand Copht our Founder, I was taught the means of regenerating degenerate man.

Q. How did you spend your time within that place?
A. In glorifying God and in completing the tasks ordained by our great founder and Master.

CHAPTER TEN

A COMMENTARY ON CAGLIOSTRO'S EGYPTIAN RITUAL

> CAGLIOSTRO'S EGYPTIAN FREEMASONRY was worth the lot of them, for he tried to render it not only more wonderful, but more *honourable* than any other Masonic Order in Europe.
> BARON DE GLEICHEN

When interpreting any ritual, it is important to note that there is no one given meaning. Therefore one person's interpretation is as valuable as another's. One of the purposes of symbolism is to express things that can't be expressed through words alone and therefore symbolism and allegory are open to numerous interpretations, so the opinions expressed here are by no means intended to be taken as definitive.

The commentary offered here combines both a Masonic and an esoteric understanding of the ritual.

UNDERSTANDING THE MYSTICAL RITES OF EGYPTIAN FREEMASONRY

The ritual of Count Cagliostro reveals far more about him, his aims and how he viewed the world than anything else we can find. After all this is the text that he felt summed up his teachings of the higher philosophies of life.

The first thing that struck us about the ritual is that there does not appear to be anything remotely Egyptian about it, but we need to read between the lines to make sense of it and also make ourselves aware of some crucial factors. Firstly, all forms of Egyptian tradition, or indeed any spiritual tradition that was not Christian, would have to be hidden in the cloak of Christian terminology. This was the only way in Cagliostro's time one could avoid persecution. And secondly, the spread of ancient Egyptian knowledge and mysteries had been limited to oral tradition – the majority of the ancient papyruses had been destroyed in the fires at Alexandria and what had been rescued was available in Greek and Latin translations.

The *Rosetta Stone* had not yet been discovered and those who still knew the language of the hieroglyphs were few and far between.[1] Until the French scholar Jean-François Champollion cracked the code of the Rosetta

Stone in 1822, any papyrus or stele that had been removed from Egypt would have remained undeciphered. So Cagliostro could not have known of the Egyptian Mysteries *unless* he had been taught, either during his travels in Egypt or by someone who had intimate knowledge of the teachings. There is certainly documentation regarding those temple priests who converted to Christianity and rather than discard all their previous wisdom, chose to hybridize it with their new faith. Ancient knowledge gradually filtered down through the Greek writings, indeed Plato and Socrates are both said to have been taught in ancient Egypt. Either way, if Cagliostro had genuine Egyptian knowledge he probably wouldn't have known the precise Egyptian terminology that we use and know nowadays; he would have used the Greek terms or the alchemical symbols as his means of expression, for alchemy is said to be the symbolic form of the ancient teachings from the land of the Pharaohs.

Any modern Freemason would find the Ritual a rather confusing text and on first reading it he could be forgiven for stating that much of the text appeared to be gibberish. This would be rather appropriate as the word 'gibberish' itself comes from a reference to the spiritual language used by the ancient alchemist Jabir ibn Hayyan (c.721–c.776, also known by his Latin name of Geber) and the whole text is rich is alchemical symbolism. The Ritual has far more akin with magic and the occult than it does the aims of moral regeneration that modern Freemasonry has as its focus. It draws much of its content from the medieval grimoires, particularly a text called the *Greater Key of Solomon*. Much of it is clothed in the language of alchemy and Hermeticism but the Masonic reader will, however, with study, find there are many areas of philosophical and symbolic overlap that would explain why Cagliostro felt that his Egyptian Freemasonry was both an improvement and a restoration of regular Freemasonry. In fact the Ritual of Cagliostro may help the modern Mason see the hidden alchemy in his own Lodge.

To enter Cagliostro's realm we need to picture a divine force running through and underpinning everything in the universe. This force constructs everything and controls everything that is around us. It is both around us and within us — in fact we are 'it'! This force connects everything in such a way that both we and every other person are a small reflection of the entire universe — a microcosm. Everything that is constructed externally is also constructed inside you with the same spiritual forces. And because we are created in the image of God, the power to control it is within our grasp. There are also hidden creatures and beings that exist on this level, such as angels. These angels represent the perfect purity of the divine force and are appointed by God himself. The ritual and philosophy of Cagliostro depicts these forces as being planetary in nature.

The Mysteries of the Planets

In our ancestors' earliest imaginings the planets represented gods or spirits travelling across the sky. Each planet had been associated with different attributes depending on its appearance, movement and the emotions it invoked in the people viewing it. To Cagliostro the whole of existence was underpinned by these seven divine forces represented by the planets. Every personality trait, every action and every object was instructed, controlled and influenced by these forces under the government of God's seven heavenly angels.

As The Proverbs of Solomon (9:1) states:

Wisdom has built her house;
she has hewn out its seven pillars.

This, to the Count, was a clear reference that existence was created from the seven planetary forces, and because the human personality was constructed of these seven forces, spiritual advancement could only be achieved by purification, adjustment and evolution. In regular Freemasonry, he saw the inner structure as being that of balancing the positive and negative, the Jachin and the Boaz of the human personality. He viewed this as the alchemical process of joining mercury and sulphur, which some alchemists term the 'chemical wedding'. He understood from his knowledge of alchemy that human spirit is constructed of the seven planetary forces. Freemasonry was full of references to the number seven – seven working tools (modern English Freemasonry has added two new tools that mar this symbolism); seven virtues; seven Officers of the Lodge and even the seven-pointed, bright and morning star was prominently contained in Freemasonry.

For Cagliostro, to truly bring the human personality and indeed the human spirit into a divine balance, one needed to work directly with these forces. Where regular Freemasonry sought to bring the personality into balance by the harmony of opposites, Egyptian Freemasonry was far more focused, or to Cagliostro's mind, was restored to what Freemasonry was always meant to be doing. It was not just intended to be a reference to rebirth but was a pointer to the original aims of the Craft before it became 'corrupted'. The Egyptian Ritual was often considered to be 'apocalyptic' or 'revelatory' as were the writings of its patron, Saint John the Evangelist.

Freemasons still refer to themselves St John's Masons. His feast day falls on 27 December. Its place in the calendar at the time of the winter solstice is opposite to that of the feast day of Saint John the Baptist, which falls on 24 June shortly after the summer solstice. These two saints represent the two pillars that stand beside the Masonic 'point within the circle'. This alludes to the symbol that all Freemasons are to endeavour to emulate, both physically and spiritually, the ability to balance one's desires and passions in the pursuit of knowledge.

Freemason Gregory Stewart makes this observation:

> Saint John the Baptist, represented as the inverted pyramid, the Alchemical sign for water, representing the spiritual and emotional love. St. John the Evangelist, represented as the pyramid pointing up symbolizing fire that is the drive and will of action. When placed together, they symbolize the perfect balance of darkness and light, life and death, passion and constraint, will and emotion, winter and summer. Together both represent the interlocked star of Solomon, or the Square and Compass.[2]

The spiritual relevance of the number seven is universally known and you can see references in the following from the Revelation of John, chapter 1. There are also references to immortality, another key aspect of the ritual:

> 4 John, to the *seven* churches which are in Asia: Grace be unto you, and peace, from him which is, and which was, and which is to come; and from the *seven* Spirits which are before his throne;

12 And I turned to see the voice that spake with me. And being turned, I saw *seven* golden candlesticks;
13 And in the midst of the *seven* candlesticks one like unto the Son of man, clothed with a garment down to the foot, and girt about the paps with a golden girdle.
14 His head and his hairs were white like wool, as white as snow; and his eyes were as a flame of fire.
15 And his feet like unto fine brass, as if they burned in a furnace; and his voice as the sound of many waters.
16 And he had in his right hand *seven* stars: and out of his mouth went a sharp two-edged sword: and his countenance was as the sun shineth in his strength.
17 And when I saw him, I fell at his feet as dead. And he laid his right hand upon me, saying unto me, Fear not; I am the first and the last:
18 I am he that liveth, and was dead; and, behold, I am alive for evermore, Amen; and have the keys of hell and of death.
19 Write the things which thou hast seen, and the things which are, and the things which shall be hereafter;
20 The mystery of the *seven* stars which thou sawest in my right hand, and the *seven*

golden candlesticks. The *seven* stars are the angels of the *seven* churches: and the *seven* candlesticks which thou sawest are the *seven* churches.

This use of the number seven is not coincidental and has been used in every branch of religion and esotericism over the centuries – in the Bible, seven is the number of sacrifice, purification and consecration; it is represented by the seven branches of the golden candlestick; the seven churches, seven spirits (angels), seven stars, seven seals and so on.

We also see this tradition reflected in the 'Divine Poimandres' (the second book of The Hermetica) Chapter 2 verse 13, when the Mind of God creates the *Seven Governors,* meaning the seven planets.

> For the Mind being God, Male and Female, Life and Light, brought forth by his Word another Mind or Workman; which being God of the Fire, and the Spirit, fashioned and formed seven other Governors, which in their circles contain the Sensible World, whose Government or disposition is called Fate or Destiny.

It was the Count's wish to bring each and every planetary quality or metal (as Cagliostro phrases it) into balance, this being symbolized by a marriage of two opposites – the combining of mercury and sulphur.

This again is reflected in the Divine Poimandres where there is a creation myth describing how the mind of God falls in love with the Earth or physical existence and, as a result of their union, man is created. This was undoubtedly the source of both the focus on marital symbolism and the planetary focus of the Count's 'Egyptian' Freemasonry.

As the Poimandres reads:

18 But the Father of all things, the *Mind* being *Life* and *Light*, brought forth *Man* like unto himself, whom he loved his proper *Birth*; for he was all beauteous, having the image of his *Father*.

19 For indeed God was exceedingly enamoured of his own form or shape, and delivered unto it all his own Workmanships. But he, seeing and understanding the *Creation* of the Workman in the whole, would need also himself *fall to work*, and so was separated from the Father, being in the sphere of Generation or Operation.

20 Having all Power, he considered the Operations or Workmanships of the *Seven*; but they loved him, and everyone made him partaker of his own order.

21 And he learning diligently, and understanding their Essence, and partaking their Nature, resolved to pierce and break through the *Circumference* of the Circles, and to

understand the power of him that sits upon the Fire.

22 And having already all power of mortal things, of the Living, and of the unreasonable creatures of the World, stooped down and peeped through the *Harmony*, and breaking through the strength of the Circles, so showed and made manifest the downward-born Nature, the fair and beautiful Shape or Form of God.

23 Which, when he saw, having in itself the insatiable Beauty, and all the operations of the *Seven Governors*, and the Form or Shape of God, he *smiled* for love, as if he had seen the shape or likeness in the Water, or the shadow upon the Earth, of the fairest Human form.

24 And seeing in the Water a Shape, a Shape like unto himself, in himself he loved it, and would cohabit with it, and immediately upon the resolution ensued the operation, and brought forth the unreasonable Image or Shape.

25 Nature presently laying hold of what it so much loved, did wholly wrap herself about it, and they were mingled, for they loved one another.

26 And from this cause *Man* above all things that live upon earth is double: *Mortal*,

because of his body, and *Immortal,* because of the substantial Man. For being immortal, and having power of all things, he yet suffers mortal things, and such as are subject to Fate or Destiny.

27 And therefore being above all *Harmony,* he is made and become a servant to *Harmony,* he is *Hermaphrodite,* or Male and Female, and watchful, he is governed by and subjected to a Father, that is both Male and Female, and watchful.

28 After these things, I said, *Thou art my mind, and I am in love with Reason.*

29 Then said *Poimandres,* This is the *Mystery* that to this day is hidden and kept secret; for Nature being mingled with man, brought forth a Wonder most Wonderful; for he having the nature of the *Harmony* of the *Seven,* from him whom I told thee, the Fire and the Spirit, Nature continued not, but forthwith brought forth seven Men, all *Males* and *Females,* and sublime, or on high, according to the Natures of the seven Governors.

The planets or seven spheres mentioned above are said to be in charge of different areas of life and existence; their corresponding attributes are as follows:

Luna (the Moon)

Luna is a Roman name identified with Diana, goddess of the Moon. The Moon embodies the primary female principle and women in general. The Moon's action changes and fluctuates. The Moon is primarily in charge of human emotions and imagination. When the force is expressing itself positively in a human soul its attributes are dreaminess and imagination, it gives us an adventurous spirit, it makes us spontaneous and alluring. It also controls the intuition and the quality of self-reconciliation and self-understanding. Its negative qualities or vices are those of impulsivity, instability and mental agitation. Unbalanced and unchecked it gives us mood-swings, idleness and obsession.

The Moon as also said to rule over the trades of farming, sailing and child care. In the human organism, it governs the breasts, pancreas, and the female reproductive organs.

The angel of the Moon has the power to assist in smoothing domestic problems, the growing of plants, ensuring safe journeys and acquisition of merchandise by water, successful embassies, conception, and is connected with messages, dreams, and cycles.

Mercury

Mercury is named after the wing-footed Roman messenger god. This planet's action is unpredictable and explosive. The positive attributes associated with Mercury are all things fluid such as movement, ingenuity, eloquence and precision; also the art of communication, intelligence, intuition, skill, analysis and the ability to make good judgements. Negative attributes include: craftiness, deceit, impatience, being critical, aloof and divisive.

If you are influenced by Mercury you will be drawn towards professions or activities such as teaching, lecturing, writing, advertising or communication in general; science, theatre (especially comedy), all aspects of business and commerce. In summoning the positive forces of Mercury you will find aid in acquiring knowledge. You will attract intellectual friends due to your ability to communicate intelligently and fluidly. You will achieve success in business. Mercury is also useful for magical working, apparitions and divination, for obtaining information or making calculations. Mercury also provides safety in travel. Symbols commonly associated with Mercury include: The Winged Staff (Caduceus) and the Hermetic Scroll. Within the body, Mercury has rulership over the brain, nervous system and breathing, and due to the 'quicksilver' nature it is attributed to mental alertness and concentration, helping to concentrate intellectual expression and reasoning powers.

Venus

Venus, the Planet of Love, was named after the Roman goddess. She represents all that is gentle, harmonious, beautiful and kind. Due to her link with love, she corresponds to all things connected with relationships and nurturing. Venus assists in matters of the heart and all pleasurable activities pertaining to friendships and social affairs. These positive aspects are creative and joyful. However, if these qualities are unbalanced the response can be self-indulgence and selfishness; unchecked emotions of jealousy and possessiveness. Her symbols include seashells, the mirror and the girdle. Venus presides over the human bodily functions of the kidneys, throat and para-thyroid. She helps keep balance of calcium levels and the emotions.

Sol (the Sun)

Sol is taken from the Roman name of the Sun deity, representing the primary masculine principle and men in general. The Sun is energizing and stimulating, giving us warmth and light essential for life. Self-confident leadership and power are reflections of the Sun's energy; it also promotes mental creativity, illumination and clarity. The positive outlets are loyalty, harmony and compassion; mastery through peace and spiritual enlightenment which in turn helps to prevent war, promoting friendship and harmony. Good health is also a benefit of attuning to the planetary action of the Sun. However, if these attributes are contrary, negative traits such as arrogance, egocentrism and control dominate, leading to dangerous supremacy and battle. To aspire to the Sun, you will find acting or anything where you take centre stage or a position of superiority such as executive, director and politician, appealing. Symbols associated with the Sun are the solar diadem, sunburst or Sacramental Cup. The Sun governs the heart, spine and thymus and helps to maintain youthfulness and good health in general.

Mars

The planet Mars, named after the Roman god of war. The action of this planet is sudden, forceful, and disruptive. The positive energy of Mars is competitive, dynamic and vital; also constructive anger, enthusiasm, valour and willpower. Negatively the energies can be used violently and destructively, emanating as manipulation or destructive anger, cruelty and hostile aggression. Martian traits lead to military professions or hard manual work such as blacksmithing, fire fighting or engineering using iron and steel. Mars gives the ability to be critical when making decisions, for confidence and empowerment help to destroy unwanted influences and banish enemies. Within the body, Mars governs the sex organs and the muscles and leads to a strong, magnetic aura. Symbols associated with Mars are primarily of warfare, the lance, shield and helmet.

Jupiter

Jupiter, named after the primary Roman god. Jupiter's action is order, efficiency, growth and increase. It enables good judgement, direction of benevolent power, mercy and generosity and the ability for spirituality and devotion. The opposite traits are expressed as hypocrisy, pride, smugness and greed; also dogmatism. These qualities are reflected in the kind of activities of those closely linked to Jupiter, such as philosophy and religion (priests), politics and law, civic duties, insurance and banking and academia. To be at one with Jupiter can bring good fortune in general, advancement, health, prosperity, a successful career or spiritual enlightenment. Jupiter's influence within the human organism is with the liver, pituitary glands and hormones.

Saturn

Saturn was originally named after the Roman god of agriculture. This planet is known as the taskmaster or teacher of the horoscope, influencing the ability to carry out one's duties in life; to create endurance and stability, making proper foundations. Saturn is the planet of equilibrium and limitations, teaching higher intuition and patience. Negatively the energies are hatred, impatience and coldness, brooding and autocratic. The kind of work that would suit someone attuned to Saturn would be politics and business; masonry, plumbing or clock-making; funerary preparations and the making of wills. Saturn can provide the traits useful for political activity, an aid to study for exams, to acquire esoteric knowledge, understanding the process of death and dying.

Symbols we tend to associate with Saturn are the scythe and hourglass (the Grim Reaper) the compasses and the double axe. Saturn's influence within the body is over the skin, teeth, bones, gallbladder, also the mind: passages of time (ageing and dying) and depression.

ANALYSIS OF THE RITUAL

The Ritual itself is a system of angel magic and there is very little resemblance to the regular three degrees in Freemasonry. It includes many aspects that not just Freemasons would find very uncomfortable – swearing blind allegiance to the superiors in the Order; dipping items in the blood of different creatures to give them magical powers; evocation of planetary angels during special hours of the day.[3] Most of these seem to be derived either directly or indirectly from the medieval grimoires perhaps via a text called *The Three Books of Occult Philosophy* by Heinrich Cornelius Agrippa which was written in 1533. It was in Latin so most educated people, no matter what country they resided in, could read it, including the Count. The means of magic, however, have changed little. Indeed a modern occult practitioner would find himself in familiar territory in Cagliostro's rituals. The closest existing equivalent is the planetary magic now practised by the modern occult order the *Aurum*

Solus.[4] The main difference in the Aurum Solus system is that personal contact is made directly with the planetary angels, whereas Cagliostro used a medium in the form of a young boy or girl referred to as a 'dove' in the Ritual text. The idea being that a pure child would be able to go into a trance and receive communication directly from the divine beings. This is a very common idea in both mediaeval sorcery and the traditions of ancient Egypt. We shall learn more about this later.

The rituals of Cagliostro are not the most important part of his teachings; they were merely introductions into an alchemical and occult school. We know from the documents that Apprentices met every seven weeks, Companions every five weeks and the Masters every three weeks. We also know that Apprentices trained for three years before becoming Companions, who in turn trained for a further two years before becoming Masters. In these meetings the real secrets would have been taught and one can only wonder at the inner alchemical teachings of the art taught in these Lodges.

The Ritual however does give us some exciting hints. It is probable that the students were being taught spiritual evolution through the forces of the seven planets. It may well be that the seven planets represented various Egyptian deities which were not mentioned in the Ritual for fear of persecution from the Catholic Church. Indeed it is likely that the whole Ritual has been encoded for this very purpose; as mentioned previously there is barely a mention of anything Egyptian or of a deity from that country. It is also probable that the candidate was being taught how to make magical items in the degree of Egyptian Apprentice, in which it is mentioned that the different energies of the planets can be imbued into objects if they were plunged into the blood of the corresponding animal at the correct hour of the day. By the time the candidate becomes a Master he is taught how to make a magical circle. The magic circle is a very common tool and is pictured in mediaeval grimoires exactly as the Count's ritual dictates, with four flaming pots in each quarter. The incense recommended by the Count represents the four elements – earth, air, fire and water. It is probable that from this degree the candidate was taught how to control the angels. Indeed frequent reference to controlling angels is made throughout the rituals from Egyptian Apprentice onwards, making it clear that this was a very important element in the entire text.

The First Degree – Egyptian Apprentice

Seven knocks are made on the door of the Lodge – these seven knocks represent the seven angels and seven planetary forces.

The aim of the first degree of Egyptian Freemasonry was to teach the candidate the true nature of himself, to show him of which matter he is constructed, in order that he gained self-knowledge and recognized who he truly was, vices and all. This stage in alchemy is known as *Nigredo* (blackening). It is one of the two stages of what the alchemists call the *Lesser Work*. The second stage is that of *Albedo* (whitening), a cleansing and transformational process.

If you are to be initiated into Egyptian Freemasonry the first thing you would witness would be a beautiful painting. In Freemasonry these paintings, full of mysterious symbolism, are known as *tracing boards*. Originally these images were painted on the floor of Lodges. Early Freemasons were known as 'mop and bucket' Masons because of their requests, at the taverns in which they met, for a mop and bucket to remove the markings they made on the floor. Tracing boards teach true contemplation and symbolism. They are symbols for the candidate and indeed all membership of the Lodge to speculate and contemplate upon.

In the case of Egyptian Freemasonry, the first tracing board was in the *Room of Preparation*. Depicted on it was a representation of the Great Pyramid, making a firm statement about the origins of the Order's spirituality. This is a four-cornered pyramid and the four elements (earth, air, fire and water) were said to correspond with its four corners. The fifth point is the apex of the pyramid which represents spirit. The spiritual always rules over the four elements. The meaning given is that the divine part of the man should be in charge of his will, his mind, his emotions and his body. This is the same point of symbolism that Cagliostro called *Becoming the Pentagon,* which will be covered in depth later on. The pentagon represents the spiritual aim of Egyptian Freemasonry. That of becoming a divine being ruled by the Holy Spirit.

On this tracing board was also pictured a figure of 'Time' standing outside a cavern. Many writers in the past have interpreted this as 'Time' guarding the cavern. However with the translation of the actual Ritual we discover that this is not what the intention was. 'Time' is supposed to be looking distraught, pictured as an old man having difficulty entering the cavern. The message to the candidate is that he is about to find his true self and that his true self is beyond the limitations of time; the cavern represents the inner nature of man.

The Ritual also tells us that on the left of the picture is a cornucopia, a horn of plenty. This is an object from Greek legend which is a magic horn made from a seashell that gives unlimited food and sustenance; this points to the great spiritual rewards on the path of spiritual development. We are also told that on the right there are pictured some chains and some philosophical instruments. The chains represent the limitations of our perceptions and of our negative attributes. The philosophical instruments (unfortunately we are not informed as to their exact nature) most likely represent the tools that one would use to free oneself from the chains. In reference to this, the candidates are prepared for their Masonic ritual, as are modern Masons, by having all metals removed from their person. In this case the metals represent the removal of the chains that hold back the candidate from his spiritual aspirations. This is a quite a different interpretation to that of modern Freemasonry which tends to describe this as reference to the building of King Solomon's Temple when no metal tool was heard.

The candidate having been prepared was then introduced into the temple by virtue of his ordinary Masonic qualifications, and proclaimed as a seeker of the true Freemasonry which first flourished amongst the wise of Egypt. Some references speak of the candidate kneeling before the Grand Copht, or in his absence the Master of the Lodge who then breathed upon him. There is no reference in our version of the Ritual of this happening at this particular point.

The candidate is then led into the temple which is decorated in white and blue and filled with swinging censers filled with incense to help effect moral regeneration. The white symbolizes the candidate's purity. The blue is sky-blue and is here to represent the universal nature of the spiritual goal. As the candidate changes himself he changes the world because he and the whole of existence are interlinked and interconnected.

The candidate is then led to an altar which has depictions of the Sun and Moon upon it; on the left is the Moon, on the right is the Sun and in the centre is a brazier containing a sponge saturated with alcohol. He then kneels and takes an oath of obedience to the order to keep the secrets communicated to him and to obey his superiors.

At the moment that he has taken his oath, the alcohol in the brazier is set on fire and the candidate's hand is held above the flame, between the Sun and the Moon. This represents the divine aim of alchemy – to bring all the forces in the spirit and consciousness of the candidate into divine balance and harmony. So the masculine force of the Sun and the feminine force of the Moon combine together to form a balance represented by Mercury, in this case by the divine flame under the candidate's hand. It is worth noting that although the Sun and the Moon are the most powerful of the planets, here they are representing the total sum of all the planetary forces and their opposites combining into a third great state. In fact all planets and the planetary forces must be brought into harmony – the Sun with the Moon, Mars with Venus, Jupiter with Saturn. When this is achieved there is a rebirth in the individual and he becomes divine. This is symbolized in many ways in alchemical writings, sometimes this balance is depicted by the hermaphrodite or more often it is depicted as the philosopher's stone or as Hermes. Mercury is often used as the symbol of this process and it is said to be the only planet in balance with itself.

After the oath the candidate is clothed in white with a white cloth. He is then struck three times on the right shoulder with a sword. The white cloak represents both the purity of the candidate and also his next aim which is that of self-purification. Interestingly, the word 'candidate' (from the Latin *candidatus*) actually means 'one who is robed in white'. The three strikes of the sword on the right shoulder represent the work that the candidate must undertake in the three degrees of Egyptian Freemasonry; the right arm being the arm of work and strength.

There is then delivered a catechism (a series of questions and answers) which explains much of the symbolism of the degree. The catechism of the first degree was primarily that of alchemy but the Apprentice was also entreated to enter into a search for God and to examine the self; all of this work was to be undertaken as being for the promotion of the Divine Glory. Other subjects for study were natural and supernatural philosophy. Natural philosophy was explained as the marriage of the Sun and the Moon and knowledge of the seven metals.

Question: what is signified by natural philosophy?

> *Answer: the marriage of the sun and the moon and the knowledge of the seven metals.*

The marriage of the Sun and the Moon has already been explained, however the seven metals deserve some discussion.

The seven metals and planetary correspondences are as follows:[5]

Saturn – Lead

Jupiter – Tin

Mars – Iron

Sun – Gold

Venus – Copper

Mercury – Quicksilver

Moon – Silver

or in *The Greater Key of Solomon:*[6]

> Saturn ruleth over Lead; Jupiter over Tin; Mars over Iron; the Sun over Gold; Venus over Copper; Mercury over the mixture of Metals; and the Moon over Silver.

These metals are said to have affinity with the planet that they correspond with. In fact it is a common point of magical philosophy to believe that higher forces have resonances with certain items on this Earth.

Henry Cornelius Agrippa describes it thus:

> It is manifest that all things inferiour are subject to the superiour, and after a manner (as saith *Proclus*) they are one in the other, viz. in inferiour are superiour, and in superiour are inferiour: so in the Heaven are things Terrestriall, but as in their cause, and in a Celestiall manner; and in the Earth are things Celestiall, but after a Terrestriall manner, as in an effect.

Each planet has various stones, herbs and incenses all ascribed to it. Here Cagliostro is focusing on the metals. The metals are the most important because they are used in magical ceremonies to take on the energy and spirit from the planet. But also because they represent the constructive energy of the planet that everything is created from, and in this case both forms of knowledge are suggested. The Count intends the student to know about the metals' affiliation with the divine forces of the planets but he is also, more importantly, talking about self-knowledge. When alchemists made reference to metals they meant spiritual forces manifested as matter. At this point Cagliostro is talking about the whole purpose of the first degree of Egyptian Freemasonry, which is to know one's self. So to know the seven metals is to know the seven manifested planetary forces that make up your very soul, your personality and everything about you.

The maxim given in this particular version of the manuscript is: *'Qui agnoscit martem, cognoscit artem'* – 'whoever recognizes Mars, knows art'.

'To know Mars is to know art'

There have been many interpretations of this saying. We personally believe that the main purpose of this motto is to install in the spiritual seeker the knowledge of his true self and the nature of the work ahead of him. Man is a martial creature. To fight and to struggle is in his nature. It is iron that flows in his blood – the metal of Mars.

In order to make a change to the external world, you need to struggle. All art is a fight between the way things are and the way you want them to be; in the spiritual quest, self-transformation is the objective, and in alchemy we must face all our negative qualities and win. The art which is Masonic or alchemical requires struggle, discipline and tenacity.

Another version of Cagliostro's maxim – *'Qui agnoscit mortem, cognoscit artem'* which translates as 'he who has knowledge of *death*, knows the art of dominating it', has been found in other accounts of the Ritual.[7] This also ties in perfectly with the regeneration theme of the Ritual, however, in this particular manuscript it is clearly written as *'martem'* – Mars. Whether this was a 'typo' by the French scribe or was a deliberate second meaning we shall probably never know.

The Apprentice was required to have three years of study between being initiated and becoming a Companion. During this period of learning he would delve into the alchemical teachings. It is mentioned in the text that there are workshops for the Apprentice and Companion Masons within the Lodge building. These would no doubt have been used for the various magical and alchemical tasks required of them, such as the consecration of implements and preparation of talismans, etc. The Apprentice was also required to spend three hours in meditation of the Divine every day, which by anyone's standards is a significant dedication to one's spiritual progress. The catechisms continue in the same lofty way, talking about the use of *primal matter* which can lead to immortality. The primal matter is the divine spark within each person, and of course Cagliostro saw it as his God-given task to show people how to use it.

He instructs the students on the seven-stage process which will lead to the discovery of their own divinity and states:
Seven are the transitions for perfecting the matter.

Seven are the colours.

Seven are the effects that shall complete the philosophical operation.

The seven colours he refers to are the seven colours associated with the planets, which are as follows:

Sun – Yellow or Gold

Moon – White or Silver

Saturn – Black

Mars – Red

Jupiter – Blue

Mercury – Orange or Yellow

Venus – Green, Purple or Pink

These are the colours listed by Cagliostro's contemporaries. It seems likely that Cagliostro had assigned his own colours, as later on in the Ritual we hear mention of seven steps each coloured with a planetary colour. Then in a rather confusing and typical Cagliostro-ish phrase he mentions the first five are the primary colours. Of course there being only three primary colours, this makes it very hard to decode his colour system, unless he has included black and white, which then gives us five.

He may have been using those given in *The Greater Key of Solomon* from which he appears to draw much of his teaching:

> Wherefore unto Saturn the colour of Black is appropriated; Jupiter ruleth over Celestial Blue; Mars over Red; the Sun over Gold, or the colour of Yellow or Citron; Venus over Green; Mercury over Mixed Colours; the Moon over Silver [white], or the colour of Argentine Earth.

The seven processes which Cagliostro goes on to list in rather cryptic terms refer to the initiate's own personal journey through the planets. Each planet comes with its own test and the initiates must climb the seven-stepped stairway of the planets to attain perfection.

The test of Saturn is to face your own fear of death and the temporary nature of all physical beings. Indeed, you must face a symbolic spiritual death, leaving behind the 'old' you.

The test of the Sun represents the first rebirth of the initiate. You must learn to express your ambition, your creativity and your inner beauty in harmony with the other aspects of your personality and all things around you. You must also, of course, at each stage learn to understand this force's expression in the external world. So part of the challenge of the Sun would be to learn to appreciate beauty in all things.

The challenge of the Moon is to control your imagination, to correct your mind to avoid delusion, and to become at one with the feminine aspects of your personality. The test of Mars is to master your inner aggression. People who are too aggressive would have to learn to retain their aggression; people who do not have enough aggression will have to learn to face things using anger as a tool. The challenge of Mercury is that of intellect and of learning, and to bring these into balance with the rest of the whole personality. Your intellect and your knowledge should be your servants, not the other way round.

The test of Jupiter is that of fatherhood and learning to look after yourself and those around you, and to bring these aspects into a divine balance with the other parts of the personality. And the final challenge, which is that of Venus, would be of mastering your love and sexuality. Indeed one of the biggest challenges of this stage of development would be to develop divine love and love of all things around you, who interconnect in this existence.

It should be noted that these seven steps are merely summarized above; this is to give the reader an idea of what is involved in the process. Each stage for the initiate would be an exciting, yet individual journey into both the very nature of his self and the forces underpinning the universe. It is impossible to describe the depth of experience or the nature of each challenge that would await him. In a sense this is one path that can only be understood by walking it.

The cryptic phrases associated with each of these steps are deliberately obscure. It is not a rare occurrence in any mystical path for the student to be given riddles to solve which lead to inner knowledge of the subject matter. Interestingly, the two Latin phrases represent the two processes that the candidate should master before moving on to the next degree. This is why in the next degree, the Master stands at the bottom of the stairway of five steps rather than seven. This shows that the candidate has already taken the first two steps. He has gone through a death; or rather he starts in a state of death and unawareness, which is represented by the sleeping Hermes. Hermes (Mercury) represents the spiritual self rather than the planet Mercury and in this case is threatened by the Master of the Lodge. This symbolizes the spiritual awakening being brought about by the teachings of Egyptian Freemasonry. Once the candidate is 'awake' in himself then he will discover the true nature of his self. He will discover the true nature of metal, in both himself and the world around him. Of course we all know the key to this discovery is through recognition of the beauty of divine creation represented by the Sun.

We then have a rather large section of catechisms explaining how Cagliostro believes his philosophy is superior to those published by others, his version of the history of Freemasonry, and the real meaning behind Masonic symbolism. He talks of the first matter being symbolized by the Masonic acacia, while its mercurial part is represented by the rough or unhewn stone. It is this which must be transformed via philosophical putrefaction and which then becomes the philosopher's stone.

He goes on to explain that the Masonic symbol of the blazing star has a meaning that most Masons do not know about and that it represents supernatural philosophy and is symbolized by the *heptagram* (seven-pointed star). But this being a ritual by Count Cagliostro we must have some sorcery thrown in. He goes on to explain that the star also signifies the seven angels who surround the throne of God. These angels are the intermediaries between mankind and the Divine, and to contact these beings it was required that the Egyptian Apprentice spent three hours daily in solitary meditation and prayer so as to acquire the divine aid necessary for their advancement towards perfection. This whole process is similar to that of regular Masonry in the first degree, with the notable difference of explicit esoteric practice. There is still the element of overcoming base human traits and advancing to a higher level of moral standing. The difference in Egyptian Freemasonry is that your aim is to become at one with the angels. They are the examples the seven forces your soul is to emulate.

One of the greatest difficulties that magicians encountered with the Church was their contention that angelic beings could be summoned to assist in magical practice. The seven angels, corresponding with the seven planets, were the primary spirits to be invoked. Cagliostro does not name the angels but they are called:

Kassiel – the ruler of Saturn

Michael – angel of the Sun

Raphael – ruler of Mercury

Gabriel – angel of the Moon

Zamael – ruler of Mars

Sachiel – angel of Jupiter

Anael – ruler of Venus

These seven spirits were the same as those that the Brahmans of ancient India called the seven Devas, in Persia they were called the seven Amaschapands, in Chaldea they were named the seven Great Angels, and in Jewish Cabalism we know them as the seven Archangels. These spirits are considered more perfect in essence than humans, and they are believed to be on Earth to help mortals spiritually progress. It is thought that they work out the pattern of trials that each human being must pass through, and they give an account of the individual's actions to God when the mortal has passed from the earthly plane. They are unable to interfere with human free will; it is up to the individual to make the choice between good and evil. However, when called upon, angels can assist humans in various ways. When the Egyptians wished to invoke a spirit they used something called *hekau* – 'word of power'. The word of power, when spoken aloud, would release a vibration capable of summoning spirits. Therefore the most powerful *hekau* for calling up a specific spirit in ceremonial magic is that spirit's own name.

Cagliostro has not finished his sorcery. He goes on to start educating the newly made initiate in methods of magical practice that would not seem out of place in medieval grimoires, such as *The Lesser Key of Solomon*.[8] He explains that magical implements can be made that are in resonance with the planets. He doesn't list the full range of items but he does explain how they are to be created. The process is a well-known one which has been described in works of the occult since the Middle Ages.

In order to consecrate these items, they are plunged in the blood of an animal (whether this is real or allegorical we are uncertain) corresponding to the planet. Like metals and colours, these are believed to have resonance with the planets' forces, so certain animals are supposed to have a kinship and resonance with a certain planet. The animals are never listed in the Ritual but these are the ones which are traditionally associated:

Saturn – crow, raven, spider, goat

Jupiter – eagle, swan, whale, white bull

Mars – ram, wolf, woodpecker, wasp

Sun – lion, bantam, hawk, salmon

Venus – cat, dove, dolphin, bee, tortoise

Mercury – jackal, ibis, ape, swallow

Moon – wild cat, hare, dog, owl

The hour of the planet is calculated by dividing each day into 12 equal parts. From sunrise each hour is assigned a planetary correspondence. This is normally done in accordance with the planetary orders of the days of the week but Cagliostro gives his own running order. The method is indeed given in *The Greater Key of Solomon* but the running order varies:

OF THE DAYS, AND HOURS, AND OF THE VIRTUES OF THE PLANETS

WHEN thou wishest to make any experiment or operation, thou must first prepare, beforehand, all the requisites which thou wilt find described in the following Chapters: observing the days, the hours, and the other effects of the Constellations which may be found in this Chapter.

It is, therefore, advisable to know that the hours of the day and of the night together, are twenty-four in number, and that each hour is governed by one of the Seven Planets in regular order, commencing at the highest and descending to the lowest. The order of the Planets is as follows: ShBThAI, Shabbathai, Saturn; beneath Saturn is TzDQ, Tzedeq, Jupiter; beneath Jupiter is MADIM, Madim, Mars; beneath Mars is ShMSh, Shemesh, the Sun; beneath the Sun is NVGH, Nogah, Venus; beneath Venus is KVKB, Kokav, Mercury; and beneath Mercury is LBNH, Levanah, the Moon, which is the lowest of all the Planets. It must, therefore, be understood that the Planets have their dominion over the day which approacheth nearest unto the name which is given and attributed unto them – viz., over Saturday, Saturn; Thursday, Jupiter; Tuesday, Mars; Sunday, the Sun; Friday, Venus; Wednesday, Mercury; and Monday, the Moon.

The rule of the Planets over each hour begins from the dawn at the rising of the

Sun on the day which takes its name from such Planet, and the Planet which follows it in order, succeeds to the rule over the next hour. Thus (on Saturday) Saturn rules the first hour, Jupiter the second, Mars the third, the Sun the fourth, Venus the fifth, Mercury the sixth, the Moon the seventh, and Saturn returns in the rule over the eighth, and the others in their turn, the Planets always keeping the same relative order.

However, the medieval sorcery has only just started. Next, Cagliostro explains to students about the 'paper of art'. His explanation makes it clear that this is in fact what the magicians call 'virgin parchment'. *The Lesser Key of Solomon* says in its second book:

OF VIRGIN PARCHMENT, OR VIRGIN PAPER, AND HOW IT SHOULD BE PREPARED

VIRGIN paper, or card, is that which is new, pure, clean, and exorcised, never having served for any other purpose.

Virgin parchment is necessary in many Magical Operations, and should be properly prepared and consecrated. There are two kinds, one called Virgin, the other Unborn. Virgin parchment is that which is taken from an Animal which hath not attained the age of generation, whether it be ram, or kid, or other animal.

Unborn parchment is taken from an animal which hath been taken before its time from the uterus of its mother.

Take whichsoever of these two classes of animals thou pleasest, provided only that it be male, and in the day and hour of Mercury; and take it to a secret place where no man may see thee at work. Thou shalt have a marshreed cut at a single stroke with a new knife, and thou shalt strip from it the leaves, repeating this Conjuration.

This paper is said to have no previous spiritual influence and thus makes it ideal to be drawn on and charged with the magical effect — in this case the pentagon is inscribed on the paper. Interestingly the pentagon is not used as a protective symbol as the pentagram is in more recent times; in Cagliostro's rites it is a symbol of divine authority, of strength and power.

The whole Ritual ends with a personal statement of evidence, the Orator stating that he has seen the Grand Chief or Cagliostro himself working miracles. It not hard to imagine what would be taught to the Entered Apprentice after a ritual such as this; the whole Ritual includes both the inner and outer exploration of the qualities of the planets. The initiate has been taught to recognize planetary energies and forces within himself and, in turn, that the spiritual path is one of progressing through the different planets. He has been informed that in time, using various magical implements charged with the influences of the planets, he will be able to summon angels and control them. He has been taught how to make virgin parchment and to purify himself and it is probable that within his first year of apprenticeship he will learn how to make magical talismans using the blood of an animal corresponding to the planet, in the hour of the planet, from the metal of the planet and using the magical name of the angel of the planet. Utilizing all this he can change his life favourably and, as the Count put it, 'realize wishes'.

The whole Ritual is a beautiful mix of alchemy and sorcery. In fact the outer workings being so reflective of the inner, one cannot help but to see its beauty. The inner and outer planets are discovered at the same time and the influences and powers mastered internally and externally. But once the candidate has seen his new self and has seen that the world is constructed by the divine forces, what then is the next step? This is the subject of the second degree or Degree of the Egyptian Companion.

The Second Degree — Egyptian Companion

The first thing a candidate to the second degree of Egyptian Freemasonry would notice is that the Lodge is decorated in a very similar manner to the first degree, save that it has some additional gold decoration. All represents the aim of alchemy. In this sense it is not symbolizing the Sun, with which the metal has resonance, but something more. It is symbolizing the spiritual goal of alchemy. Gold is a wonderful symbol of this because of its preciousness and also because of its resistance to both fire and water. Gold cannot oxidize like other metals and therefore is seen as being immortal.

On the tracing board is a figure of Mercury fighting with the Master of the Lodge. In fact the Master on the board is killing Mercury. This represents the process which the candidate must go through. Once he has 'woken up' and become aware of himself and has gained enlightenment as to how he and the world really works (first degree), then he must kill all of the 'old' self and finally, in the third degree, be reborn. The whole second degree is about 'spiritual death'. We also have, pictured on the tracing board, three stones – the first being the rough ashlar, the second the smooth ashlar and the third is a pyramid-shaped stone. This is a perfect example of how the Count felt that regular Freemasonry fell short. In Freemasonry, the candidate is depicted as a *rough* ashlar, a stone in its natural unhewn shape. The process of regular Freemasonry is for the candidate to gain virtue and, through self-control and discipline, to knock off any vices or negative aspect of his personality so that he can then become the *smooth* or *perfect* ashlar; a stone worthy to fit in the temple walls and able to work with the rest of society for the better good of mankind. To Cagliostro this was one step short of what the true aim should be. He wanted to go beyond being a 'good man' and to become divine. This is what the third pyramid stone, which only appears in Egyptian Freemasonry, represents.

During the ceremony the Worshipful Master holds the sword made of gold and silver. The reader will not be surprised here that it is not uncommon for magical swords to be charged and used in magical ceremonies. In this case the sword is made of silver and gold, which is extremely significant as the ancient Egyptians used to combine the two metals into a third metal called *electrum* which symbolized their divine ideal. The magic sword described here seems to have already been charged spiritually. We suspect it was charged, as in the previous ritual, by immersing it in the blood of an appropriate animal and possibly in the way illustrated in *The Key of Solomon* below.

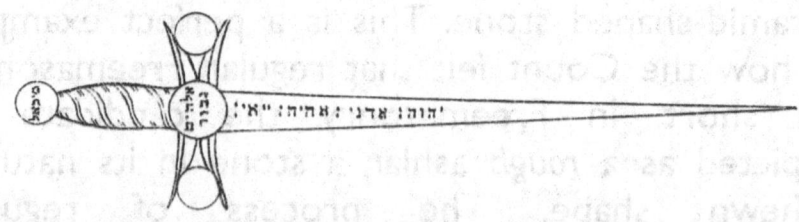

Figure 11 Magical Consecration of a Sword from The Key of Solomon

The flame-coloured ribbon that everyone wears in this degree signifies that they have gone through the vilification and dedication process in the first degree of Egyptian Freemasonry, when they held their hands over the sacred flame. It is also an allusion to the tongues of fire (Acts 12:1-4) that the disciples of Jesus had rest 'on each one of them. And they were filled with the Holy Spirit.'

The rose plaque placed on the ribbon is a symbol of the spiritual path. It is a beautiful and circular form. It makes the environment around it more pleasant by its sense and appearance. But it also has thorns. This holds the meaning that you can create something beautiful and wonderful and change the inner and outer world, but great challenges and pains are to be borne in this process. The rose is also an allusion to the ideals of the Rosicrucians, the Hermetic esoteric Order of the Rose-Cross and a branch of para-Freemasonry.

On the altar there were two glasses, one filled with wine and the other filled with leaves of gold, the symbolism of which we shall examine shortly.

The candidate is led into the *Chamber of Reflection* and taught, directly by the Orator, spiritual lessons required in order to enter this degree. The Apprentice degree was about knowing who you are and having a lesson about how the spiritual world works. It was a waking-up process. This degree was about self-purification and self-transformation.

The candidate then knocks on the door. Having mastered the first two planets, which in Cagliostro's eyes correspond to the first part of the Lesser Work of alchemy, namely the blackening process, the candidate was only required to knock five times – representing the five remaining planets.

The Lodge is then opened and the candidate is led to the foot of the throne of the Worshipful Master. He holds in his right hand a candle which represents that he has achieved the enlightenment required to pass to this degree; the Master's speech summarizes perfectly the purpose of the first degree in the work undertaken, explaining that the candidate has both learned about himself and about the nature of the intermediaries to God. He is of course referring to the seven angels.

The candidate is then fumigated using two small burners containing incense. The process of using incense to purify and bless exists in almost every spiritual tradition. The idea being that the positive spiritual energies of the incense and the intent of the fumigator will drive away any negative influences or energies within the person. This is a form of sympathetic magic; as the scent makes a person perfumed, so too does it change the spiritual qualities within him.

Henry Cornelius Agrippa describes the process:

> Some Suffumigations also, or perfumings, that are proper to the Stars, are of great force for the opportune receiving of Celestiall gifts under the rayes of the Stars, in as much as they do strongly work upon the Aire, and breath. For our breath is very much changed by such kind of vapours, if both vapours be of another like: The Aire also being through the said vapours easily moved, or affected with the qualities of inferiours, or those Celestiall, daily, and quickly penetrating our breast, and vitals, doth wonderfully reduce us to the like qualities.[9]

This is also purification by air, the second of the four elements after fire. This shows the many different levels of symbolism contained within Cagliostro's Ritual. In the first degree the candidate is purified by fire and in the second degree by air and there is a strong implication of water in the third degree.

The candidate then kneels and makes his obligation to blindly observe and obey, as in the first degree.

The Worshipful Master then clothes the candidate in a completely white robe representing his purity, and he is struck by the sword on the shoulder three times as in the previous degree. Again this represents the hard work that he should undertake using the secrets of the three degrees of Egyptian Freemasonry.

Then follows a beautiful but brief speech performed by the Master to the newly made Companion:

> By the power that I hold from the great chief, the Founder of our Order, and by the grace of God, I confer upon you the degree of Companion, and constitute you a guardian of the knowledge which we shall communicate to you by the sacred names of Helios (Sun), Mene (Moon), Tetragrammaton (sacred name of God).

This is a rendering of completeness. We have the Sun and Moon and then finally the Hebrew four-letter name of God. This name of God was said to have been received by Moses at the burning bush. It is spelt *IHVH* – the name of the God of Israel as it appears in the original Hebrew Bible. These four Hebrew letters [יהוה] are often collectively called the *Tetragrammaton* (from the Greek Τετραγράμματου, meaning 'four-letter') and is usually transliterated into *IHVH, YHWH, YHVH, JHWH* (German) or *JHVH* (English).

This name is unpronounceable because it has no vowels. Magicians and sorcerers have always been obsessed by it as it is said that he who knows how to pronounce the true name of God will gain power over him and be able to act as God. Cagliostro used to proclaim, 'To name is to define!' The belief that knowing the name of something allows you to control it has ancient roots and this is why when Moses asked God his name he answered 'I AM that I AM', in order to avoid giving his name to him. Traditionally this word was never pronounced by the Hebrew priests, it was known to very few and was a great secret and 'He who can rightly pronounce it, causeth heaven and earth to tremble, for it is the name which rusheth through the universe.'

The Tetragrammaton, *IHVH*, intrinsically means 'to be'. It represents the four elements, the four cardinal points and the four worlds of the Cabala. This magical name contains many mysteries. The four letters were arranged one above another to look like the image of a man. The different combinations of the four letters and indeed the repeating letter 'H' have great meaning. One consistency through all traditions though is that this word is powerful and can create wonderful effects. The 2nd-century BC cabalistic text *The Sefer Yetzirah*[10] describes the way that these letters were used to create the universe, and each letter corresponds to the elements air, fire and water.

> He selected three letters from the simple ones, and sealed them as forming his great Name, *I H V* and he sealed the universe in six directions.
>
> Five – He looked above, and sealed the height, with *I H V*.
>
> Six – He looked below, and sealed the deep, with *I V H*.

> Seven – He looked forward, and sealed the East, with H I V
>
> Eight – He looked backward, and sealed the West, with V H I
>
> Nine – He looked to the right, and sealed the South, with V I H
>
> Ten – He looked to the left, and sealed the North, with H V I
>
> Twelve – These are the ten ineffable existences, the spirit of the living God, Air, Water, Fire, Height and Depth, East and West, North and South.

This is interesting, given the suspected elemental structure of Cagliostro's three degrees. The Count certainly would have been aware of *The Sefer Yetzirah,* as he had a personal obsession with the Cabala. In this case Cagliostro was using the name of God to create a new universe within the candidate.

The use of the number seven is again prominent in the cabalistic teachings that were so obvious in the Ritual:

> The seven double letters produced the seven planets, the 'seven days', and the seven apertures in man (two eyes, two ears, two nostrils, and one mouth). Again, as the seven double letters vary, being pronounced either hard or soft, so the seven planets are in continuous movement, approaching or receding from the earth. The 'seven days', in like manner, were created by the seven double letters whereat they change

in time according to their relation to the planets. The seven apertures in man connect him with the outer world as the seven planets join heaven and earth. Hence these organs are subject to the influence of the planets, the right eye being under Saturn, the left eye under Jupiter, and the like.[11]

Following the speech from the Master in the Ritual the candidate is then imparted with further symbols of the primal matter in the form of gold and wine. He was given red wine to drink, which has great reflection with the Eucharist ritual of Christianity where wine is drunk representing, and indeed to some people transforming into, the blood of Jesus Christ, and bread is given to represent his body. In a sense this is Cagliostro's form of Eucharist. We imagine that to Cagliostro Jesus Christ was a symbol of spiritual rebirth just like Hermes or Adoniram. In this case both wine and gold leaf is used. The text doesn't mention it specifically, but we suspect that the gold leaf was mixed in with the wine at this point in the ritual. Gold has long been considered able to hold a magical charge. In traditional occult techniques all recipes are potentized by having heated gold plunged into them, which allows them to take on the spiritual force.

The two crystal glasses that hold the wine represent two of the pillars on the cabalistic tree – the *Pillar of Force* and the *Pillar of Form*. One pillar represents the spiritual energy of existence, while the other pillar represents both the structure and knowledge of the structure of existence. They symbolically relate to the two pillars that guided the Jews out of Egypt. The *Pillar of Force* is the pillar of flame that lit their way during the night, in this case represented by the glass of wine. The *Pillar of Form* is the pillar of smoke that slowed the pursuant Pharaoh and this is represented by the glass of gold leaf.[12] Once more we have another symbol of the 'chemical marriage' and the achievement of the alchemical goal. In this case showing to the candidate he must gain control of the forces of the universe and his self, but also gain the knowledge of the structure of existence. Knowledge and power must be combined to achieve his goal. It is also likely that the mixture was spiritually charged with divine energy or 'blessed' as the Church calls it. By experiencing this divine energy firsthand it would allow students to sense and become resonant with it in the future.

Cagliostro then explains that Adoniram is also the primal matter and must be killed. This demonstrates the great overlapping of symbolism used by the Count, the killing of Hermes/Mercury or the killing of Hiram Abiff is one and the same process, as is being reborn in the Christian faith. It's the same spiritual process but presented in a different way.

The whole presentation seems a paradox. Cagliostro is talking about the removal of the liquid part which the candidate has received in the form of the wine. How can this be? If you are supposed to kill Mercury, and killing Mercury involves removing the liquid part, which is then given to you as wine, how can Mercury represent yourself? The whole thing seems self-contradictory. The paradox is deliberate. The truth is that to gain yourself, you must first kill yourself (not in the literal sense!), and you must undergo a symbolic death. To be reborn you must first die. Before you can become one with the Divine, you must 'kill your spirit' – i.e. conquer the hold that our ego/lower self has over us.

At this point in the ceremony the Worshipful Master breathes three times on the candidate to make him a Companion. Other references to the Count's Ritual describe this happening on an initiate's reception as Entered Apprentice, but our Ritual does not state so. It is also stated that Countess Cagliostro, in her capacity of Grand Mistress of the female Lodge, breathed upon the faces of her initiates.[13] The symbolism of breathing on the surface seems obvious in references to the Christian Bible. God breathed life into Adam. In this degree the Worshipful Master breathes new life into the candidate. But could there be an Egyptian dimension to the symbolism?

The use of 'breathing' on the candidates by the Count and Countess holds a very interesting significance. It would appear at first analysis to be reminiscent of the ancient Egyptian *Opening of the Mouth* ceremony, which was used literally to open the mouth of the deceased so that they may 'breathe' once more in the afterlife, thus conferring immortality upon the soul. For the ancient Egyptians, there was nothing more terrifying than the prospect of being 'dead' i.e. not achieving the status of becoming immortal and walking with the gods. However, there is another book that was used by the Egyptians to confer immortality on the recipient and that was the Book of Breathings. It was used in a similar way to the Book of the Dead, in that it was buried with the mummified bodies and was a similar guide for the soul to achieve immortality. It was during the Greco-Roman period that the Book of Breathings became more prevalent – it was deemed to be a composition of various texts including the Book of Passing through Eternity and possibly The Book of Transformations. It would seem that this text began to supplant the lengthier Book of the Dead as the ancient Egyptian Empire began to draw to a close. Hugh Nibley writes:

> Almost any funerary text could safely be called a 'Book of Breathing', since all deal with with renewal of life and resurrection of the flesh, which for the Egyptian means breathing first of all.[14]

In *The Hor Book of Breathings* translated by Michael Rhodes, it states:

> The Document of Breathing ... shall be buried ... under his left arm near his heart

... if this book is made for him, then he will breath like the souls of the gods forever and ever.

Isis was reputed to have made the book for her brother and husband Osiris, so that it would 'cause his soul to live, to cause his body to live, to rejuvenate all his limbs'. It implores the owner to hide it and keep it secret and not to let anyone read it for it is 'effective for a man in the gods' domain so that he may live again for millions of years'.[15]

The text also talks of the need to be cleansed both mentally and physically – the heart should be purified, the front in a state of purity and the back in a state of cleanliness. It even states that the midsection should be cleansed with natron (salt) until no part of the body or mind is polluted by sin. It mentions entering the *Hall of the Two Truths* and being purified by the *Two Goddesses of Truth* (the goddess Ma' at in her twin form) also in the *Hall of Geb* (earth) and the body cleansed in the *Hall of Shu* (air). They ask that Amun breathes on him and that Ptah fashions the limbs and that he can join Re (Sun) on the horizon and his soul appears in heaven as the disc of the Moon. The soul is then made divine in the Hall of Geb.

There are also some notable biblical references to 'breath' or 'breathing on' a person that can be applied to this practice. The Bible is said to be 'the breath of God' – when the word is spoken, it is breathed out and this imbues it with the spirit. The word for 'breath' in the Bible (Hebrew *ruach* and Greek *pneuma*) can be translated as 'spirit'. The Holy Spirit is the immortal side of us, and is also called the breath of the Divine. *YHVH* – means the 'selfexistent one'; *HVH* in Hebrew means 'to breathe' or 'to become'. So *YHVH* could be interpreted as 'he who causes to breathe' or 'he who causes to become through breathing'.

St John states in John 20:22, after he has witnessed the post-Resurrection appearance of Jesus, 'When he had said this, he breathed on them and said "Receive the Holy Spirit".' So the breath and breathing is obviously a very potent symbol for imbuing the Holy Spirit onto another; by breathing life into the candidate the Master is 'making' him divine.

The Egyptian word for breathing is *SnSn*. There appears to be a wealth of meaning to this word – to smell, breathe; to exude an odour; to inhale air or the breath of life; the breath of life itself; the stench of a corpse. *SnSn* is also, conversely, the word meaning to mingle; to kiss; to unite. If it is duplicated (*snsn.s*) or written with the image of a double harpoon, it can then mean to join a company; to unite, fraternize, become a friend of, to enter a bond of brotherhood. In fact the word 'mingled' (*snsn.s* or *snsn.n.s*) when evaluated by E Otto, shows that in one instance it was actually represented by a picture of two men shaking hands – an early sign of brotherhood, of Freemasonry?[16]

Continuing with the Ritual, we are then told that a catechism is given. But it is rather disappointing as we don't seem to have the catechism of the second degree in the manuscript. We suspect that it would be very much focused on alchemical processes and those of self-purification and regeneration.

We know that from other sources Cagliostro claimed that, by the first matter when it had been transmuted into the philosopher's stone, and by the acacia (which is a symbol of immortality), the Masons would be able to enter a state of renewed youth. It would involve an ascetic existence, combined with the use of herbs and alchemical potions to quite literally purge the body of all toxins and impurities and restore it to that of an infant child's constitution. On becoming a Master, the Mason would be given the chance to take part in two 'quarantines' of Cagliostro's design, which would incorporate these processes; this we will discuss in section entitled "Cagliostro's Quarantines".

This second degree is concerned with moral and spiritual regeneration and the candidate is required to purify himself from within. There should be five years of study and digestion of the knowledge between the degree of Companion and Master. But after he has undergone this spiritual death, it is time for a glorious rebirth. This is the subject of the third and final degree of Egyptian Freemasonry.

The Third Degree – Egyptian Master

The whole third degree ceremony corresponds with the alchemical process of *Rubedo*, which means 'reddening'. This represents the total union of spirit and matter into one enlightened divine form.

In this third ceremony, things became much more complex and somewhat dramatic. The temple would be arranged as follows – on the tracing board the main symbol of the whole ceremony is the phoenix, sitting in the middle of a burning fire. The phoenix is also an Egyptian symbol for rebirth known as the *Bennu* Bird.[17] Myth has always shown the phoenix as a bird that consigns itself to the flames, only to hatch again from the ashes with beautiful plumage, able to live for a second time. It is a perfect symbol of divine regeneration and immortality. Depicted below the phoenix is a *staff of Mercury* or *caduceus* (a wand with serpents intertwined upon it). The serpents represent the two forces combined to become the 'Great Work'.[18] Below all this is a figure of 'Time', now in the form of a man looking strong and aggressive, beside which is a depiction of the Master of the Lodge ready to cut off the wings of Time. Strewn on the ground are the tools of Time, the inverted hourglass and the broken scythe. All this symbolizes the fact that the Master Mason is about to destroy the control that time has over him and become immortal.

The throne, at this time, is raised on only three steps. This represents that in Cagliostro's system the student will have now progressed through four of the planets with only three remaining to complete his final alchemical goal.

On a cushion is the magical sword of gold and silver, engraved with the magical seals of all the planets. Interestingly, in this degree we have two Worshipful Masters, both of whom wear the names of the seven angels embroidered on golden spangles.

The Lodge is opened with prayers; the first are to the Master making particular reference to the seven angels who surround the throne of God, invoking them and asking that divinity makes them compliant with the divine demands, meaning of course *their* demands.

The first part of the process of making a Master of Egyptian Lodge is asking whether anyone has any cause to believe that he is not ready, or if any other grievances may exist against the candidate. The elect then test the candidate; to see if he is patient and obedient, they tell him that in spite of the time and hard work that he has put in he is not ready to become a Master. This of course is a test to see if he really is a Master. If he has mastered himself, his emotions will not control him and he will accept the judgments of the elect without arguing. After all, he has sworn twice now to obey his superiors blindly, something no modern Mason would do. The affirmative response to the candidate's proficiency is also required from the seven angels; once this has been received the making of the Master Mason can continue.

After this process, which must be a great test to the candidate, he is then brought to the Worshipful Master. He is then dressed in the clothing of the degree, which is a white tunic with white shoes edged and knotted with a white ribbon, a girdle of blue silk and a red cordon from right to left. The symbolism of the clothing is the same as in the former degree, except in this one the blue silk represents the trial by water which is of course in balance with the trial by fire in the first degree. Note that the trial by water has not yet happened, that will be discussed later in the Ritual.

The candidate is then made to kneel and makes a solemn prayer to God and, of course, the Great Chief Cagliostro himself. The Worshipful Master, as in all the degrees of Egyptian Freemasonry, then blows over the head of the candidate three times to make him a Master Mason. The candidate is then conducted to the *tabernacle*, which in this case must have been a small room or tented area. Traditionally the Tabernacle was a portable dwelling place for the Divine presence during the Exodus of the Hebrews from Egypt to Canaan. The *Shekinah* (presence of God) resides within the Tabernacle and it becomes the 'Holy of Holies', the inner temple into which only the high priests may enter.[19] In this ritual, having in his previous degree performed his own form of Eucharist, Cagliostro is not only opening the tabernacle but is placing a person within it. This of course is blasphemy of the highest order. Not only is he having the candidate represent the spirit of God, he is placing him in the House of God. The candidate *is* God.

It is not described within the Ritual but one practice that is well known is that Cagliostro used to use a pure young boy or girl as a medium. The idea that young children are more in touch with the spirit world is not a new one and it is probable that the child would have been given something to stare into in order to be able to see angels appear. This practice is known as scrying, and the scryer often used a crystal ball or a bowl of water as the instrument to 'see'. The Egyptian demotic magical texts often made references to young boys being used for scrying purposes. A traditional practice involved the magician taking the hand of the young boy and drawing mystical figures on the palm of the hand in ink, until there was a small well of liquid. Incense was then burned and sometimes magic words were said or a piece of parchment with figures burned. The boy would then start to see figures and forms move in the ink.

It is also known that this boy was placed in a box or a tabernacle. So it is likely that within the tabernacle of the temple, the candidate was not alone, the young child known as the 'dove' was probably dressed all in white and seated before him. It is indeed mentioned in the catechism of the third degree that the candidate does meet the 'dove' within the 'inner temple'. Interestingly the symbol of a dove is often used to represent the Holy Spirit *(Shekinah),* so this meeting of the candidate and 'dove' within the inner temple is very symbolic. St Paul said:

> You are a temple of the Holy Spirit within you ... So glorify God [the spirit] within your body.

Therefore the man and the temple are the 'dwelling place' of God; he then receives the blessing of the Holy Spirit, possibly via the conduit or 'dove'. Outside the tabernacle a great prayer is made, with every member of the Lodge facing the holy name of God that is placed within the blazing star.

It is then said that the Worshipful Master shall use the power which the Great Chief has given him to cause the angel Anael (angel of the Sun) and the other divine planetary angels to appear before the candidate; most certainly this would be through the medium of the 'dove' or young child. The angels are then asked whether the candidate is ready to be received to the degree of Master. On receiving the affirmative, divinity is thanked for its grace and the candidate is retrieved from the tabernacle and led back outside the Lodge to the Chamber of Reflection.

We then come to the second stage of the ceremony of Egyptian Master. Firstly, a magic circle is made. The magic circle is an extremely common practice to all familiar with magic, witchcraft and other allied arts. It has been so for many years and continues to be used to this day. The circle represents the space wherein the magic can be worked. It represents the whole of the universe and within the circle the magician is god. The circle, because of its unity being without point and without end and having only one side, represents the divine nature and the ongoing nature of the whole of existence. In addition, the circle represents a force of protection and limitation, and because the line is unbroken the magician's energy is kept within the circle and the negative forces are kept without. Various magical texts give different techniques of drawing a circle but the principle is always the same.

In this case the circle is formed in a very similar way to that described in the *Greater Key of Solomon*. First, one of the Worshipful Masters with his magical sword goes to each quarter and draws a circle in one of each of the cardinal points. It is not mentioned, but we suspect that some elemental symbol representing each one of the four elements of earth, air, fire and water were made in each one of these circles. It is an extremely common practice in magic to summon the four elements to their respective quarters when opening a circle. Then the circle is drawn about the head of each person present. The reason for this is mysterious as it is not usual to do this in any spiritual tradition, as all those taking part in the Ritual will ordinarily be within the main circle. We infer, in this case, that it was a form of sympathy to be created with the candidate who is to be in the main large circle. The next part of the procedure is quite standard; first a nail is placed in the centre of the chamber on which a cord is tied. The cord is 6 feet long and attached to it is a piece of chalk by which a circle is drawn as the designated place for the candidate. It is the normal practice in most magical texts for the cord to be the length of the magician. We wouldn't be surprised if the cord was in fact measured to the height of the candidate so as to make the circle represent his own spirit. We then have burners with incense placed at the four quarters; each one of the four censers represents one of the four elements which will be invoked upon the circle being opened. This procedure is often prescribed and is recommended in the *Greater Key of Solomon*. Just like the planetary correspondence, the elements themselves have plants and scents which are in sympathy with their forces.

After this is completed the candidate is then fetched from the Chamber of Reflection; when he returns to the Lodge he is led to the centre of the circle and he then receives the same speech as he did upon his reception as an Apprentice. After completing the speech the

Worshipful Master speaks to the candidate – an interesting paragraph showing that some of the Count's views have a distinctly Gnostic feel to them. It ends in a sentence:

> ...you must agree to promise and vow to renounce your past life and so to arrange your affairs that you can become a free man.

This demonstrates that, to the Count, the 'free' part of Freemasonry refers to gaining freedom from the limitations of being human. Cagliostro's teachings often include the Christian premise that humans are 'sinners' and need to be restored to the state of innocence that was known before the fall of man. He believed Freemasonry was a means of becoming divine – of overcoming our limitations, weaknesses and gaining spiritual freedom.

The candidate then kneels and repeats the words exactly as the Master dictates to him. When the oath is finished all the brethren kneel and the candidate lies upon the full length of the cord, his face on the ground. At this point the candidate, who is lying within the circle, represents the entirety of himself and the entirety of the universe in one. The cord represents the creative force that made him and the universe. A pinch of each of the perfumes is then put into the fires representing the creation of the universe; the depiction of the universe being created from the four elements occurs both in the Divine Poimandres of Hermes Trismegestus and in the Christian Bible. The biblical description starts with the element of fire and the words 'let there be light' and then the creation of space and air and then the water. Finally Earth is created and the candidate is now truly a new being, a new universe.

As the candidate lies there, the Worshipful Master puts his hand on his head and Psalm 50 from the Bible is read over him. This psalm is about rebirth and about leaving the old self behind. It makes mention of purification with hyssop water. In the traditional texts on magic and sorcery this psalm is indeed read during a purifying wash with the herb hyssop mixed with holy water. Though it is not mentioned in the Ritual text, we think it is probable that at some point in the evolution of the Cagliostro Ritual, hyssop water was used and sprinkled on the candidate at this point.

The candidate is then brought to his feet, conducted to the throne, and the Worshipful Master blows over him three times, passing the red cordon around his neck, after which he shall have been blessed and touched by the angels. It is tempting to believe that this red cordon may have been the same length of twine the candidate lay on during the process in the magical circle; if so, the symbolism would be complete.

The ceremony then concludes with a speech by one of the Worshipful Masters explaining how divinity has made an agreement with Count Cagliostro to bestow on his students divine wisdom and allow them, like the biblical Jacob, to walk the ladder of the angels to heaven. This of course has a strong implication of the vision of Jacob's ladder, when he saw the angels ascending and descending to and from heaven. Jacob was at that time sleeping with his head on a rock, which has Masonic symbolism. The rock is the beginning point, the rough ashlar. The angels represent the seven angels and planetary forces, which is the path Count Cagliostro teaches you to walk.

Almost as an afterthought it is stated that the angels will now appear before the candidate and when informed (by the dove) they are in his presence the Worshipful Master and all those present shall in their hearts give thanks to the Great God. We then receive a catechism of the Master of an Egyptian Lodge, which, perhaps wisely, attempts to describe only the most obvious of the symbolism involved in the former ritual.

Cagliostro's Quarantines

Once the Egyptian Freemason had been raised to the degree of Master, he was then given the opportunity to partake in Cagliostro's famous 'Quarantines'. These two operations of rejuvenation and transmutation would each last 40 days. The French word *quarantaine* means 'a period of 40 days' and relates to the historical detention imposed on those afflicted with plague or sickness. The time period is also symbolic of other mystical or religious trials, for example, Noah's flood lasted 40 days, Kings Saul, David and Solomon ruled for 40 years, Moses spent 40 days on Mount Sinai receiving the Commandments and Jesus spent 40 days and 40 nights in the desert where he was sorely tested. It is also believed that this could possibly have been taken from the ancient Egyptian tradition of embalming the deceased for the same period of time – in *Talisman: Sacred Cities, Secret Faith*, Graham Hancock and Robert Bauval state that Cagliostro's regime was:[20]

> ...clearly modelled on the forty days of embalming in ancient Egypt reported by classical authors such as Diodorus, who called this period 'the remedy which confers immortality'...[21]

Hancock and Bauval also point out the interesting biblical quote observing when Jacob dies in Egypt:

> Joseph threw himself upon his father (Jacob), weeping and kissing his face. He ordered the physicians in his service to embalm his father ... and they did so, finishing the task in forty days, which was the usual time for embalming.

The goddess Isis is also revered for her invention of embalming and rejuvenation rites and it is no surprise that Cagliostro maintained that his Egyptian Freemasonry had also been divinely inspired by the goddess herself.

The First Quarantine

How to achieve the Pentagon and become morally perfect

Whatever his detractors may say, Cagliostro was definitely a stickler for discipline, particularly with his Egyptian Freemasons who were expected to follow a tough regime to show they were willing to transcend the levels of other mere mortals and to attempt to achieve physical and spiritual perfection. They were encouraged to engage in a strict daily routine of meditation, prayer and study, six hours of reflection, three hours of prayer and nine hours involved in the holy operations of Egyptian Freemasonry. The remaining hours were at the disposal of the individual. Cagliostro devised a plan for a building that would be specifically used for spiritual practice. He originally designed it for a house he occupied in Switzerland – it was called 'The House of Regeneration' and was equipped with rooms for meditation and seclusion.

The first Quarantine was for moral and spiritual rejuvenation and involved *How to Achieve the Pentagon*, which would lead to moral perfection. It was to be practised by 13 Master Masons together and involved a combination of magical and cabalistic elements occasionally reminiscent of the Sacred Magic of Abramelin the Mage, which would have the purpose of instructing the Mason in the teachings necessary for the understanding of the second Quarantine – *How to Rejuvenate and Become Physically Perfect*.

The Symbolism of the Pentagon

By studying and understanding the symbolism of the pentagon, they would be able to achieve the state of primitive innocence 'of which man has been deprived by sin'. This would have been through mastery of the five elements and the communication with the seven angels who were said to have impressed their ciphers and seals upon the pentagon, as in the Ritual.

The pentagon is a geometrical figure of five sides and five angles. Its essential meaning is the same as the pentangle (pentagram) which is a very common magical symbol. The top point represents the spirit, the other four represent Earth, Air, Fire and Water. Each one of these elements represents a different aspect of the human personality. Earth symbolizes the body and the instinct; air – the intellect; fire – the will; water – the emotions. They also represent, just like the planets, different aspects of physical existence – the fire element represents all energy, the air element represents matter in its gaseous form, the water element is matter in its liquid form, the earth element is matter in its physical form. Everything can be corresponded and analysed using the four elements. The pentagon points out that the correct arrangement is an interaction of the spirits and elements within a human. The idea being that the spirit should be ruling the four elements and the four elements should be in their places and doing their correct jobs, and then the human spirit is completely in line with the divine order of things. This ultimately is the aim of the Hermetic path.

Eliphas Lévi analysed the Quarantine of the Pentagon in detail:

> The precepts of moral regeneration according to the Grand Copht were as follows; 'You shall go up to Mount Sinai with Moses; you shall ascend Calvary; with Phaleg you shall climb Thabor, and shall stand on Carmel with Elias. You shall build your tabernacle on the summit of the mountain; it shall consist of three wings or divisions, but these three shall be joined together and that in the centre shall have three stories. The refectory shall be on the ground floor. Above it there shall be a circular chamber with twelve beds round the walls and one bed in the centre; this shall be the place of sleep and dreams. The uppermost room shall be square, having four windows in each of the four quarters; and this shall be the room of light. There, and alone, you shall pray for forty days and sleep for forty nights in the dormitory of the Twelve Masters. Then you shall receive the signatures of the seven genii and the pentagram traced on a sheet of virgin parchment. It is the sign which no man knoweth, save him who receiveth it. It is

the secret character inscribed on the white stone by the youngest of the Twelve Masters. Your spirit shall be illuminated by the divine fire and your body shall become as pure as that of a child. Your penetration shall be without limits and great shall be also your power; you shall enter into that perfect repose which is the beginning of immortality; it shall be possible for you to say truly apart from all pride: I am who he is. The three chambers represent the alliance of the physical life, religious aspirations and philosophical light; the Twelve Masters are the revealers whose symbols must be understood; the signatures of the seven spirits mean the knowledge of the Great Arcanum. The whole is therefore allegorical, and it is no more a question of building a house of three stories than a temple of Jerusalem in Masonry.

The Second Quarantine
How to rejuvenate and become physically perfect
This account gives a good idea of the rather punishing regime involved:
The Aspirant has to retreat with a friend in the countryside on a full Moon night in May and locked inside a room he has to suffer from a very exhausting diet for forty days' time. The diet consists of scarce food based on light soups and tender cooling laxative vegetables, distilled water

beverages or May rain. Each meal must start with a liquid, a drink and end with a solid snack as a biscuit or bread crust. On the seventeenth day of this retreat after a small emission of blood, he will start taking some white drops of secret composition. He will have to take six of them in the morning and evening, adding two a day till the thirty-second day. Another blood emission is taken this day at sunset, the following day he stays in bed till the end of the Quarantine. Then he starts taking the first grain of Original Matter, the same that God has created in order to give man immortality. Because of sin, man has lost the knowledge of it. It can't be conquered other than by a favour from the Eternal, and Masonic work. After having taken this grain the one who is going to rejuvenate becomes unconscious for three hours and in convulsions he sweats and evacuates continuously. After having come to him self and changed bed he must be fed with a pound of fat-free beef and cooling herbs. If this food makes him feel better on the following day he is given the second grain of Original Matter in a cup of broth that besides the effect of the first grain will cause him a very strong delirious fever. He will lose the skin, and the teeth and hair will fall out. On the following thirty-fifth day if the patient recovers his strength, he will soak in a bath for one hour in neither cold nor hot water. On the thirty-sixth day he will have his third and last grain of Original Matter in a glass of vintage and generous wine that will make him sleep quietly and peacefully. Then the hair grows back, the teeth too and the skin gets healed. When he wakes up he soaks in new aromatic bath and on the thirty-eighth day he will have a bath in plain water mixed with nitre. Later on he gets dressed and starts walking in his room, then on the thirty-ninth day, he takes ten drops of Balsam of the Great Master along with two spoons of red wine. On the fortieth day he will leave the house, rejuvenated and perfectly recharged.[22]

As a Phoenix rising from the ashes, the regenerated man or woman could be a:

...spirit filled with divine fire. His body as pure as that of the most innocent babe, his insight will be unlimited, his power immense. He will help to spread truth over the whole globe. Finally he will have perfect knowledge of the great chaos, as well as of good and evil, of time past, present and future.[23]

In conclusion we can see that Cagliostro's Ritual of Egyptian Freemasonry and the corresponding Quarantines were no mere trifles. It was a deeply esoteric and spiritual system of enlightenment and regeneration, hardly one that could be disregarded, as borne from neither sheer ignorance nor pride. The revelation of this work will cast a whole new light upon the life and work of Count Alessandro di Cagliostro.

CONCLUSION

During the writing of this book we have been constantly amazed at the intricate twists and turns that the challenge of unravelling Count Cagliostro's life and personality has generated. We all like to think that, after months of research, we are in the position to be able to reasonably judge the person or persons that we are writing about. After all, it is a very in-depth affair; day after day getting to know their character, their idiosyncrasies, the nuances and direction of their language and way of thinking. It is a labour of love and an intense 'friendship' that develops from this scrutiny and immersion in the very mind and soul of our subject. We have grown to like the Count; to us, he has been (as Trowbridge, Evans and Hall have all stated previously) 'a victim of calumny and ignorance'. But previous perceptions aside, we have encountered a perfect example of the metamorphoses of one man, an enigma who has left us his legacy of esoteric mastery and wisdom in the form of his life and work.

Our conclusion therefore consists of four main points.

What was 'Egyptian' Freemasonry and what did it reveal?

The discovery of an old text written in French, consisting of 110 pages written in an elegant hand and entitled 'Egyptian Masonry' excited our curiosity.

What it contained had never before been examined or analysed in great detail – what indeed was Egyptian Freemasonry and what did it reveal? These are the questions we set out to answer and here, for the first time, we have presented a complete copy in English translation. The revelation of the manuscript was quite extraordinary; we did not expect it to be such a comprehensive and esoteric masterpiece. Its foundation lies within the realm of traditional Freemasonry but its countenance is purely magical. A system of personal and spiritual rejuvenation encapsulated within the wisdom and morality of Masonry, and Chapter 5, explains what is known of the origins and development of the oldest lodges in the world. The ideas and concepts were, we argue, implanted into these lodges by William Schaw. More important, however, is the connection between Schaw's Renaissance concepts and those contained within Cagliostro's Egyptian Rite in Chapter 9.

From finding this authentic treasure, donated by Charles Morison's widow to the Grand Lodge of Scotland's Library, we have tried to prove an exciting fact – could the manuscript Ritual actually have been written by Cagliostro himself? If so, this would be a discovery of major significance. We had to know whether the manuscript we had been studying was indeed written in the hand of Cagliostro. The rumours were there and so we set about attempting to trace any document that may also have been written by Cagliostro, a task that was not to be made any easier by the lack of material left to us after the Inquisition burnt his belongings.

However, hidden away in Harvard University, was a letter from Cagliostro to his wife Seraphina. At last we would be able to compare the handwriting and hopefully be the first to prove whether the manuscript had been personally scribed. When we saw the letter we knew instantly that the manuscript of Egyptian Freemasonry in the Grand Lodge of Scotland was not written in Cagliostro's hand. We initially felt disappointed but realized that this discovery did not make the manuscript any less authentic in context, but merely showed that it was a copy of the Ritual most likely scribed by one of the brethren of the Mother Lodge of Triumphant Wisdom in Lyons. But on reading the text again we realized that we had overlooked the obvious – it had been dictated by Cagliostro. The manner in which he gives instructions makes it obvious that he was repeating the Ritual word for word and someone was copying it with great accuracy (there are but a few minor errors). Here then we have the actual words of the Masonic Magician.

Heretic or Martyr?

This book started out as a quest to find out what was in Cagliostro's Egyptian Freemasonry Ritual and, indeed, to discover what it was that infuriated the Catholic Church enough to make such an example of him. Was it because he was a Freemason? Assuredly, but so were thousands of others. Was it because he was a heretic? By the Church's standards most definitely, but so were *millions* of others.

Here we are concerned with the bigger picture. In Chapter 2 we saw that Cagliostro was banished from Paris after the Diamond Necklace Affair, despite his innocence. He was known to be a Freemason (he rarely hid his light under a bushel) and had established a Lodge of the Egyptian Rite. As he prepared to leave Paris he made some predictions (see section entitled "BANISHED FROM FRANCE") which uncannily came as close to the truth as did not matter. Yet still he and Freemasonry were not in any way considered to be part of the pre-Revolution turmoil. When the Revolution began and the mob ruled the streets, most Freemasons were executed as they were considered part of the *Ancien Régime* and not the new system of government then being forged. It was not until years after the main events had taken place that

Barruel suggested that Freemasonry was the driving force behind the Revolution. This is an identifiable feature of conspiracies – most are created after it is too late to speak to the principal witnesses or access crucial evidence. Up to this point then we have the curious situation where no one before, during, or immediately after the French Revolution suggests that Freemasonry was in any was involved, until a Jesuit priest, Barruel, writes a book at almost exactly the same time that a respected Scottish academic makes similar claims in his book. For two such eminent individuals to come to similar conclusions, at almost exactly the same time, meant to the readers that there was some truth in their claims. The hare had started running and run it still does. Everybody knows that the Freemasons were behind the French Revolution even if we can't quite prove it...

During much of the 18th century, large parts of Europe also suffered from anti-Semitism with which Freemasonry was often associated. The reasons why are beyond the scope of this book, but it is clear that using Freemasonry and anti-Semitism served a variety of purposes including religious prejudice, political ideology, personal vendettas, as well as much wider sociopolitical manoeuvrings. Some of these instances were relatively minor, petty politics used for short-term political gain; some were used for more terrifying reasons. If we combine anti-Freemasonry, anti-Semitism and being a 'heretic, dogmatic, heresiarch and propagator of magic and superstition' it is obvious why Count Cagliostro was doomed. But there was so much more to it. Cagliostro was in possession of something the Church wanted to destroy – he offered mankind a chance to reach divine enlightenment *without* a church, *without* a priest and without fear. By examining the treatment of Cagliostro we have seen how an individual Freemason has been treated because he was a Freemason.

Through this process we believe we have reached a crucial and fundamental understanding of why Freemasonry was, and still is, treated in that way. As we have seen previously (see section entitled "THE 1700s – THE NEW SYSTEM OF FREEMASONRY"), when James Anderson wrote the first constitutions for the Grand Lodge of England in 1723 and an updated version in 1738 he claimed that Freemasonry was not a religion but was another, better, way for men of all backgrounds to come together to try and improve their moral and spiritual attitudes. This concept, from a man of the cloth, must have terrified leaders of all Churches, all political parties and every other group who thought that they had the true 'message' as to how best to advance mankind. It seems to us that it was from this point that Freemasonry came under sustained attack from all quarters and those attacks have not ceased.

When Andrew Ramsay, by then a convert to Roman Catholicism, approached Cardinal de Fleury (see section entitled "A LEGACY OF PERSECUTION") he seems to have done so in the belief that the Church could make use of this new organization known as Freemasonry and even went so far as to seek the Cardinal's opinion as to what he proposed to say to an assembly of Freemasons. As we now know, Ramsay was too late and the Church had, in secret, decided to turn its face against Freemasonry. Yet one curious fact remains. As time passes, individuals and groups and their alleged errors are allowed to fade away, to be forgotten or are simply ignored. This is not the case with Freemasonry which after more than 300 years remains the subject of attack by a multitude of groups and people and for a whole host of reasons.

Balsamo and Cagliostro

Enough has been said about Joseph Balsamo. Authors, both old and new, are still divided over the dilemma — it would seem that people have been either jealous, vindictive or just plain confused with regards to the subject. Count Cagliostro was doing nothing different from many of the nobles and travellers of the era, playing around with names and heritage. The Comte de St Germain was a perfect example, in fact things that Cagliostro has said and done have been overlapped with those of St Germain and vice versa.

The two identities of Balsamo and Cagliostro continue to fight for status and we wonder if anyone will ever conclusively prove whether they were one and the same. We have never attempted to prove that Balsamo and Cagliostro were two different people, born of different parents, but what we do contend is that if they were one and the same they later became 'different people'. Balsamo's disreputable spectre has never ceased to haunt Cagliostro, but that in itself highlights the differences between the two characters. If we look at the 'official' evidence it would appear that Cagliostro, although still the bombastic bon viveur, began his biggest metamorphoses soon after he became a Freemason. There is a saying:

> Given time Freemasonry can make the spark in a good man a blazing fire.

Within a few years the negative traits of Balsamo had disappeared and the phoenix of benevolence and humanity had arisen from the blazing fire in the form of the healer, spiritual Master and evolutionary Freemason – Cagliostro! If Freemasonry had caused such an epiphany and consequent change in character, then perhaps the Craft has been seriously underestimated by some, whereas others are well aware of the potential of Freemasonry and so consider it a threat to them and their position. If this is the case, then perhaps a little compassion and admiration for the Count's transformation are in order.

The Masonic Magician

Cagliostro has been continually painted as an ignorant charlatan with no real spiritual insight or experience. He is regarded by modern Freemasons and historians as yet another historical embarrassment, a casualty of his own folly. Within this book we have been able to discover a different character – a man with superior knowledge of the occult, who was able not only to create a system of personal and spiritual development but also to leave a legacy of alchemical and metaphysical genius that has largely been ignored. It is our belief that not only was Cagliostro responsible for his unique Ritual of Egyptian Freemasonry; he was also the author of a rare occult/alchemical text known as *The Most Holy Trinosophia*. This book is usually attributed to the Comte de St Germain, but from careful study it is almost certainly the work of Count Cagliostro. So not only did Cagliostro instigate a vitally important Masonic ritual but he wrote one of the most important occult documents to ever survive. This man was a victim of gross misjudgement and blatant defamation – the friend of humanity was probably one of the greatest adepts of the past 500 years and we have allowed him to become tarred with the slurry brush of infamy through ignorance, prejudice and persecution.

When wrongs are committed, the first normal human reaction is to deny them, to forget them and to encourage others to do the same. Time, however, has a way of changing denial into shame, guilt and remorse. The Church, 400 years after the execution of Giordano Bruno, announced an official expression of 'profound sorrow' and an acknowledgement that Bruno's death was an error. This statement was made during the papacy of John Paul II (1978–2005; b.1920).

Will Cagliostro, condemned to death for being a Freemason, receive a similar posthumous expression of regret? We can but wait and hope.

ENDNOTES

Introduction

[1] During the course of researching for this book we came across many, many examples of that hatred and prejudice and so we resolved to create a new word which truly reflects that fact. We encourage other authors to adopt this more accurate term.

Chapter One

[1] *Souvenirs de Charles-Henri, Baron de Gleichen,* Paris, 1868
[2] *Memorial, or Brief for Cagliostro in the Cause of Card. de Rohan, &c.* (Fr.) by P Macmahon, 1786
[3] *Courier de l'Europe* (Courier of Europe) was a Franco-British twice-weekly periodical published successively in London, in Boulogne-sur-Mer, then again in London from 1776–92.
[4] Trebizond is a city on the southeast shore of the Black Sea. It was originally a Greek colony. It is an important centre for the converging trade routes from Central Asia and the far East.

[5] Mufti, the title of a scholar who is an interpreter or expounder of Islamic law (Sharia).

[6] The Sherif (from Sharif – meaning 'noble' or 'highborn') is a descendant of Muhammad via his daughter Fatima.

[7] Memorial, *or Brief for Cagliostro in the Cause of Card. de Rohan, &c.* (Fr.) by P Macmahon, 186

[8] www.rosicrucian-order.com

[9] Lettre du Comte de Cagliostro au people anglais: Pour server de suite à ses memoirs, London, 1786

[10] *Courier de l'Europe*, 1786

[11] Kenneth Mackenzie, *Royal Masonic Cyclopedia*, Aquarian Press, 1987, p.100

[12] *Souvenirs de Charles-Henri, Baron de Gleichen*, Paris, 1868

[13] Ibid p.30

[14] 'Sacred Marriage' in alchemical terms relates to the union of the Sun and Moon; our divine spirit with the soul and finally the body.

[15] *Memoires de la Baronne d'Oberkirch sur la Cour de Louis XVI et la Societe Francaise avant 1789*

[16] *Souvenirs de Charles-Henri, Baron de Gleichen*, Paris, 1868

Chapter Two

[1] http://en.wikipedia.org/wiki/Magic_%28paranormal%29

[2] Timothy Freke & Peter Gandy, *The Hermetica, The Lost Wisdom of the Pharaohs*, p.12

[3] It is mentioned by Idries Shah in his book *The Sufis*, that Al Hallaj may have been the inspiration for Hiram Abiff in Masonic legend – the link he believes may be the Sufi sect Al-Banna ('The Builders').

[4] Also known as *Poemandres, Poemander* or *Pimander* – meaning Man-Shepherd, an attribute to God.

[5] Anon. *Lives of the Alchemystical Philosophers*, 1815

[6] A E Waite, *The Secret Tradition in Freemasonry*, vol.2, p.152

[7] http://www.blavatsky.net/magazine/theosophy/ww/setting/mesmer.html

[8] Bergquist, 1999, pp.431–46

[9] *Mémoires de la Baronne d'Oberkirch sur la Cour de Louis XVI et la Societe Française avant 1789*

[10] www.rosicrucian-order.com

[11] The term *elixir*, has only been in use since the 7th century ad. It derives from

[12] Eliphas Lévi, *Transcendental Magic: It's Doctrine and Ritual,* Rider & Co., 1896
[13] F Ribadeau Dumas, *Cagliostro,* p.96
[14] Jean-Benjamin La Borde, *Lettres sur la Suisse,* Paris, 1783
[15] Eliphas Levi, *History of Magic,* 1860
[16] www.rosicrucian-order.com/revista_artcagl.htm

Chapter Three

[1] Manly P Hall, *The Secret Teachings of All Ages,* 1928, p.cxcviii
[2] Paul Christian, *The History and Practice of Magic,* 1870
[3] A *Lettre de Cachet* was a letter signed by the King of France, countersigned by one of his ministers, and closed with the royal seal, or *cachet.* They contained orders directly from the King, often to enforce arbitrary actions and judgments that could not be appealed.
[4] *Universal Register* became *The Times* in 1785.
[5] This was a private letter sent to a friend in France, dated 20 June 1786, but published on both sides of the Channel

and deemed to be a premonitory text outlining the downfall of the monarchy.

[6] *The Life of Joseph Balsamo* – Inquisition Biography English Translation, London, 1791
[7] W H Trowbridge, *Cagliostro – The Splendour & Misery of a Master of Magic*, Chapman & Hall, 1910
[8] F Ribadeau Dumas, *Cagliostro* p.293
[9] Ibid p.297
[10] *L'Evangile de Cagliostro*, pp.277–93
[11] Ibid p.138
[12] *The Life of Joseph Balsamo* – English translation 1791
[13] *Ist Cagliostro der Chef der Illuminaten?*, 1790
[14] *The Life of Joseph Balsamo*, p.88
[15] Ibid p.89
[16] Ibid p.85
[17] Ibid p.137
[18] Extract of a letter sent to the Judge of Strasburg by Count de Vergennes, 13 March, 1783
[19] www.theosophytrust.org
[20] Ibid

Chapter Four

[1] The Rose on the Cross relates to the Rose of Sharon (Christ) in Christianity, the Rose Croix in Freemasonry also has symbolic meaning for the Rosicrucians among others.

[2] W H Trowbridge, *Cagliostro – The Splendour & Misery of a Master of Magic*, 1910

[3] Various list – see bibliography

[4] Thomas Carlyle, 'Count Cagliostro: in Two Flights', *Historical Essays*, 1833

[5] Baring-Gould, pp.7–8. This version dates from 1228, and can be found in Roger of Wendover's *Flores Historiarum*.

[6] Ibid pp.14–15

[7] *The Life of Joseph Balsamo* – Inquisition Biography London 1791

[8] Sax Rohmer, *The Romance of Sorcery*, 1914. Rohmer was a member of the Hermetic Order of the Golden Dawn.

[9] Theosophy.org/tlodocs/teachers/cagliostro.htm

[10] The Illuminati have long been linked with Freemasonry, often erroneously. Founded in 1776 (that is almost 200 years after the first Masonic records appear) by Adam Weishaupt in Bavaria without any

Masonic authority or acknowledgement. Masonic ceremonial and practice were pirated and a number of prominent Freemasons joined their ranks. All this certainly did nothing to dissuade people that the two were closely connected.

[11] *Lucifer,* vol. V, no.29, January, 1890, pp.389–95

Chapter Five

[1] The debate has been ongoing for many years and the most comprehensive journal dealing with this subject and many others relating to all aspects is *Ars Quatuor Coronatorum (AQC)* being the *Transactions of Quatuor Coronati Lodge,* No.2076 the oldest Lodge of Research in the world.

[2] Unfortunately few remain, at least in their entirety, but the Great Hall at Stirling Castle is a lasting testament to his skill.

[3] Reproduced in full in *The Rosslyn Hoax?*, 2006

[4] The Reformation in England by comparison was not only earlier but was a consequence of the dynastic and political machinations of Henry VIII (1509–47, b.1491).

[5] Most other trades had Incorporations but, with the exception of the stonemasons, none had lodges.

[6] It would be unfair to ignore geniuses in other countries who emerged during the Renaissance. Scotland and England produced their own. Examples are Gavin Douglas, William Dunbar, Francis Bacon, Inigo Jones and William Shakespeare. Yet others such as Hans Holbein transcended national boundaries.

[7] The first mention of the Rosicrucian Order was a document: *Fama Fraternitatis Rosae Crucis* published in 1614 in Kassel, Germany.

[8] The adoption of Vitruvius's work as the 'gospel' of architecture was not immediate as it was hampered by the fact that the text was not supported by illustrations. An illustrated edition was published by Giovanni Giocondo (c.1433–1515) in 1511. The version translated into Italian by Daniele Barbaro (1513–70) in 1556 and illustrated by the architect Andrea Palladio (1508–80) became the best known because of the quality of both the translations and illustration.

[9] One of the five classical orders of architecture, the others being: Ionic,

Corinthian, Tuscan and Composite, which play a part in modern Masonic ritual.
[10] Vitruvius, *De architectura* vol.3.
[11] Platonic thought or philosophy is grounded on realism and was ideally suited to Renaissance investigative methods.
[12] *L'idea del Theatro*, 1550, briefly explains its function and construction. Frances Yates also showed that it was based on classical Roman theatre designs as described by Vitruvius. See: The Art of Memory, pp.129–59.
[13] See his epitaph above.
[14] Quoted in: *Giordano Bruno and the Hermetic Tradition* by Frances A Yates, Chicago and London, 1991, p.205.
[15] *De umbra rationis & iudicii, siue de memoriae virtute Prosopopaeia*, London, 1583/4. Quoted in: *The Art of Memory*, p.266 et seq. and *Giordano Bruno and the Hermetic Tradition* both by Frances A Yates, Chicago and London, 1991, p.199.
[16] It is a matter of conjecture but it has been suggested that because the authors of these and later manuscript rituals were not illiterate they did not feel bound by Schaw's instruction intended for illiterate stonemasons.

[17] As mentioned before, the Tower of Babel, although predating KST, was built of brick not stone and so would not have been relevant to stonemasons.

[18] An official expression of 'profound sorrow' for Bruno's death was made during the papacy of John Paul II.

[19] Exact dating was rarely given and the texts were often attributed to 'the time of Moses'.

[20] *De Rebus sacris et ecclesiaticis exercitiones XVI*, London?, 1614.

[21] See, for example: *The Origins of Freemasonry – Scotland's Century (1590–1710)*.

[22] The search and discovery of a ritual of the Scottish sort but which is clearly English in origin is the holy grail of some Masonic historians.

[23] For example see: 'A New Masonic Catechism: The Arlie MS 1705', *AQC* vol.117 which, as well as discussing the second oldest Masonic ritual in the world, provides the three oldest rituals in parallel.

[24] This also suggests that alchemists had some vague understanding of the geological process.

[25] This reached in England in 1349 and Scotland the following year.
[26] The Greeks held the belief that everything was made from Earth, Air, Fire and Water and the body humours were closely allied with these.
[27] *Exercitatio anatomica de motu cordis et sanguinis in animalibus*, Frankfurt, 1616.
[28] The lodge was said to be at 'D' and the document is for that reason also known as the Dundee MS.
[29] Freemasons know them as 'exposures' and they are usually published for profit despite the protestations of the authors.
[30] It is immediately noticeable that the document is much fuller than the earlier rituals but also that its language is much less Scottish.
[31] The left 'oxter' is the most logical being the closest to the heart!

Chapter Six

[1] See, for example, *The Temple and The Lodge* and *The Hiram Key* to name but two.
[2] *The Rosslyn Hoax?* is one of the more recent publications to seriously undermine this theory.

[3] We confess to a dislike of the term 'speculative Freemason' in this particular debate as it obscures the argument. Either the individuals concerned were stonemasons or they were not.
[4] Members of the lodge were then besieging Newcastle on Tyne and held a special meeting for this purpose.
[5] Grand Lodge MS No.2
[6] Albert Mackay, *Encyclopedia of Freemasonry*, p.1122
[7] It is perhaps significant that this Lodge, founded in 1670, contained less than 20 per cent of working stonemasons, the remainder consisting of members of the aristocracy, the Church, and numerous professions.
[8] The appeal was also directed to other religious groups but they were numerically few.
[9] There are always exceptions, Scotland being one, where Lodges regularly confer four degrees, the additional one being the Mark.
[10] Kipling was a prominent Freemason.
[11] The origins of the Royal Society lie in an 'invisible college' of natural philosophers who began meeting in the mid-1640s to discuss the ideas of Francis

Bacon. Founded officially on 28 November 1660, at Gresham College after a lecture by Christopher Wren, it was 'a College for the Promoting of Physico-Mathematical Experimental Learning'.

[12] *Nous* definition: philosophical term meaning mind/intellect or cosmic reason/mind of God.

[13] Another version of this ritual has recently been discovered. See: 'The Airlie MS 1705' in *AQC*, vol.117.

[14] Kenneth Mackenzie, *Royal Masonic Cyclopaedia*, 1877, p.96

[15] *Lucifer*, Journal Vol. V, no.29, January, 1890, pp.389–95

[16] Occasionally claimed to be Charles Edward Stuart (Bonnie Prince Charlie).

[17] Illuminism, derived from the French *illuminer*, referring to spiritual enlightenment.

Chapter Seven

[1] The papal declaration of his death is shown in the plate section and a translation is to be found on page 61. We wish to place on record our most grateful thanks to Bernardino Fioravanti, Grand

Librarian of the Grand Orient of Italy for the use of this image.

[2] If this was truly what Scottish Lodges were attempting to do then the ramifications for modern Masonic Lodges are significant.

[3] The English Reformation took place for dynastic and political reasons whereas the causes in Scotland were primarily religious.

[4] Eugen Lennhoff, *The Freemasons*, 1994, p.283

[5] He was initiated in the Horn Lodge (now known as the Royal Somerset and Inverness Lodge, No.4) the same Lodge as his fellow Scot – James Anderson.

[6] For an excellent and detailed discussion of the Oration (two of which exist) see: 'Andrew Michael Ramsay and his Masonic Oration', *Heredom* vol.1 (The annual journal of the Scottish Rite Research Society). This was followed by an interesting letter by Cyril N Batham in vol.2 regarding when and if the Oration had been delivered.

[7] It is not the purpose here to debate the theological aspects regarding Freemasonry and religious organizations but we are sure that this would be a most interesting area of research.

[8] Although some credit him as including in the Oration the idea that Freemasonry descended from the Knights Templar he never mentioned them in his Oration.

[9] Some years ago an attempt was made to count the number of Orders, Rites, ceremonies, degrees, grades, etc. which had some claim to be Masonic. The counting ceased when the figure exceeded 1,000.

[10] It is not clear if this was his real name or one he assumed in order to join a Lodge.

[11] When using the term 'anti-revolutionary' it is essential to bear in mind that French Freemasons were not actively campaigning, *as Freemasons,* against revolutionary groups, and were obeying the Masonic precepts laid down in 1723 to be a peaceable subject and obey the law of the country (paraphrased from Anderson's Constitutions).

[12] In early 1787 Charles-Alexander de Calonne (1734–1802) called an 'Assembly of Notables' and it is generally accepted as being the first specific event which led to the Revolution.

[13] Fear of the French Revolution spreading to Britain led to numerous new laws and reviews of military capabilities.

[14] James Watt was also a Freemason.

[15] The wordy title was, in full: *Proofs of a Conspiracy against all the Religions and Governments of Europe, carried on in the secret meetings of Freemasons, Illuminati and Reading Societies.* He appears to have started work on the book a couple of years prior to publication.

[16] The French title was: *Mémoires pour servir à l'histoire du Jacobinisme,* London, 1797, and was published in English under: *Memoirs of the History of Jacobinism and Freemasonry of Barruel,* translated into English by the Hon. Robert Clifford, London, 1798.

[17] It is not possible to be a true Freemason without having taken such an obligation.

[18] A Frenchman Martinez Pasquales (1727–74) was a mystic and theurgist whose writings provided the basis of the Order which was revitalized in 1890. Despite the disruptions caused by war and other upheavals the Order is today in good health.

[19]   Warrant for Genocide – the myth of the Jewish world conspiracy and the Protocols of the Elders of Zion.

[20]   Norman Cohn and his book: Warrant for Genocide, for example.

[21]   There is no doubt, however, that they would have discussed the case and applied the Masonic precepts as taught in their Lodges.

[22]   The book was published in two volumes – the first in 1925 and the second in 1926.

[23]   Named after where the government was based.

[24]   We make no implications whatsoever of motives here, merely stating the facts so far as we are aware of them.

[25]   For more details see the recently published: Two Lives, Janet Malcolm, Yale University Press, 2007

[26]   Much research requires to be done in this area and we suggest, and it is only a suggestion, that: 'the Masons might not come out looking good so why bother?'

[27]   German Freemasons were after all German and unlike Freemasons in occupied countries were permitted more latitude – e.g. they were not shot or

sent to concentration camps – certainly not in the same numbers as elsewhere.

[28] Spain was an exception in that it was not involved in the war but Freemasons suffered none the less.

[29] These measures, taken by a totalitarian Fascist regime, began just at the time *Mein Kampf* (My Struggle) by Adolph Hitler was published.

[30] Interestingly, the Gestapo was never sent to the islands and the small population may account for the lack of interest in Freemasonry.

[31] Many Freemasons, especially those in public positions (teachers, postmen and other civil servants) lost their jobs or were demoted. It is also known that a considerable number were executed.

[32] In 1942 Eichmann attended the Wannsee Conference where he acted as Secretary. This conference planned the Nazis' official policy of the Final Solution to the Jewish Question (which included many non-Jews).

[33] Of course that very act supplied the regimen with names of thousands of Freemasons.

[34] Chapter 11 – Race and Nation.

[35] This is yet another area that requires further research. What has been attempted in recent years has been hampered by a wall of silence. There is some information. See for example: http://www.grandlodgescotland.com/index.php?option=com_content&task=view&id=277&Itemid=126

[36] His son is still alive and is an active Freemason.

[37] *The Sufferings of John Coustos* 1746, reprinted at Birmingham in 1790. Editions in German and French were published in 1756, as were two editions in Boston in 1803 and 1817.

[38] Henry Wilson Coil, *Coil's Masonic Encyclopaedia*, Richmond, Virginia, Macoy Publishing & Masonic Supply Co., Inc., 1996, p.56.

[39] Reichssicherheitshauptamt – Office of the High Command of Security Service

Chapter Eight

[1] *Sabbatianism* was a 17th-century Jewish messianic movement formed around the figure of Sabbatai Zvi/Zebi (1626–76).

[2] Hiram Abiff, in Masonic ritual, is the Chief Architect of King Solomon's Temple who

was murdered by three ruffians in an unsuccessful attempt to force him to reveal the secrets of the Master Mason. This allegorical story is reconstructed in the third degree of Craft Freemasonry.

[3] C E K von der Recke, *Memoirs*, pp.116–26

[4] An invaluable 20th-century course in Hermetics is available for the serious student in Franz Bardon's *Initiation into Hermetics – The Path of the True Adept*, Merkur Publishing, 1999

[5] Manly P Hall, *The Secret Teachings of all Ages*, 'The Mysteries and their Emissaries', p.197

[6] John Hogg, *Royal Masonic Cyclopedia*, London, 1877

[7] A piece of religious music set with Psalm 50/51 to be sung within the Sistine Chapel during Holy Week, all other uses of this piece were punishable by excommunication until Mozart gave his rendition of the Miserere to Dr Charles Burney who published it in London; subsequently the ban was lifted.

[8] A E Waite, *New Encyclopedia of Freemasonry*, vols. I & II

[9] The reference to 22 letters and 'arcanum' may reflect an association between Hermeticism and the Tarot which was

used for a more profound purpose than that of mere 'fortune-telling'.

[10] *Mosaic Genesis* – the Christian version of the fall of man, similar in many ways to the Egyptian Genesis of creation.

[11] Paul Christian, *The History & Practice of Magic*, 1870

[12] Manly P Hall, *Rosicrucian and Masonic Origins*, pp.408–9

[13] *Magi* – (plural of Magus – Magician) a sacred caste of priests, originating from Egypt, Chaldea, Samaria and Persia.

Chapter Nine

No notes

Chapter Ten

[1] The *Rosetta Stone* is an ancient Egyptian artifact from c.196BC that has been instrumental in the understanding of hieroglyphic language. It is inscribed with two Egyptian scripts (hieroglyhs and Demotic) and Classical Greek. Discovered by the French in 1799, it was deciphered initially by French scholar Jean-François Champollion and has since made our understanding of the Egyptian hieroglyphs much simpler.

[2]   http://www.freemasoninformation.com/esoterica/saintjohntheevangalist.html
[3]   We are unsure as to whether this is allegorical or not!
[4]   Denning & Phillips, *Planetary Magick*, Llewellyn Publications, 1995
[5]   Henry Cornelius Agrippa, *The Three Books of Occult Philosophy*
[6]   *The Greater Key of Solomon*, Clavis Salomonis 16th-century grimoire spuriously attributed to King Solomon, involves the invocation of angels and spirits.
[7]   F Ribadeau Dumas, *Cagliostro*, English translation, George Allen & Unwin Ltd., 1967, p.140.
[8]   *The Lesser Key of Solomon*, 17th-century Grimoire inspired by *The Greater Key of Solomon*.
[9]   Henry Cornelius Agrippa, *The Three Books of Occult Philosophy* Chap. XIIII. *Of Perfumes, or Suffumigations, their manner, and power*
[10] Sefer Yetzirah, Book of Creation
[11] http://en.wikipedia.org/wiki/Sefer_Yetzirah
[12] 'And in the morning watch The Lord in the pillar of fire and of cloud looked down upon the host of the Egyptians,

and discomfited the host of the Egyptians' (Exodus 14:24 RSV)
[13] A E Waite, *Secret Traditions in Freemasonry*
[14] Hugh Nibley, 'What is The Book of Breathings?', *BYU Studies*, vol.11, no.2 (Winter, 1971), pp.153–87
[15] Michael D Rhodes, *The Hor Book of Breathings: A Translation and Commentary*, Foundation for Ancient Research and Mormon Studies, Provo, Utah, 2002
[16] E Otto, *Das 'Goldene Zeitalter' in Religions en Egypte*
[17] The Bennu Bird represents the 'soul of Ra', 'He Who Came Into Being by Himself' – the Egyptian phoenix.
[18] *Great Work* – the last two stages of alchemical transmutation (*Coagulatio* and *Rubedo*) *Lesser Work* – the first stages of alchemical transmutation (*Nigredo* and *Solutio*).
[19] *Shekinah* – Hebrew word used to denote the dwelling or settling presence of God, believed by some to represent the feminine principle of God.
[20] In the mummifying process it took 40 days for the body to be completely dried out and safe from decay. Often a further 30 days were needed for

beautifying and dressing the body, hence the often quoted 70 days for the full embalming process.
[21] Hancock & Bauval, *Talisman: Sacred Cities, Secret Faith*, Element Books, p.362
[22] Eliphas Lévi, *The History of Magic*, 1860
[23] F Ribadeau Dumas, *Cagliostro*, 1967, p.148

APPENDIX I

A list of those influenced by the Hermetic tradition (by no means exhaustive)

The Artists

Sandro Botticelli (c.1444–1510) – Italian Renaissance painter
Leonardo da Vinci (1452–1519) – Tuscan polymath
Albrecht Dürer (1471–1528) – German painter and mathematician
Girolamo Francesco Maria Mazzola (1503–40) known as Parmigianino – Italian painter and printmaker
Philippe Jacques de Loutherbourg (1740–1812) – English painter (of French origin), inventor and alchemist
William Blake (1757–1827) – English poet, visionary, painter and printmaker

Scientists, Doctors and philosophers

Plato (c.428–348BC) – Greek philosopher
Roger Bacon (1214–94) – English Franciscan Friar and philosopher
Nicolaus Copernicus (1473–1543) – Polish astronomer and founder of heliocentric cosmology

Tycho Brahe (1546–1601) – Danish astronomer, astrologer and alchemist

Giordano Bruno (1548–1600) – Italian priest, philosopher, cosmologist and occultist

Sir Francis Bacon (1561–1626) – English philosopher, statesman and essayist

Galileo Galilei (1564–1642) – Italian physicist, mathematician, astronomer and philosopher

Michael Maier (1568–1622) – German physician and alchemist

Sir Thomas Browne (1605–1682) – English author and expert in medicine, religion, science and esoterica

Elias Ashmole (1617–92) – English antiquary, politician, astrologer, alchemist and early speculative Freemason

Sir Isaac Newton (1642–1727) – English physicist, mathematician, astronomer, natural philosopher and alchemist

Carl Jung (1875–1961) – Swiss psychiatrist and founder of analytical psychology

Herbert Silberer (1882–1923) – Viennese psychologist, contemporary of Freud, Adler and Jung

Writers and poets

Olympiodorus of Thebes (born c.380, active c.412–25) – Egyptian historical writer and poet

William Shakespeare (1564–1616) – English playwright and poet

John Donne (1572–1631) – Jacobean poet and preacher

Alexander Pope (1688–1744) – English poet and satirist

Percy Bysshe Shelley (1792–1822) – English Romantic poet

Mary Shelley (1797–1851) – English writer, including the novel Frankenstein

William Butler Yeats (1865–1939) – Irish poet, dramatist and member of the Hermetic Order of the Golden Dawn

Occultists, Magicians and Alchemists

Maria the Jewess also known as Maria Prophetissa (c.3rd century AD) – an early Western alchemist and inventor of important alchemical apparatus including the three-armed distillation chamber or still

Abu Musa Jābir ibn Hayyān, also known as Geber (c.721–c.815) – Muslim polymath and alchemist

Abu Nasr Muhammad ibn al-Farakh al-Fārābi (c.872–950/951) – Persian scientist, philosopher and alchemist

Abū Alī al-Husayn ibn Abd Allāh ibn Sīnā (980–1037), known as Avicenna – Persian polymath, alchemist and physician

Artephius (c.12AD) – attributed author The Secret Book of Artephius

Albertus Magnus (1193–1280) – German Dominican friar, scientist and alchemist

Thomas Aquinas (1225–74) – Italian Roman Catholic priest and student of Albertus Magnus

Arnold de Villeneuve (Villanova) (c.1240–1311) – French healer, doctor and alchemist

Pope John XXII (1244–1344) – French Prelate and friend and student of Villeneuve

Pietro D'Apone (b.1250) – Italian physician, alchemist and astrologer, tortured (died in prison) and consequently burned in effigy by the Inquisition

Raymond Lully (c.1235–1316) – Spanish scholar and alchemist

Jean de Meung (c.1250–c.1305) – French author, poet and alchemist

Alain de L'Isle (b.c.1128–d.1298) – French alchemist known as the 'Universal Doctor'

Nicolas Flamel (c.1330–1417?) – French alchemist

Christian Rosenkreuz (c.1378–1484?) – legendary founder of the Rosicrucian Order (Order of the Rose Cross)

Bernard of Treves (1406–90) – German alchemist

Johannes Trithemius (1462–1516) – German Abbot and occultist, his students included Agrippa and Paracelsus

Dr Johann Georg Faust (1466–c.1540) – German alchemist, astrologer and magician

Henry Cornelius Agrippa von Nettesheim (1486–c.1535) – German magician, writer, alchemist and Astrologer

Paracelsus (1493–1541) – Swiss alchemist and doctor

Sir George Ripley (1415?–1490) – English alchemist, wrote The Compound of Alchymy; or, the Twelve Gates leading to the Discovery of the Philosopher's Stone

John Dee (1527–1609) – English occultist, philosopher and mathematician

Edward Kelley (1555–97) – English magician

Robert Fludd (1574–1637) – English physicist, astrologer, alchemist and mystic

Jacob Böhme (1575–1624) – German Christian mystic

Emanuel Swedenborg (1688–1772) – Swedish scientist, theologian and Christian mystic

Count de St Germain (c.1710–c.84) – inventor and alchemist

Dom Antoine Joseph Pernety (1716–96) – French Dominican monk and alchemist, created the Swedenborgian Rite

Martinez Pasqually (c.1727–74) – French Freemason and mystic, founded Ordre des Chevalier Maçons Élus Cohen de L'Univers/Order of Knight Masons, Elect Priests of the Universe

Franz Anton Mesmer (1734–1815) – German-born healer

Louis-Claude Saint-Martin (1743–1803) – French philosopher known as le philosophe inconnu

Eliphas Lévi (1810–75) – French occult author and magician

John Yarker (1833–1913) – English Freemason, author and occultist

Gérard Encausse, known as Papus (1865–1916) – Spanish-born physician and occultist, founder of the modern Martinist Order

George Ivanovich Gurdjieff (? 1866–1949) – Armenian-Greek mystic

Aleister Crowley (1875–1947) – English occultist, writer and mystic, member of the Hermetic Order of the Golden Dawn

Manly Palmer Hall (1901–90) – Canadian author and mystic

Israel Regardie (1907–85) – English occultist and author

Franz Bardon (1909–58) – Czech naturopath and magician

APPENDIX 2

Planetary Correspondences used by Cagliostro and his Contemporaries

	Planet	Archangel	Intelligence	Spirit	Hebrew	Greek	Colour
1	Saturn	Kassiel	Agiel	Zazel	Shabbathai	Kronos	Black
2	Jupiter	Sachiel	Iophiel	Hismael	Tzedeq	Zeus	Blue
3	Mars	Zamael	Graphiel	Bartzabel	Madim	Ares	Red
4	Sol	Michael	Nakhiel	Sorath	Shemesh	Helios	Gold
5	Venus	Anael	Hagiel	Qedemel	Nogah	Paphié	purple
6	Mercury	Raphael	Tiriel	Taphtartharath	Kokab	Hermes	yellow
7	Luna	Gabriel	Shelachel	Chasmodai	Levanah	Mene	Silver

	Planet	Element	Pillar	Animals	Mythological
1	Saturn	Earth	Boaz	crow, raven, spider, goat	chimæra
2	Jupiter	Water	Jachin	eagle, swan, whale, white bull	unicorn, hippogriff
3	Mars	Fire	Jachin	ram, wolf, woodpecker, wasp	basilisk, werewolf
4	Sol	Air	Yang	lion, bantam, hawk, salmon	phoenix, griffin
5	Venus	Fire	Boaz	cat, dove, dolphin, bee, tortoise	mermaid, siren
6	Mercury	Water	Both	jackal, ibis, ape, swallow	twin serpents
7	Luna	Air	Boaz	wildcat, hare, dog, owl	harpy, hydra

	Planet	Trees	Herbs/plants	Incenses/perfumes
1	Saturn	yew, cypress	ivy, hemlock, amaranth, nightshade, hemp	asafoetida, scammony
2	Jupiter	fig, oak, cedar, chestnut	sage, nutmeg, hyssop	saffron
3	Mars	pine, holly	wormwood, ginger, nettle, basil, radish	dragon's blood, pepper
4	Sol	acacia, bay, rowan	sunflower, marigold, peony, saffron	olibanum, cinnamon
5	Venus	elder, fruit trees	rose, hyacinth, geranium, thyme, myrtle, liquorice	sandalwood, myrtle
6	Mercury	birch, aspen, mulberry	marjoram, caraway, fennel, mandrake, lavender, dill	mastic, storax, white sandal
7	Luna	willow, almond, coconut palm, bay, hazel, papaya	lotus, gourds, mushroom, opium poppy, moonwort	camphor, aloes, jasmine

	Planet	Gemstone	Metal	Day
1	Saturn	black onyx, jet, anthracite	lead, antimony	Saturday
2	Jupiter	amethyst, sapphire, lapis lazuli	tin, zinc	Thursday
3	Mars	ruby, garnet, bloodstone	iron, all steels	Tuesday
4	Sol	topaz, chrysolite, heliodor, zircon	gold, gold-like alloys	Sunday
5	Venus	emerald, turquoise, jade, malachite	copper, all bronzes	Friday
6	Mercury	opal, fire opal, agate, serpentine	quicksilver, aluminium	Wednesday
7	Luna	moonstone, pearl, quartz, fluorspar	silver, platinum	Monday

GLOSSARY

alchemy The word is derived from the Arabic *al-kimia,* which refers to the preparation of the stone or elixir by the Egyptians. *Kimia* comes from the Coptic *khem* alluding to the fertile black soil of the Nile delta. The word refers to the primordial or first matter, the 'One Thing' through which all creation manifests. Alchemy, then, is the Great Work of nature that perfects this chaotic matter.

apron Main item of Masonic regalia (others being jewels, sashes/cordons, badges of office). The Masonic apron is almost certainly descended from the stonemason's apron but is now only of symbolic importance.

arcana Arcana ('magical secrets') are archetypal influences that transcend time and space.

ashlar, rough An undressed stone as delivered from a quarry.

brother/brethren The terms by which Freemasons refer to each other singularly and collectively.

candidate A person who seeks, or is nominated for, initiation/office in Freemasonry.

cowan A non-Freemason often considered to be someone seeking to obtain the 'secrets' of Freemasonry without passing through the normal degrees.

elixir The elixir of the alchemists is essentially a liquid version of the philosopher's stone – it may then perfect any substance. When applied to the human body, the elixir cures diseases and restores youth.

entered prentice 'Prentice' is the original Scottish word for apprentice. When joining a lodge (and taking the first ceremony) the prentice was entered (written) into the lodge records, thereby becoming an entered prentice.

Entered Apprentice The first degree of Freemasonry.

Fellow Craft The second degree of Freemasonry

first matter The primordial chaos that is fashioned into reality – it is the physical manifestation of the 'One Thing'. In alchemy it is the base material for all creation – *materia prima*.

Five Points of Fellowship Contained in the earliest Masonic rituals it is a lesson about relationships between Freemasons. Occasionally symbolized by a five-pointed star.

freemasons Stonemasons who worked in 'sandstone' – 'freely worked stone'.

Freemasons Men, today, who are members of a Masonic Lodge and who have no connection with working stonemasons.

Freemasonry The organization which is comprised of Masonic Lodges and which descended from earlier stonemasons' lodges.

gavel A small hammer, usually wooden, often seen in auction houses or courts, and used by the Master and Wardens to keep order within the Lodge. Scottish Lodges normally use a maul rather than a gavel.

gold Gold is the most perfect of the metals. For the alchemist, it represented the perfection of all matter on any level, including that of the mind, spirit, and soul.

Grand Copht(a) Title taken by Egyptian high priests, used by Cagliostro as founder and Chief of Egyptian Freemasonry.

Grand Lodge The 'head office' of a group of Lodges and their members. Usually having jurisdiction over a specific geographic area. There are exceptions where several Grand Lodges coexist in some countries.

Grand Orient Almost identical to a Grand Lodge except that many do not strictly adhere to the ancient landmarks of Freemasonry (such as the belief in a Supreme Being).

heresy A theological or religious opinion or doctrine maintained in opposition, or held to be contrary, to the Roman Catholic or Orthodox doctrine of the Christian Church, or, by extension, to that of any Church, creed, or religious system, considered as orthodox. By extension, heresy is an opinion or doctrine in philosophy, politics, science, art, etc., at variance with those generally accepted as authoritative.

heretic A heretic is a person who expresses or acts on opinions considered to be heresy.

Hermes Trismegistus (Thrice Greatest) Syncretism of the Greek god Hermes and the Egyptian god Thoth – both deities of writing and magic in their respective cultures.

Hermetics (Hermeticism) A system of philosophical and religious beliefs based primarily on the teachings of Hermes Trismegistus.

Installation The ceremony whereby the Master of a Lodge is 'installed' into office.

lodge (stonemasons) The meeting place of stonemasons where other stonemasons were initiated. These admitted non-stonemasons until some became recognizable as modern Masonic Lodges.

Lodge (Masonic) Most people accept that a Lodge is a meeting place of Freemasons and is the basic 'unit' of Freemasonry where the first three degrees are conferred. It is not a place. Whist this is true, a Lodge is more accurately described as a gathering of Freemasons who are meeting for the purposes of Freemasonry. In that sense the place is of secondary importance.

maul A stonemason's primary working tool. A small, very heavy bell-shaped hammer used to strike a chisel or other working tool in order to shape stone in a particular way. Scottish Masonic Lodges tend to use this instrument rather than a gavel in recognition of their stonemasons' ancestry.

Mason A Freemason.

mason A stonemason.

Masonist A term used to describe an anti-Mason. **Masonophobe** A term also describing an anti-Mason.

mercury (metal) Mercury, also known as quicksilver. Alchemists believe that mercury transcends the solid and liquid states, heaven and Earth, life and death. It symbolizes the god Hermes.

Mercury Name of the planet and also the Greek god.

natron Salt. Used by the Egyptians for embalming and cleansing.

Ouroboros The serpent that devours itself. An ancient symbol of eternity and the principle that 'all is One'.

passed/passing Having taken the Fellow Craft degree the Freemason is said to have been *passed* to the second or Fellow Craft degree.

pentagon A five-sided shape used in geometry and Hermetics (five elements in balance).

preceptory The meeting place of Knights Templar, also the basic 'unit' of the Masonic Order of Knights Templar.

prentice Scottish word for apprentice.

raised/raising Having taken the third or Master Masons' degree the Freemason is said to have been raised to the High and Sublime degree of Freemasonry.

speculative A word used to differentiate a Freemason from a stonemason but this can cause confusion where someone is employed as a stonemason but is also a member of a Masonic Lodge. Increasingly writers are using the terms stonemason and non-stonemason to make it clear exactly what kind of individual is under discussion.

temple Masonic Lodges are frequently referred to as being Masonic Temples. This causes confusion when it is assumed (as it often is) that Freemasonry must be a religion because it holds meetings in a temple. However this is quite incorrect. The earliest rituals refer to masons meeting in the porch or entrance to King Solomon's Temple. The entrance is not sacred and there is no religious observance. The meetings did not take place in the Temple but it seems laziness had led Masons as well as others as to incorrectly refer to Lodges as Temples.

traditional history Each 'branch' of Freemasonry has an emphasis which is uniquely it own. Modern Craft Lodges concentrate on the building of King Solomon's Temple whereas another branch of Freemasonry will deal with something quite different – the chivalric ideals of the Knights Templar, for example. Freemasonry is therefore like a family, a unit, but each individual member has its own character.

Thoth/Djehuti Ibis-headed Egyptian god of writing and magic – he is known as the *scribe of Ra*.

Worshipful Master The Master Elect of the Lodge.

BIBLIOGRAPHY

Agrippa Von Nettesheim, Heinrich Cornelius. *The Three Books of Occult Philosophy: A Complete Edition*, Llewellyn Publications, US, 1993

Andrews, Richard, *Blood on the Mountain*, Weidenfeld and Nicholson, 1999

Ashlar Magazine, various vols. – 1997 to date, Circle Publications Ltd., Helensburgh

Auld & Smellie, *The Free Masons Pocket Companion*, Edinburgh, 1765

Balsamo, Giuseppe, calling himself Count Alessandre di Cagliostro, *Memoires Authentiques pour servir a l'histoire du Comte de Cagliostro*, Paris, 1785

Baigent, Michael, and Leigh, Richard, *The Temple and the Lodge*, Corgi Books, 1997 (First published by Jonathan Cape, 1989)

Baigent, Michael, and Leigh, Richard, *The Elixir and The Stone – Unlocking the Ancient Mysteries of the Occult*, Penguin Books Ltd. 1998 (First published by Viking, 1997)

Baigent, Michael, and Leigh, Richard, *The Inquisition*, Viking, London, 1999

Barber, Malcolm, *The New Knighthood – A History of the Order of the Temple*, Canto, 1998 (First Published by Cambridge University Press, 1994)

Barberi, Monsignor, *The Life of Joseph Balsamo, commonly called Count Cagliostro: containing the Singular and Uncommon Adventures of that extraordinary personage, from his Birth till his Imprisonment in the Castle of Saint Angelo*, translation from original proceedings published at Rome by Order of the Apostolic Chamber, Dublin, 1792

Bardon, Franz, *Initiation into Hermetics*, Merkur Publishing Inc., 2001

Bardon, Franz, *The Practice of Magical Evocation*, Merkur Publishing Inc., 2002

Bardon, Franz, *The Key to the True Kabbalah*, Merkur Publishing Inc., 2002

Barrett, David V, *Secret Societies – from the Ancient and Arcane to the Modern and Clandestine*, Blandford, A Cassell Imprint, London, 1997

Bombast von Hohenheim, Philipp Aureolus Theophrastus, also called Paracelsus, *Hermetic and alchemical writings. Now for the first time faithfully translated into English edited with a biographical preface, elucidatory notes, a copious hermetic vocabulary and index*, edited by Waite, Arthur Edward, London, 1894

Bredin, Jean-Denis, *The affair: the case of Alfred Dreyfus*, Sidgwick & Jackson, London, 1987, translated by Jeffrey Mehlman

Bronner, Stephen E, *A Rumour about the Jews. Reflections on Antisemitism and the Protocols of the Learned Elders of Zion*, St. Martin's Press, New York, 2000

Budge, E A Wallis, Sir, *The Book of the Dead*, (rev. ed.), Arkana, London, 1985

Burns, James, *A Sketch of the History of the Knights Templars*, Edinburgh, 1837

Calcott, Wellins, *A Candid Disquistion of the Principles and Practices of the Most Ancient and Honourable Society of Free and Accepted Masons*, London, 1769

Calmet, Augustine, *The Phantom World*, Wordsworth Editions Ltd., Ware, 2001. First published as: *Dissertations sur les apparitions des anges, des démons et des esprits. Et sur les revenans et vampires de Homgrie, de Boheme, de Moravie et de Silésie*, Paris, 1746

Chailley, Jacques, *The Magic Flute Unveiled: Esoteric Symbolism in Mozart's Masonic Opera*, Inner Traditions Int., 1992

Cheyne, W, *The Free-Mason's Pocket Companion*, Published by the Printer, Edinburgh, 1752

Christian, Paul, *The History and Practice of Magic*, 1870

Churton, Tobias, *Freemasonry – the Reality*, Lewis Masonic Publishing Ltd, Surrey, 2007

Churton, Tobias, *T he Golden Builders: Alchemists, Rosicrucians and the First Freemasons*, Weiser, 2005

Clarke, J R, 'A new look at King Solomon's Temple and its connection with Masonic Ritual', in *Ars Quatuor Coronatorum (AQC)* Vol.88, London, 1975

Cohn, Norman, *Warrant for Genocide. The Myth of the Jewish world-consiracy and the Protocols of the Elders of Zion*, 1st edition, Eyre and Spottiswoode, London, 1976

Cohn, Norman, *The Pursuit of the Millennium*, Frogmore, 1978

Cooper, Robert L D, *Freemasons, Templars and Gardeners*, ANZMRC (Australian and New Zealand Masonic Research Council), Melbourne, 2005

Cooper, Robert L D, *The Rosslyn Hoax?*, Lewis Masonic Publishers Ltd., 2006

Cooper, Robert L D, *Cracking the Freemason's Code*, Rider, London, 2006

Cornwell, Rupert, *God's banker: an account of the life and death of Roberto Calvi*, Victor Gollancz Ltd, London, 1983

Coustos, John, *The Sufferings of John Coustos for Freemasonry*, printed by W Strahan, for the author, London, 1746

Daraul, Arkon, *Secret Societies – A History*, Tandem, London, 1969

David, Rosalie, *Religion and magic in ancient Egypt*, Penguin, London, 2002

Davies, Peter, and Lynch, Derek, *The Routledge Companion to Fascism and the Far Right*, Routledge, London, 2002

Donaldson, Gordon, *Scottish Historical Documents*, Neil Wilson Publishing Ltd., Glasgow, 1997

Dumas, F Ribadeau, *Cagliostro*, Translated by Elisabeth Abbott, George Allen & Unwin Ltd, London, 1967

Dyer, Colin, *Symbolism in Craft Freemasonry*, Lewis Masonic Publishers Ltd., Shepperton, 1976

Eched, Sam, *Authentic or Distorted Hebraism*, Privately printed. (A gift to the authors for which we are extremely grateful)

Evans, Henry Ridgely, 'Cagliostro and his Egyptian Rite of Freemasonry', *The New Age Magazine*, The Scottish Rite, Southern Jurisdiction, Washington DC, 1919

Faÿ, Bernard, *Revolution and Freemasonry 1680–1800*, Little, Boston, 1935

Firminger, Rev. W K, 'The Romances of Robison and Barruel', in *AQC*, Vol.50, London, 1940

Fischer, Klaus P, *The History of an Obsession – German Judeophobia and the Holocaust*, The Continuum Publishing Group Inc. New York, 1998

Flanders, Judith (ed.), *Mysteries of the Ancient World*, Seven Dials, 1999 (First published by Weidenfeld & Nicolson 1998)

Freke, Timothy, and Gandy, Peter, *The Hermetica: The Lost Wisdom of the Pharaohs*, Piatkus, 1997

Fry, Lesley (Mrs Lesley Shishmarev), *Waters flowing Eastward. The war against the kingship of Christ*, Editions R.I.S.S. Paris, (2nd edition) 1933

Funck-Brentano, Frantz, *The Diamond Necklace*, trans, Greening & Co. London, 1911

Gilbert, Adrian, *The New Jerusalem – Rebuilding London: The Great Fire, Christopher Wren and the Royal Society*, Bantam Press, London, 2002

Grand Conclave [of Scotland], *Statutes of the Religious and Military Order of the Temple as Established in Scotland*, Privately printed, 1843

Hall, Manly P, *The Secret Teachings of All Ages*, H S Crocker, 1928

Hall, Manly P, *The Most Holy Trinosophia*, The Phoenix Press, California, 1933

Hall, Manly P, *Freemasonry of the Ancient Egyptians*, The Philosopher's Press, Los Angeles, 1937

Hamill, John, *The Craft: A History of English Freemasonry*, Auarian-Crucible, 1986

Hamill, John, and Gilbert, Robert (eds.), *Freemasonry – A Celebration of the Craft*, Greenwich Editions, London, 1998

Hannah, William W T, *Darkness visible, A revelation & interpretation of Freemasonry*, Saint Austin Press, London, 1963 (10th edition)

Haslip, Joan, *Madam Du Barry – The Wages of Beauty*, Tauris Parke Paperbacks, London, 2005

Haven, Dr Marc, *L'Maître Inconnu Cagliostro. Étude Historique et Critique sur la Haute Magie*, Éditions Pythagor, Paris, 1932

Heckethorn, Charles William, *The Secret Societies of All Ages and Countries*, 2 vols., New York University, 1965

Henderson, George David, *Chevalier Ramsay*, Thomas Nelson & Sons Ltd., London, 1952

Hoffman, Robert L, *More than a trial – the struggle over Captain Dreyfus*, New York Free Press, New York, 1980

H.R.H. Prince Michael of Albany, *The Forgotten Monarchy of Scotland – The True Story of the Royal House of Stewart and the Hidden Lineage of the Kings and Queens of Scotland*, Element Books Ltd., 1998

Holden, Andrew, *Jehovah's Witnesses – Portrait of a Contemporary Religious Movement*, Routledge, London, 2002

Hollis, Christopher, *A History of the Jesuits*, Weidenfeld & Nicolson, London, 1968

Jacob, Margaret C, *Living the Enlightenment: Freemasonry and Politics in Eighteenth-Century Europe*, Oxford University Press, Oxford, 1991

Jung, Carl Gustav, *Answer to Job*. [Researches into the relation between psychology and religion by means of a study of the Book of Job and of the incarnation of Christ] Trans. R F C Hull, Routledge and Kegan Paul, London, 1979

Jung, Carl Gustav, 'Answer to Job', in *Psychology and Religion: West and East*, London, 1981

Kaplan, Aryeh, *Sefer Yetzirah: The Book of Creation*, Jason Aronson Inc., 2000

Kallis, Aristotle A (ed.), *The Fascism Reader*, Routledge, London, 2003

Khaler, Lisa, 'Andrew Michael Ramsay and his Masonic Oration', *Heredom*, Vol.1 (1992), Scottish Rite Research Society, Washington DC

Knight, Stephen, *The Brotherhood: The Secret World of the Freemasons*, Granada Publishing Ltd., London, 1984

Knoop, Douglas, and G P Jones, *The Scottish Mason and the Mason Word*, Manchester University Press, 1939

Knoop, Douglas and G P Jones, *A Short History of Freemasonry to 1730*, Manchester University Press, 1940

Knoop, Douglas, and G P Jones & Douglas Hamer (eds.), *The Early Masonic Catechisms*, published for the Quatuor coronary Lodge, No.2076, London by Manchester University Press, 1963 (2nd Edition)

Knoop, Douglas, and G P Jones, *The Genesis of Freemasonry*, Manchester University Press, 1947

Lane, John, *Masonic Records 1717–1894 by John Lane*, 2nd edition, London, 1895 (First published in 1887)

Laurie, Alex, *The History of Freemasonry drawn from Authentic Sources of Information with an Account of the Grand Lodge of Scotland from its Institution in 1736 to the Present Time*, Edinburgh, 1804

Lennhoff, Eugene, and Frame, Einar (trans.), *The Freemasons*, Lewis Masonic Publishing, Middlesex, 1978

Lévi, Eliphas, *Transcendental Magic*, Weiser Books, (new edition), 1968

Lévi, Eliphas, *The History of Magic*, trans. A E Waite, Weiser Books, 1999

Lomas, Robert, *The Invisible College – The Royal Society, Freemasonry and the Birth of Modern Science*, Headline Book Publishing, 2001

Longerich, Peter, *The Unwritten Order – Hitler's Role in the Final Solution*, Tempus, Stroud, 2003

Lyon, D Murray, *History of the Lodge of Edinburgh (Mary's Chapel), No.1. Tercentenary Edition*, The Gresham Publishing Co., London 1900

Memoires de la Baronne d'Oberkirch sur la Cour de Louis XVI et la Societé Francaise avant 1789

Mackenzie, Kenneth, *Royal Masonic Cyclopedia*, Aquarian Press, 1987

MacKenzie, Norman (ed.), *Secret Socities*, Holt, New York, 1967

Mathers, S Liddell MacGregor, *The Key of Solomon the King* (Clavicula Salomonis), London, 1888

McCalman, Iain, *The Seven Ordeals of Count Cagliostro*, Century, 2003

Mecklenburg, Counseiller du Duc de, *The Temple of Solomon with all its Porches, Walls, Gates, Halls, Chambers, Holy Vessels, the Altar of Burnt-Offering, the Molten Sea, Golden-Candlesticks, Shew-Bread, Tables, Altar of Incense, the Ark of the Covenant, with the Mercy-Seat, the Cherubims, &c. As also The Tabernacle of Moses* ... London, 1725

Meikle, Henry W, *Scotland and the French Revolution*, MacLehose & Sons, Glasgow, 1912

Messori, Vittorio, *The Ratzinger Report* (trans. Salvator Attanasio & Graham Harrison), Ignatius, San Francisco, 1985

Nilus, Sergyei Professor, *The Jewish peril: Protocols of the learned elders of Zion*, anonymously printed London, 1920 (subsequently translated by George Shanks)

Parker, Derek, *Casanova*, Sutton, Stroud, 2002

Phillips and Denning, *Planetary Magick*, Llewellyn Publications Ltd., Woodbury, MN, 1995

Photiadès, Constantin, *Les vies du Comte de Cagliostro*, Editions Grasset, Paris, 1932

Piatigorsky, Alexander, *Who's Afraid of Freemasons?*, Harvill, London, 1997

Plaidy, Jean, *The Queen of Diamonds*, Robert Hale, London, 1995

Prichard, Samuel, *Masonry dissected: being a universal and genuine description of all its branches from the original to this present time. As it is deliver'd in the constituted regular lodges ... To which is added, the author's vindication of himself*, London, 1730

Ridley, Jasper, *John Knox*, Clarendon, Oxford, 1968

Ridley, Jasper, *The Freemasons*, Constable, London, 1999

Roberts, J M, *The Mythology of Secret Societies*, Secker & Warburg, New York, 1972

Robison, John, *Proofs of a conspiracy against all the religions and governments of Europe, carried on in the secret meetings of Free Masons, Illuminati, and reading societies. Collected from good authorities by John Robison*, Edinburgh, 1798

Robinson, John J, *Born in Blood – The lost secrets of Freemasonry*, M Evans and Company, Inc., 1989

Rohmer, Sax, *The Romance of Sorcery*, Methuen, London, 1914

Rosslyn, The Earl of, *Rosslyn Chapel*, The Rosslyn Chapel Trust, 1997

Ruddiman, Auld and Company, *The Free Masons Pocket Companion*, Published by the Printer, Edinburgh, 1761

Short, Martin, *Inside the brotherhood: further secrets of the Freemasons*, Granada Publishing Ltd., London, 1983

Smout, T Christopher, *A History of the Scottish People 1560–1830*, Fontana Press, 1985 (First published by Collins Publishers 1969)

Souvenirs de Charles-Henri, *Baron de Gleichen*, Paris, 1868

Stewart, T M, *Symbolism of the Gods of the Egyptians*, A Lewis, London, 1978

Stevenson, David, *The First Freemasons – Scotland's Early Lodges and their Members*, Second Edition, The Grand Lodge of Scotland, 2001 (First published by the Aberdeen University Press 1988)

Stevenson, David, *The Origins of Freemasonry – Scotland's Century 1590–1710*, Cambridge University Press, 1988

Stewart, Trevor, *English Speculative Freemasonry: Some Possible Origins, Themes and Developments*, Prestonian Lecture 2004, privately printed, Sunderland, 2004

Tait, Peter, Brown, James and Tait, John, *The Freemasons Pocket Companion*, published by the Printers, Glasgow, 1771

Todd, Margo, (ed.) *Reformation to Revolution – Politics and Religion in Early Modern England*, Routledge, London, 1995

Trowbridge, William R H, *Cagliostro*, Brentano's, New York, 1910

Tyson, Donald, *The Power of the Word: The Sacred Code of Creation*, Llewellyn Worldwide, Woodbury, MN, 2004

Waite, Arthur Edward (ed.), *The Alchemical writings of Edward Kelly* (translated from the Hamburg edition of 1676), London, 1893

Waite, Arthur Edward, *The Book of Ceremonial Magic including the rites and mysteries of Goetic theurgy, sorcery and infernal necromancy*, Rider, London, 1987 (new edition)

Waite, Arthur Edward, *Devil-worship in France or the question of Lucifer. A record of things seen and heard in the secret societies according to the evidence of initiates*, Thomas Vaughan, London, 1896

Waite, Arthur Edward, *The Brotherhood of the Rosy Cross: being records of the House of the Holy Spirit in its inward and outward history*, Rider, London, 1924

Waite, Arthur Edward, *The Secret Tradition in Freemasonry*, Kessinger Publishing Co, Facsimile edition (Aug 1997)

Walker, D P, *Spiritual and Demonic Magic. From Ficino to Campanella*, Sutton Publishing, Stroud, 2000

Wartski, Lionel, *Freemasonry and the Early Secret Socities Acts*, privately printed, Natal, South Africa, 1983

White, Michael, *The Pope and the Heretic, A True Story of Courage and Murder at the Hands of the Inquisition*, Little, Brown & Company, London, 2002

Yates, Frances A, *The Art of Memory*, Routledge and Paul, London, 1966

Yates, Frances A, *Giordano Bruno and the Hermetic Tradition*, University of Chicago Press, Chicago, 1964

Index

A
Abbey of St Germain de Prés, 75
Aberdeen Lodge, 249
Adam, 325
Adoniram, 395, 396, 415, 485
Adoptive Freemasonry, 26, 27, 335, 337
Affair of the Diamond Necklace, 2, 23, 97, 99, 101, 122, 129, 162, 175, 180
Affair of the Necklace (film), 186
African Architects, 75, 271
Agardi, Endreinek, 171
Age of Enlightenment, 35, 63, 258, 261, 262, 263, 273
Agrippa, Henry Cornelius, 45, 75, 203, 452, 479
Ahasuerus (Ahasverus), 166
Airlie MS, 224, 229
Aitcheson's Haven Lodge, 241
Akhenaton, 46
Al Hallaj, 39
Albedo, 455
Albertus Magnus, 54, 229
alchemy, 18, 20, 56, 58, 60, 75, 80, 84, 86, 89, 92, 210, 212, 228, 229, 232, 234, 236, 237, 275, 341, 342, 437, 439, 455, 476
  bans on, 58
  Emerald tablet, 46, 48, 54
  and Scottish stonemasonry, 228, 229, 232, 234, 236, 237
Aleph, 92
Alexander, Anthony, 241, 243
Alexander, William, 241, 243
Alexander the Great, 37
Althotas (tutor), 6, 8, 11, 12, 92, 93
America or United States, 175
  Freemasonry in, 89, 178

American Constitutions, *273*
American Revolution, *175*
Amis Réunis Loge, Paris, *297*
Ananiah, *320*
Anderson, James, *249, 251, 253, 254, 258, 263, 266, 273*
angel,
   see seven angels,
Angiolini, Luiggi, *156*
animal magnetism, *71*
animal spirit, *234*
Anne of Denmark, *190, 218*
Antonini, Carlo, *120*
Apollo, *92*
Apple Tree Tavern, *249*
Aquino, Chevalier Luigi d'*, 11, 12, 31*
Arcane Schools (Yarker), *322*
architecture, *205*
   and the human body, *205*
Art of Memory, *198, 208, 210, 215, 216, 218, 220, 224, 239*
'as above, so below', *41, 46, 48, 54, 73*

Ascent of Elijah, The (Loutherbourg), *180*
Ashmole, Elias, *241, 245*
astrology, *54, 60, 210, 232, 275*
Aurum Solus, *453*
Austria, *69, 71*
   Masonophobia in, *289, 313*

B
Bacon, Roger, *54, 58*
Baghdad House of Wisdom, *39*
Balsamo, Guiseppe 'Joseph', *106, 108*
Balsamo, Lorenza, *106*
Bannockburn, Battle of, *239*
Barclay, Archibald, *192, 195*
Bardon, Franz, *171*
Barruel, Abbé Augustin, *293, 295, 297, 299*
Bartolozzi, Francesco, *83*
Bastille, *31, 97, 105, 175, 177*
Bauval, Robert, *501*
Bavarian Illuminati,
   see Illuminati,

Bellonne, Sir, *12*
Benedict XIV, Pope, *112, 287, 289*
Benedictines, *75*
Berardi, Matteo, *120*
Bester, Alfred, *186*
Bhagavad Gita, *258*
Bienfaisante Lodge, *335*
Bible, *258, 443, 487, 499*
Big Bang theory, *42*
Bismark, Duke of, *271*
black death, *234*
Black Magic (film), *185*
Blake, William, *73, 180*
Blavatksy, Helena Petrovna, *158, 177, 178, 183*
Blevary, Madame, *18*
blood-letting, *234*
Bode, J Johann Christoph, *129*
Boehme, Jacob, *67, 203*
Boileau, Pierre, *15*
Boticelli, Sandro, *203*
Bottini, Lorenzo Prospero, *122, 152, 156, 158*
Bourbon, Duchesse de, *337*
Bourges, Archbishop of, *114*

Boyle, Robert, *203*
brain, *234, 236*
Bramante, Donato, *205*
'breathing', *485, 487, 489*
Brotherhood of Luxor, *71*
Brunelleschi, Filippo, *203*
Bruno, Giordano, *171, 203, 215, 216*
Brussels, *20*
Buccleuch, Francis Scott, Duke of, *251*
Buddhism, *37*
Bulwer-Lytton, Baron Edward, *180*
Burrows, Simon, *102*

C

caduceus, *448, 492*
Cagliostro, Count Alessandro di, *224, 263, 273*
  Acharat (given name), *6, 92*
  Affair of the Diamond necklace, *2, 23, 97, 99, 101, 122, 129, 162, 175, 180*
  and alchemy, *18, 20, 56, 84, 86, 89, 92*

and alphabet of the Magi, *348, 350, 352, 354, 355*
arrest by Inquisition, *106, 110, 122*
assumes name Count de Cagliostro, *11*
banishment from France, *101, 162, 291*
Barruel's references, *295, 297*
Bastille imprisonment, *2, 31, 97, 175*
Bordeaux vision, *331, 333*
and Cardinal de Rohan, *80, 83, 86*
Castel Sant'Angelo imprisonment, *110, 124, 156*
Catholic re-education, *116, 118*
character, *160, 162, 164*
death and burial, *154, 156*
death sentence commuted, *145, 158*
Declaration of Sentence, *112, 114*
Egypt, Asia and African travels, *11, 18*
Egyptian Freemasonry, see Egyptian Freemasonry,
escape rumours, *171*
European travels, *20, 21, 23, 26, 27, 29, 31, 162*
and elixir of life, *86, 89*
and Freemasonry, *15, 16, 18, 63, 241, 258, 271, 275, 341, 342, 344, 346*
'Friend of Mankind', *41, 95*
Giuseppe Balsamo identity, *106, 108, 110*
good name vouchsafed, *142*
as Grand Copht, *78, 101, 102, 122, 133, 135, 323, 342*
healing powers, *23, 26, 29, 31, 83, 84, 86, 89*
and Hermeticism, *6, 11, 35, 45, 83, 341, 342*
Illuminati revolutionary theory, *128, 129, 174, 175, 177, 180*

immortality claims, *167, 169*
influence on creative minds, *178, 180, 183, 185, 186, 355, 356*
interrogation and trial by Inquisition, *75, 92, 114, 128, 129, 131, 133, 135, 137, 139, 140, 142, 145, 167*
Jesuit agent theory, *177, 178*
Letter to the English People, *15, 108*
Letter to the French People, *105, 175*
love for Jews, *137, 139*
in London, *15, 16, 18, 20, 101, 102, 105, 106, 108, 110*
and Lord George Gordon, *105, 106*
in Lyons, *31, 333, 335*
marriage, *12, 15*
and Masonic Convention in Paris, *31, 95, 97, 267, 269*
in Mecca, *8, 11*
memorial, *102*
mission, *33, 41, 63, 120, 122, 322, 323*
New World Order theory, *178*
papers burned, *112*
parentage, *2, 4, 6*
in Paris, *83, 84, 95, 97, 99, 101*
pommade pour la visage, *86*
and Prince Raimondo di Sangro, *75*
psychic powers, *77, 78, 80, 83, 84, 354*
Quarantines, *501, 503, 506, 507*
religious nature, *137*
in Rome, *12, 15, 110, 112, 114, 116, 118, 120, 122*
Rosicrucian connection, *93*
Rue St Clair house, *95, 101*
and Saint Germain, *63, 64, 65*
San Leo imprisonment, *145, 146, 148, 150, 152, 154, 156, 158*
seal, *16, 18, 89, 92, 185*
séances, *26, 77, 78, 80, 95*

Seraphina's betrayal, *118, 120, 122, 124*
Supreme Council of France speech, *342, 344, 346, 348, 350, 352, 354*
Cagliostro, Countess Seraphina Feliciani, Countess di, *106, 110, 118, 162*
   Bastille imprisonment, *99*
   betrayal of Cagliostro, *118, 120, 122, 124*
   Convent of Santa Appolonia, *110, 145*
   Egyptian Grand Mistress, *20, 21, 337, 339, 341, 485*
   escape rumours, *171*
   European travels, *20, 21, 23, 26, 27, 29, 31, 162*
   initiation into Freemasonry, *15, 16*
   Inquisition testimony, *124, 126, 128*
   insanity and death, *158*
   in London, *15, 18, 20, 102*
   Lorenza Balsamo identity, *106, 108*
   marriage, *12, 15*
   reasons for return to Rome, *114, 116*
   reversion to Catholicism, *116*
   Saint Germain visit, *63*
Cagliostro (Carpi), *186*
Cagliostro (comic book), *186*
Cagliostro, Aventurier, Chemiste et Magicien (film), *185*
Cagliostro – Liebe und Leben eine Grossen Abenteurers (film), *185*
Cagliostromantheum (magic show), *185*
Camillo, Giulio, *215*
Cappello, General, *309, 313*
Caramaniea, Princess of, *11*
Cards of Cagliostro, *183*
Carlyle, Thomas, *162*
Caroly, *185*
Carpi, Piero, *186*
Carr, William Guy, *299*
Cartaphilus, *166*

Casanova di Seingalt, Count Giacomo, *108*
Casaubon, Isaac, *222*
Casket of Cagliostro, *183, 185*
Castel Sant'Angelo, *110, 124, 156*
Catherine II (the Great), *27, 29, 313*
Catholic Mass, *140*
Catholicism, *279*
   Cagliostro's 'conversion', *116, 118*
   Seraphina's reversion, *116*
ceremonial magic, *322, 323*
Champollion, Jean-François, *437*
Channel Isles, *309*
Charles VI, *289*
Cheiro (Count Louis Hamon), *183*
chemical wedding (conjunctio), *27, 439, 443, 444, 485*
Chetwode Crawley MS, *224*
Chinese alchemy, *58, 86*
Christian IV, *190*
Christian mysticism, *45*
Christian occultism, *322*
Christianity, *37, 437, 484*
   and Hermeticism, *222*
   Swedenborg's reform, *73*
Church, *63, 162, 453*
   anti-Semitism, *139*
   case against Cagliostro, *140, 142, 145*
   Egyptian Freemasonry condemned, *133, 135, 137, 139, 140, 142, 145*
   heretic and schismatics, *285, 287*
   hostility to Freemasonry, *75, 110, 112, 128, 129, 131, 269, 271, 279, 282, 283, 285, 287*
   proposed amalgamation with Egyptian Freemasonry, *116, 120*
   toleration of Hermeticism, *222*
Church of Scotland, *216*
Clemenceau, Georges, *301*
Clement V, Pope, *16*

Clement X, Pope, *279*
Clement XII, Pope, *112, 282, 283, 285, 313*
Clement XIII, Pope, *271*
Clement XVI, Pope, *12*
conspiracy theories, *174, 175, 177, 178, 180, 183, 185, 186, 299*
Constantine, Emperor, *39*
Constitutions of the Free Masons (Anderson), *273*
   first (1723), *249, 251, 253*
   second (1738), *254*
Convention of Wilhelmsbad, *271*
Copley Medal, *258*
Cordier de Saint-Fermin, l'Abbé, *174*
Cosi fan Tutte (Mozart), *71*
Coston (Cofton), George, *18, 320, 322*
Count Cagliostro (Tolstoy), *180*
Courier de L'Europe (newspaper), *4, 16, 102, 105, 106*

Courland, Duchy of, *23, 323*
Court de Gébelin, Antoine, *174*
Coustos, John, *313*
Coxe, Daniel, *273*
Cranmer, Bishop, *129*
Crata Repoa, *75, 77, 271*
Crillon, Duc de, *31*
Cromwell, Oliver, *129*
Crowley, Aleister, *183*
Crown Ale House Lodge, *247*
Crudeli, Tommaso, *269*
Cruz, Carlos, *186*

D

da Costa, Hippolyto Joseph, *313*
Da Vinci, Leonardo, *203, 205*
Darwin, Erasmus, *263*
DC Comics, *186*
De Architectura (Vitruvius), *205*
de Conti, Prince, *293*
de Fleury, André-Hercule, Bishop of Fréjus, *279*

de Lasalle, Commandant, 31
de Morande, Charles Theveneau, 15, 16, 102, 105, 106, 108, 110, 183
De Postate et Sapientia Dei (Ficino), 41
de Ricci, Scopio, Bishop of Pistoria, 287
De umbris idearum (Bruno), 216
De Vita Libra Tres (The Three Books of Life) (Ficino), 325
Deceived, The (Catherine the Great), 27
Deceiver, The (Catherine the Great), 27
Dee, Arthur, 203
Dee, John, 45, 203
Démeunier, Jean-Nicolas, 273
Denmark, 215
Desaguliers, John Theophilus, 249, 251, 258, 263, 287, 289
Di Sangro, Prince Raimondo, 75
Diana, goddess, 446
Dicson (Dickson), Alexander, 203, 216
Diocletian, 58
Divine Cagliostro, The (sculpture), 178
Divine Code, 258
Dombrowski, General, 156
Donatello, Donato, 203
Doria, Cardinal, 145, 146, 148, 150, 152, 154
Doric architecture, 205
doves (child mediums), 26, 77, 93, 339, 341, 432, 453, 493, 495
Dreyfus Affair, 299, 301, 305
Druids, 258
du Barry, Madame, 78, 80, 97, 102
Dumas, Alexander père, 89, 180
Dunfermline Abbey, 201
Dunkerly, Thomas, 263

E

Eco, Umberto, *186*
Edict of Nantes, revocation (1685), *287, 289*
Edinburgh Lodge, *192, 241, 243*
Edinburgh Register House (ERH) MS, *220, 224, 261, 262*
Egypt, *11, 18, 261*
Egypt, ancient, *46, 247*
   alchemy origins, *56*
   and Freemasonry, *261, 262*
   Hermeticism in, *45, 222, 367, 369*
   hieroglyphs, *41, 212, 215*
   initiation rituals, *75, 77*
   Opening of the Mouth ceremony, *487*
Egyptian Book of Breathings, *487*
Egyptian Book of the Dead, *18, 261*
Egyptian Freemasonry, *120, 128, 177, 188, 192, 243, 297, 320, 322, 323, 325, 327, 329, 331, 333, 335, 337, 339, 341, 342, 344, 346, 348, 350, 352, 354, 355, 356*
   alleged influence on fraternal societies, *178*
   Cagliostro's inspiration for, *11, 18, 320*
   Cagliostro's lectures on, *327, 329, 331*
   Church amalgamation proposed, *116, 120*
   Church condemnation, *112, 133, 135, 137, 139, 140, 142, 145*
   female initiates, *180, 335, 337, 339, 341*
   Leipzig refusal, *23*
   and Magic Flute, *180, 355, 356*
   and Order of Philalethes, *95, 97, 267, 269*
   in Poland, *29*
   Seraphina's disinterest, *114, 116*
   structure, *335, 337, 339, 341, 342, 344, 346, 348, 350, 352, 354, 355, 356*

in The Hague, *20, 21*
Egyptian Freemasonry Ritual, *93, 323, 357, 359, 361, 363, 365, 367, 369, 371, 373, 375, 376, 378, 380, 382, 384, 386, 388, 390, 392, 395, 396, 398, 400, 402, 404, 406, 408, 410, 412, 413, 415, 416, 418, 420, 422, 423, 425, 427, 429, 430, 432, 433*
    analysis, *450, 452, 453, 455, 458, 459, 461, 462, 464, 466, 468, 470, 472, 474, 476, 478, 479, 481, 484, 485, 487, 489, 492, 493, 495, 497, 499, 501, 503, 506, 507*
    Cagliostro's Quarantines, *501, 503, 506, 507*
    degrees,
        first (Apprentice), *327, 335, 365, 373, 375, 376, 378, 380, 382, 384, 386, 388, 390, 392, 395, 396, 398, 400, 402, 404, 406, 408, 453, 455, 458, 459, 461, 462, 464, 466, 468, 470, 472, 474, 476*
        second (Fellow Craft or Companion), *329, 335, 365, 408, 410, 412, 413, 415, 416, 453, 476, 478, 479, 481, 484, 485, 487, 489, 492*
        third (Master), *335, 365, 418, 420, 422, 423, 425, 427, 429, 430, 432, 433, 453, 492, 493, 495, 497, 499, 501*
        fifth, *329*
    understanding, *435, 437, 439, 441, 443, 444, 446, 448*
Egyptian Genesis, *325*
Eichmann, Adolf, *309*
electrum, *478*
Elias, *133, 390*
Elijah, *322, 325, 327*
elixir of life, *86, 89, 229*
Elected Cohens (Elus-Cohens), Rite of, *65, 67, 69, 93*
Emerald Tablet, *46, 48*
    commentary, *54*
    Newton's translation, *48*

Encausse, Gerard (Papus), *69*
Encyclopaedia Britannica, *291, 293*
England, *215, 216*
    Freemasonry in, *108, 224*
    Grand Lodge of, *243, 245, 247, 249, 253, 263, 266, 273, 277, 287, 289*
Englund, Robert, *186*
Enlightenment, *63, 258, 261, 262, 263, 266, 267, 269, 271, 273*
Enoch, *86, 133, 322, 325, 390*
Erotic Rites of Frankenstein (film), *186*
Esperance Lodge, *15, 16, 108, 162*
Eucharist, *484*
Evans, Henry Ridgley, *185*
Exodus, *167, 169*

F

Falk, Rabbi Hayyim Samuel Jacob, *320, 322*
Faÿ, Bernard, *302, 305*

Fénelon, François, Archbishop of Cambrai, *279, 287*
Ferdinand V, *287*
Feuille Villageoise, *114*
Ficino, Marsilio, *41, 325*
Figuier, Louis, *97*
First World War, *69*
Flamel, Nicolas, *86*
Flamel, Pernelle, *86*
Florence Lodge, *269*
Florentine Inquisition, *313*
Foucault's Pendulum (Eco), *186*
Founding Fathers, *273*
Fowler, William, *216, 218*
France, *71, 73, 215, 311*
    Cagliostro's Supreme Council speech, *342, 344, 346, 348, 350, 352, 354*
    Freemasonry in, *266, 267, 301*
    Grand Lodge (Grand Orient) of, *89, 174, 266, 279, 291, 335, 342*
    Masonophobia (Vichy France), *302, 305, 307*

see also French Revolution,
France, Anatole, *301*
Franco, General Francisco, *266, 287, 313*
Franklin, Benjamin, *174, 175, 273, 302*
Fratres Lucis, *71*
Frauenfeld, *73*
Frederick II, *75, 190, 271*
Freemasonry,
    Adoptive, *26, 27, 335, 337*
    and alchemy, *56, 437*
    alleged role in French Revolution, *139, 175, 289, 291, 293, 295, 297, 299, 302*
    and ancient Egypt, *261, 262*
    Cagliostro and, *15, 16, 18, 63, 241, 258, 271, 275, 341, 342, 344, 346*
    Church hostility, *75, 110, 112, 128, 129, 131, 269, 271, 279, 282, 283, 285, 287*
    degrees,
        first (Entered Apprentice), *16, 224, 256*
        second (Fellow Craft), *16, 224, 256*
        third (Master Mason), *16, 256*
    establishment of (1717), *243*
    famous Freemasons, *262, 263*
    global spread, *178, 263, 266, 267, 269, 271, 273*
    and Hermeticism, *41, 60, 63, 222, 224, 239, 341, 342*
    ideals, *253, 254, 256, 258*
    Judeo or Masonic 'conspiracy', *299, 305, 309, 311, 313*
    Knights Templar theory, *239*
    Masonic Convention, Paris, *31, 95, 97, 267, 269*
    mystical and spiritual elements, *258, 261*
    new system, *243, 245, 247, 249, 251, 253, 254, 256, 258*
    persecution, *275, 277, 279, 282, 283, 285, 287, 289,*

291, 293, 295, 297, 299, 301, 302, 305, 307, 309, 311, 313
speculative, *241, 245, 256*
transition from stonemasonry, *224, 239, 241, 243, 256*
Freke, Timothy, *39*
French Revolution, *101, 112, 120, 122, 164, 357*
  alleged role of Freemasonry, *139, 175, 289, 291, 293, 295, 297, 299, 302*
  Cagliostro conspiracy theory, *174, 175, 177*
Fry, Miss, *18, 20*

G
Galen, Claudius, *234*
Gandy, Peter, *39*
Gébelin, Antoine Court de, *174, 342, 344, 346, 348, 350, 352, 354*
Genesis, *199*
George I, *249*
George II, *313*
Gerard, M, Judge of Strasburg, *142*
Germany,
  Freemasonry in, *75, 271, 273*
  Nazi Masonophobia, *301, 302, 309, 311, 313*
Gestapo, *302, 305, 309*
Ghezzi, Father, *116*
Gillray, James, *108*
Gleichen, Baron de, *2, 21, 29, 31, 164, 269, 435*
Goebbels, Joseph, *313*
Goering, Herman, *309, 313*
Goethe, Johann Wolfgang von, *180*
gold, *229, 232, 461, 476, 478, 484*
Golden Dawn, Hermetic Order of the, *167*
Goose & Gridiron, *243, 245, 247*
Gordon, Lord George, *105, 106*
Graf von Cagliostro, Der (film), *185*
Grand Charity, *245*
Great Arcanum, *92*
Great Architect of the Universe, *258, 344*
Great Britain, *277*

Great Pyramid, *11, 455*
Great White Brotherhood, *93*
Great Work, *92*
Greater Key of Solomon, *75, 437, 461, 464, 472, 497*
Greeks, ancient, *37, 325, 437*
Gross Cophta, Der (Goethe), *180*
guilds, *198*

H

Hague, The, *20, 21*
Hall, Manly P, *337, 354*
Hamilton, Alexander, *243*
Hamilton, George, *287*
Hancock, Graham, *501*
Hannibal, M d', *169*
Hapsburg, House of, *289*
Hardivilliers, 'Brother', *16*
Harranian Sabians, *39*
Harvey, William, *236*
Haydn, *71*
heart, *234, 236, 237*
hekau (word of power), *470*
Helvétius, Adrien, *174*
Helvétius, Anne-Catherine, *174*
  'salons', *174, 175*
Henry IV, *58*
Hermes Trismegistus ('Thrice-Great'), *6, 35, 37, 39, 46, 48, 54, 60, 86, 325, 344, 346, 499*
Hermes (Mercury), *468, 485*
Hermetic alchemy, *75*
Hermetic Ritual of Perfection, *75*
Hermetic Scroll, *448*
Hermetica (Corpus Hermeticum), *33, 37, 39, 41, 42, 45, 222, 258, 262, 325*
  see also Poimandres,
Hermeticism, *11, 18, 41, 45, 46, 60, 63, 92, 178, 203, 215, 234, 239, 275, 331*
  and Cagliostro, *6, 11, 35, 45, 63, 341, 342*
  and Freemasonry, *41, 60, 63, 222, 224, 239, 341, 342*
  Scottish, *215, 216, 218, 220, 222*

Hiram Abiff, *322, 346, 485*
Historical Illuminatus Chronicles, The (Wilson), *186*
Hitler, Adolf, *69, 301, 302, 305, 309, 311, 313*
Holocaust, *307, 311, 313*
Holocaust Memorial Day Trust, *307*
Holy Roman Empire, *289*
Hor Book of Breathings, *487*
Horn Lodge, see Rummer & Grapes,
Houdon, Jean-Antoine, *83, 174, 178, 273*
House of Regeneration, The, *503*
Hugo, Victor, *301*
Huguenots, *287*
'humours', *234*
Hungary, Masonophobia in, *301, 313*
Hussein, Saddam, *313*
Hymns to the Aten, *46*

I

Idris, *325*

Il Mesatro Sconosciuto – the Unknown Master (comic book), *186*
Il Ritorno de Cagliostro (film), *186*
Illuminati, *112, 118, 128, 129, 139, 174, 175, 177, 180, 271, 273, 295*
    Bavarian, *128, 129, 271, 273*
Illuminati of Avignon, *75*
immortality, *140, 142, 164, 167, 169*
Incorporations (Scottish guilds), *198, 199*
Indian alchemy, *86*
Ingolstadt University, *69*
Innocent VIII, Pope, *325*
Inquisition, *75, 89, 92, 106, 110, 112, 114, 120, 122, 124, 126, 128, 129, 131, 133, 135, 137, 139, 140, 142, 145, 167, 287, 320*
    Florence conference (1737), *279*
I N R I, *344, 346*
Irish freemasonry, *266*
Isis, *175, 322, 487, 501*
Isis, Lodge of, *337, 339*

Islam, *39*
Italy,
   Grand Oriente of, *309*
   Masonophobia in, *269, 271, 307, 309, 313*

J
Jabir ibn Hayyan, *437*
Jacob's ladder, *499*
Jacobites, *249, 251, 266, 285*
James II, *249*
James VI (I), *188, 190, 195, 216, 218, 241*
Japan, *313*
Jenner, Edward, *263*
Jesuit agent theory, *177, 178*
Jesuits, *75*
Jesus Christ, *67, 92, 137, 164, 166, 167, 169, 171, 322, 325, 327, 478, 484, 501*
Jewish Cabala, *45, 92, 178, 354, 470, 484, 485*
Jewish Diaspora, *166*
Jews, *137, 139, 254*
   Judeo or Masonic 'conspiracy', *299, 305, 309, 311, 313*

Joachin (Jakin) and Boaz, *92, 392, 395, 396, 439*
Joan of Arc, *171*
John, Gospel, *166, 489*
John XXI, Pope, *58*
John XXII, Pope, *58*
John the Baptist, *327, 441*
   feast day, *441*
John the Evangelist, St, *135, 243, 441*
   feast day, *110, 135, 192, 243, 371, 441*
Joseph II, Emperor, *118, 289*
Joseph, Father, *114*
Josephine, Empress, *337, 339*
Judaism, *37*
Jupiter, *215, 402, 450, 452, 459, 466, 470*

K
Kempeitai, *313*
Kilwinning Lodge, *192, 195, 225*
King Solomon's Temple (KST), *220, 222, 247, 261, 262, 458*
Kings, Book of, *325*

Kings Chapel, Boston, *273*
King's Head Tavern, London, *15*
Kipling, Rudyard, *258*
Knights of Malta, Order of, *12, 116, 118*
Knights Templar, Order of, *16, 239, 263, 266, 267, 271, 390*
Knights Templar Freemasonry, *285*
Kun, Bela, *301, 313*
Kuzmin, Mikhail, *185*

L

La Motte, Comtesse de (Jeanne de Valois-Saint-Rémy), *97, 99, 101, 102, 186*
Laborde, Jean-Benjamin de, *89*
Lafayette, Marquis de, *174, 175*
Lalande, Joseph Jérôme Lefrançais de, *174*
Lamballe, Princesse de, *337*
Langes, Savalette de, *95, 97*
lap of my liver, *232, 237*
Lavater, Johann, *89*
LDP, *16, 18, 92*
Leipzig, *23, 75*
Lêogane Lodge, *67*
Lesser Key of Solomon, *75, 470, 474, 478*
Lettres de Cachets, *97, 101, 105, 175*
Lévi, Eliphas, *89, 92, 183, 506*
Library of Alexandria, *37, 39*
Life of Joseph Balsamo, The (Inquisition publication), *128, 133*
Life of Sethos, The (Terrasson), *77, 356*
L'Initiation, *323*
Literary Low-Life Reassessed, A (Burrows), *102*
liver, *234, 236*
Lives of the Alchemystical Philosophers, *63, 64, 65*

Lodge of Antiquity, Bloomsbury, *108*
Lodge Original No 1 (Lodge of Antiquity No 2), *247*
Lodges of Adoption, *26, 27*
London, *15, 16, 18, 20, 101, 102, 105, 106, 108, 110*
Lorraine, Duke of (Holy Roman Emperor), *287*
Louis VI, *97*
Louis XV, *78, 97, 102*
Louis XVI, *99, 101, 162, 175, 291, 297*
Louis Phillipe, King, *185*
Louis Philippe II, Duke of Orleans, *291*
Loutherbourg, Philippe Jacques de, *180*
Lyons, *31, 333, 335*

M

Mackey's Encyclopedia of Freemasonry, *69*
Macmahon, Parkyns, *4, 102*
Magi, alphabet of, *348, 350, 352, 354, 355*
magic, *33, 171, 210, 437*
   black (goetia), *60*
   ceremonial, *322, 323*
   stage, *183, 185*
   see also theurgy,
magic circle, *458, 495, 497*
Magic Flute (Mozart), *92, 178, 180, 355, 356*
magician, *33*
Magician's Seal (Serpent Seal), *16, 18, 89, 92, 185*
Maier, Michael, *54*
Malchus, *166*
Malta, *11, 12, 31*
Maravian Church, *287*
Marcello, Father, *114, 124*
Maria Theresa, Empress of Austria, *29, 80, 289, 313*
Marie Antoinette, *73, 97, 99, 162, 175, 180, 297*
Marini, Corporal, *150, 152*
Marlborough, Duke of, *279*
Mars, *215, 402, 450, 459, 466, 470, 472*
   'to know Mars is to know art', *380, 462*
Marsh, Brother, *108*
Martinist Order, *67, 69*

Marvel Comics, *186*
Marvellous Life of Giuseppe Balsamo, Count Cagliostro, The (Kuzmin), *185*
'Mason's Confession, The', *236, 237*
Mason's Word, *277*
Masonic Square, *262*
Masonophobia, *275, 277, 279, 282, 283, 285, 287, 289, 291, 293, 295, 297, 299, 301, 302, 305, 307, 309, 311, 313*
  timeline of persecution, *313*
Masonophobic Exhibition, *289, 291, 293, 313*
Master Mariners, *199*
Matthew, Gospel, *166*
McCalman, Iain, *186*
Mecca, *6, 8, 11*
Medici, Cosimo de, *39, 41*
Medina, *6*
Mein Kampf, *302, 309, 311, 313*
Mémoires de la Baronne d'Oberkirch, *80*
Memoirs of a Physician (Dumas), *180*
Memorial or Brief for the Count Cagliostro (Macmahon), *4, 6*
memory, natural and artificial, *210*
Memory Theatre, *215*
Mercury (planet), *215, 402, 448, 459, 466, 468, 470, 472*
Mercury (spiritual self)), *375, 410, 468, 476, 485*
Mesmer, Franz Anton, *31, 67, 69, 71, 73, 78, 162*
metals,
  see seven metals,
Metatron, *325*
Methodism, *287*
Methuselah, *327*
Middlesex, Charles, Duke of, *269*
Mind of God, *41, 42, 171*
Mirabeau, Comte de, *174*
Miromesnil, Marquis de, *142*
Mittau, *23, 26, 27*
Molay, Jacques de, *16*
Moniteur Universel, *112*
Montagu, Duke of, *243, 249, 251*

Montgolfier, Jacques-Etienne, *263*
Montgolfier, Joseph-Michel, *263*
Montmorency-Luxembourg, Duke of, *174*
Moon (Luna), *63, 215, 402, 410, 446, 448, 458, 459, 466, 470, 472*
   marriage with Sun, *380, 384, 395, 459*
Moray, Robert, *243*
Morison, Charles, *357*
Mormon Church, *178*
Morning Herald, *108*
Mosaic Genesis, *325, 352*
Moses, *322, 327, 481, 501*
Most Holy Trinosophia (?Cagliostro), *356*
Moszynski, Count, *27, 29*
Mother Earth, *232*
Mouchy, Maréchal de, *31*
Mozart, Wolfgang Amadeus, *31, 71, 92, 178, 180, 355, 356*
Musaeum Hermeticum, *54*
Mussolini, Benito, *301, 307, 309, 313*
mystery plays, *199*

N

names, *346, 348*
Napoleon, *93, 171*
natural spirit, *234*
Nazi Masonophobia, *301, 302, 305, 307, 309, 311, 313*
Neo-Platonism, *35, 210*
New World Order, *178, 299*
Newton, Isaac, *48, 54, 258*
Nibley, Hugh, *487*
Nigredo, *455*
Nile, *232*
Nine Sisters (Neuf Soeurs) Lodge, *174, 273*
Noah and the Ark, *199*
Nous, *41*
Nuremberg, *21, 23*

O

Oberkirch, Baroness Henriette Louise d', *80*
occultism, *23, 27, 71, 437, 453*
Oil of Wisdom, *26*
Ordeal of Water, *126*
organs of the body, *232, 234, 236, 237*

Orphic Hymns of Orpheus, 45
Orsini, Cardinal, 12
Osiris, *171, 322, 487*
Ouroboros, *21, 23*
'pagan' philosophy, *35*

P

Palance, Jack, *185*
Palladio, Andrea, *205*
papal bulls against Freemasonry first, *271, 287*
  second, *287, 289*
Papal States, *110, 118, 129*
Paracelsus, *45, 69, 75, 89, 203, 354*
Paravent de Cagliostro (Cagliostro's Folding Screen) (film), *185*
Parfaite Intelligence Lodge, Liège, *293*
Paris, *31, 67, 75, 78, 83, 95, 97, 99, 101, 105, 162, 174, 266*
Paris Moniteur, *171*
Pasqually, Martinez de, *31, 65, 67, 322*
Paul, St, *495*
Payne, George, *251*
Pentagon, *178*
pentagon symbolism, *455, 503, 506*
Perfect Equality Lodge, The Hague, *20*
Pernety, Dom Antoine Joseph, *31, 75, 114*
Pétain, Philippe, *302*
Phantom, The (comic book), *186*
Philalethes (Lovers of Truth), order of, *95, 267, 269*
Philip, King of France, *16*
Philip V, *287*
Philippe II, Duke of Orléans, *174*
philosopher's stone, *46, 54, 56, 229, 384, 386, 489*
phoenix, *410, 416, 432, 433, 492*
pillar symbolism, *262, 485*
Pinto, Grand Master of Malta, *4, 11, 12*
Pius VI, Pope, *110, 122, 131, 145*
planets,
  see seven planets,
Plato, *37, 45, 322, 437*

pneuma, *234*
'Poimandres', *41, 42, 45, 46, 443, 444, 446, 499*
Poland, *27, 29*
Poniatowski, King Stanislas Augustus, *29*
Poninski, Prince Adam, *27, 29*
Pontius Pilate, *166, 167, 169*
Port-au-Prince Lodge, *67*
Portuguese Inquisition, *313*
Prost de Royer, M, *335*
Protestantism, *199, 277, 287, 289*
Protocols of the Elders of Zion, *299*
Proverbs of Solomon, *439*
Psalm 50, *499*
Psalm 104, *46*
Psychoshop (Bester and Zelazny), *186*
Ptolemy II, *37*
pyramid stone, *476*
Pythagoras, *37, 45, 234, 348*

Q
Queen of Sheba, *329, 339*
Queen's Necklace, The (Dumas), *180*
Quesnel, Pasquier, *287*
Quietism, *279, 287*
Qur'an, *258, 325*

R
Raleigh, Walter, *203*
Rameses II, *261*
Ramsay, Allan, *285*
Ramsay, Andrew M, *279, 329*
Ramsay's Oration, *279, 285*
Reformation, *201, 249*
Reformed Church in Scotland, *199*
Reformed Rite of the Beneficient Knights of the Holy City, *271*
Renaissance, *39, 41, 56, 162, 203, 205, 210, 212, 215*
Renan, Ernst, *301*
Revelation of John, *441, 443*
Ricciarelli, Count, *15*
Richelieu, Duc de, *167, 169, 335*

Richmond, Charles Lennox, Duke of, *249*
Robert I, *239*
Robert-Houdin, *185*
Robison, John, *291, 293, 295*
Rochester, Bishop of, *251*
Rohan, Cardinal Louis René Édouard de, *29, 78, 80, 83, 86, 97, 99, 114, 116, 122, 140*
Rohan, Bailiff de, *12*
Rohmer, Sax, *167*
Roman architecture, *205*
Roman Art of Memory, *208, 210*
Roman Empire, *37, 39*
Romance of Cagliostro, The (Cheiro), *183*
Rome, *12, 15, 110, 112, 114, 116, 118, 120, 122, 285*
Rose-Croix Masonry, *69, 93, 322*
Rose-Cross, *344, 346*
Rosenkreuz, Christian, *203*
Rosetta Stone, *437*
Rosicrucianism, *78, 89, 93, 164, 203, 263, 478*
rough ashlar, *56, 375, 395, 476*
Rousseau, Jean-Jacques, *287*
Roussel, Geuydan de, *302, 305*
Roveredo, *116*
Royal Society of London, *247, 258*
Royal Society of Edinburgh, *243, 291*
Rubedo, *492*
Rummers & Grapes (Horn Lodge), *247, 251*

S

Sabbatianism, *322*
Sacchi, *31*
Sagesse Triomphante (Triumphant Wisdom) Mother Lodge, Lyons, *31, 95, 262, 323, 333, 335, 359, 361*
    Statutes and Regulations, *363, 365, 367, 369, 371, 373*
Sahib, Guru Granth, *258*

Saint Germain, Count de, *63, 64, 65, 71, 86, 93, 164, 167*
Saint Martin, Louis Claude de, *31, 67, 69, 93*
Saint Maurice, Father François-Joseph de, *118, 120, 122*
Salahaym, Mufti, *6, 8, 11*
San Domingo, *67*
San Leo prison, Urbino, *145, 146, 148, 150, 152, 154, 156, 158, 185*
Saturn, *215, 404, 452, 459, 466, 468, 470*
Savalette de Langes, Paul, *174*
Sayer, Anthony, *243*
Scaliger, Joseph Justus, *222*
Schaw, William, *188, 190, 192, 195, 198, 205, 210, 215, 216, 218, 220, 224, 228, 277*
   tomb of, *201, 203*
Schaw Statutes, *190, 192, 195, 198, 199, 201, 203, 225, 228, 229*
Schikaneder, Emmanuel, *355, 356*
Schroeder, Friedrich Joseph Wilhelm, *69*
Scieffort, Herr, *23*
Scot, 'Lord', *18, 20*
Scotland, *188, 190, 216, 224, 239, 241*
   Grand Lodge of, *266, 323, 357*
   union with England, *241, 277*
Scots, The, *237*
Scott, Francis, 2nd Duke of Buccleuch, *251*
Scottish Freemasonry, *263, 266, 285, 293*
Scottish Hermeticism, *215, 216, 218, 220, 222*
Scottish Rectified Rite (Chevaliers Bénéficients de la Cité-Sainte), *69*
Scottish Rite, *89, 93, 267*
Scottish Reformation, *198, 199*
Scottish stonemasonry, *190, 192, 195, 198, 199, 201, 203, 241, 247*
   'accepted' brethren, *245, 277*

alchemy connection, *228, 229, 232, 234, 236, 237*
Art of Memory, *198, 208, 210, 218, 220, 224*
degrees,
 first (Entered Prentice), *198, 224, 225*
 second (Fellow Craft), *198, 224, 225*
early lodges, *224, 225, 228, 229, 232, 234, 236, 237*
passwords and handgrips, *243, 245*
secrecy, *218, 220, 277*
transition to Freemasonry, *224, 239, 241, 243, 256*
Second World War, *69*
Sefer Yetzirah, *481, 484*
Segur, Marshal de, *142*
Semproni, Sempronio, *145, 148, 150*
Serpent Seal, *16, 18, 89, 92, 185*
Serrano, Teodoro Serrano, *313*
Seton, Alexander, *201, 203, 215*
seven, *384, 386, 439, 441, 443, 444, 446, 464, 484*
seven colours, *395, 464*
Seven Ordeals of Count Cagliostro, The (McCalman), *186*
seven angels, *398, 408, 439, 468, 470, 479, 492, 495*
seven metals, *380, 461, 462*
seven planets, *215, 410, 439, 441, 443, 444, 446, 448, 450, 452, 453, 459*
 angelic rulers, *468, 470*
 animal correspondences, *470, 472*
 colour correspondences, *464*
 days and hours governed, *402, 404, 472*
 initiatory tests, *464, 466*
 metal correspondences, *461*
Shekinah, *93, 493*
Siberian Shaman, The (Catherine the Great), *27*
Sicily, *12*

Sigillus Sigillorum (Bruno), 215, 216
silver, 232, 461, 478
Simonini, J B, 299
Skull and Bones, Order of, 178
Skull of Cagliostro, 185
Smith, Hélène, 183
Smith, Joseph, 178
smooth ashlar, 56, 476
Socrates, 437
Solomon, King, 220, 224, 329, 339, 392, 395, 396, 418, 501
Sophie, Queen, 190
soul, 236
Spain, 266
    Grand Orient of, 313
    Masonophobia in, 287, 313
Spanish Civil War, 313
Spawn (film), 178, 186
St Andrews University, 216
St John, Order of, 128
St Paul's Cathedral, 247
St Petersburg, 27
stage magic, 183, 185
star (blazing star), 396, 398, 408, 432, 439, 468

Stein, Gertrude, 305
Stevenson, David, 224, 275
Stewart, Gregory, 441
stonemasonry,
    see Scottish stonemasonry,
Strachan, Alexander, 243
Strasburg, 29, 31, 86
Strauss, Johann, 180
Strict Observance, Order of, 15, 16, 18, 69, 162, 169, 271
Stuart, House of, 249
Stukely, William, 258
Sufis, 39
Suhrawardi, Yahya, 39
Suidas, 232
Sun (Sol), 63, 215, 402, 410, 450, 458, 459, 466, 468, 472
    marriage with Moon, 380, 384, 395, 459
Supreme Council of France, 342, 344, 346, 348, 350, 352, 354
Suspense (US series), 185
Swank, Hilary, 186
Swedenborg, Emanuel, 31, 67, 73, 75

Swedenborg, Rites of, 75, 93
Swedenborgians, 287
Swinton, Samuel, 102
Switzerland, 110
    Masonophobia in, 287, 313
sword, magical, 410, 478, 492
Sybils, 335, 354
symbols, 41, 58, 228, 229, 232

T

tabernacle, 493, 495
Talisman: Sacred Cities, Secret Faith (Hancock and Bauval), 501
tarot, Cagliostro deck, 185
Tarrubia, Joseph, 287
Tempettio, Rome, 205
Terrasson, Jean, 77, 356
Tetragrammaton (IHVH), 481, 484
Theosophical Society, 71, 183
theurgy (divine magic), 54, 60, 67
Theveneau de Morande, Charles, 102, 105, 106, 108, 110, 183
Thomas Aquinas, 58
Thoth, 6, 35, 37, 39, 86
Three Books of Occult Philosophy, The (Agrippa), 75, 452
Three Firing Glasses Lodge, 289
Three Skulls Lodge, 289
Thun, Prince Pietro Virgilio (Bishop of Trent), 116, 118, 145
Times, The, 101
Toklas, Alice B, 305
Tolstoy, Count, 180
Torah, 258
Tories, 249, 253
Torrigiani, Grand Mason, 307, 309
tracing boards, 373, 375, 392, 410, 432, 455, 476, 492
Trebizond, Empire of, 4, 6, 8, 12
Trebizond, Prince of, 4
Trinity doctrine, 73
Triptaka, 258
Trithemius, Johannes, 54

Trowbridge, W H R, *106, 114, 160, 175, 177*

U

Union of Parliaments, *277*
Unitarians, *285, 287*
United States, see America,
Universal Register, *102*
Urabis Raham, *395, 396*

V

van Swieten, Dr, *69*
Vannetti, Clemontino, *116*
Vatican, *116, 118, 128, 154, 156*
Venus, *215, 402, 448, 459, 466, 470, 472*
Vernon, Howard, *186*
Vie de Joseph Balsamo, La (Barberi or Marcello), *114*
Vienna, *69, 71*
virgin paper, *406, 474*
vital spirit, *234*
Vitruvian Man, *205*
Vitruvius, Marcus Pollio, *205*
Vivaldi, Marquise, *120*
Voltaire, *174, 273, 287*
von der Recke, Charlotte Elisabeth Konstantia (Elisa), *23, 26, 27, 327*
von Hundt, Baron Karl Gotthelf, *16, 271*
von Koppen, Frederick, *75, 271*
von Medem, Counts, *23, 26*

W

Waite, Edward, *177, 339*
Walken, Christopher, *186*
Wandering Jew, *65, 164, 166, 167*
War of the Austrian Succession, *289*
War of the Spanish Succession, *279*
Warsaw, *27, 29, 84, 86*
Washington, George, *175, 302*
Watt, James, *263, 293*
Webster, Nesta, *299*
Weishaupt, Adam, *271*
Welles, Orson, *185*

Wesley, *285, 287*
Wharton, Phillip James 1st Duke of, *251, 266*
Whigs, *249*
Whitfield, *285, 287*
Wiccans, *35*
Willermoz, Jean-Baptiste, *69*
Wilson, Robert Anton, *186*
Winton, George Seton 5th Earl, *285*
'Wizard of the South', *185*
Worker, Norman, *186*
women, *26, 27, 67, 69, 180, 335, 337, 339, 341*
Wren, Christopher, *247, 249*

Y

Yale University, *178*
Yarker, John, *322*
Yates, Frances, *224*
Yeats, W B, *73*

Z

Zanoni (Bulwer-Lytton), *180*
Zelazny, Roger, *186*
Zeleda, Cardinal de, *122*
Zola, Emile, *301*
Zoroaster, *45, 60*
Zoroastrianism, *37*

www.ingramcontent.com/pod-product-compliance
Lightning Source LLC
Chambersburg PA
CBHW011712290426
44113CB00018B/2653